W9-AOP-670

FLORIDA STATE
UNIVERSITY LIBRARIES

MAR 7 2003

TALLAHASSEE, FLORIDA

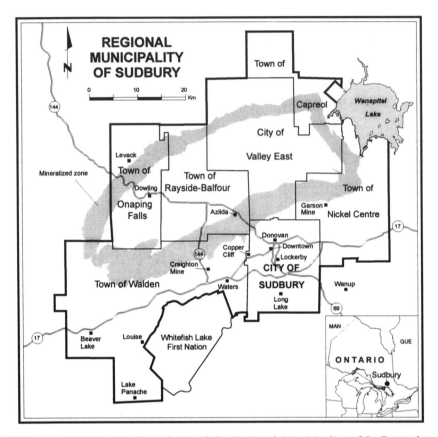

This map illustrates the boundaries of the Regional Municipality of Sudbury, the geographic context for much of this study. Situated in Northern Ontario, the municipality comprises the cities of Sudbury and Valley East and the towns of Capreol, Nickel Centre, Onaping Falls, Rayside-Balfour and Walden. Shown also are the locations of the Finnish working-class districts and rural enclaves discussed in the text. The shaded and oval-shaped mineralized zone is where the mines operated by Inco and Falconbridge can be found.

Between a Rock and a Hard Place

A Historical Geography of the Finns in the Sudbury Area

Oiva W. Saarinen

Wilfrid Laurier University Press

WLU

This book has been published with the help of a grant from the Humanities and Social Sciences Federation of Canada, using funds provided by the Social Sciences and Humanities Research Council of Canada. We acknowledge the support of the Canada Council for the Arts for our publishing program. We acknowledge the financial support of the Government of Canada through the Book Publishing Industry Development Program for our publishing activities.

Canada

Canadian Cataloguing in Publication Data

Saarinen, Oiva W., 1937-

Between a rock and a hard place : a historical geography of the Finns in the Sudbury area

Includes bibliographical references and index.
ISBN 0-88920-320-2 (bound)   ISBN 0-88920-353-9 (pbk.)

1. Finnish Canadians—Ontario—Sudbury Region—History. 2. Finns—Ontario—Sudbury Region—History. I. Title.

FC3099.S83Z7 1999   971.3′13300494541   C98-932487-7
F1059.5.S83S22 1999

F
1059.5
.S85
S23
1999

© 1999 Wilfrid Laurier University Press
Waterloo, Ontario N2L 3C5

Paper Edition 1999
Second impression 2000

Cover design by Leslie Macredie using photographs supplied by the Finnish Canadian Historical Society

∞

Printed in Canada

All rights reserved. No part of this work covered by the copyrights hereon may be reproduced or used in any form or by any means—graphic, electronic or mechanical—without the prior written permission of the publisher. Any request for photocopying, recording, taping or reproducing in information storage and retrieval systems of any part of this book shall be directed in writing to the Canadian Reprography Collective, 214 King Street West, Suite 312, Toronto, Ontario M5H 3S6.

Contents

Contents   vii

List of Tables, Figures, Maps, Aerial Photograph and Biographies

Tables

Figures

Maps

Aerial Photograph

Biographies

Acknowledgments

I would like at the outset to acknowledge the people who have contributed to the development of the field of Finnish immigration history. One advantage of working with Finnish historical geography is the fact that this ethnic group can lay claim to having one of the richest archival heritages extant. Indeed, few other ethnic groups reflect such an appreciation for their ethnic heritage. There has clearly been a whole-hearted desire within the Finnish Canadian community to ensure that its rites of passage into Canadian society are well documented and available to the general public.

In Canada, organizational records and the desire to keep a good set of books can be dated as far back as 1890. This trait has continued to the present day. That the Finnish community has been able to create such an abundance of historical documentation is largely the result of the almost universal literacy of its members and their propensity to develop an ingenious process for the creation, preservation and dissemination of archival materials. This rich heritage consists of a wide variety of source materials, including personal, family and business records; organizational records; documentation by the Finnish Canadian press; unpublished hand- and typewritten manuscripts, booklets and pamphlets; academic books, theses and journal articles; and formal archives. For the early immigrants, who lived behind a linguistic barrier, newspapers were especially important. Started as early as 1896 in the form of a handwritten or "fist" press (*nyrkki-lehti*), they served as a "guide, an interpreter, a teacher, and an intimate friend."[1] Sudbury was blessed in this regard, as it served for many years as the focal point for Finnish journalism in Canada. The study of Finns in the Sudbury area has likewise been the subject of numerous M.A. and Licenti-

Notes to the Acknowledgments are on p. 279.

ate theses written by Finns and others. Sudbury can thus lay claim to being one of the most intensely studied Finnish communities in Canada. I have relied heavily on these academic works. With respect to the creation of archives, Sudbury is noteworthy as it served as the original depository for the two main Finnish archives in Canada—the Finnish Canadian Archives now in the Public Archives of Canada in Ottawa and the records of the Finnish Canadian Historical Society now at the Archives of Ontario. Much archival material from Sudbury has also been collected by the Multicultural History Society of Ontario.[2]

Another pleasure in researching the story of the Finns in the Sudbury area was the spirit of co-operation shown by the people who worked with me throughout this undertaking. Their willingness to share information and constructive criticism proved to be a great experience and contributed significantly to the completion of the book. To all of them, I express my deep and sincere gratitude. I would like to extend special thanks to the many individuals who went out of their way to share memories of their immigrant experience for the biographies or regarding their upbringing as native Finnish Canadians. To Léo Larivière, I am grateful for his wizardry in computerized cartography and help in developing the maps found in the book. I wish to acknowledge the invaluable help that I received from Professor Gerry Tapper of Laurentian University and Keijo Kaitila, D.C., who read earlier drafts of the manuscript and made a number of cogent suggestions. Jules Päiviö, former chairman of the Department of Architecture at Ryerson Polytechnic University in Toronto, offered valuable suggestions and gave additional insights regarding the history of the Finnish Organization of Canada. Appreciation must also be extended to Lennard Sillanpää, Ph.D., formerly of the Department of Indian Affairs and Northern Development in Ottawa and now Docent, Åbo University, Finland; Varpu Lindström, Ph.D. and past Master, Atkinson College, York University; and Börje Vähämäki, Ph.D. and visiting professor of Finnish, University of Toronto, who graciously offered their insights and criticisms of the text. Acknowledgment must likewise be given to the personnel of the Sudbury Land Registry Office for their assistance regarding the arduous task of searching Finnish land ownership patterns.

Financial assistance for this undertaking was received from the Finnish National Society of Sudbury and from the Office of the President, Dean of the Faculties of Humanities and Social Sciences and the Institute of Northern Ontario Research and Development at Laurentian University. Finally, I would like to extend a deep and sincere appreciation to my wife, Edith, for her ongoing assistance and co-operation, including the onerous task of proofreading the text.

I wish to dedicate this book to the memory of my father and mother, who came to Canada as Finnish immigrants in the 1930s. While I grew up as a Canadian, my parents nevertheless passed on to me a sense of pride in my Finnish heritage. Because of them, I have had the pleasure of savouring life from the vantage of two different worlds. *Kiitos*!

Introduction

Why write a book on the Finns of the Sudbury area? There are several reasons. First, the story simply deserves to be told. Since 1883 Finns have played an integral part in the transformation of the Sudbury area from a rail town to its present-day role as the regional capital of northeastern Ontario. In a variety of ways, as pioneering agricultural settlers, labour reformers, hardworking citizens, builders of churches, halls, saunas and athletic fields, Finns left an indelible imprint on the physical and human landscape. Throughout the first half-century of Finnish settlement in Canada "there was no other locality . . . where the Finns had held such a pivotal role in history as in the community of Sudbury."[1] In like fashion, Jim Ashcroft, former Ontario Division president of Inco, has remarked that "the story of the Finns in Sudbury is a noble and uplifting chapter in our regional history."[2] Second, there is the question of "roots." For myself and others of Finnish origin, the book is intended to serve as a path of discovery, leading not only to a greater appreciation of our heritage but also to an understanding of how "carry-over effects" from Finland and elsewhere were influenced by domestic factors in Canada and Northern Ontario. Third, the time is right. A century of the Finnish experience has passed— time enough for a thoughtful review of the historical record. The rapid aging of the Finns as an ethnic group makes it imperative that their past aims, aspirations and achievements be duly recorded for future generations. As one insightful observer once reminded me, "it is fine for you academics to deal with ethnic institutions, processes, patterns and all those sorts of things, but you must never forget that, in the final analysis, it all comes down to people."[3] The book is also intended as a celebration of the concept of multiculturalism. It is this aspect of the Canadian way of life—our

---

Notes to the Introduction are on p. 279.

1

ability to live with varying ethnic groups and cultures—that serves to differentiate Canada from most other countries in the world. Finally, it is hoped that this book will serve as a useful framework for comparable studies involving other ethnic groups in North America.

The book is approached from two distinctive viewpoints. First, it examines the Finnish experience in the Sudbury area from the vantage point of an academic geographer who has great empathy for the historical perspective. The Finnish Canadian experience has been intimately interwoven with geographical influences, such as the homeland setting, adaptation to a new living environment, the fashioning of distinctive rural and urban landscapes and the creation of landmarks intended for the celebration and sharing of the collective ethnic experience. None of these geographical features, however, can be divorced from the perspective of history. The book can thus be considered as an attempt to assess Finnish ethnicity in terms of the integration of space and time. Second, it reflects concern for those readers whose primary interest lies not so much in the search for trends, processes and patterns but rather in the development of Finnish personalities, landmarks and landscapes. The book acknowledges these interests through the incorporation of maps, photographs and biographical sketches.

The title for this book deserves comment. The Canadian environment was extremely difficult for Finnish immigrants. While the book gives ample evidence that Finns participated in many of the happier pursuits of life—sports, theatre, music, dancing, singing and the like—the reality was that everyday existence was harsh. Finns who came to Sudbury found themselves caught "between a rock and a hard place." Rock defined the physical reality of the Sudbury setting, whether in the form of rugged hills, hardrock mines or farms and forests intimately linked with the Precambrian Shield. The human setting, however, was equally hard. Assimilation brought with it many dangers, especially where employment and politics were concerned. In forestry and mining, Finns were given jobs that required great endurance and a tolerance for hazardous conditions. In agriculture, they were relegated to the rural fringes that others had rejected. To improve their lot in life, Finns turned to the only two options available to them—the labour movement and political activism. It was in this fight for improved working and living conditions that the hardness of Canadian society proved to be the greatest.

The book consists of six chapters. As the immigrant experience cannot be divorced from the national setting, Chapter I establishes the Canadian perspective for events that took place in Sudbury over the past century. This chapter provides the necessary geographical and historical context for the subsequent chapters. Chapter II focuses on the geographical setting of the Sudbury area and describes the pattern of Finnish settlement from the 1880s to the present. The important role played by Copper Cliff, Sudbury and Garson as the cradles of urban settlement is established. It is shown how the Finns began to define their own territory, whether as distinctive working-class "Finntowns" in the urbanized areas, or in the form of "ethnic islands" in the rural areas. It is concluded that many of these enclaves have managed to retain part of their ethnic character to the present day. Attention is also directed to Lake Panache and Florida as unique forms of summer and winter retreats. Chapter III deals with the most controversial feature linked to Finnish institutional development in the Sudbury area— the rise of a "Great Divide" between the leftist and conservative sections of the community. The chapter proposes that many of the root causes behind this factionalism evolved out of influences derived from four geographical settings: Finland, Russia/Soviet Union, the United States and Canada.

The contribution made by Finns to the economic well-being of the Sudbury area is examined in Chapter IV. Attention here is directed to several topics: the initial appearance by Finns as blue-collar employees in the resource industries; the promotion by Finns of workers' rights and the union movement; the remarkable contribution made by Finnish women in the workplace; and the upward mobility exhibited by the native-born generation after World War II. Chapter V outlines how Finnish ethnicity has served as a major force, enhancing cultural activity in the Sudbury area through sports, the theatre, choral singing, fraternal/club groupings and the rest home movement. Other contemporary aspects of the cultural setting are examined as well, such as the growing role of "symbolic and voluntary ethnicity" and the rapid decline in the use of the Finnish language. Chapter VI provides a summary of the book and concludes with a perspective of the future of the Finnish community in the Sudbury area. It is argued that while the present culture and identity of the Finns continues to show dynamism and vitality, the new millennium will bring with it major changes.

Interspersed throughout the book are twenty biographical sketches. Based on the legacies they have established within the community, the following individuals have been selected for detailed treatment: Thomas Jacobson, Frank and Margaretta Anderson, Karl Lehto, Rev. Arvi Heinonen, Lempi Johnson, John Ahlqvist, Aku Päiviö, Bruno Tenhunen, William Eklund, Rev. Lauri Pikkusaari, Oliver Korpela, Sulo and Bertha Heino, Bill Johnson, Risto Laamanen, Paul Villgren, Maija Ceming, Laila Rintamäki, Wilf Salo, Arne Ritari and Judy Erola. Maps and photographs are used to illustrate landmarks and landscapes of visual and cultural importance to the

Finnish community. It is pertinent to note here that the settlement dates shown on many of the maps refer specifically to the time of official registration of property by the Land Titles Office of the Province of Ontario; they cannot be used to pinpoint the actual times of arrival, which, in most cases, occurred many years previously. An annotated bibliography has been included outlining the sources of information used for the undertaking of this book.

Some reference must also be made here to the use of Canadian surnames by immigrant Finns. Many surnames referred to in the text and maps differ from those used in Finland—some do not appear to be of Finnish origin at all. There are several reasons for this historical trait. Some Finns considered their surnames to be alien and long compared with English names, thereby constituting for them a burden for everyday living in a Canadian setting; for those in business, Finnish names often served to complicate normal dealings. Thus many names (1) lost their initial component, e.g., from Kurkimäki to Mäki, or from Hakojärvi to Järvi; (2) were shortened, especially if they ended in (i)nen, e.g., Saarinen to Saari, Ahonen to Aho, Poikolainen to Laine and Kautiainen to Kannen; or (3) took their English equivalents, e.g., Mäki to Hill or Järvi to Lake.[4] In some instances, new names were given to Finns by immigration officials or by bosses at their place of work. One foreman at Inco, for example, found the Finnish names of his workers so difficult that he arbitrarily changed them to Wilson, Johnson and Nelson![5] The use of English names was occasionally adopted as a deliberate means of eliminating traces of their past for various personal, political or marital reasons.

Another surname trait that deserves comment is the tradition of using male names only to depict patterns of land and business ownership in assessment and registry records. One of the unfortunate consequences of this form of institutionalization has been to minimize the important role of women who often ran farms, or conducted businesses such as bootlegging and boarding houses. Thus, the use of Finnish surnames often does not depict the real situation with respect to gender and power within the Finnish community. Finally, it should be noted that the spellings of family surnames as shown on the settlement maps may not always be accurate as personnel working in provincial Land Registry or municipal assessment offices frequently misspelled Finnish names; as well, the umlaut marks ä and ö associated with the language were usually ignored.

Chapter I

Finnish Settlement in Canada

An understanding of the evolution of Finnish settlement in the Sudbury area requires some reference to the development of the Finnish community in Canada. From a national perspective, immigration and ethnic diversity have always constituted important aspects of Canadian life; indeed, Canada has portrayed itself to the rest of the world as a model of multiculturalism. It is not surprising, therefore, that the Canadian government has made available a wealth of census data and other forms of information to reflect this multicultural orientation. With some one hundred distinct ethnic and cultural communities, Canada has been described as an international nation that features a "cultural mosaic" tradition in contrast to that of the United States, which has been depicted as a "melting pot" society. This chapter reviews the role played by Finns in the fashioning of the Canadian ethnic mosaic from the latter stages of the nineteenth century to the 1990s.

Immigration

Canada was first brought to the attention of Finland by Pehr Kalm, who made the initial contact with this part of North America in 1749-50 and later acquired fame through the writing of his travel diary, known as *Travels in North America*, and issued in 1770.[1]

Despite the interest shown in Kalm's travels to Canada, immigration to North America from Finland was directed totally to the United States. The first immigrants to Canada did not arrive until early in the nineteenth century, by way of the United States and Alaska, rather than directly from Finland. These pioneers found temporary employment in the construction of the Lachine Canal in Quebec and the Welland Canal in Ontario between 1829

Notes to Chapter I are on pp. 279-81.

Shown here is the Emigrant Hotel in Hanko, Finland, which housed Finns awaiting ship departure. Hanko, located southwest of Helsinki, was a popular point of emigration from Finland. (National Museum of Finland)

Prior to World War II, emigrants used a variety of shipping lines to come to North America, e.g., Allan, CP, Cunard, Dominion and White Star. In this picture taken in 1927, it is evident that seasickness was one of the hazards of ocean travel. (National Museum of Finland)

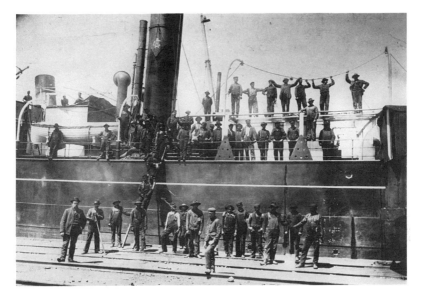

As early as 1887, Finns were attracted to Sault Ste. Marie when the construction of the Canadian lock began. Others followed later, including those shown above who became harbour workers with the Algoma Steel Company. (Multicultural History Society of Ontario)

One of the most recognizable Finnish streetscapes in Canada is Bay Street in Thunder Bay. Striking forestry workers are shown here in 1935 in front of the Big Finn Hall and the famous *Hoito* Restaurant. (Multicultural History Society of Ontario)

Many Finnish immigrants were attracted to a variety of construction projects such as the Chelsey Falls dam in Quebec, 1915. Two days after this photograph was taken, five Finns died when the dam collapsed. (Multicultural History Society of Ontario)

Not all Finns were employed in mining, forestry or construction. At Sointula, along the coast of British Columbia, many Finns pursued fishing in their distinctive white and blue boats, 1920. (Multicultural History Society of Ontario)

Some Finnish families migrated to the Prairie provinces. Shown here is Mikki Myllymäki's homestead in New Finland, Saskatchewan, 1897. He came here from Sudbury using funds from the sale of his farm to a mining company. (New Finland Historical and Heritage Society)

Veikko and Reino Koski are shown here standing in front of their family's sod-covered home in Dinsmore, Saskatchewan, c. 1918. (Aili Koski, private collection)

and 1887.[2] Others came following the acquisition of Alaska by the United States in 1867. After this purchase, many of the five hundred Finns residing in Alaska moved south to British Columbia.[3] In 1876 a small migration of Finnish settlers began from the United States to the Thunder Bay area.[4]

Despite recruitment efforts as early as 1874, direct emigration from Finland did not start until the 1880s (table 1). At the beginning, agents were used in the migration process:

> There were also agents in Finland telling young Finns that America was a grand place to go. These agents were hired by foreign governments, including Canada's; by railway and steamship companies, including the Canadian Pacific Railway; and by private companies . . . who needed cheap labor.[5]

Table 1
Immigration to Canada (1883-1994)

Year	Origin Overseas	Origin United States	Total	Year	Origin Overseas	Origin United States	Total
1883	19	58	77	1940	3	29	32
1884	305	125	430	1941	1	19	20
1885	2	10	12	1942	—	21	21
1886	2	26	28	1943	—	18	18
1888	53	34	87	1944	1	7	8
1889	4	10	14	1945	6	20	26
1890	1	16	17	1946	22	34	56
1891	—	—	—	1947	43	38	81
1892	—	—	—	1948	200	27	227
1893	—	—	—	1949	236	31	267
1894	—	—	—	1950	483	21	504
1895	9	—	9	1951	4130	28	4158
1896	—	—	—	1952	2293	15	2308
1897	12	—	12	1953	1232	20	1252
1898	88	—	88	1954	697	20	717
1899	669	63	732	1955	632	20	652
1900	544	122	666	1956	1094	34	1128
1901	600	113	713	1957	2829	55	2884
1902	1716	93	1809	1958	1258	38	1296
1903	1427	23	1450	1959	890	54	944
1904	825	124	949	1960	993	54	1047
1905	1312	99	1411	1961	350	31	381
1906	1417	154	1571	1962	340	45	385
1907	1420	128	1548	1963	285	40	325
1908	453	251	704	1964	415	61	476
1909	1348	509	1857	1965	580	76	656
1910	2262	1570	3832	1966	636	60	696

Table 1 (continued)

Year	Origin Overseas	Origin United States	Total	Year	Origin Overseas	Origin United States	Total
1911	1637	2626	4263	1967	703	56	759
1912	2135	1245	3380	1968	—	—	740
1913	3508	746	4254	1969	—	—	700
1914	637	184	821	1970	—	—	604
1915	91	85	176	1971	—	—	398
1916	276	618	894	1972	—	—	275
1917	129	922	1051	1973	—	—	323
1918	15	342	357	1974	—	—	320
1919	25	81	106	1975	—	—	256
1920	1198	58	1256	1976	—	—	237
1921	460	50	510	1977	—	—	177
1922	654	50	704	1978	—	—	260
1923	6019	28	6047	1979	—	—	169
1924	6123	36	6159	1980	—	—	191
1925	1561	56	1617	1981	—	—	167
1926	4721	84	4805	1982	—	—	181
1927	5154	113	5167	1983	—	—	63
1928	3674	84	3758	1984	—	—	81
1929	4614	98	4712	1985	—	—	73
1930	2749	62	2811	1986	—	—	68
1931	100	36	136	1987	—	—	96
1932	32	30	62	1988	—	—	79
1933	45	22	67	1989	—	—	78
1934	63	16	79	1990	—	—	67
1935	38	26	64	1991	—	—	58
1936	50	11	61	1992	—	—	63
1937	73	21	94	1993	—	—	106
1938	67	14	81	1994	—	—	103
1939	63	19	82				

Sources: The figures for 1883-1967 are taken from William Darcovich, ed., *A Statistical Compendium on the Ukrainians in Canada*, 1891-1976 (Ottawa: University of Ottawa Press, 1980), pp. 539-49; information since 1968 has been derived from Citizenship and Immigration Canada, *Immigration Statistics* (Ottawa: Citizenship and Immigration Canada, 1968-94).

There is uncertainty regarding the date of the first settlers. While passenger lists in Finland suggest that a group of twelve men emigrated to Thunder Bay in 1880, some sources indicate that the first official arrivals from Finland came to Canada in 1882-83, to work for the *Siipiaar* (Canadian Pacific Railway or CPR) in the Ottawa and Sudbury area.[6] According to Canadian census returns, however, Finnish settlement in Northern Ontario had already started by 1881, as fifty-one Finns were recorded as residing in the northwest part of the province at Silver Islet, Port Arthur and Dryden,

where surveying and construction were being done for the CPR transconti-
nental line.[7] By 1891 the number of Finns in Northern Ontario had grown
to almost four hundred. New pockets of settlement could now be found in
northeastern Ontario, at Sault Ste. Marie, the Sudbury mining area, Algoma
Mills and along the CPR line northwest of Mattawa.[8] It appears that many of
these settlers had come from the United States without being recorded as
official immigrants. Among the early settlers was Thomas Jacobson, who
came to the Sudbury area in 1885 (biography 1).

Between 1883 and 1891, some 754 Finnish immigrants came to
Canada. Of this total, 60 percent came from Finland and 40 percent from
the United States. The United States thus played an important role in shaping the early migration of Finns into Canada. New Finland in Saskatchewan
illustrates this point. In the 1891 annual report of the federal Department of
Agriculture, C.K. Hendrickson, an immigration agent for the CPR, wrote
the following:

> New Finland is another colony which I located two years ago, while in
> the employ of the Canadian Pacific Immigration Department in Win-
> nipeg. Until this spring there were only three families . . . in the colony,
> but by my special efforts during last winter and spring, when travelling in
> the neighbouring states of Minnesota and Dakota, on immigration busi-
> ness, on behalf of the C.P.R., I induced several of the families in those
> states to the new colony. . . . I hope to see a good many of them arriving
> in the next season, as some delegates from two of the largest Finnish
> settlements in North and South Dakota visited this district during the
> past summer, and were well pleased with the land and the prospects
> generally.[9]

The exodus to Canada from Finland was not significant at this time as it
represented only about 1 percent of that country's total overseas
emigration.[10] As the century drew to a close, pockets of settlement emerged
in the farming areas of Saskatchewan and the mining districts of Vancouver
Island. A small group of Finns was also drawn to the construction of the
Canadian locks at Sault Ste. Marie between 1887 and 1995.[11] Finns also
started to settle in the burgeoning community of Toronto as early as 1887.
While not reflected in the census returns, it is known that hundreds of
Finns were temporarily attracted to the Yukon following the start of the
Klondike Gold Rush in 1896.[12]

Some of the early arrivals, however, became disenchanted with Canada
and returned to Finland or went back to the United States. Due to harsh
working conditions in the mines and forests, up to 25 percent of all immigrants who came to Canada eventually migrated back to Finland.[13] One
study has even suggested that almost as many Finns may have moved from
Canada to the United States as moved in the opposite direction.[14]

Biography 1
Thomas Jacobson: The First Pioneer

Thomas Jacobson (formerly Karppi) was born on 9 September 1866 at Vähäkyrö, Finland. He emigrated as a child to the United States. Jacobson was among a group of eleven who travelled from New York to Collingwood and then by ship to Algoma Mills, where they expected to find work with the CPR on the railway line being constructed to Sault Ste. Marie. As construction at that time was suspended, the group walked the tracks to Sudbury, arriving on 24 June 1885. Jacobson was hired by the Canadian Copper Company (CCC) where he remained for the next fifteen years, working at various places such as the Copper Cliff mine, Evans mine, Blezard mine and in the roast yards. He was a supporter of the *Oikeuden Ohje* (Golden Rule Temperance Society) and a founding member of the *Copper Cliffin Suomalainen Evankelis-Luterilainen Wuoristo-Seurakunta* (Copper Cliff Wuoristo Finnish Evangelical Lutheran Church). A deeply religious man, it was said that only the worst blizzards kept him and his family from attending church. He served for twenty-one years on the church council between 1897 and 1930, and also taught Sunday school and Finnish language classes. While in Copper Cliff he married Susanna Franssi, who came from Ylistaro, Finland. In 1893 he made a brief trip to Finland with his wife and one child. He returned to Copper Cliff and resumed work with the Canadian Copper Company.

In 1899 he acquired a farmsite consisting of 144 acres on Lot 7 in Concession 3 of Waters Township and moved there permanently in 1901. He started with mixed farming and later became a dairy farmer. While Jacobson has sometimes been labelled as the first rural landholder in the area, it was actually Mikki Myllymäki who gained this distinction in 1885, having purchased a farmstead and mining property near the Mond Smelter in Denison Township.[15]

The leading role played by Jacobson within the Finnish community did not go unnoticed by *The Sudbury Star*:

> Thomas Jacobson was in the van of that migration from Finland which, within the next few years, was to bring to Sudbury and Copper Cliff some of their best miners, most progressive farmers, and finest citizens, migration whose contribution to the development of the mining industry in Sudbury can hardly be measured.[16]

When Waters Township was incorporated in 1903, he was acclaimed as a councillor. He served on the township council for many years and was active in developing local roads. His wife passed away in 1934. Thomas and Susanna had seven children: Anna (born 1892), Hilda (1895), Jacob (1896), Carl (1901), Maria (1902), Niilo (1905) and Vieno (1910). With his splendid patriarchal figure and his beard extending down to his waist, he emerged as an unforgettable Finnish personality. He left a powerful legacy as all his children eventually resided in the Sudbury area. One of his grandchildren is Judy Erola, who became a member of the federal cabinet in the 1980s. Jacobson died on 26 December 1938.

A group photograph of Thomas Jacobson (1866-1938) and his family (c. 1920s). Thomas (see biography 1) is shown seated at the left front row beside his wife, the former Susanna Franssi. (R. Kujala, private collection)

A marriage photograph of Frank (1880-1944) and Margaretta Peltoniemi Anderson (1882-1966) (see biography 2), taken in Copper Cliff in 1901. (Anderson Farm Museum)

This group photograph taken in 1944 shows many of the early volunteers who helped to establish the tradition of the Finnish Canadian Grand Festival. Karl Lehto (1888-1985) (see biography 3) is shown here second from the left in the front row. (Finnish Canadian Historical Society)

Rev. Arvi Heinonen (1887-1963) (see biography 4) was the dynamic Finnish-speaking minister of the Presbyterian (United) Church who won many converts from Lutheranism in the area between 1913 and 1923. (Finnish Canadian Historical Society)

With the appointment of Sir Clifford Sifton as the minister of the Interior in the new Liberal government in 1896, the focus of Canadian immigration shifted from the United States to Europe. The resulting Finnish migration to Canada came in three major waves (figure 1). The first, consisting of more than 20,700 settlers, occurred between 1901 and World War I. The relative significance of Canada as a destination for Finns had by then increased considerably, and it now accounted for about 17 percent of Finland's emigration.[17] The migratory movement, however, was certainly larger than the official statistics indicate, as Finns were often classified as Swedes or Russians. Many Swedish-speaking Finns, for example, adopted a tradition of referring to themselves either as Swedes or Canadians rather than Finns. Indeed, this tendency was so strong that it appears to have continued up to the 1990s.[18] The open border between the United States and Canada before the 1920s also created a floating labour force that made it difficult to determine an immigrant's real country of residence.

Figure 1
Finnish Immigration to Canada (1901-91)

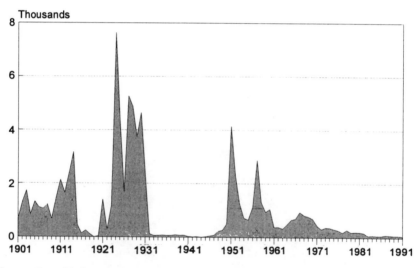

Source: See table 1.

A second wave began in 1921. The momentum of the 1920s could be attributed largely to the immigration restrictions imposed south of the border by the United States Quota Act (1921-24) and the Immigration Act (1924), which reduced the number of Finns permitted to enter the country to 566.[19] More than 37,000 Finns arrived throughout the decade and by 1930 Canada was the leading country of destination for Finnish emigrants. It appears, however, that many of those who came to Canada during the

1930s subsequently reemigrated to the United States. The third flow took place between 1950 and 1960, when another 17,000 Finns arrived. The reduction in migration after the 1960s was influenced by the introduction of a point system and the abolition of discrimination in Canadian immigration policy. These changes were significant as they made it more difficult for Finns to emigrate to Canada. The growing popularity of Sweden as an alternative destination for Finns was another factor minimizing the emigrant flow across the Atlantic Ocean. Immigration records indicate that more than 87,500 Finnish immigrants came to Canada between 1901 and 1991. This number constituted approximately 0.8 percent of the total immigration flow to Canada for the period.[20]

The character of Finnish immigration throughout the century reflected other changes as well. Whereas women constituted only 30 percent of the total number of Finns in Canada at the turn of the century, by 1967 they exceeded the number of male arrivals. By 1991 the female proportion rose to more than 53 percent. Of the 5,724 Finnish immigrants who arrived in Canada between 1968 and 1992, for instance, 3,090 (54 percent) consisted of females. A number of other trends also involved women. In the earlier years, the majority of women were young and single, a feature that helped to foster among them a high degree of self-dependence. Those who were attracted to rural areas or resource towns found themselves greatly outnumbered by men. By 1931, Finnish women had become more urbanized than their male counterparts, as opportunities to work as live-in maids or in the service industries such as restaurants, hotels and hospitals proved to be more plentiful in the large urban centres. Finnish women dispersed themselves as follows:

> [I]t is important to remember that there were three distinct categories of Finnish immigrant women, the largest group being urban women, often single, and mainly domestic servants. A second group encompassed those who lived in or near the resource towns and catered to the needs of the male labourers. . . . In this group I would also include the "stump farmers," those rural women who lived within commuting distance of cities such as Sudbury and Thunder Bay. The third group, and the smallest, were the women on the prairies.[21]

Another change involved the Swedish-speaking Finns. Prior to the 1930s, it is estimated that up to 20 percent of the immigrants from Finland may have been Swedish-speaking; this proportion, however, then dropped significantly. Of the nearly 100,000 Finns recognized in the 1991 census, Swedish-speaking Finns accounted for only 975, or a mere 1 percent of the total.[22] These Swedish-speaking Finns are now concentrated in the Vancouver and Toronto area. A more recent trend involves the number of non-immigrant Finns with temporary status. In 1987, for instance, there were more than nine hundred Finns in Canada with student/employment author-izations or visitor status, whereas only ninety-six arrived as immigrants. Since Finland's reorientation towards the European Union in the 1990s, the number of Finns with temporary status has dropped to less than three hundred. The contemporary pattern of migration, therefore, can no longer be described as a search by immigrants for permanent employment or a new lifestyle; rather, it consists essentially of temporary movers who come to Canada for short-term jobs, personal visitations or educational opportunities. Whether or not this new trend will have any major long-term consequences for the Finnish Canadian community remains to be seen.

Distribution

The distribution of Finns in Canada between 1901 and 1996 is shown in table 2. From 2,502 in 1901 their numbers peaked at 43,885 in 1931 before declining slightly in 1941. The figures then increased again, culminating in a record high number of 59,436 in 1961. This level remained constant during the 1960s before dropping in the 1970s and 1980s; by 1996 only 33,590 persons were recorded as having single Finnish ancestry.

The statistical interpretation of who constitutes a Finn, however, has recently become more complicated. Traditionally, the number of Finns has been determined from ethnic data based on a single-origin concept. Until the 1971 census, it was the respondent's paternal or father's ancestry that was reported, and only one origin could be identified. In the 1981 census both of these restrictions were removed. One effect of these changes was a sizable reduction in the number of Finns responding in the previous single-origin category; another result was the appearance of a new and larger group of multiple-origin persons with only one parent of Finnish background. The results of these changes were striking (figure 2 and table 3). In the 1996 census, 108,720 respondents indicated some linkage with Finnish ancestry. Of this total, 33,590 (30.9 percent) viewed themselves as single-origin Finns. The remaining 75,135 (69.1 percent) consisted of individuals with only a partial attachment to the ethnic group. According to Statistics Canada, it is the Finnish immigrant group that tends to report single origins, whereas native-born Finns generally indicate multiple origins. Due to the passing away of the older immigrants, the ratio of single to mixed ancestry in Canada has shifted significantly in favour of the latter in recent years.

The distribution of Finnish settlement by province and territory was established early in the century. Unlike Finland, where the population was evenly distributed throughout the southernmost parts of the country, the Finns in Canada found themselves dispersed in a huge territory that was almost thirty times the size of their homeland. Ontario, the Prairie provinces (Alberta, Saskatchewan and Manitoba) and British Columbia emerged

Table 2
Finnish Settlement in Canada by Province/Territory (1901-96)

Province/Territory	Census year										
	1901	1911	1921	1931	1941	1951	1961	1971	1981	1991	1996
Nfld.	—	—	—	—	—	31	36	45	70	15	20
P.E.I.	—	—	1	1	—	7	16	—	10	15	10
N.S.	6	43	45	99	96	159	254	235	260	120	135
N.B.	2	24	35	135	109	149	165	145	95	100	95
Quebec	115	216	76	2,937	2,043	1,600	2,277	1,865	1,140	735	645
Ontario	1,225	8,622	12,835	27,137	26,827	29,327	39,906	38,515	33,395	25,470	21,940
Manitoba	76	1,080	506	1013	808	821	1,070	1,450	1,060	665	605
Sask.	137	1,008	1,937	2,313	1,940	1,805	1,891	1,725	1,275	1,045	840
Alberta	99	1,588	2,926	3,318	3,452	2,958	3,662	3,590	4,135	2,365	1,825
B.C.	780	2,858	3,112	6,858	6,332	6,790	10,037	11,510	10,810	8,620	7,415
Y.T.	62	61	21	34	55	50	72	95	30	55	20
N.W.T.	—	—	—	4	20	48	50	35	45	35	30
Total	2,502	15,500	21,494	43,885	41,683	43,745	59,436	59,215	52,315	39,320	33,590

Note: These figures refer to single origins only.

Source: Statistics Canada, *Censuses of Canada* (1901-96).

Figure 2
Finns in Canada by Origin and Birthplace (1901-96)

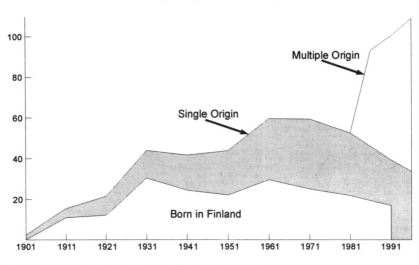

Source: Statistics Canada, *Censuses of Canada* (1901-96).

Table 3
Finnish Settlement in Canada by Single and
Multiple Origins (1996)

Province	Single origin	Multiple origin	Total
Newfoundland	20	125	150
Prince Edward Island	10	75	85
Nova Scotia	135	530	665
New Brunswick	95	540	635
Quebec	645	1,350	1,995
Ontario	21,940	39,280	61,220
Manitoba	605	2,255	2,865
Saskatchewan	840	2,795	3,640
Alberta	1,825	9,180	11,005
British Columbia	7,415	18,735	26,150
Yukon Territory	20	140	165
Northwest Territories	30	120	150
Total	33,590	75,135	108,720
Percentage	30.9	69.1	100.0

Source: Statistics Canada, *Census of Canada* (1996).

as the most favoured destinations. Before World War I, more than one-half of all Finnish settlement was found in Ontario. While the prairies served as the secondary destination until 1921, this position was gradually taken over by British Columbia. The Atlantic provinces (New Brunswick, Nova Scotia, Prince Edward Island and Newfoundland and Labrador), Yukon and the Northwest Territories were never successful in attracting permanent Finnish immigrants.[23] In Quebec, only Montreal served as a magnet. The provincial distribution of the Finnish population at the peak period of Canadian settlement in 1961 is illustrated in map 1. Since 1961 there have been changes to the provincial distribution of Finnish settlement. While Ontario's position remained supreme in 1996 with 65 percent of the total Finnish Canadian population by single origin (56 percent including multiple origins), British Columbia's proportion rose to 22 percent by single origin (24 percent including multiple origins). In contrast, the share for the remaining provinces declined.

The rural and urban distribution of the Finnish population fluctuated over the years. In the early years of the century, Finns developed a strong preference for rural and resource-based areas. In 1921, two-thirds of them could be found in these districts, many of them in rural or urban *pesäpaikat* (nesting places known as Finntowns) similar to those found in Michigan and Minnesota.[24] This geographical orientation has sometimes been attributed to the Finns having "an urge for land in their blood."[25] The fact that land was often free or available at a cheap price in these areas was another attraction. For others, land was sought as a stabilizing influence. According to one Finnish vice-consul in Canada, immigrants were "warned by those who have come before him and who write home, to keep away from the city because unemployment always exists there."[26] Farming districts were favoured as they provided complementary sources of employment to those of forestry and mining. While urbanization of the Finns officially rose to 46 percent by 1931, the reality was that more than four-fifths of these urban dwellers could still be found in small communities of 30,000 or less. Regardless of where they lived, Statistics Canada reported that the Finns at the time exhibited a higher than average propensity towards segregation and a lower tendency to become naturalized Canadian citizens.[27]

The initial phases of Finnish occupance favoured rural/resource settlements, many of which flanked the national railway lines. Among them were included the coal-mining areas of Wellington and Nanaimo on Vancouver Island, the farming districts of Salmon Arm, Solsqua and White Lake in the interior of British Columbia, the mixed-farming areas around Sylvan Lake, Eckville, Radway and Smoky Lake in central Alberta, New Finland and

Map 1
Distribution of Finns in Canada (1961)

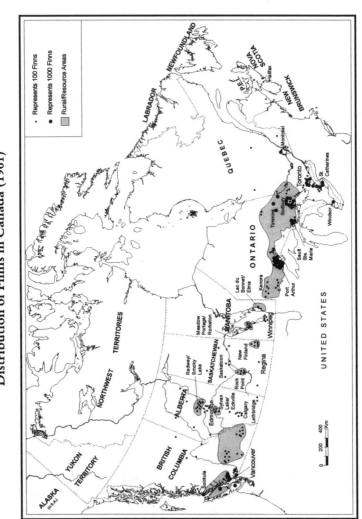

Source: Statistics Canada, *Census of Canada* (1961).

Rock Point in southern Saskatchewan, Selkirk, Lac du Bonnet, Elma, Meadow Portage and Rorketon in Manitoba and virtually all of Northern Ontario straddling the CPR and Canadian National Railways (CNR) railway lines in the wilderness between Sudbury and Kenora.

Some settlements had interesting origins. Sylvan Lake and Eckville, for example, attracted Finns from the United States beginning in 1902. New Finland, encompassing the area around Tantallon and Wapella, served as the first Finnish settlement on the prairies, and it had the distinction of being the first and only block agricultural settlement offered to the Finns.[28] Rock Point was unique as it served as the largest agrarian settlement in western Canada up to the 1980s.[29] Mention must also be made of the utopian socialist experiment founded on Malcolm Island in British Columbia. Known as Sointula ("a place of harmony"), this colonization scheme started by Matti Kurikka and A.B. Mäkelä in 1901 succeeded in attracting hundreds of Finns. The project, however, was beset with difficulties and it ultimately failed in 1904-1905; many of the settlers then moved on to create a smaller colony at Webster's Corners near Vancouver.[30]

Despite this preference for rural and resource settings, some large Finnish urban centres did emerge. Among the first to develop in the 1880s and 1890s were Thunder Bay (Port Arthur and Fort William) and Copper Cliff. After the turn of the century, both Toronto and Vancouver began to attract immigrants as well. By 1911 Thunder Bay, Toronto and Vancouver had established themselves as the three main urban centres for the Finns in Canada. World War I wrought considerable change to the existing pattern of settlement, as it fostered the expansion of Finnish settlement in the mining and manufacturing centres of Northern Ontario, such as Sault Ste. Marie, Cobalt, Timmins, Sudbury and North Bay.

The migratory infusion of the 1920s greatly reinforced the existing Finnish centres of Thunder Bay, Toronto, Vancouver, Sudbury and Timmins. For the first time, places such as Montreal, Winnipeg, Hamilton, Windsor, Calgary and Kirkland Lake also began to draw large numbers of Finns. The emergence of Montreal at this time is noteworthy. Its growth can be partly explained by the restrictions on immigration to the United States that were introduced in the 1920s, which led to Montreal becoming the first destination point for most Finns coming to North America. According to Laine, support by the Finnish State was also important in reinforcing the new role played by Montreal:

> Its base of operations in Canada was the consulate that it had established in Montreal during the early 1920s and upgraded to the status of consulate general in 1925. Akseli K.L. Rauanheimo, who served first as consul and then as consul general until his death in the early 1930s, became the chief instrument in achieving his government's aims. For example, he cham-

pioned the establishment of *Montrealin Pyhän Mikaelin Suomalainen Luterilainen Seurakunta* (St. Michael's Finnish Lutheran Congregation of Montreal) and *Montrealin Suomalainen Seura* (Finnish Society of Montreal). He also enlisted the aid of the *Suomen Merimieslähetysseura* (Finnish Seamen's Mission Society) in Helsinki . . . with a mandate to establish and maintain a *Suomalainen Siirtolaiskoti* (Finnish Immigrant Home) in Montreal.[31]

Montreal was distinctive as the Finns who lived there were predominantly female, the great majority of them serving as maids.[32] The latter was not surprising, given the fact that Finnish women were allowed into Canada only as farmers' wives and daughters, or as domestics.

Table 4
Finnish Population by Census Metropolitan Area (1996)

CMA	Single origin	Multiple origin	Total
Toronto	6,070	8,060	14,135
Thunder Bay	4,840	7,490	12,340
Vancouver	3,825	7,820	11,645
Sudbury	2,450	4,115	6,560
Calgary	610	2,810	3,420
Edmonton	495	2,385	2,885
Ottawa-Hull	545	2,050	2,595
Victoria	530	1,425	1,960
Winnipeg	385	1,395	1,780
Montreal	490	925	1,415
Hamilton	275	1,030	1,305
London	295	850	1,140
St. Catharines-Niagara	245	835	1,080
Kitchener	230	840	1,070
Oshawa	180	785	960
Windsor	245	550	800
Saskatoon	165	600	770
Regina	85	500	595
Halifax	80	345	425
St. John	25	95	120
St. John's	20	60	80
Chicoutimi-Jonquière	0	30	35
Sherbrooke	0	25	30
Quebec	10	10	20
Trois Rivières	0	0	0
Total	22,095	45,030	67,165
Percentage of Canadian Finnish Population	65.8	59.9	61.8

Note: Totals may vary because of rounding.
Source: Statistics Canada, *Census of Canada* (1996).

The emergence of the Finns as an urbanized group after World War II signalled a sharp break from the past. As the 1950s tide of immigrants came largely from urban areas in Finland, the previous attraction of farming and employment in resource areas no longer held the same pull. Thus, there was an increasing trend for this ethnic group, like other Canadians, to settle in the larger centres. In fact, by 1996 more than 60 percent of all Finns in Canada resided in one of Canada's metropolitan centres (table 4). Within this metropolitan framework, two-thirds of the Finnish population could be found in the four major centres of Toronto, Thunder Bay, Vancouver and Sudbury. Other changes occurred as well. The historical role previously played by Montreal as a port of entry for Finns disappeared. On the other hand, newer settlements such as Calgary, Edmonton and Victoria in western Canada had become much more significant. The most important trend, however, was the rise of Toronto as Canada's premier centre for Finnish activity. Whereas Thunder Bay had long served as the largest Finnish centre up to 1991, by 1996 it had been superseded by Toronto:

> It should also be noted that many national Finnish organizations have their head offices and/or presidents in Toronto. These include Canadian Friends of Finland, Finnish Association for Seniors in Canada, Finnish Canadian Cultural Federation, Finnish Organization of Canada, Finnish Language School Teachers Association, and Finnish War Veterans in Canada. Both of Toronto's Finnish newspapers also have national distribution. Toronto's influence, therefore, extends far beyond the city and affects, on some level, all Finnish Canadians.[33]

Demographic Characteristics

The Canadian censuses provide insights regarding the demographical character of the Finns, such as birthplace, mother tongue, home language, religion and gender-based age groupings. The proportion of Finnish Canadians whose birthplace is shown as Finland has already been illustrated in figure 2. During the early years of the century, more than 70 percent of the Finnish population reported birthplaces in Finland; by the 1950s and 1960s, however, this proportion had dropped to around 50 percent. By the 1991 census, only 43 percent of the 39,230 Finns of single origin indicated Finland as their birthplace. Thus the contemporary Finnish population has now become dominated by individuals who are non-immigrants.

Among the types of language data provided by the census are those that pertain to the concepts of mother tongue and home language. Mother tongue refers to the first language learned at home and still understood by an individual. Mother tongue data was first collected in 1921 for Finns over ten years of age; thereafter, it covered the entire ethnic group. Home language, on the other hand, is defined as the language currently spoken, or most often spoken, at home. Information dealing with home language is available from 1971. A comparison of mother tongue and home language is vital in assessing the process of language maintenance and transfer. Language maintenance occurs when Finnish is used both as a mother tongue and home language, whereas language transfer is said to have taken place when the language most often used at home differs from the mother tongue.

Figure 3
Finnish Population in Canada by Mother Tongue
and Home Language (1901-91)

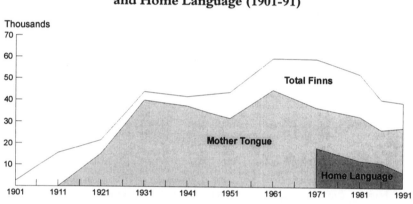

Source: Statistics Canada, *Censuses of Canada* (1901-91).

The retention of Finnish as a mother tongue remained high until World War II (figure 3). By 1961 the proportion of Finnish Canadians with some knowledge of the language had declined to around 75 percent. According to the 1991 census data, the comparable figure for Finns of single orgin is 71 percent. The use of Finnish as a home language, however, reveals a much different picture. Only 31 percent of Finnish Canadians in 1971 used the language regularly at home; by 1991, this number had dropped to 18 percent. These trends indicate that the cords of linguistic transmission between the generations by 1991 had been cut to such an extent that Finnish was well on its way to becoming an endangered language. Even where the language is spoken at home, it often reflects a modified version of Finnish and English referred to as *fingliskaa*. While some view this hybrid form of the Finnish language in a humorous vein, others have been saddened by the *siansaksaa* (gibberish) trend.[34] Regardless of the point of view, this trend portends that the continuance of Finnish ethnicity in the new millennium will not be accompanied by any substantial language component.

The above tendency has already forced some Finnish-based institutions to make significant language adjustments.[35] In some churches, however, the increased use of English has met with resistance:

> [E]xisting Finnish ethnic congregations, meaning those whose main language is Finnish, are struggling with their English ministry. As it looks now, some have already passed the point beyond which their survival as independent congregations is very unlikely. . . . The present situation in Canada among the Finnish Lutheran congregations does not support the assumption that the general history of North-Americanization will repeat itself. For a reason, unknown to me, Finnish congregations do not seem to follow the well-travelled path of . . . Canadianization.[36]

Within the Finnish media, though, both *Vapaa Sana* (The Free Word) and *Kaiku/Echo* publications have accepted the need for some use of English. The declining usage of everyday Finnish has likewise spurred the rise of a heritage language school movement in places such as Toronto, Thunder Bay and Sudbury.

Table 5
Religious Affiliation of Finnish Canadians (1931-81)
(in percentages)

	Year					
Affiliation	1931	1941	1951	1961	1971	1981
Lutheran	87.7	85.5	75.8	70.2	60.3	59.4
United	3.9	5.6	10.3	12.8	12.6	10.9
Roman Catholic	1.3	2.0	3.7	4.9	5.9	4.8
Pentecostal	0.0	0.4	—	1.3	2.2	4.2
Anglican	1.5	2.2	3.8	4.4	4.3	3.3
Presbyterian	2.1	2.0	2.5	1.8	2.1	1.6
Other/No preference	3.4	2.1	3.9	4.5	12.4	15.7
Total	43,885	41,683	43,745	59,436	59,215	52,315

Source: Statistics Canada, *Censuses of Canada* (1931-81).

Information regarding the religious affiliations of the Finnish Canadian population is unfortunately available only for the 1931-81 censuses. The majority of Finns have nominally remained proponents of the Lutheran faith (table 5). This official support ranged from a high of 88 percent in 1931 to a low of 59 percent by 1981. The United Church served as the second affiliation of choice, and support for it grew from 4 to 11 percent in the same interval. While of lesser importance, some adherence has been given to the Roman Catholic, Pentecostal and Anglican faiths. A notable trend was the growing importance of the Pentecostal Church during the 1960s and 1970s. A secularization tendency can likewise be observed as the proportion of Finns indicating no religious affiliation grew from 3.4 percent in 1931 to more than 15 percent by 1981. This latter figure, however, understates the real situation, as many Lutherans rarely attend church.

Table 6
Finnish Ethnic Origins by Selected Age Groups (1931 and 1991)
(in percentages)

	1931		1991 (Single origin)	
Age	Male	Female	Male	Female
Less than 15	10.1	9.9	3.4	3.3
15 to 24	9.9	10.4	4.4	4.4
25 to 44	28.0	16.8	14.9	15.3
45 to 64	8.8	4.7	15.6	17.6
65 and over	0.8	0.5	8.5	12.6
Total	57.6	42.3	46.8	53.2

Source: Statistics Canada, *Censuses of Canada* (1931 and 1991).

Finally, census data permits the temporal analysis of the Finnish population by gender-based age groupings. Table 6 provides a revealing comparison of this characteristic for the two census years 1931 and 1991. The age-group comparison affirms the male-to-female transition of the community and its maturation from a youthful to an elderly population. In 1931 some 20 percent of the Finnish Canadian population was fifteen years of age or less; by 1991 the comparable figure was less than 7 percent. In contrast, only 1.3 percent were sixty-five years of age or over in 1931; this proportion is starkly different from the figure of more than 21 percent shown for 1991. The high ratio of seniors portends significant drops in the 2001 census for the number of Finns showing single origin and Finnish mother tongue and home language responses. The contemporary manifestation of this maturation process is evidenced by the rise of the seniors' rest home movement in Toronto, Vancouver, Thunder Bay, Sudbury and Sault Ste. Marie.

CHAPTER II

Geographical Pattern of Finnish Settlement in the Sudbury Area

This chapter examines the origins of Finnish settlement in the Sudbury area and illustrates how the Finns dispersed themselves into distinctive urban working-class "Finntowns" and agriculturally based "enclaves." Unfortunately, little census data are available regarding Finns who settled here prior to World War I. While inferences can be made from the census manuscripts of 1891 and 1901, it was not until 1921 that consistent data became available. A summary of the number of Finns in the Sudbury District, the Sudbury Census Metropolitan Area (CMA) and the City of Sudbury between 1921 and 1996 is given in table 7.

A number of observations can be gleaned from these data. In relative terms, Finns were most important between World Wars I and II. For the territorial District of Sudbury, they constituted the largest non-French/English ethnic group from 1921 to 1951, accounting for 5 to 8 percent of the population. After the 1950s, the highest-ranking ethnic position was taken over by the Italians. The ranking of the Finns in the CMA fell below the Italians and the Ukrainians in 1971, but rose above the latter after 1981. In the town/city of Sudbury, Finns were the main ethnic group in the 1930s, at which time their relative proportion stood at over 7 percent. By 1941 Ukrainians had emerged as the largest ethnic group with the Italians following in second place by 1951. In the 1960s Germans moved into third place over the Finns.[1] While the proportion of Finns had dropped to 2.4 percent by 1991, they regained their position as the second-largest ethnic group after the Italians. The rise in the ranking of the Finns from fourth to second place in the city between 1971 and 1981 can be attributed in part to the enlargement of its boundaries to include Broder and part of Dill Townships after the formation of regional government in 1973.

Notes to Chapter II are on pp. 281-85.

Table 7
Number of Finns in the Sudbury Area (1921-96)

Year	Sudbury District			Sudbury Census Metropolitan Area			Town/City of Sudbury		
	No.	%	Rank	No.	%	Rank	No.	%	Rank
1921	2,517	5.8	(1)	—	—	—	206	2.4	(2)
1931	4,633	8.0	(1)	—	—	—	1,374	7.4	(1)
1941	4,704	5.8	(1)	—	—	—	1,241	3.9	(2)
1951	5,411	4.9	(1)	—	—	—	1,478	3.5	(3)
1961	7,446	4.5	(2)	—	—	—	2,994	3.2	(4)
1971	7,095	3.6	(2)	5,470	3.5	(3)	2,750	3.0	(4)
1981	—	—	—	4,490	3.0	(2)	3,000	3.3	(2)
1986	—	—	—	3,760	2.5	(2)	2,455	2.8	(2)
				2,695★					
1991	—	—	—	3,340	2.1	(2)	2,200	2.4	(2)
				3,330★					
1996	350			2,450			1,700		
	470★			4,155★			2,360★		

Note: Rank refers to ethnic ranking, excluding the British and French. This concept of
       ethnicity has been retained for the rest of the text. The asterisk (★) refers to multi-
       ple rather than single Finnish origins.
Source: Statistics Canada, *Censuses of Canada* (1921-96).

The Finnish population reached its zenith of more than 7,400 in 1961.
By 1996, however, their numbers by single origin had dropped to 2,450 for
the CMA and 1,700 for the city of Sudbury. If census figures for multiple
origins are included, the total number of people with links to the Finnish
heritage in the Sudbury area in 1996 was approximately the same as it was
in 1961. Of this total, almost all constituted Finnish- rather than Swedish-
speaking Finns.

Migration to the Sudbury Area

Why did Finns choose to leave Finland and the United States to come to
Sudbury? A number of "push" and "pull" factors caused this movement.
For those who left Finland prior to World War I, economic conditions
related to overpopulation in agricultural areas, the paucity of industrial
employment and the rise of a large landless rural class were of paramount
importance. Since these factors were most important in Ostrobothnia, this
western region of Finland served as the point of origin for most of the early
immigrants. Both Pikkusaari's and Krats's studies support Kero's description of this region as "Emigration Finland."[2] Non-economic considerations

such as the desire for political and religious freedom, the fear of Russification and the dislike of military conscription served as other spurs to migration.[3] Those who came to the Sudbury area were largely male farmers and agricultural workers from communes such as Kauhava, Kurikka, Vähäkyrö, Ilmajoki, Jalasjärvi, Nurmo, Kauhajoki, Ylistaro and Lapua in the province of Vaasa. The pattern of male dominance at the time can be partly explained by the fact that many men came to Canada alone with the understanding that they would either return to Finland or send for their families at a later date.

The pull element associated with Canada was clear-cut—the country was a favoured destination because it offered employment and high wages in unskilled jobs at construction sites and in the extractive industries. The availability of land to men over eighteen years of age was also significant. As early as 1885, the minister of Agriculture, who was in charge of Canadian immigration, was quoted as saying that "many of the Finns . . . who immigrated to this country . . . will use their very considerable earnings to enable them to settle on land, and this is in addition to the large sums which many have remitted to enable their friends to come to this country."[4] This view was supported by the well-known geologist A.P. Coleman, who noted in a speech made in Sudbury in 1912 that "Every Finlander, as soon as he can, takes up 160 acres and builds him a shack and gets a cow or two. He is never satisfied until he does that."[5] The movement of Finns to the Sudbury area was affected both by the phenomenon of chain migration and indirect migration via the United States. Chain migration can be defined as the encouragement and assistance of friends and relatives to immigrate to Canada by those compatriots and family who had already settled here.[6] This was an important linkage that sustained the outflow of Finns from Ostrobothnia throughout the 1920s. Another aspect of the migratory move to Sudbury was the complicated pathway between an emigrant's point of origin and final destination (figure 4). As was the case for Frank Anderson (biography 2), emigration may have involved the United States as a stepping stone. Immigrants often came here from the Minnesota Mesabi Range and Michigan Copper Country, where blacklisting and negative labour experiences encouraged them to seek alternative destinations. Many Finns crossed and recrossed the Canada-United States border before deciding on the Sudbury area as their ultimate "Eldorado." This open border concept between the United States and Canada applied equally well to Finland, as it was not unusual for Finns to make several trips overseas before deciding on permanent residency in Sudbury. Women, however, were less peripatetic than the men, and moved more directly from their origin to their destination.

Figure 4
Immigration Paths to Beaver Lake
in Lorne Township (1900-45)

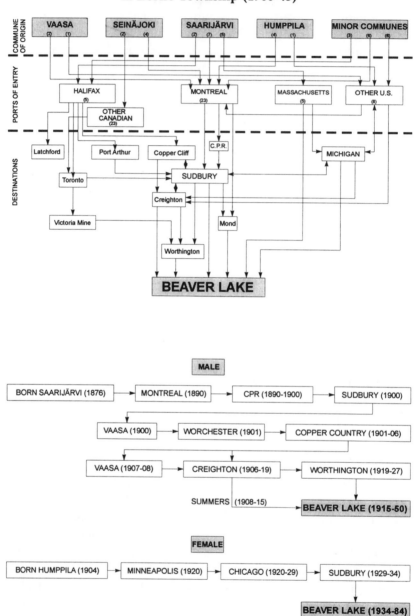

Source: Oiva Saarinen and G.O. Tapper, "The Beaver Lake Finnish Community: A
Case Study of Ethnic Transition as Influenced by the Variables of Time and
Spatial Networks, ca. 1907-1983," in *Finns in North America*, pp. 170-71.

Biography 2
Frank and Margaretta Anderson: The Dairy Farmers

The Anderson Farm Museum is one of the outstanding historical landmarks in the town of Walden, located just west of Copper Cliff. The farm was founded by Frank and Margaretta Anderson. Born in Kauhava, Finland, in 1880, Frank left Finland for the United States in 1897 and came to Copper Cliff via Minnesota in 1901. In the latter year he married Margaretta Peltoniemi who was born in Oulu, Finland, in 1882. After working several years as a miner and shift boss for the Canadian Copper Company at Copper Cliff, he became a general foreman for Inco at the Crean Hill mine (1906-10). In 1908 his future with the company was secured when he found and returned a payroll. He was assured that he would never again have to look for a job. In 1910 he transferred to Creighton. In the following year, he retired temporarily from mining to build up his health and acquired a quarter lot (forty acres) where the museum now sits. He later returned to Creighton and worked there until 1921.

Margaretta assumed control over the operation of the farm while Frank cleared the land and undertook other duties, such as serving as a municipal coun-cillor for Waters Township for five years between 1922 and 1927. In 1926 he returned to mining and became a shift boss at Frood Mine. By 1932 the Anderson farm had grown to 366 acres. *The Sudbury Star* claimed at the time that their model farm, consisting of ninety head of cattle, was the best dairy herd in North-ern Ontario and one of the best in Ontario.[7] The farm had a permanent staff of six plus the family; at its peak, it had a staff of fifteen. A dairy operation was estab-lished in 1935 to serve the Creighton townsite. After Frank's death in 1944, the dairy plant was sold to Copper Cliff Dairy; the Anderson farm, however, continued to supply milk until 1958. Margaretta passed away in 1966.

Most of the Anderson property was purchased by Inco in 1950, excluding the 13.89 acres where the farm buildings were situated. The town of Walden acquired the remaining parcel and the farm buildings in 1977 as a museum site for heritage purposes. In 1981 a master plan was approved, which identified the site both as a farm museum and as a central point "for the collection, preservation, and display of material related to the history of the Town of Walden."[8] The Anderson Farm Museum opened on 2 June 1985. In 1987 a Board of Management was appointed; two years later, a full-time curator was hired. The museum eventually became part of the provincial operating grant system in 1990. Since its inception, the heritage site has played a vital role in preserving aspects of the township's his-tory through its promotion of publications, cultural exhibits, fairs, guided tours, craft workshops and live theatre. It also served as a venue for FINNFORUM V, an academic conference that was held in Sudbury in 1995. The museum is supported by a large number of dedicated volunteers.

Immigration in the 1920s was substantially different from that which had taken place previously. The Bolshevik Revolution in Russia, Finland's Declaration of Independence in 1917 and the Finnish Civil War of 1918 created conditions of economic and political uncertainty and divided the nation into conservative "White Guard" and socialist/communist "Red Guard" factions. Restricted from going to the United States because of new immigration laws, adherents of both factions migrated to the lumber camps of Northern Ontario and the industrial towns of Thunder Bay and Sudbury. Among them was a group of political refugees who went to New Liskeard. They comprised fifty Red Guard leaders, including the former head of the coalition government when Finland was still a Grand Duchy, Oskari Tokoi.[9] While emigration from Ostrobothnia continued, more of the newcomers now came from the urban centres of Helsinki, Turku and Tampere in southern Finland. Another contrasting feature was the increased proportion of housewives and young women seeking employment as domestics.

The influx of the 1950s was underlain by push-and-pull factors linked to the overbearing influence of the USSR in Finland, an uncertain economic future and the powerful attraction of the Canadian economy. With respect to the latter, the expansion of the mining and construction industries in Sudbury and Elliot Lake and the lure of forestry jobs drew hundreds of Finns to the area. While Ostrobothnia remained a favoured point of origin, the postwar immigrants came from all parts of Finland as well as from the ceded area of Karelia.

Distribution

As early as 1882-83, Finns are known to have worked for the CPR at its various railway construction camps in the Sudbury area. While their stay was relatively short, their appearance received favourable comments from government officials:

> I wish particularly to call your attention to a very valuable class of immigrants who have this year come . . . and who bid fair to become most desirable and thrifty settlers, viz.: Finlanders who were directed here by Mr. Dyke [Liverpool agent] and who being pioneers of a large body of their countrymen, whose intention it is to leave Europe next year, it was very desirable should be induced to settle here. These men went to work on the Canadian Pacific Railway at Sudbury, under Mr. Worthington, who pronounced them amongst the best workers he has ever had.[10]

These temporary railway employees served as the forerunners of the larger flow of Finns who later came to the area to seek permanent work opportunities in agriculture and in the resource industries.

Copper Cliff rather than Sudbury served as the first site of permanent Finnish settlement. It was second only to the Thunder Bay area as *the* destination for Finnish immigrants coming to Ontario. From Copper Cliff, settlement spread out into other areas, in the form of four distinctive types of urban Finntown clusters and rural enclaves that permitted them to be near their fellow Finns. The first spread consisted of those miners who moved in groups to temporary camps that lasted only as long as the mines were operational. The second outflow involved the shift of miners to permanent mining towns such as Garson and Creighton. The third dispersion was the drift to Sudbury and its environs in the 1920s and 1930s. Within and around this emerging hub, three working-class neighbourhoods evolved: a downtown community centred around the Elm-Spruce Street area, the Donovan district situated between Frood Mine and the downtown core and the Lockerby area, found south of the built-up part of Sudbury in McKim Township. The final ripple effect was directed to the *farmikontri* (farming country) in the townships of Lorne, Louise, Waters, Broder, Dill, Cleland, Laura and Secord.

Copper Cliff

Permanent Finnish settlement in the Sudbury area started in 1885 when a group of eleven men arrived at the Copper Cliff mining camp on June 24. Four men in this group acquired immediate employment with the Canadian Copper Company as miners at the Copper Cliff No. 1 mine: Jacob Ollila, Eerik Karppi, Jacob Kari and Tuomas Karppi. Tuomas Karppi, who adopted the name of Thomas Jacobson, later emerged as a key figure in both Copper Cliff and Waters Township. Others who may have been in this original group included Juho Lauttamus and Mikki Myllymäki.[11] These pioneers were joined later in the year by a larger group of their countrymen and Finns quickly became an integral part of the local labour force.[12] According to one reminiscence, there was a "score of huge Finlanders" who could be found in the village seeking their wages in 1886-87.[13] In 1887 the first Finnish woman immigrant, Kustaa Pölkki, arrived in Copper Cliff. Her marriage soon thereafter, the birth of a daughter (claimed by Finns to have been the first child born in the community) and the arrival of other Finnish women heralded the normalization of family life. When the smelter and roast heap operations started in 1888, the community was transformed into an industrial village. Additional workers were attracted, and according to Lutheran church statistics there were more than sixty Finns living in the settlement. While they were good workers, one company official at the time complained that some of them were unsanitary and lived "like hogs."[14] Everyday living was made difficult by sulphur fumes from the nearby roast-yards that were so thick that Finnish women often shouted from the doors of their houses so their husbands could find their way home.[15] During the 1890s Copper Cliff continued to serve as the heart of Finnish settlement in the Sudbury area. As one Finnish chronicler noted:

[W]e hold Copper Cliff to be the cradle of [Finnish] material and spiritual efforts which have occurred. Herein was born the first congregation and the church built for it. The first temperance society was founded in Clif [*sic*], which then aspired to spread its influence to other of the Nickel region's new communities. The first youth organization was founded there; as well, therein began the first appearance of socialist ideas among the Finns. It also witnessed the first grim struggles between the new and old ideas and standpoints.[16]

When Copper Cliff was incorporated as a town in 1901, it served as the home for 350 to 400 persons classified as Russian and Lutheran; since Lutheran Finland existed as a Grand Duchy of the Russian Empire at the time, these figures can be taken as an indication of the number of resident Finns. Many Finnish residents, however, were floating workers who remained in the community only for the duration of construction projects. As Copper Cliff was located near other mining campsites where there were men who were single or had families in Finland, it served as a popular gathering place during the weekends.

Map 2
Finns in Copper Cliff (1915)

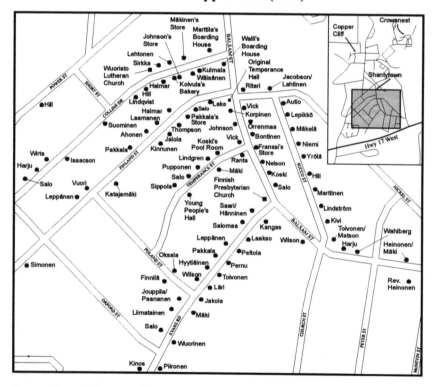

Source: Town of Copper Cliff, *Assessment Roll* (1915).

The Finnish presence in the town manifested itself as a distinctive community (map 2). This visibility was due in part to the Canadian Copper Company's (and later Inco's) policy of concentrating its ethnic labour force in six different parts of the town: Copper Cliff, Shantytown, the East Smelter Hamlet, Crow's Nest, Orford and Evans Mine. The Copper Cliff, Orford and Evans Mine settlements housed the Anglo-Saxon miners and Canadian Copper Company officials, while Shantytown was the home of the Finns, Poles, Ukrainians and French Canadians. Italians were relegated to Crow's Nest.[17] Such segregation was a clear manifestation of the Canadian Copper Company's complete domination of the town:

> [C]ontrol of land leases and privately-owned buildings allowed the company to foster a pattern of occupational segregation in Copper Cliff, as the settlement of "particular occupations, in particular houses, on particular streets" made visible "a hierarchy based on occupational status." Equally important was the company's ability to turn land ownership to the task of ethnic segregation, as immigrants were steered away from housing reserved for Anglo-Saxon employees to the outskirts of the village, and there left "to develop on their own in Shantytown."[18]

This form of corporate dominance, however, was not unique to the Sudbury area; Finns who previously worked in the mining towns of the Lake Superior region of the United States with the Calumet and Hecla Mining Company had also faced similar forms of control.[19]

The construction of the area's first Finnish hall in 1895 was followed by the building of a second hall in 1903 and a Finnish church in 1908. One calculation shows that 574 Finns resided in Copper Cliff in 1915.[20] Life for them at this time has been described as follows:

> 'Cliff' was, however, for us like another Finland. The Finnish language was heard everywhere. The Finns had settled in the same part of the village. To earn a living, and perhaps entertaining the hope of getting rich, Finns set up boarding houses. . . . There were three stores, a bakery, a shoemaker, and a tailor shop, and two public saunas. There was also a billiard room, a movie theatre, two churches and a spacious hall in the middle of the residential area. There was also a Finnish policeman in the Finnish area.[21]

Copper Cliff set the stage for the emergence of the *poikatalo* (boarding and rooming house) as an integral feature of the Finntown settlements. This was a natural development given the fact that the majority of Finns were young single males. Many commercial enterprises sprouted in Shantytown, geared to serving the practical needs of the ethnic group. These included tailors, shoemakers, barbers, small construction operations, midwifery services, two public saunas and taxi services.[22] Other enterprises of note included general stores owned by John Wilson, Herman Koski,

Copper Cliff served as the "cradle of Finnish settlement" in the Sudbury area. One of the first institutions to develop was St. Timothy's (Wuoristo) Evangelical Lutheran Church. Constructed in 1908, it also served for a time as the home of the *Oikeuden Ohje* Temperance Society. (Finnish Canadian Historical Society)

The former Finnish Presbyterian Mission in Copper Cliff around World War I. It was frequently referred to as "Franssi's Church." (Finnish Canadian Historical Society)

A number of successful Finnish business enterprises were established in Copper Cliff, such as Tuomas Franssi's General Goods Store, c. 1915. (Finnish Canadian Historical Society)

Another large business enterprise was Copper Cliff Dairy. It is shown here (c. 1940s) on the former site of the Finnish Presbyterian Mission. (Bill Johnson, private collection)

Finnish miners were attracted to Garson as early as 1908. Numerous boarding houses were established in the townsite, such as the one above, owned by W. Bontinen, 1910. (Ray Kaattari, private collection)

Among the many miners who worked at the Garson mine were Heikki Kallio (left) and Selim Kolari (right), 1919. (Finnish Canadian Historical Society)

The Hollinger mine disaster in 1928 was a watershed event for the Finnish working-class movement. Eight Finns died in this tragedy; as well, their common-law widows and children were denied compensation. *Vapaus* and the FOC used this calamity to promote workers' rights in the Sudbury area. (Multicultural History Society of Ontario)

The 1928 cave-in at Inco's Worthington mine dramatized the image of mining as a dangerous industry. Fortunately, all of the Finns working at the mine were safely evacuated. (John Passi, private collection)

One of the outstanding landmarks in Copper Cliff was Finland Hall, owned by the Young Peoples' Society of Copper Cliff. Erected in 1903, it was destroyed by fire in 1915. (Public Archives of Canada)

From Copper Cliff, Finnish settlement spread into outlying mining camps, such as Sellwood. Shown here is the Finnish Socialist Organization of Canada Hall, 1911. (Public Archives of Canada)

Among the many temporary mining camps to attract Finns was that of Mond. The Mond townsite, formed in 1901, existed until 1923. (John Passi, private collection)

The Finnish Socialist Hall was a centre of activity at Mond. Shown here is a gymnastics display by a group of miners in front of the hall, c. 1914. (John Passi, private collection)

Tuomas Franssi, Henry Mäkinen, Herbert Johnson and Andrew Pakkala, Werne Koivula's bakery and the Copper Cliff Dairy. The Koivula Bakery was a substantial operation that employed up to twenty people. Started around the turn of the century, its reputation grew to such an extent that its products were shipped throughout Canada, as far west as British Columbia. Another major enterprise was Copper Cliff Dairy. Established in 1924, it became the first of several Finnish-based dairies to appear in the Sudbury area.

The Finnish presence in Copper Cliff declined after World War I, following the opening of a street railway connection with Sudbury, the promotion of Sudbury by Inco as the preferred residential site for its workers and the decline of the work force in Copper Cliff from 1,450 to 725 between 1919 and 1923.[23] Finns who previously resided in the rooming and boarding houses of Copper Cliff moved to Sudbury and elsewhere.

Temporary Mining Camps

Prior to World War I, there were more than forty mining camps scattered throughout the Sudbury area (map 3). The oldest camp, Worthington, dated from 1885. Mond, Victoria Mines, Nickelton, Chicago Mine, North Star Mine, Blezard, Gertrude, Crean Hill and Sellwood were other examples. These villages played a significant role as they dispersed early settlement throughout the Sudbury basin. Often, they were homes to hundreds of people, many of them Finns. Within this floating network of minesites, Finnish miners and construction workers exhibited a high degree of mobility—they simply followed job opportunities regardless of location. In 1921, for instance, only five Finnish families remained at the North Star site following the closure of the mine as most miners left to try their hands at farming, forestry and fishing.[24] Among the camps to attract Finnish workers was Mond village situated near the Victoria mine, the Mond roastyard and the Mond smelter in Denison Township north of the Algoma Eastern Railway (AER) and Highway 17 West. These operations formed part of the Mond Nickel Company. The village of Mond was located two miles north of the Victoria Mines townsite and smelter. Few Finns, however, lived at the Victoria townsite, which had been established by Mond Nickel as a planned 320-acre community; they preferred to live in the more ethnically based Mond townsite, closer to Victoria mine itself (map 4). Mond was a virtual League of Nations settlement with Finns, Ukrainians, Poles, Italians, French and British comprising most of the population.

During its lifespan from 1901 to 1923, the village featured many elements of Finnish occupance such as a hall, public sauna, athletic club and boarding house.[25] Many log houses, such as that built by Kalle Sillanpää, were built by means of *talkoot* (communal bees). Like the other mining

Map 3
Early Mining Camps in the Sudbury Area before 1917

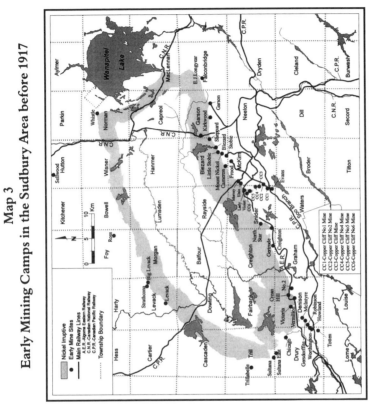

Source: Royal Ontario Nickel Commission, *Report* (Toronto: Legislative Assembly of Ontario, 1917), p. 104.

Map 4
Finns in Mond Townsite (1917-18)

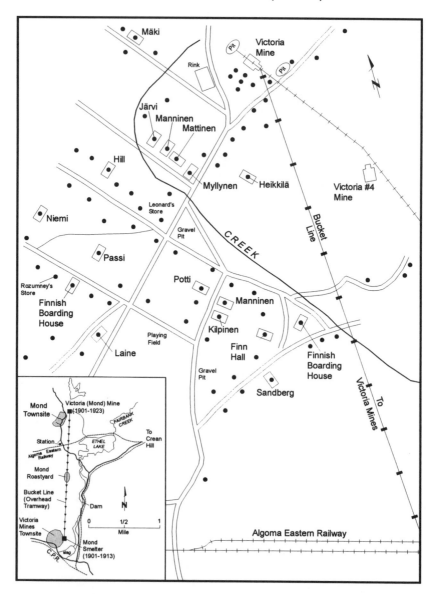

Source: W.H. Mäkinen, "The Mond Nickel Company and the Communities of Victoria Mines and Mond," pp. 30-31; interview with John Passi, Sudbury, 1995.

camps in the Sudbury area, the population of Mond village rose and fell in accord with the dictates of the mining industry. In 1914 there were an estimated 110 Finns residing in the camp. By 1921, however, the *Vapaus* (Liberty) newspaper reported the following situation: "Some years ago Mond was one of the most active of the small mining towns in the area in terms of Finnish presence and activity. But employment in the mine began to decline and the Finns then sought forestry employment or turned to farming."[26] The nearby community of Victoria Mines floundered following the move of the roastyard and smelter to Coniston in 1913. While the village of Mond continued to operate, it was profoundly effected by the deaths of sixteen Finns who lost their lives in the *Empress of Ireland* disaster in the St. Lawrence River on 29 May 1914. It was estimated that fifty Finns from the Mond, Copper Cliff and Garson areas were on the ship.[27] Mond townsite declined after the closure of the mine in 1923 and most of the Finnish workers left for Worthington. Olavi Mattinen was the last resident to leave in 1936.[28]

The community of Crean Hill was a close neighbour of the Mond village. Finns were among the first arrivals following the opening of the mine by the Canadian Copper Company in 1905. By 1908-1909 they numbered more than 250 and constituted one-half of the total population.[29] The Finns immediately proceeded to erect a hall and established a library and athletic club. The gradual cessation of mining, however, dropped the Finnish population to less than one hundred by 1914 and to only forty-five by 1920. When mining ceased, the Finnish hall was dismantled and sold to the Vermilion River Finns located further south.

Company Towns of Garson and Creighton

Not all of the mining camps proved to be temporary. Around the larger mining deposits, settlements of more substantial size arose. Among these could be included Garson and Creighton. Finnish settlement in Garson started after the opening of the Garson mine in 1906-1908 and the development of the Kirkwood mine in 1913-16. Both properties were owned by Mond Nickel. According to school records, Finns were attracted to the area as early as 1908, many coming directly from Copper Cliff. Garson's Finnish population rose from seventy persons in 1908 to more than two hundred in 1913. In the latter year, eighty-three persons, or 40 percent of the total, consisted of single Finnish men.[30] Finns at the time comprised approximately one-third of Mond's labour force. Settlement occurred both as rural farmsteads in Garson and Neelon Townships and as part of the Garson townsite itself (map 5). Finns, however, rarely chose to reside in the smelter town of Coniston situated further south in Neelon Township.

Map 5
Finns in Garson and Neelon Townships (1935)

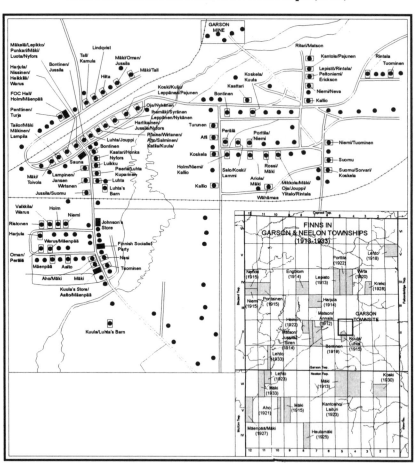

Source: Ray Kaatari, *Voices from the Past*, pp. 36-37; Town of Nickel Centre, *Assessment Rolls* (1911-36); Sudbury Land Registry Office.

The first large Finnish landholder to appear on the local scene was Kalle Annala in 1912. In the following year, he was followed by Urho Lepistö and Sam Mäki. Eleven Finnish farmers arrived around the World War I period. During the decade of the 1920s, another nine farmsteads were developed.[31] In the early 1930s, Oscar Mäki acquired two large parcels of land in nearby Neelon Township, which eventually became part of the "New Sudbury" community. These farmsteads remained active up to the 1950s, at which time many were subdivided for urban residential purposes, as occurred with the Luhta (1934-38) and Matson (1954) farmsteads.

The Finnish occupancy of the Garson townsite occurred both in the business section and company town; however, the most notable concentration developed in "Finntown" north of the business section and astride the CNR railway which ran from the Garson mine to Sudbury. This land was owned by Mond Nickel and leased to residents at a nominal charge. Included in Finntown were twenty-five dwellings and five boarding/rooming enterprises that housed eighty-eight individuals in 1912.[32] These boarding houses, which were generally run by women, housed the single Finns who worked with Mond Nickel either as miners or labourers.

A number of Finnish enterprises sprouted in the townsite, among them a tailor, a public sauna and grocery stores (owned by Emile Jauhiainen and Oscar Kuula). Koivula's Bakery from Copper Cliff and A. Niemi from Sudbury catered to local bakery and photographic needs. N. Matson was well known for the Finnish mats she wove from strips of used clothing and sold to many local homeowners. One of the more colourful entrepreneurs was Wester Tuominen, who devised a unique method for cutting up cordwood or timbers resurrected from mining operations:

> Residents who lived in Garson in the thirties and forties will remember Wester Tuominen, the "machine doctor" dragging behind his car, a portable sawmill. . . . He would hie up to their yard, remove one of the vehicle's rear wheels, replace it with a homemade pulley, attach a long rubber belt to it and to his saw machine, start the engine and begin cutting. Hundreds of cords of wood were cut this way for the residents. . . . Eventually his saw machine was a self contained portable unit. Tuominen served the company for 31 years and amazingly according to company records, he never missed a shift during that time.[33]

There was also the ubiquitous Finn Hall, built in 1911, that provided the only location for party gatherings and served as the home of the Garson Athletic Club.

While Finnish occupancy in the village remained strong until World War II, its relative significance then declined due to the aging of the population and the out-migration of younger Finns. In the former company-owned part of the townsite, many Finns opted to purchase their homes from Inco in 1974, following the introduction of regional government.[34] Thus this part of the settlement sustained some degree of Finnishness until the 1980s.

Finnish miners were likewise among the first group of workers to be attracted to Creighton mine in Snider Township after its opening in 1899. At least forty Finns were present in 1910 and by this time a hall had been constructed. Around the same time a Finnish clubhouse was established by Frank and Margaretta Anderson. It was expanded into a boarding house during World War I. The number of Finns increased to more than two hundred by 1914, at which time Creighton was proclaimed to be the "greatest nickel mine in the world."[35] The Rent Rolls for 1915 reveal that the forty-eight Finnish families in Creighton were distributed rather evenly along Albert, George and Jaffre Streets.[36] Shortly thereafter, a Finnish sports group called *Yritys* (Endeavour) appeared. The Finnish population at the mine site ranged as high as eight hundred before falling to around 150 by 1930. Other Finnish enterprises in the townsite included a public sauna and a dairy plant run by Frank Anderson between 1938 and 1945 and later by Copper Cliff Dairy up to 1954.[37] Creighton continued to flourish after World War II until the 1980s, at which time the village, for economic reasons, was dismantled by Inco.

Sudbury and Environs

Sudbury itself did not attract Finns until after World War I (table 8). At the time, its Finnish population was less than that found in the town of Copper Cliff and the townships of Waters, Lorne, Broder and Louise. Beginning in the 1920s, however, the regional pattern of Finnish settlement changed as three working-class Finntowns began to emerge in and around Sudbury, in the downtown, Donovan and Lockerby districts.

There were several reasons for the belated emergence of Sudbury as a node of Finnish settlement. These included the rise in urban-based migration from Finland in the 1920s, the opening of the Sudbury and Copper Cliff Suburban Electric Railway in 1915 and the decision by Inco to encourage its workers to build homes in Sudbury. Inco's preference for a labour force that commuted to Copper Cliff from Sudbury via the street railway system was reinforced by its decision not to provide any more housing in the townsite:

> When, in 1914, the eight-hour day was introduced to all Canadian Copper Company operations, the Company openly stated it would not be providing housing for the increased work force necessitated by the shorter working day. These employees were expected to live in Sudbury, and commute via the new street railway system.[38]

In 1929 Inco even authorized the sum of $500,000 in loans for its employees to assist them in constructing homes in Sudbury.[39]

As in Copper Cliff and Garson, Finns in Sudbury resided in close-knit, working-class neighbourhoods. Another parallel was the appearance of rooming and boarding houses, halls and commercial enterprises as part of the ethnic landscape. A distinguishing feature, however, was the appearance of *koiratorpat* (bootlegging, or blind pig) establishments that catered to single and married male and, on occasion, to female Finnish workers. The Finnish presence was sufficiently distinctive to pique even the interest of the distinguished magazine *National Geographic*:

Table 8
Finnish Settlement in the Sudbury Area (1921-41)

Municipality/ Township	1921 No.	1921 Percentage of total population	1931 No.	1931 Percentage of total population	1941 No.	1941 Percentage of total population
Rural						
Baldwin	25	7.8	59	20.8	45	17.9
Balfour	0	0.0	3	1.1	2	0.3
Blezard	37	7.4	14	2.7	14	2.6
Broder	237	52.9	341	64.6	355	62.0
Burwash	10	2.6	30	3.3	64	5.9
Cartier	4	0.9	3	0.7	8	2.0
Denison	98	22.8	31	16.3	44	24.0
Dill	48	24.0	104	33.4	103	41.9
Dowling	0	0.0	0	0.0	4	1.0
Drury	104	22.0	126	34.6	71	22.3
Falconbridge	0	0.0	3	0.6	6	0.7
Garson	167	23.5	320	26.3	254	12.9
Graham	7	5.2	47	24.4	6	6.4
Hanmer	0	0.0	0	0.0	5	0.7
Hutton	17	5.7	0	0.0	0	0.0
Levack	65	25.8	50	11.9	0	0.0
Lorne	279	85.1	280	85.4	242	87.7
Louise	217	78.1	0	0.0	0	0.0
McKim	20	4.5	42	7.9	365	7.1
Nairn	19	9.4	20	11.1	17	8.9
Neelon	8	0.5	43	1.8	48	4.7
Rayside	15	1.6	52	4.9	37	3.8
Snider	193	16.7	153	10.4	195	11.3
Waters	285	62.6	368	70.2	694	10.4
Urban						
Sudbury	206	2.4	1,374	7.4	1,241	3.8
Capreol	0	0.0	1	0.0	4	0.2
Chelmsford	0	0.0	0	0.0	1	1.0
Copper Cliff	267	10.3	491	15.5	394	10.6
Frood Mine	0	0.0	10	5.8	8	11.4
Coniston	0	0.0	0	0.0	1	0.0
Levack	0	0.0	0	0.0	77	8.6

Source: Statistics Canada, *Censuses of Canada* (1921-41).

Go to Sudbury, home of the great International Nickel Company and of the Frood Mines, and the rush and roar is the same. Here still more Finns, a "Finnlandia" café, and Finns buying talking-machine records of Finnish songs, and Finns squatting about shoe shops and cigar stands, playing more Finnish tunes on mandolins and singing boisterous Finnish songs in a "beverage bar."[40]

Downtown

As noted previously, Sudbury remained a peripheral site for Finnish settlement prior to World War I. Shortly thereafter, a working-class neighbourhood began to develop in the downtown area west of the CPR tracks. As shown on map 6 and aerial photograph 1, this residential development grew to encompass a zone that extended from the CPR mainline to the east, Queen's Athletic Field, Elm Street Public School and the Children's Aid Society to the west, Pine Lane to the north and Oak Street to the south. Finnish interest in the downtown surfaced in 1913 when John Ajola acquired two lots at the corner of Alder and Elm Streets.[41] Ajola was the secretary-treasurer of the first Western Federation of Miners (WFM) local organized in Sudbury. These properties were later purchased by the Finnish Socialist Organization of Canada (FSOC) in 1917; due to site difficulties, however, were eventually sold in 1936-38. In 1920 two other developments started the transformation of the area into an urban Finntown. The first was the purchase of a site in 1921 by the Liberty Hall Company on Lorne Street between Spruce (now Applegrove) and Elm Streets. This company had been formed earlier to find a permanent home for the *Vapaus* newspaper and the Sudbury local of the Finnish Organization of Canada (FOC). A building was erected in 1921 with the basement housing the printing presses of the newspaper and the main floor serving as a hall.[42] Spurred by the increase in the number of Finnish newcomers, the site was expanded in 1923. By the late 1920s the hall portion of the building had become a beehive of activity for dancing, teaching seminars, concerts, athletics, reading, theatrical presentations (forty-two in 1925 alone) and meetings. Activity was sufficiently brisk to warrant the hiring of permanent theatre and music teachers.

The Great Depression and its accompanying unemployment weakened the financial position of the company. Nevertheless, the hall was still made available to unemployed single men for overnight lodging purposes. In December 1932 Liberty Hall was sold to Sudbury Lodge 282 of the Independent Order of Odd Fellows. After World War II, the building was acquired by the Finnish Pentecostal Church (1958-68) and the site was expropriated by the province in 1968. The space formerly occupied by the hall is now a grassed lot.

The second event in 1920 was the acquisition of Elm House on the corner of Dufferin (now Pine) and Elm Streets. Elm House was erected in 1893 and from 1894 it functioned as Sudbury's second hospital, the Algoma and Nipissing (later Sudbury General) Hospital.[43] The building was subsequently transformed into a rooming house and run by Finnish managers until 1926, when it was rented by *Kuluttajain Yhdistys* (The Consumers' Society). Spearheaded by Hannes Sula, August Kannisto and Ida Koivula, the Society renovated the building, started a consumers' restaurant and improved the rooming house facilities. A small co-operative store was added later. Between 1929 and 1937, Elm House became the headquarters of the Sudbury FOC local and housed various tenants, such as John Lievonen's Tailoring, Lindberg Taxi and Carl Sundholm's Watch Repair. After the building was sold, Vern Piispanen for a time operated a men's clothing store on the site.

Map 6
The Finnish Downtown Landscape (c. 1920s-1940s)

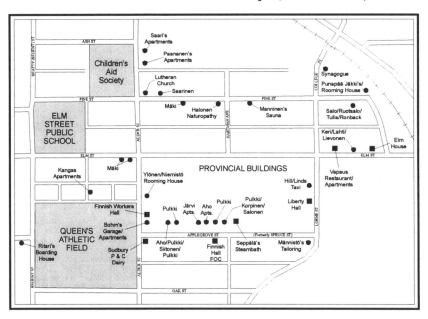

Source: Sudbury Land Registry Office.

The Finnish character of the area was given added dynamism between 1928 and 1932 through the construction of three institutional buildings— the *Vapaus* building, the Finnish Workers' Hall and a co-operative dairy. The *Vapaus* building, situated on Elm Street, was built in 1928. Owned by *Vapaus* Publishing Company, the main floor served as the headquarters for the

Vapaus newspaper and several apartments were rented on the upper floor. Adjacent to the printing operations on the main floor there was a co-operative store that had been relocated from the Elm House; this store, however, closed in 1932 and its space was taken over by a privately owned restaurant known as *Finlandia*. It was later transformed into a co-operative restaurant known as the *Kuluttajat Ruokala* (Consumers' Restaurant). Run by a board of directors, the co-operative consisted of a restaurant on the Elm Street side and a boarding-house kitchen on the lane side. The latter was open twenty-four hours a day. The meals served at the boarding house became legendary, and it was claimed that no patron ever left hungry. The restaurant was run by several managers, including John Raivo, Jallu Saari and Bill Kivinen. In 1952 the co-operative era came to an end when the operation was bought by Bill and Pearl Kivinen; it was resold to Sulo and Bertha Heino, who renamed it the Uptown Restaurant. The restaurant lost its Finnish character in 1958 when it was bought by a Chinese owner. In 1974 the printing operations of *Vapaus* were shifted to Toronto; the building was sold two years later. The paper was published in Toronto until 11 March 1991.

Aerial Photograph 1
The Downtown District of Sudbury (1946)

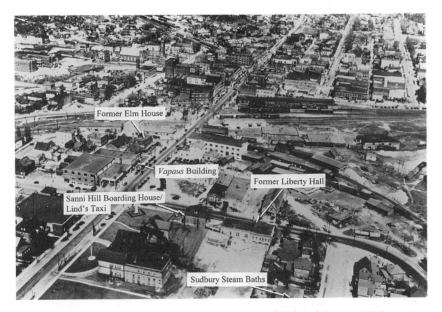

Source: Government of Canada, *Department of Mines and Technical Surveys* (1946).

The second addition to the Finnish landscape was a hall on Alder Street built in 1929 by the Copper Cliff Finnish Social Society. This Society had previously owned two other halls, one in the Copper Cliff area and another between Sudbury and Copper Cliff. Known as the Workers' Hall, the Alder Street building attracted workers who had close affiliations with the Industrial Workers of the World (IWW, or the "Wobblies") union. The hall served as a centre for dancing and theatrical performances until 1938, when it was sold to the Slovak National Society. The third institutional feature was a Finnish co-operative dairy on the corner of Alder and Spruce Streets. This enterprise was rooted in the rise of consumer dissatisfaction with milk prices and the decision to create the Co-optas (Co-operative Trading Association of Sudbury) in 1927. Two lots were purchased on behalf of Sudbury FOC Local 25 which were later transferred to Co-optas in 1928. Pasteurization equipment was bought from Emil Ojala, who owned a small dairy on Kelly Lake Road. The dairy building was constructed in 1928. Within a year, the operation was enlarged to include butter as well as milk production, and apartments were constructed on the second floor. The ownership changed in 1931 due to a major split within the FOC regarding the role of the co-operative movement. Supporters of the FOC lost to a dissenting faction, which assumed control of the dairy in 1932 and ran it as a private company. This effort, too, failed, and in 1934 the dairy was revived as a co-operative known as *Sudburyn Tuottajain ja Kuluttajain Osuusmeijeri* (Sudbury Producers and Consumers Co-operative Dairy), with most shareholders being Finnish farmers. The co-operative ran as a successful operation until 1963 when the dairy equipment was acquired by Palm Dairies. The property was sold in 1971 and the profits were distributed among the shareholders of the co-operative.

Elm House, Liberty Hall, the *Vapaus* building and the co-operative dairy served as a gravitational pull for other Finnish enterprises. In 1921, on Spruce Street, K. Asiala and Jack Seppälä erected the Sudbury Steam Bath building, which also served as a rooming house.[44] After 1953 the ownership of the building passed into other Finnish hands. Paavo and Martha Manninen ran another sauna on Pine Street. Bohm's Garage, at the corner of Alder and Spruce Streets, opened in 1930 with apartments on the second floor that housed Finnish tenants. On Pine Street could be found J. Halonen's Chiropractic and Drugless Clinic. Often referred to as "Smokey Joe," Halonen was well known for his habit of winter dipping in Lake Nepahwin, even as a senior citizen. The concentration of Finns in the area encouraged other entrepreneurs such as Karl Lehto to set up businesses in the nearby downtown district (biography 3).

The downtown area of Sudbury supported many Finnish businesses. Shown here is the Eagle Café and Boarding House on Elm Street owned by Frank Snellman, 1919. Frank is shown standing in the front with his wife Olga and son Karl. The others are boarders. (Archives of Ontario, F1404-15-124/MSR 12234-20)

One of the enterprises found on Spruce Street near the downtown was Bohm's Garage and Apartments. Built by a Finnish businessman, D. Bohm, in 1930, it also housed numerous tenants on the second floor. (Oiva Saarinen, private collection)

Public saunas and steam baths were popular up to the 1960s. Shown here is the Sudbury Steam Bath located on Spruce Street, 1926. Lempi Johnson is the woman on the left. (Lempi Johnson, private collection)

Sports were a major part of the Finnish cultural scene. Athletes and gymnasts are shown here at the first Finnish-Canadian Amateur Sports Federation Festival held at Union Field near Victoria Street west of the downtown. (Wilf Salo, private collection)

The Donovan was a major Finnish working-class district. Erected in 1935 by the Finnish National Society of Sudbury, *Sampo* Hall served for decades as a major landmark in the area. (Archives of Ontario, F1405-15-15/MSR 2029-21)

Sampo Hall was refurbished in the 1970s and finally sold in 1994. (Antti Haaranen, private collection)

From 1932 until 1952, Kaskela's Athletic Field in the Donovan served as the track-and-field site for the Finnish National Society of Sudbury. (Finnish Canadian Historical Society)

From the 1930s until its sale as a park in 1971, the Workers' Park in Lockerby south of the city served as a popular site for the members of the Finnish Organization of Canada. (Elvi Duncan, private collection)

Biography 3
Karl Lehto: Merchant-Wrestler

Karl Lehto was born in Tampere, Finland, in 1888. As a youngster he practised on gymnastics equipment built by his father. This allowed Karl to experiment with the sport even before attending elementary school. He spent his spare time at the local Sports Palace, where wrestling was the chief attraction. At the age of seventeen he succeeded in placing third in the Finnish wrestling championships. In 1906 he migrated to the United States and worked at a lumber camp in Minnesota where he wrestled under the title of the "Mysterious Finn." He quickly forged his way to the top of the wrestling profession and met the greats of his day, falling just short on two occasions of the world's championship. In 1911 he returned to Finland where he became the Finnish wrestling champion. A tour of the North American vaudeville circuit brought him to Copper Cliff in 1914.[45] He fought all comers in more than two hundred matches between 1911 and 1914. One of his more famous and successful matches, billed as a "fight with death," was in Duluth with a Japanese jiu-jitsu expert. His fame was such that an entire issue of a Finnish sports magazine was devoted to his exploits. After experiencing injuries in some of his later matches, he came to the conclusion that his future resided more in business than in wrestling.

Karl wrote a book in Finnish called *Catch as Catch Can* and edited a sports magazine entitled *Sporting Message*. He settled in the upper peninsula of Michigan and purchased a farm, with the intention of bringing his parents there from Finland. The war, however, interfered with this resolve. Karl then attended a college known as Ferris Institute in Big Rapids, Michigan. In 1916 he revisited Sudbury, where he established a clothing store in the Balmoral Hotel building. Two years later, he married Lillian Semblia. Karl maintained his interest in wrestling and promoted other sports such as skiing and skating. He continued wrestling more for the love of the sport than for any monetary consideration. The local newspaper claimed that a bout in 1922 against George Walker of Port Arthur was the most exciting match ever held in Sudbury. His last wrestling match was held in 1925 when he battled Wilf Salo. In 1928 he erected a building on Durham Street that became the site of his second store. In 1937 Karl purchased the Blue Block on the same street and moved his clothing store there for the third and final time. He ran his clothing store until 1944, when it was sold to J.T. Paquette. Karl also owned an eighteen-apartment building in the city and two apartment buildings in Windsor.

Karl served as a major spokesperson for the Finnish community during World War II. In 1939-40, serving as the association's treasurer, he assisted the Sudbury District Finnish War Aid Association in rendering wartime assistance to Finland. In 1940 he was elected president of the FCAA *Voima* and helped organize the first of the Grand Festivals. In 1944 he was given the distinction of formally opening *Voima's* new hall, *Suomi Ranta* (Finland Beach). After his retirement, he spent much time in Florida. Karl and Lillian had four children: Edith, Joyce, Bobby and John. He died in Sudbury on 11 September 1985 at the age of ninety-seven.

The community was enlivened by the presence of colourful Finnish personalities who were given nicknames depicting their origins, physical features or general characters. Among them were *Punapää Jäkki* (Red-headed Jack), *Ikaalisten Tatu* (Tatu from Ikaalinen), *Savon Piiti* (Peter from Savo), *Pikku Konsta* (Little Konsta), *Härmän Iita* (Ida from Härmä), *Lapuan Sanni* (Sanni from Lapua), *Kauhavan Tynne* (Tynne from Kauhava), *Tampereen Anni* (Anni from Tampere) and *Puipuli Eeriksonni* (Cheating Erickson).[46]

Apartments and rooming houses sprouted to accommodate the growing Finnish population. Situated between Bohm's Garage and Sudbury Steam Bath were three apartment buildings owned by Otto Järvi, Nestori Aho and Kusti Pulkki. The Pulkkis were well known in the Sudbury area, as Kusti and his wife Hilja operated the North Cafe in the old Borgia district of the downtown. Other Finnish apartment buildings also appeared on nearby Alder and Cypress Streets. Among the rooming houses were those run by Rudy Lind and Jack Hankaanpää on Pine Street, Ida Ylönen on Alder Street beside the Workers' Hall, Justiina Ritari on Spruce Street west of Queen's Athletic Field and Sanni Hill on Lorne Street between Liberty Hall and the Cenotaph. The latter also served as the site of Lind's Taxi. While many single-family residences were constructed by Finns, perhaps the most interesting was the Uuno Salonen home found on Spruce Street, built out of round stones from a nearby gravel pit. Many of the Finnish properties on Spruce and Lorne Streets were expropriated by the government of Ontario for its courthouse and jail in the middle 1970s.

In 1938 yet another landmark appeared with the construction of the Finnish Hall. After the sale of Liberty Hall in 1932, many FOC members turned to the nearby Ukrainian Hall, run by the Ukrainian Labour Farmer Temple Association, as a gathering place. This switch in halls was understandable given the history of close co-operation that existed between the FOC and the Temple Association.[47] Some Finns, however, shifted their allegiance to the Workers' Hall on Alder Street. To compensate for the loss of Liberty Hall, the FOC purchased another property adjacent to the Ukrainian Hall, and in 1938 the first theatrical performance was held in the new Finnish Hall. Numerous plays were presented in 1939 and indoor gymnastics blossomed under the schooling of Jack Hymander. The hall was temporarily closed by the federal government between 1940 and 1943. Shortly after its reopening in January 1944, it was destroyed by fire. The hall was quickly rebuilt and inaugurated in November of the same year.[48] While the building continued to operate at a lively pace during the 1950s and 1960s, it experienced a decline in use due to the aging of the immigrant population and the greater attraction of *Sampo* Hall for the newer Finnish arrivals. The building was sold in 1981 to the Association of United Ukrainians; in 1990 it became the Sudbury Women's Centre. Traces of the past still exist, however, as the Finnish Senior Citizens' Club continues to use the hall on a regular basis.

During the peak period of occupance in the late 1930s, approximately 200 Finns lived in this part of the downtown; another 150 could be found nearby in the West End. The Finnishness of the area remained until the 1960s; in the ensuing decades, the landscape lost much of its ethnic character. Following the expropriation of Finnish properties, the sale of the Finnish Hall and the co-operative dairy and the outflow of Finnish residents, little is left to reflect the existence of what was once a vibrant and dynamic centre for the Finnish population.

Donovan

The second Finntown in the city developed in the Donovan, situated north of the downtown. Known as *Kittilänmäki*, this neighbourhood developed in the late 1920s, peaked during the 1950s, and declined after the 1970s. Two events in the 1920s prompted Finns to move into this area. The first was the aforementioned Inco decision that Copper Cliff would no longer serve as a dormitory town for its new company employees. The second was the discovery of new ore at Frood Mine in 1926 and the resulting decision by Inco and the Mond Nickel Company to merge their operations in 1929. The expansion of Frood Mine provided opportunities for employment that were rapidly filled by Finnish miners.

A perusal of the *Vernon's Directory* indicates no record of any Finns in the neighbourhood before 1911. By 1920, though, a small vanguard of pioneers had appeared—among them John Kannisto, manager of the *Vapaus* Publishing Company, and Oscar Koivula, a well-known merchant tailor. The initial settlement of the Donovan was thus linked to employment in the downtown. During the Great Depression, the geographical setting changed substantially as the Donovan had by this time become the favoured residential site for Finnish miners employed at Frood mine. The revamped setting, in turn, fostered the growth of Finnish services such as bakeries, tailors, grocery stores, a dairy and drug store, a men's-wear shop, boarding/rooming houses, public saunas and the ever-present bootlegging establishment.

The Finnish permeation of the Donovan by the late 1930s is shown on map 7. Finns by this time were well established in the core area found between Kathleen Street to the south, Frood (Bartram) Road to the west, the unbuilt Northern Heights area to the north and Tedman Avenue to the east. In 1938 more than six hundred Finns resided in the area. Of this total, 25 percent were residential owners and the remaining 75 percent were renters. Many Finns also rented their properties as sources of income while working in mines elsewhere; others owned empty lots intended either for selling or construction purposes. A review of assessment rolls for other years and the *Vernon's Directory* makes it clear that there was a high degree of internal residential mobility, with similar household names appearing on different streets from one year to the next.

Map 7
Finns in the Donovan (1938)

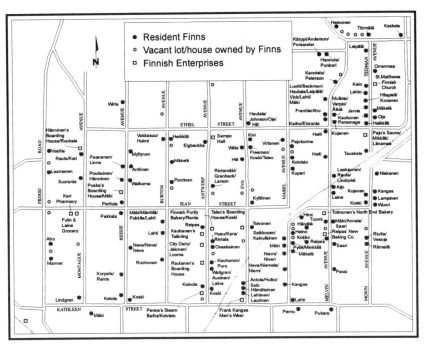

Source: City of Sudbury, *Assessment Roll* (1938); Sudbury Land Registry Office.

Finnish establishments of all kinds could be found interspersed within the residential fabric. Antwerp Street was the focal point for these enterprises. A. Penna operated a public bathhouse that later became known as Alavo Steam Baths. On the same street could be found H. Kauhanen's tailor shop, City Dairy, S. Rautanen's boarding house, Urho Ranta's Finnish Purity Baking Company (also known as Karju's Bakery) and *Sampo* (Magic Mill) Hall. Other businesses included Frank Kangas Men's Wear and Joseph Talso's boarding house on Eva Street, Elmer Tolmunen's North End Bakery and John Reipas's New (Northern) Baking Company on Melvin Avenue, A. Paju's Sauna and St. Matthew's "pikku kirkko" (small church) and parsonage on Tedman Avenue, D. Hänninen's boarding house, Fulin and Laine's grocery store and E. Kari's pharmacy on Montague Street and Nestor Puska's boarding house on Bessie Street.

Sampo Hall, with its hilltop location on Antwerp Street overlooking the Donovan, served as the centre of Finnish cultural activity in the Donovan from 1935 to 1994. The hall was allied with the *Sudburyn Suomalainen Kansallisseura* (Finnish National Society of Sudbury, or FNSS) and with the *Kanadan Kansallismielisten Suomalaisten Keskusliitto* (Central Organization of Loyal Finns in Canada, or COLFC). The construction of the hall in 1935 was followed by a burst of activity that included the formation of a choir, theatre group and library. Additional land was acquired and the building expanded in 1937. Summer sporting activities were promoted through the construction of a sports field known as *Kaskelan Kenttä* (Kaskela's Athletic Field) at the corner of Bruce and Dell Streets. This site remained in use until the early 1950s.

Settlement of the Donovan continued after World War II. The neighbourhood was given added vitality when *Sudburyn Pyhän Matteuksen Suomalainen Evankelis-Luterilainen Seurakunta* (St. Matthew's Finnish Evangelical Lutheran Church) was erected at the corner of Bloor and Mackenzie Streets in 1948. Also important was the preference among the postwar immigrants to support *Sampo* Hall rather than the Finnish Hall on Spruce Street. This was especially true of the younger arrivals, who established the *Sampo* Athletic Club and participated in rhythmic gymnastics and folk dancing. These activities were brought to a temporary halt when the hall was destroyed by fire in 1958; with the aid of volunteers who were on strike at the time, a new building was erected by the following year. For another decade, the hall continued to serve as a centre of activity; by the 1970s, however, it was evident that the younger Canadian-born Finns had lost interest in the Finnish National Society and its activities. To meet this challenge, the hall was refurbished and enlarged with the assistance of a Wintario grant in 1976-78.

The new initiative met with some initial success. Throughout the 1980s, the revamped hall served as a meeting place for the *Sampo* Rhythmic Gymnastics Club, the Sudbury Finnish Male Choir, the Knights and Ladies of Kaleva, the Senior Citizens' Friendship Circle and as the site for *Kalevala* Day and Finnish Independence Day celebrations. In 1990 the Sudbury *Suomi* Lions Club began using the hall as its official den; two years later, the service club purchased the hall. The transfer of ownership, however, proved to be short-lived. The building was returned to the Society and later resold to Grace Outreach Ministries. The *Läksiäistanssi* (Farewell Dance), held on 29 October 1994, brought a tear to the eyes of many a Finn with the realization that a major feature of Finnish immigrant history in the Sudbury area had just passed into history.[49]

While the loss of *Sampo* Hall marked the symbolic passage of the Donovan as a Finnish working-class neighbourhood, this demise had been forecast years previously by the outflow of younger Finns to other parts of the city, and the closing of businesses such as Frank Kangas Men's Wear in 1975 and Alavo's Sauna around the turn of the 1980s (table 9). Even those who remained in the vicinity chose to reside in the nearby and more modern Northern Heights residential area that had developed in the 1960s. By 1991 there were fewer than fifty Finnish households in the Donovan area. The process of neighbourhood decline continued in 1996 when Leinala's Bakery relocated to the southern end of the city. Having acquired an excellent community-wide reputation for Finnish baked goods since its founding in 1961, the shift of Leinala's Bakery marked yet another stage in the passage of the Finnish era in the Donovan.

Table 9
Finns in the Donovan Neighbourhood (1911-91)[a]

Street	No. of households by street (per year)								
	1911	1921	1931	1941	1951	1961	1971	1981	1991
Frood	0	2	3	2	3	2	1	2	1
Montague	0	1	4	5	5	4	5	5	5
Bessie	0	0	12	10	13	13	13	6	7
Burton	—	0	9	13	14	13	17	10	8
Antwerp	—	0	12	15	17	21	19	7	7
Eva	0	1	10	18	25	30	19	14	11
Mabel	0	2	21	32	24	27	24	22	1
Melvin	0	4	15	17	17	20	6	4	4
Tedman/Morin	0	0	8	18	24	22	20	8	1
Edith	0	3	3	2	0	0	0	0	0
Dell	0	0	1	4	3	2	2	1	0
Kathleen	0	1	4	4	6	6	7	4	4
Total	0	14	102	140	151	160	133	83	49

a Based on name recognition.
Source: Vernon Directories Limited, *Sudbury Directories* (1911-91).

Lockerby

In the late 1920s Finns started to show an interest in the attractive Trout (now Nepahwin) Lake area situated in Lockerby in McKim Township. This tract of land south of Sudbury consisted of virgin territory owned in the form of large hand holdings by William Turcotte (1904), the Leckie family (1910) and Florence MacLeod (1923). In 1925 Sydney Pottle opened the first subdivision on the north shore of Nepahwin Lake. Most of the Finns who came to the Lockerby area obtained their properties from either Pottle or MacLeod. In July 1925 Karl Lehto was the first Finn to register property in the Pottle subdivision on the site now occupied by the Bel Lago condominium building. He was followed by Dr. Heikki Koljonen, who bought properties on both sides of Long Lake (now Paris) Road. Koljonen, a Finnish doctor in Sudbury with close ties to the FOC movement, often purchased land on behalf of the organization. In 1933 he acquired 3.5 acres of land on the west shore of Nepahwin Lake and transferred it to FOC Local 16 in 1938 for use as a recreational and cultural centre. The property became popularly known as *Työn Puisto* (Workers' Park). By 1937 the site featured a sauna, dance platform, restaurant, six-room main building and a small residential dwelling. A large diving tower and summer camp for children were added later. With its attractive setting, the property emerged as a popular place for summer activities sponsored by the FOC. The site was so well known nationally that on one occasion it was visited by the Canadian doctor and political activist Norman Bethune, who later became famous as a hero in China and Spain.

On the other side of Paris Road, Dr. Koljonen acquired additional land and opened a subdivision in 1938 along both sides of Alerts (Caswell) Drive. While part of the subdivision was used for residential purposes, the largest land parcel passed into the hands of FOC Local 16 for use as an athletic field by the *Kisa* (Alerts) Athletic Club. Both the Workers' Park and Koljonen's subdivision were temporarily vested in the hands of the Custodian of Canada during World War II. After the war the two sites were returned and they continued to be intensely used by FOC and Alerts members up to the 1960s. Due to suburban expansion and rising taxes, the FOC was forced to sell the athletic field in 1961. The land was purchased by David Caswell (1969) and Zulich Enterprises (1989). Part of the former track-and-field site is now owned by the Rockview Senior Co-operative Homes, Inc. A similar fate befell the Workers' Park, which was later sold to the city of Sudbury.

The Workers' Park and the track-and-field site drew other Finns to the existing Pottle subdivision and to the newer MacLeod subdivision which opened in 1939 on Mäki Avenue. Harold and Elena Pernu also opened a subdivision between Nepahwin Avenue and Walford Road in 1941. Commercial uses that sprouted as a result of this residential development included the Koski Bros. meat and grocery store on the east side of Long Lake Road and Paul Jansson's sauna on the site formerly owned by Karl Lehto. The high degree of residential mobility among the Finns was also used by some enterprising individuals as an opportunity to erect, rent and sell homes for generating income.

Finns soon dominated the geographical area framed by Nepahwin, Paris, Indian (formerly Ethel), Wagner, Caswell Drive, Mäki and Old Burwash Roads (map 8). Those who lived close to the Workers' Park or the athletic field were mainly Finns who worked with the *Vapaus* newspaper or

Map 8
The Lockerby Finnish Settlement (1946)

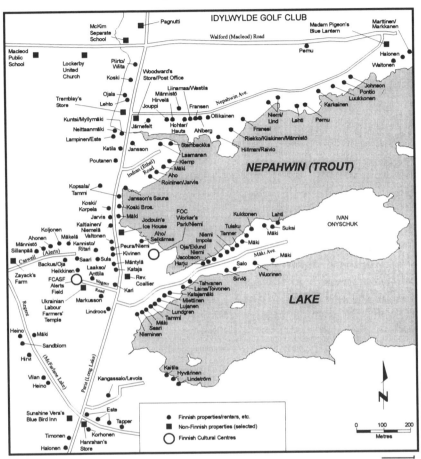

Source: Township of McKim, *Assessment Roll* (1946); Sudbury Land Registry Office.

who had links with the *Canadan Suomalainen Järjestö* (Finnish Organization of Canada) or the *Suomalais-Canadalaisen Amatööri-Urheiluliitto* (Finnish-Canadian Amateur Sports Federation, or FCASF), for example, William Eklund, Edwin Suksi and Elvi Duncan (Salo). The assessment records for McKim Township suggest that many Finnish households in the area featured common-law relationships as many of the resident females were referred to as "housekeepers" rather than spouses. According to one resident, these arrangements may have evolved out of the fact that few Finns had any form of inherited wealth and thus saw little need to legally formalize their relationships.[50] In this connection, Lindström has suggested that these relationships can be taken as proof of the strong class and anticlerical stances held by women.[51] As many couples did not have children, one outcome was a rapid shift of land ownership after World War II to residents of non-Finnish extraction.

Finnish life in Lockerby was coloured by the presence of noteworthy personalities. One was *Koljos Kassu*, a husky man, who worked as a herder for Dr. Koljonen's goats, which were located for a time on his subdivision. Another was Armas Lindberg who taught swimming at Prete's Steam Bath and Swimming Pool in downtown Sudbury during the winter months and at the Workers' Park in the summer. He was instrumental in having a three-storey diving tower erected on the shoreline. Armas had a favourite stunt which he performed on the diving tower. After donning a heavy fur coat, he would climb the tower and dive into the water, surfacing with only his swimming trunks on. This stunt was performed later at Sault Ste. Marie where he dove off the swinging bridge into the water below. Paul Jansson, whose name became synonymous with skiing in the Sudbury area after 1923, also earned respect because of his habit of travelling the twenty-kilometre round trip from his Trout Lake home to Copper Cliff by bicycle or on skis for eighteen years until his retirement in 1964.

The Lockerby landscape included major non-Finnish features as well, such as the Idylwylde Golf and Country Club property found north of Nepahwin Avenue, the Jodouin Icehouse located on the present-day site of Lakeshore Manor Apartments, the fenced-in Catholic retreat south of the Workers' Park, which was owned by Rev. J.N. Coallier between 1935 and 1958 (now Casadolfo Apartments), the Woodward (formerly People's) and Hanrahan's Stores, the Zayack homestead and the "Madam Pigeon" and "Blue Lantern" establishments, situated on Nepahwin Avenue and the Four Corners intersection, respectively. The latter site, run by the Radicioni family, had previously been owned by Juha Korhonen in 1935-37. The entire eastern part of the Mäki peninsula was owned by the Sisters of St. Joseph of the Diocese of Sault Ste. Marie from 1956 until 1971. It has since been transformed into Sudbury's most prestigious subdivision. Further west could be found the Bouchard farm and dairy, which supplied the Lockerby Finns with milk.[52]

Despite the recent decline in the Finnish population, aspects of the Finnish legacy remain. Most noteworthy was the sale of Workers' Park to the city in 1971. Now known as Nepahwin Park, it continues to exist with the understanding that it will forever be used as a park for the enjoyment of the general public. As well, the presence of the Finnish Pentecostal Church, Leinala's Bakery/Scandinavian Foods and the large number of elderly Finns who continue to reside in local apartments all attest to the ongoing attraction of this area for the Finns.

Rural Enclaves

Most of the Finns who came to the Sudbury area after the turn of the century were not attracted to the urban centres; most sought the farming lands and rural environs associated with forests and lakes. In these rural districts, agricultural enclaves similar in nature to the Finntown neighbourhoods found in Sudbury and Copper Cliff also appeared. These bucolic settings all manifested a high degree of political independence and cultural unity. They often consisted of marginal lands; in fact, Finns became respected for their ability to "make prosperous farms out of areas no one else would work at."[53] There was some compensation, however, as the environment of these areas was similar to that of Finland. Geographically, the enclaves were associated with the broad swath of territory south of Copper Cliff and Sudbury that stretched from Lorne Township in the west to Cleland Township in the southeast.

A number of reasons can be advanced for this spatial orientation. First, the pattern of Finnish settlement clearly followed employment opportunities in the mining industry. The Worthington mine in Drury Township, Creighton mine in Snider Township, Crean Hill mine and the Victoria mine, smelter and roastyard in Denison Township and the Garson mine in Garson-Neelon Township all offered Finns mining employment adjacent to agricultural areas. These areas served as spatial opportunity zones, where land and the availability of alternative jobs could be relied upon to ensure a reasonable standard of living. Second, the opening of the Algoma (Soo) Branch of the CPR in the 1880s, the AER, and the CPR and CNR lines to Toronto before World War I provided access to hitherto isolated farming lands west and south of Sudbury. Third, there was the issue of land availability. The early Finns discovered that the best agricultural land in the "Valley" north of Sudbury had already been settled by French farmers after the construction of the CPR main line in 1883. Land to the south was also restricted by the creation of the Burwash Industrial Farm in 1913, a provincial correctional facility, which resulted in the removal of some 14,000 hectares (34,594 acres) of land from the market in the unorganized townships of Laura, Secord, Servos and Burwash. Another limitation was the withdrawal from public sale in 1915-21 of crown lands west and east of the Sudbury area to minimize sulphur damage from the O'Donnell and Coniston roastyards and to reduce payments by mining companies for agricultural losses. Fourth, new Finnish immigrants were constantly advised by others to keep away from the city because unemployment always exists there.[54] Fifth, there was the feeling among many Finns that agricultural land could always be relied on to provide a safe haven in the event of unemployment or economic depression.[55] Sixth, the fact that many immigrants who came to Canada were rural landless peasants introduced an intense personal desire for land ownership. Seventh, there was the availability of free crown land in the Sudbury area. As did many others, Finns took advantage of the Free Grant and Homesteads Act passed in 1868 that made free land available subject to certain settlement conditions. This enticement lasted until 1941, when free land grants were suspended. As early as 1912, money was also given by the Northern Development Branch of the province for settlement assistance and road construction in rural areas. Yet another attraction was the passage by the federal government in 1932 of the Relief Land Settlement Act to spur a "back to the land" movement; for unemployed Finns, such an alternative was preferable to deportation to Finland. This relief initiative was important locally as it stimulated Finnish settlement in the townships of Drury, Cleland and Dill.[56] Finally, many Finns preferred these rural areas simply because they were unorganized, thereby ensuring a minimum of government involvement with their daily lives.

Waters Township

The first rural enclave to develop outside Sudbury was the Finnish Settlement in Waters Township found west of Copper Cliff. This township was opened for settlement in 1882 when the CPR began construction of its Algoma Branch westward from Sudbury to Sault Ste. Marie. In 1885 timber rights were granted to the Booth and Gordon Lumber Companies and lumbering operations came into being. These activities attracted French- and English-speaking settlers who bought rural land from the lumbering companies. As a result of this spurt in growth, the township of Waters was incorporated in 1903. By this time Finns had discovered the township; for example, Thomas Jacobson had already been an active farmer for several years. In Jacobson's wake came three other Finnish farmers: Solomon Mäkelä, Antti Pleuna and John Lahti. These four farmers formed the beginning of a small colony along Black Lake Road that became known as the Finnish Settlement.[57]

Other Finns were drawn to the area during the first decade of the century, many of them acquiring rural properties from the original French and English settlers. According to the township's 1909 voters' list, fifteen Finns were shown as being voters; in addition, there were numerous other resident Finns who lacked citizenship and thus could not vote.[58] By World War I the township had become solidly Finnish. According to the township's Assessment Roll for 1916 (all earlier records were destroyed in a fire), Finns had acquired more than 60 percent of the rural farmland and comprised a similar percentage of the assessed population.[59] In 1921 the Canadian census revealed that more Finns lived in Waters Township (285) than in any other settlement in the area.

By World War I, Finnish farmsteads had expanded beyond the original confines of the Finnish Settlement to encompass virtually the entire township, especially along the routes covered by Black, Fielding (Kelly Lake), Kantola and Long Lake Roads south of the CPR tracks (map 9). By this time Finns had acquired an enviable reputation for self-sufficiency: "Being very versatile and hard workers, the Finns did most of their own labour, whatever the job called for, carpenter, blacksmith, saw-mill operator, etc.; the Finns could do it, and with their strong spirit of co-operation formed a very close knit and self-sustaining community."[60] Aside from Finns, other landowners of note included the Grenon, Fielding and Moxam families. Many of these families eventually became meshed with the Finnish community through intermarriages. For a variety of reasons, such as the closeness of the Copper Cliff and Creighton townsites, the prosperity of local dairy farms, the entrepreneurial background of many of the settlers and the greater role played by the church, the township did not reflect the strong leftist tendencies among the Finns as occurred, for example, in the more outlying Beaver Lake or Wanup enclaves.

The Finnish dominance of the area was greatly strengthened during the 1920s; by 1931, more than 70 percent of its residents were of Finnish origin. Many who came to Waters Township used the profits from previous boarding-house operations in Copper Cliff and Creighton to finance the purchase of a farm; these included Henry Nelson (Pynttäri), Victor Mäkelä, Samuel Niemi, Kusti Holmes and John Ritari. Others financed their rural properties by holding jobs in the mining industry at Copper Cliff, Creighton and Crean Hill. The plentiful employment prospects lessened the need for local Finns to seek jobs in the lumbering industry during the winter months. For those engaged in full-time agriculture, mixed and dairy farming provided much of the annual income. Livestock included horses, pigs and chickens, and the fields were cultivated with wheat, rye, oats, barley, potatoes, vegetables and hay. On the larger farms, dairying was important. Farmers such as Elias Kallio and John Salo sold their milk to the Copper Cliff Dairy. Others, including John Ritari, Alex Salo (Wähäsalo) and Erland Kujamäki sold milk to the Frank Anderson Dairy in Creighton. A few, such as A. Mikkola and Matti Mäkelä, even sold milk to the Co-operative Dairy in Sudbury. Before pasteurization was required, many farmers also sold milk individually. Other sources of revenue came from the sale of butter and eggs, trapping and the delivery of wood to markets such as Creighton Mill, the O'Donnell roastyards and residences in Copper Cliff and Sudbury.

The successful operation of these farms depended in no small measure on the many hours of hard labour by women who, in addition to house-cleaning and the preparation of meals, fed and milked the cattle every day.

As Lindström-Best and Sutyla have vividly depicted in their pictorial history of early Finnish life in Canada, these women were involved in the back-breaking work of clearing land and harvesting the crops.[61] One woman, Pauliina Lahti, acquired a local reputation as a midwife and veterinarian; according to the Waters Women's Institute, "many a life was saved by her skillful hands."[62] The arrival of electricity and the telephone in the late 1940s were welcome additions on the farmstead for these hardworking women.

Map 9
Finns in Waters Township (1916)

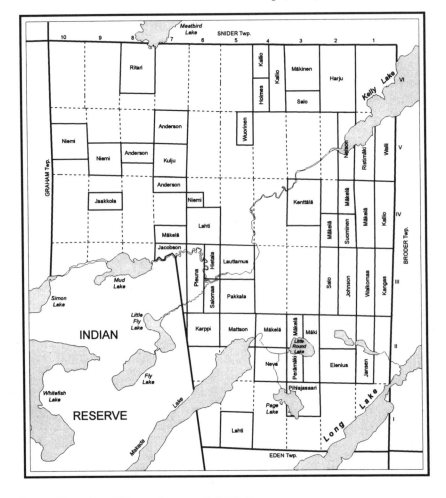

Source: Township of Waters, *Assessment Roll* (1916).

The area supported three halls. The first FOC hall was erected on Long Lake Road on property owned by Elias Kangas. It was a lively centre, and during the Great Depression it was the site of numerous dances and theatrical performances. The hall likewise supported a women's circle, choir, gymnastics group and a forty-member sports club known as *Köntys* (Bumpkins). For a time, it housed a local of the Lumber Workers' Industrial Union (LWIU) of Canada. When the hall burned in the early 1930s, two others appeared on the scene. One was erected by a small faction of FOC supporters on Black Lake Road; it appeared on the Collector's Roll in 1935, but burned shortly thereafter. The property was eventually sold because of tax arrears in 1943. The other hall was built by the remaining FOC members on John Niemi's property, and it supported a dance pavilion, ball field and the Naughton Sparks Athletic Club. After the Depression, interest in the hall waned and its assets were eventually given to the Waters Community Club.[63]

The character of the Finnish Settlement changed dramatically after World War II. Three factors were responsible for this transition. First, the suburbanization of Sudbury's population encouraged the subdividing of farms and the arrival of people from different ethnic backgrounds. Between 1931 and 1941, the proportion of the Finnish population in the township declined from 70 to 47 percent. The trend continued in the 1950s as the rapid expansion of the mining industry prompted farmers and landholders such as Esko Rauhala (1952 and 1956), Walter Mäkelä (1954), Herman Punkari (1955), Eino Mikkola (1956) and Lauri Polvi (1957) to subdivide their farms into residential lots. Second, agriculture began to suffer because of better wages in the mining industry, increased competition from southern Ontario, higher costs for farm labourers and the impact of sulphur damage from the mining operations. Many farmers found it more expedient to sell their farming properties to Inco.[64] One of these, the Harju property, became the site of Inco's Iron Ore Plant completed in 1955; as well, part of the Frank Anderson farm was sold in 1950 as the future site of the new town of Lively.

On the local political scene, Finns were influential both as councillors and reeves. From 1916 to 1959 they had continual representation on municipal council; between 1927 and 1955, the position of reeve, with only two exceptions, was assumed by one of the following: Ernest Kallio, William Kallio, Lauri Hill or Charlie Jacobson. Despite the reduced number of Finns in the township after World War II, the Finnish influence continued as evidenced by the creation of the Anderson Farm Museum in 1977 and the twinning in 1989 of the town of Walden with Ylivieskä in Finland.

Lorne Township (Beaver Lake)

Shortly after the turn of the century, another rural enclave emerged at Beaver Lake. The Beaver Lake settlement is situated in Lorne Township, approximately sixty kilometres west of Sudbury. First surveyed in 1884, the township was organized as part of the municipality of Nairn, Lorne and Hyman in 1896. In 1909 it reverted to the status of an unorganized township until it was reincorporated as part of the Regional Municipality of Sudbury in 1973. Interest in this area developed in response to logging after 1880, the construction of the CPR branch line from Sudbury to Sault Ste. Marie in 1886 and the completion of the Algoma Eastern Railway line in 1911, which connected Sudbury with Little Current. While Thomas Jutila is shown in the registry records as having acquired a lease or licence on land in the township as early as 1908, the Savolainen and Pellinen families have been accorded the distinction of being the first permanent Finnish settlers in 1912; John Savolainen was soon followed by his wife Mandi and children.[65] John Pellinen, however, was the first to register his property. Numerous other families followed in their wake.[66] By 1921 the Beaver Lake area supported 279 Finns, a figure greater than could be found either in Sudbury or Copper Cliff. During the 1920s, the number of farmsteads increased significantly.[67] Land registration slowed considerably in the next decade; however, in the 1940s and 1950s more than fifty new properties were registered.

Beaver Lake had an ethnic identity similar to the Finnish Settlement in Waters Township. The cultural landscape left no doubt as to its Finnish origins. Road names such as Suomi, Keto, Kinos, Niemi, Isaacson, Myllynen, Johnson, Jäntti, Jalonen, Wirtanen and Ronka gave tangible expression of its underlying Finnishness. Language played an important role, as the meetings of the local school board and the statute labour board were conducted entirely in Finnish. The cultural morphology associated with each farmstead reflected an interesting form of microgeography inherited from Finland. As well as a house and barn, farmsteads featured the presence of specialized structures such as saunas, haysheds, icehouses, milk houses, woodsheds, toolsheds, root houses, outhouses and garages. In contrast to construction techniques used by other ethnic groups, the buildings were constructed with hewn rather than round logs and insulated with moss and oakum instead of clay. Much technical expertise was involved in the erection of buildings, as revealed by the use of various corner joints, e.g., saddle, dovetail and locked dovetail. As was the case in Finland, local structures were often covered with homemade red iron paint and white trim.[68]

An agricultural economy developed, based on beef and dairy farming. As Sudbury grew, its market proved to be a profitable destination for meat, milk and cream deliveries. Dairy farming peaked during the 1940s. By this time, new agricultural land had become available due to the lowering of Beaver Lake and the resulting formation of two smaller lakes. Agriculture was complemented by forms of co-operative endeavour, ranging from the establishment of Co-optas branch stores at the Lempi Luopa and Victor Jutila farmsteads, barn-building bees, the loaning of horses, tractors and mechanical stump cutters and communal harvesting. Formalized organizations such as the Beaver Lake Co-op and Agricultural Club (1950-68) and the Beaver Lake Farmers' Threshing Association (c. 1930-73) also came into being. The shift to mining employment and costly provincial regulations after World War II brought an end to dairy farming and the local co-operative movement.

While it was the availability of land that initially attracted Finnish settlers, it became apparent that farming as a full-time occupation was not feasible. Fortunately, the geographical location of Beaver Lake proved to be favourable, as it was the heart of a broad economic zone that offered diverse employment prospects for the construction of hydroelectric generation stations, in mining, lumbering, the trapping of beaver and mink, general construction, carpentry, local road construction and the provision of local goods and services. A variety of enterprises surfaced: general stores, butchering, blacksmithing, painters, masseurs and masseuses, shoemaking, tanning, sawmilling and shingle planing and custom milling. These job opportunities supported the existence of the Finnish enclave until well after the 1950s.

The Beaver Lake community reflected a high degree of internal unity and cultural cohesion. This cohesiveness was prompted by the isolation of the township, the close proximity of the farmsteads to one another and the nature of the transportation networks. As late as World War I, the Vermilion River served as the "main street" of Beaver Lake. Beginning in 1920, however, a Statute Labour Board was formed; it began an active program of road construction and provided, with the assistance of the provincial government, five scows for those settlers who lived south of the Vermilion River or north of the Spanish River. The scows were phased out in the late 1960s following the stipulation by the new Local Roads Board Act that a full-time attendant was required at each site. The majority of the farmsteads were centrally situated in the township between Ella Lake and the CPR and AER railway lines (map 10). In typical Canadian fashion, land ownership assumed a checkerboard pattern, with most of the parcels occupying 160 acres (1/2 mile by 1/2 mile). Further west, Ella Lake became a summer cottage community after 1950.

Another feature that reinforced the Finnish character of the area was the existence of a community core in the centre of the township. The beginnings of this centre dated from 1915 when Local 51 of the Finnish

Socialist Organization of Canada was established; the local constructed a hall in 1918. From its inception, the hall served as the focal point for the community. The hall housed the elementary school until 1926, at which time a new building was erected. The hall/school property was considered at the time to be the "pride of the village."[69] *Jehu* (Leader) Athletic Club, organized in 1921, used a local road for sporting purposes until a track and field was constructed adjacent to the school in 1927. The importance of the nucleus was enhanced when a branch store of Co-optas was established. After the co-operative folded in the 1930s, the store ran as a private enterprise until it was relocated in the 1950s. Easily reached by foot, skis, bicycle and, later, by car, the core served as a meeting place for the local inhabitants both day and night.

Map 10
Early Finnish Settlement in Lorne Township

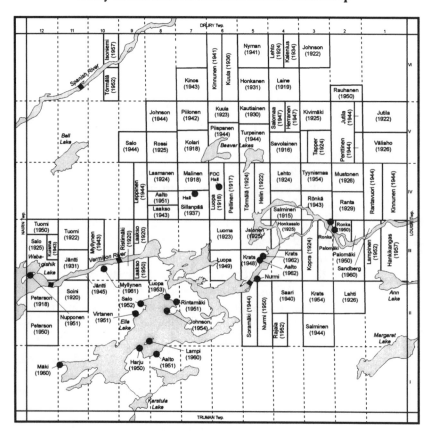

Source: Sudbury Land Registry Office.

One part of the Finnish cultural heritage that was conspicuously absent from the landscape was that of the church; aside from baptisms, weddings and funerals, organized religion exerted little influence in the daily life of the residents. This aspect of cultural life is made abundantly clear in a recently published collection of family histories where numerous references are made to the impact of institutions such as the community school, the hall and the sporting and co-operative groupings; only passing mention, however, is made to any imprint that the church may have had on the majority of residents.[70] Indeed, it was 1957 before a chapel was erected in the township in co-operation with Copper Cliff's St. Timothy's Lutheran Church. Dedicated as the Beaver Lake Lutheran Chapel in 1972, it has been faithfully supported by about twenty families. While the chapel is still used, its supporting membership has dwindled with each passing year.[71]

The conflict between the leftist and conservative forces in the community during the Great Depression briefly touched the enclave, as evidenced by the formation of another athletic club known as the Beavers, and the construction of a second hall on Lorne Falls Road in 1934, which was allied with the Finnish Canadian Workers' and Farmers' Federation. The effect of the new club and hall was short-lived as its members, unlike many of the leftist supporters in the area, failed to demonstrate any form of long-term commitment and enthusiasm.

The Finnish character of the township remained intact until the realignment of highway 17 in 1951-53. By this time Beaver Lake's island setting weakened, as the area was drawn into the expanding exurban web of the Sudbury metropolis. Finnish organizational life diminished considerably. The assets of *Jehu* and the former school building were transferred to the Beaver Lake Recreation Club in 1968. In 1972 the FOC Hall was sold and *Jehu* itself was finally disbanded in 1979 after fifty-eight years of activity. Remaining manifestations of the Finnish heritage include the erection of a historical plaque in 1989 and the formation by the local Finnish community of the Beaver Lake Historical Committee. The committee has planned a series of publications, the first scheduled for 1998.

Beaver Lake Finns were well known for their dedication to the promotion of sports and the theatre. *Jehu* represented the strongest rural club of its kind in the history of amateur sport in Canada. This was especially true for track-and-field events and cross-country skiing. In the latter sport, *Jehu* can lay claim to having produced more champions in Finnish sporting competitions than any other club. Many of its members went on to win Canadian championships. The remarkable success of the club did not come about by chance; it developed out of a philosophy based on the concept of total community involvement, including women and children as participants and older people in supporting roles. The theatre represented another area of

Shown here is the A. Linna property, which was typical of the farmstead morphology in the Beaver Lake area, 1985. The arrangement of the buildings illustrates the process of cultural transfer from the old to the new world setting. (Gerry Tapper, private collection)

Transportation by water was important for the Beaver Lake and Louise Township Finnish settlers. Shown here is a scow at the junction of Wabagishik Road and Vermilion River in Lorne Township, c. 1940s. (Gerry Tapper, private collection)

Among the early settlers in Louise Township was the Svensk family. The Svensk family is shown here in front of their summer homestead, 1913. (Ruth Svensk, private collection)

During the 1920s, Louise Township served as the site of the Presbyterian Finnish Church. Shown above is the manse of the church, c. 1920s. (Archives of Ontario, F1405-15-115/MSR 11554-6)

Agricultural activity flourished in the Wanup area until the late 1940s. Shown here is the K. Snellman farmstead in Secord Township, c. 1939-40. (Archives of Ontario, F1405-15-124/MSR 12234-5)

Hunting was another economic activity associated with the Wanup area. Trapper Arvid Salonen is shown here displaying some of his prized skins from the Lake Nepewassi area, 1936. (Finnish Canadian Historical Society)

The Long Lake area in Broder Township evolved as another focal point for Finnish rural settlement. Shown above is an aerial view of *Voima* Hall and Rauhala Island in the pre-World War II period. (Archives of Ontario, F1405-15-115/MSR 2029-34)

The Long Lake area was a popular swimming, fishing and resort destination prior to World War II. Shown here is the diving tower at Long Lake Beach, owned by Vilho Vihuri, c. 1930s. (W. Buchowski, private collection)

intense cultural activity. Interest in this artistic endeavour was so strong that a professional wardrobe was purchased and a full-time salaried director hired during the late 1920s. Between 1918 and 1961, sixty-seven plays of high calibre were produced and performed.

Louise Township (Whitefish)

The third rural enclave to develop west of Copper Cliff was in Louise Township. After this township was surveyed in 1884, a number of mining claims were staked between 1888 and 1891. These were not successful and interest in the area for mining purposes waned. French Canadians then started to farm the rolling terrain north of the Vermilion River close to Denison Township. John Lindala was the first Finnish resident. He acquired property in 1903 and moved there permanently two years later.[72] In 1906-1907 other Finns came to the area, among them Kalle Hotti. The first Finns to register property in 1916, however, were Alex Hanninen, Frans Lahti and Juha Leppänen.[73]

By 1921 about thirty Finnish residents had settled in the Grassy Lake area. Among them was Rev. Arvi Heinonen (biography 4), who had formed a Finnish Presbyterian congregation in 1915 on property acquired from Kaarlo Mäkelä. A church was dedicated in 1916, and in 1921 a manse was constructed and the church expanded. This religious element evoked considerable consternation among the leftist folk who felt that only "communism could lead the way for the oppressed small farmer."[74] The church site (now adjacent to Akela Aircraft Inc.) served as the centre for mission work among Finns and Scandinavians in Denison, Louise, Lorne and Nairn Townships. Kaarlo Mäkelä also had the distinction of being the first lay presbyter of any Finnish congregation in Canada. The siting of the church was an additional factor in fostering the early development of the township and in bringing provincial funding for road and school construction.[75]

Meanwhile, the Svensk family had started homesteading in the remote part of the township near Kusk Lake. August Svensk was the first of several tailors who came to the area following a failed strike in Toronto in 1911. A reluctant farmer, most of the work preparing the land was done by his son, Oiva. The Svensk family acquired such a fine reputation that August and Oiva became chairman and secretary respectively of the first local school board in 1917. Oiva later became head of the local roads board. Oiva Svensk, Kalle Hotti and Rev. Heinonen joined forces in getting financial help from the province to have a wooden bridge built across the Vermilion River in 1923. The opening of this bridge paved the way for the recreational development of Little Lake Panache (formerly Trout Lake) as a "summer paradise" for people from Toronto and Detroit.[76] In 1927 the well-known leftist tailor John Ahlqvist acquired a recreational property from Oscar

Biography 4
Rev. Arvi Heinonen: Anti-Socialist Zealot

Rev. Arvi Heinonen was born in 1887 in Helsinki, Finland. Following his education in Finland, he attended Oxford University in England. He worked for the Finnish National Bank for five years and was an avid sailor.[77] He went to the United States where he became editor of the Finnish newspaper *Pohjolan Tähti* (North Star) in Fitchburg, Massachusetts. After attending Congregational Church Theological College, he was ordained in 1912; he then married Cecilia Kronholm from Finland and over time they had nine children. In 1913 he received a call from the Presbyterian Church of Canada and moved to Copper Cliff where he was placed in charge of mission work from Sault Ste. Marie and Sudbury in the south to Cochrane and Timmins in the north.

Heinonen took advantage of the weak influence of the *Suomi* Synod in the Sudbury area, and with the support of the Canadian Copper Company, won many converts. In his book *Finnish Friends in Canada*, he lashed out at socialists, the state church in Finland and the *Suomi* Synod in the United States.[78] His activities resulted in a suit by Alfred Laakso and Jacob Walli, demanding that Heinonen and John Wilson, another Presbyterian, be restrained from preaching or interfering with the religious activities of the *Wuoristo* Lutheran Church.[79] Heinonen's opposition to socialists gained him national prominence through his role as a Finnish "Informant-in-Chief" for the federal government, where he used his influence to bar socialist newspapers from arriving in Canada. He also acted as an informant for Canadian companies regarding the political leanings of prospective Finnish employees. These activities were taken as proof by socialists that organized religion served the big companies rather than workers.

Using a schoolhouse provided by the Canadian Copper Company in 1913, Heinonen established the Copper Cliff Presbyterian Mission (Finnish) as a company-sanctioned church. The congregation remodelled the schoolhouse, using the ground floor as the church and the second floor for social and educational purposes. Heinonen introduced evening classes to teach English and Canadian laws and customs. The Mission at the corner of Balsam and Evans Streets (present site of Copper Cliff Dairy) was called "Franssi's Church," a reference to one of its strongest supporters, Tuomas A. Franssi, a local merchant and later the Finnish vice-consul. In 1915 Heinonen's attempts at assimilation intensified with the formation of the Finnish People's Institute, the first of its kind in Canada. It offered a variety of courses in English and Finnish in fields such as vocal and instrumental music, domestic science, industrial crafts and handiwork for the 230 members of the Mission.[80] Heinonen's prodigious attempts at winning converts to the Presbyterian cause went beyond Copper Cliff to include Finnish settlements situated in Lorne and Louise Townships. A church built in the latter township in 1916 was also used as a school until 1924. He then acquired Rauhala Island on Long Lake as a site for religious events in the summer months. After World War I, Heinonen moved to Grassy Lake in Louise Township; he built a manse there in 1921. This served as the centre of his mission work in Denison, Louise, Lorne and Nairn Townships.

In 1924 he moved to Saskatchewan where he had a pastoral charge with the United Church of Canada. Later he served the United Church at Winnipeg, Sault Ste. Marie and along the Algoma Central Railway. In 1938 he moved to the Finnish United Church in Timmins until his retirement. He passed away in 1963.

Kauppinen on the south shore of Vermilion River. Other tailors from Toronto followed. With the construction of a bridge across Little Lake Panache in 1934 and the opening of the road to Marina Bay in the same year, Louise Township evolved as the major thoroughfare for traffic between Sudbury and Lake Panache;[81] this gateway role was strengthened when an iron bridge was constructed across the Vermilion River in 1956.

In contrast to Beaver Lake, the Finnish settlement of Louise Township developed in a dispersed pattern around three local lakes: Grassy, Kusk and Little Panache (map 11). Physical geography contributed to this lack of internal cohesiveness. Large tracts of undeveloped crown lands to the southwest and the settlement of the northern part of the township by French Canadians also fostered communal separation. Given this pattern of population dispersal, it is not surprising that the township supported three halls and two athletic clubs. Shortly after its formation in 1915, Whitefish Local 20 of the Finnish Socialist Organization of Canada erected a dancing pavilion on the north shore of Little Lake Panache on land rented from J. Laine.[82] In 1924 the local acquired land from John Lievonen near the Vermilion River upstream from Grassy Lake; in 1946, some adjacent property was purchased from Martha Huhtala. A hall and sports field were constructed on this site which had the distinction of being cleared almost entirely by women. The use of this field had to be abandoned later due to annual flooding every spring by the Vermilion River.

Despite its small size, the *Kipinä* (Spark) Athletic Club formed in 1926 proved to be very successful at cross-country skiing and track-and-field meets of the Finnish-Canadian Amateur Sports Federation. After years of declining use, however, the two properties were sold to the Crean Hill Gun Club in 1968 and 1975. Further west was the Vermilion River FSOC Local 25 Hall, on the Alfred Stenman farm close to Lorne Township. It had its own athletic club, known as *Voima* (Power). A hall building was acquired from nearby Crean Hill following the closure of the mine in 1919. When this hall burned in 1925, its members drifted to the Beaver Lake and Whitefish sports clubs. The property was sold in 1975. In 1934 a local of the Finnish Canadian Workers' and Farmers' Federation built a third hall, south of the Stoney Bay cutoff, on land owned by Karl Salmi. This hall was destroyed by fire in 1940 and in 1966 the property was donated to the

Penage Road Community Centre. Feelings often ran high between the various hall factions. According to one recollection, a Finn actually refused to follow another farmer's ski trail in deep snow on Little Lake Panache asserting that he "would never ski on another . . . communist's trail!"[83]

Map 11
Early Finnish Settlement in Louise Township

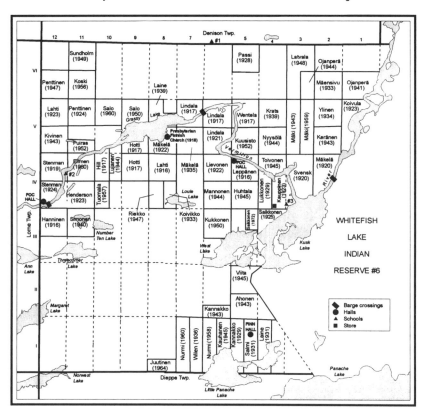

Source: Sudbury Land Registry Office.

The main form of economic activity was farming. Agriculture centred around the production of butter, cream and vegetables; later, output focused on milk production. In the 1950s agriculture declined due to youth out-migration and higher wages offered by the mining companies.

Some employment was also provided by the several stores that served the local Finnish population. Two co-operative outlets were run by Oscar Kauppinen and John Lievonen around the turn of the 1930s. Following the demise of the co-operative movement, Toivo Koivikko established a store in 1936 at the junction of Panache and Grassy Lake Roads.

The history of Louise Township is closely intertwined with that of the *Miljoonajoki* (Vermilion) River. It provided the early means of transportation; at least three ferry crossings existed to bring settlers across the river. On the Kustaa Mäkelä farm near Kusk Lake, a ferry provided campers with access to Lake Panache via a four-mile tote road that ran through the White-fish Indian Reserve. The tote road had been constructed in the 1890s by lumbering companies for the shipment of raw materials and products in and out of Lake Panache; later, it was used by campers and tourists. The other ferries were situated west of Grassy Lake and on Matti Lindala's farm. The river served an economic function as well, since fishing was used to complement agriculture.

The river wreaked havoc on the settlers during the melting season. One of the worst floods occurred in the spring of 1928, when the river rose eight to twenty feet above its normal height. As one reporter remarked, "with valleys and flatlands inundated the territory in Louise and Lorne townships skirting the banks now appears like a series of Norwegian fjords."[84] Disaster struck on 8 May when three Finnish children drowned in a scow after leaving the #2 school. As the school had been surrounded by water for several weeks, the students used a scow provided by the Northern Development Branch.[85] Eager to get home, they overloaded the boat and sank. Concern with the flooding of the river even prompted an attempt on the part of the Farmers' Club headed, by Oscar Kauppinen, to divert part of the Vermilion River through the Indian reserve into Lake Panache to ease flood conditions and to promote the earlier seeding of crops. This proposal was opposed by the camp owners at Lake Panache; they petitioned the province to stop the diversion scheme, fearing that the resulting rise in the lake level would have devastating effects on property and the fishery. The controversy went on until 1938 after which time the idea was dropped.[86]

Schooling was provided by three one-room schools. School #1, known as Den-Lou, was built along the northern border of Louise and Denison Townships. School #2 began as part of the Presbyterian church site on Grassy Lake; in 1924 it was moved to another site on the Thomas Henderson and Henry Ellmen farmsteads. Occupying the former Finnish Socialist Hall, it served students from both Louise and Lorne Townships. The late 1930s were exciting times for the isolated Finnish students; in 1938 they visited the Dionne quintuplets at Callander, and in 1939 they went to Sudbury for the visit of King George VI and Queen Elizabeth.[87] School #3 was erected in 1918 on the Kustaa Mäkelä farmstead north of Kusk Lake. The first day at school was interesting as the pupils spoke only Finnish and the teacher only English. As one student later recalled, "when she had tried everything she could do and we didn't understand a word, she went into a corner and cried."[88] This school was destroyed by fire and another one was constructed on land bought from Oscar Kauppinen. Rebuilt in 1937, the school was later sold and it now serves as part of the Penage Road Community Centre. Few students from these schools went to high school.

As was the case with the Beaver Lake settlement, there was little expression of the Lutheran faith. With few supporters outside of the Svensk family, the township lacked a Lutheran church; from time to time, however, religious services were held in the Svensk home.

While the Finnish population has declined in recent years, its heritage remains visible in the many Finnish names that can be found on the mailboxes along the Lake Panache Road.

Broder Township (Long Lake)

The Long Lake area first came to the attention of the Finns around 1901 when early settlers in the Kelly Lake area of Waters and Broder Townships discovered an elongated lake to the south some twenty kilometres in length teeming with fish and surrounded by good hunting territory. At the time, the lake's shoreline had already been settled by French farmers such as Lesperance, Labelle, Charette, Goudrieu, Pitaud, Duquette and Boileau. The Francophone influence was evidenced by the presence of the Rheault Post Office and the fact that the early minutes of the Long Lake School Board were written in French. Like other rural districts in the Sudbury area, settlement at Long Lake started because of lumbering and mining. Prior to World War I, the Victoria Harbour Logging Company lumber had a mill, office and bunkhouse situated on both sides of the bridge that now crosses the eastern part of the lake. Further west, adjacent to the Whitefish Lake Indian Reserve, was the Long Lake Gold mine, which operated from 1909 until 1916. While in existence only for a short period of time, the mine had the distinction of being Ontario's largest gold producer in 1912; at its height in 1914, the mine employed 110 employees.[89]

As the farming country west and south of Copper Cliff had already been occupied by Finns, the Kelly and Long Lake areas in Broder Township served as one of the remaining areas for agricultural activity. In 1908, Aatu Marttinen and his family came to the Long Lake area while John Freeman settled further north near Kelly Lake. From the outset, distance and topography kept the Kelly and Long Lake Finns separated from one another and there was little interaction between these two areas. By World War I the northeastern shore of Long Lake was completely dominated by the Finns.[90] While most farmsteads consisted of family units, some were owned by single men. The wartime settlers spread the Finnish population both northwards into the Kelly Lake area and southwards towards Lohi, Clearwater and Forest Lakes (map 12).

Map 12
Early Finnish Settlement in Broder Township

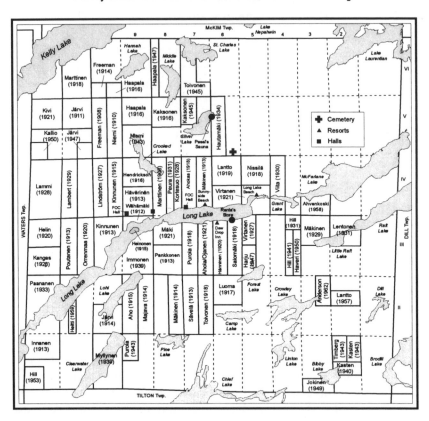

Source: Sudbury Land Registry Office; Eino Nissilä, *Pioneers of Long Lake*.

For these newcomers, agriculture was preferable to the fluctuating employment prospects associated with the mining industry. Otto Kinnonen, Arvi Mäkinen, Jaakko Hemming, Nicholai Virtanen and Kaarlo Nissilä were typical of those who came to Broder Township when mining declined or stopped at the Copper Cliff, Frood and Sellwood mines. Other properties were purchased from the original French-speaking settlers who were referred to as *härkäpoikia* (ox-boys) because they were among the last farmers in the district to use oxen for draught animals. Not all of the pioneers were farmers; the charismatic Finnish Presbyterian minister, Rev. Arvi Heinonen, for example, had a summer retreat on Rauhala Island.

Living conditions at the time were harsh. One local resident recalled:

It was the Poles and the French settlers who sold these denuded and rocky ravines. The forests had either been sold or were in a ruined state. However, since we were Finns from the Saarijärvi area, we simply proceeded to settle here with grim determination. While the men remained at home during the summer, they were forced to leave in the fall to earn money. No one was able to work at the mines so they all went to forest camps. No one knows this better than the women who were forced to remain at home with the children and the farm animals. There was no other way to travel than by skiing. One could not visit everyday with your neighbours or offer assistance regardless of any type of sickness. Go ahead and weep![91]

Other farmsteads appeared in the early 1920s.[92] Due to population growth, the school on the north shore of Long Lake (later the site of the Hart Motel), built in 1908, was sold and a new one erected on the south shore in 1923. By this time the Finnish occupation, as occurred in Waters, Lorne and Louise Townships, had moved into another rural enclave. Of the thirty-seven students enrolled in Long Lake Public School in 1924-25, for instance, 80 percent had Finnish names. Around the turn of the 1930s, more Finnish households became entrenched parts of the local setting.[93] Especially well known at the time was Matilda Virtanen, who served as the postmistress from 1919 to 1943; her story was later selected to be included in the Sudbury time capsule, which will be opened in 2083.

The dominance of the Finns continued throughout the years of the Great Depression and World War II, at which time Finnish students still constituted 80 to 85 percent of the school population. This ethnic orientation encouraged the school board to hire teachers who were Finnish in origin. After World War II the Finnish proportion in the school dropped to around one-half, reflecting the transition of the Finnish Long Lake community from one of dominance to that of a substantial minority.[94] By the end of the 1970s, Finns accounted for only about 30 percent of the school population.[95]

Changes in the settlement pattern occurred as well. The development of Long Lake for cottage purposes began in 1929-30, when Matilda Virtanen sold properties to Karl Nurmi and Matti Poutanen. Kaarina Ritari then acquired the first cottage property on Clearwater Lake in 1936;[96] she was followed by Eino Blom, who registered a summer cottage property in the following year. The promotion of the Long Lake area for seasonal purposes, however, was slowed by a poor road connection with Sudbury. The reconstruction of Long Lake Road in the late 1940s improved the situation considerably, and shoreline cottage subdivisions started to appear around all of the lakes in the township. In 1949 John Toivonen became the first Finn to register a plan of subdivision on Ester Road south of St. Charles Lake. He was followed in 1950 by Antti Kinnunen, who began to sell shoreline properties on the south shore of McFarlane Lake. At the same time, Väinö Kinnunen became the first to register a subdivision at Long Lake on Sunnyside Road west of *Voima* Hall. Others were developed on Crooked Lake by

Wilfred Niemi and Alma Bontinen (1952) and on both sides of St. Charles Lake by Viljo Jokinen (1953) and H. and L. Punkari (1954). The floodgates opened between 1955 and 1957 when numerous other subdivisions were approved as well.[97] Major improvements to Long Lake Road after 1969 enhanced the accessibility of the area further. Some properties sold by Finns evolved into institutional land uses. On Clearwater Lake, land was acquired from John Myllynen and Simo Purola for use as a Jewish retreat; in 1972 the Viljo Jokinen property on Bibby Lake was purchased by the Sudbury Fish and Game Association. The area's relative proximity to Sudbury has more recently encouraged the transformation of many cottages and lots into permanent homes.

The agricultural economy initially centred around dairy farming. Despite the isolation of the township, Finnish farmers managed to eke out a living shipping milk to the Sudbury market. At one time there were as many as ten farmers shipping milk to the Co-operative and Bouchard Dairies. Delivering milk was not an easy task as the road was a "narrow, rough, boulder strewn and rutted horse and buggy trail with many steep crooked inclines that were difficult to navigate."[98] Two of the major inclines were known as the Buchowski and Tolonen Hills. Families also maintained a few head of cattle to provide milk, cream and butter for their own use. The rural economy, however, provided only a meagre existence, and settlers were forced to turn to other activities such as the sale of gravel, the delivery of wood and lumber and employment on road construction and maintenance jobs. The economy remained marginal until the outbreak of World War II, when local farmers managed to secure employment with the mining companies.

The recreational assets of the lake provided another source of income. By the 1930s the Long Lake area had acquired a reputation as being one of the region's best fishing, swimming and resort spots.[99] Vilho Vihuri operated a summer resort known as Long Lake Beach along the northeastern shore on the site of the original elementary school. It comprised a sauna and swimming beach with a diving tower; meals and refreshments were also available. Sunnyside Beach, run by Arvi Mäkinen, could be found further west. A third resort, known as Dew Drop Inn and Beach, was operated by Victor Hänninen on the south shore. In 1954 this property was acquired by Sacred Heart College of Sudbury which, in turn, sold it to Villa Loyola of Sudbury as a religious retreat. Finally, there was the "Lily-of-the-Valley" resort on the southeast shore of the lake, where Long Lake Public School is now sited. Erected by Gilbert Rheault as the most prestigious building in the Long Lake area during World War I, it was acquired in 1939 by E. Hill, a local Finnish farmer, for non-payment of taxes. Hill leased the site to the Radicioni family who developed it as a resort. Other enterprises included Ranta's Store on the south shore of Long Lake and Passi's Sauna on the east shore of Silver Lake.

The Long Lake area was the site of three halls and two athletic fields. The first hall was erected by the Long Lake Finnish Social Society. Formed in 1920, the society built a hall and acquired property from Oscar Ahlgren along Järvi Road in 1921-22.[100] With Ahlgren and Arvi Mäkinen as trustees, membership in the society climbed to over thirty. The hall then fell into the hands of the FOC Local 35 in 1924, with the society acting as trustee. In 1932 the property was returned to Ahlgren and the building moved to another site further east. Like other FOC-owned halls, its ownership temporarily resided with the Custodian of Canada during World War II. After its return, the hall was destroyed by fire and eventually sold in 1954. The site became the property of Manitou Airways in 1963 and was later sold for residential purposes. The third hall was erected by the United Farmers' Society of Long Lake, associated with the Finnish Canadian Workers' and Farmers' Federation. It was built on property purchased from Antti Ranta in 1932. Emil Ranta and Charles Ristimäki served as the president and secretary of the society at the time. A Farmers' Hall, erected in 1933, was used extensively by local Finns. It was later taken over by the *Voima* Athletic Club in 1944. The club had roots reaching back to 1932 when it was first formed as an offshoot of the Finnish National Society based at *Sampo* Hall. Internal squabbles, however, plagued the club throughout the 1930s and it was disbanded. Spearheaded by Jack Seppälä, Antti Heiskanen and Paavo Ruohonen, the club was resurrected in 1940 as the non-political Finnish Canadian Athletic Association *Voima*. For a time, the new club met at *Sampo* Hall in the winter months and at the Farmers' Hall during the summer. In 1944 the club acquired the Farmers' Hall.

Voima Hall served as the centre for countless events including play performances, dances, wedding receptions, anniversary parties, ski races, festivals and skiing and track-and-field competitions. Silent movies featuring Charlie Chaplin were also shown. Vern Kinnonen supplied music with his accordion, assisted by Aimo Mäkinen who played drums and taps. Under the direction of Ilmari Järnefelt, a mixed choir flourished between 1941 and 1953, with as many as sixty-four members.[101] To enhance sporting competitions, additional property was acquired from the Marttinen and Ranta farmsteads in 1944-45. The building and skiing facilities were then renovated on several occasions. In 1950 a kitchen and caretaker's residence were added. Numerous improvements were made in 1969 using volunteer labour, and in 1981 a Summer Canada grant was received to expand the ski trails. The beach facilities and the hall were again improved in 1982 with the assistance of make-work job creation programs.[102]

The remaining athletic facility was built by the Long Lake Athletic Association on the south shore of Long Lake. Formed in 1951 by Finnish residents, the association acquired five acres of land from Edward Hill in 1954 on which a baseball field and skating rink were built. After the property was sold to the Sudbury Board of Education in 1973, the association disbanded.[103] The field is now part of the elementary school property.

The Long Lake area still retains much of its Finnish character. Names such as Järvi, Kivinen, Lammi, Niemi and Taipale Roads, and Lohi Lake, serve as reminders of the township's ethnic heritage. Finnish saunas continue to dot the shorelines of the township's many lakes. Financial and other considerations, however, led in 1997-98 to the sale of *Voima* Hall and its beach, athletic field and extensive ski trails. As with the *Sampo* (1994) and Finnish (1981) Halls earlier, its disappearance signalled the end of the immigrant hall as an integral feature of the Finnish ethnic community.

Dill, Cleland, Secord and Burwash Townships (Wanup)

The final rural enclave to develop was simply known as "Wanup." Located southeast of Sudbury, it was associated with the Townships of Cleland, Dill, Secord and Burwash. This district first attracted interest in 1872 when the province granted timber rights in the area. Among the lumbering firms to exploit the timber resources of the area were the Emery, Holland and Emery, Graves, Bigwood and Manley Chew Companies. The cut timber was floated down the Wahnapitei River to the French River system and from there to Byng Inlet. Manley Chew for a time had a large forest camp at the Red Pine Chutes Falls on the Wahnapitei River. The last timber operation in the area was carried on by the McFadden Company in 1938. Both the CPR and CNR also built railway lines through the area before World War I, connecting Toronto with Sudbury; two stations, known as St. Cloud (CNR) and Wanup (CPR), were established in Cleland Township.

The construction of these railway lines encouraged Finns to seek rural farmsteads on nearby lands. Dill Township was the first area to be settled. Registry records show that Antti Tainio, Frank Heino and Martti Mäntylä arrived first in 1913 and occupied land adjacent to the Wahnapitei River and the CNR line. They were followed by Jacob Mäki and Alex Salo in 1914 and John Pulkkinen in 1915. The early development of the area, however, faced two major barriers. Between 1915 and 1921, some crown lands were withdrawn in the area for environmental and economic reasons related to the mining industry. In 1913 the province also established the Burwash Industrial Farm in the unorganized townships of Laura, Secord, Servos and Burwash. Despite the land withdrawal, some Finns, including Matti Ranta and Raine Lake, settled in the area unofficially in 1916. Frank Heino was the first settler to register his property in 1921. By this time a local of the Finnish Socialist Organization of Canada had been established; its membership included half of the seventeen farmers in the area.[104]

Around World War I, laid-off men from the Mond Nickel Company and new migrants from Finland gravitated to the Wanup area.[105] The extent of Finnish influence at the time is demonstrated by the fact that of the twenty-four students enrolled in the Dill and Secord Public School in 1923, twenty-two had Finnish names.[106] There may have been as many as fifty Finnish residents at this time. During the Great Depression the number of Finns increased, due in part to the Relief Land Settlement Scheme (maps 13 and 14). Many, however, came as squatters:

> With the advent of the back-to-the-land movement, 40 Finnish families have squatted in Dryden and Cleland Townships, and displaying the spirit of the early pioneers, are hewing out homes for themselves rather than to accept relief. . . . Finnish citizens did not wait for Dryden and Cleland Townships to be opened, but squatted on arable land, each building a log house and the ever present steam bath. Some of them have 10 to 20 acres cleared. Whether by accident or design, they did not settle in a group but "spotted" all over the townships.[107]

These squatters took considerable comfort in the fact that the government had never yet evicted a squatter from a farm for the illegal occupation of land. One of these squatters was a widow known as A. Merivirta. Living alone in Dryden Township just north of Wanup, she drew admiration from *The Sudbury Star* for her tenacity in maintaining a pioneering farmstead that she had originally established with her husband:

> Hidden away among the small birches of Dryden Township, about two miles from the village of Wahnapitae, is a little log cabin and a small log stable in the midst of a clearing. . . . The cluster of log buildings in the clearing is the home of Mrs. A. Merivirta, who, as a bride, came to Dryden two years ago with her husband, but who was left a widow within six months of their settlement. Since then, she has stout-heartedly carried on alone. . . . Though there are 12 to 14 Finnish squatters in the township, she is the only woman among them. . . . The mistress of this humble estate greeted the emissaries of the Sudbury Star on a recent visit as graciously as the chatelaine of some royal castle. She wore the badge of poverty as proudly as a peeress wears her family crest. She is doing great things by her own labor, and is proud of it. She referred to things her husband had made or done. He cleared 10 acres of land and built these buildings in only three months. Destitute of money except for what they required for bare necessities of life, they could afford neither lumber nor tar paper for the shacks or for chairs or tables with which to furnish it. The roof is made of strips of birch bark, peeled from the trees on their lot. The bark is held in place by split poles, nailed over it and across the cracks. The floor is made of hand hewn logs, flattened with an axe. . . . The fireplace is a square mass of stone, with a doorless hole about a foot square and two feet from the floor as a firebox. . . . The other furniture consists of a homemade table, and homemade benches. The bed is springless, consisting of two poles of birch bark fastened between them.[108]

Map 13
Early Finnish Settlement in the Wanup Area (West)

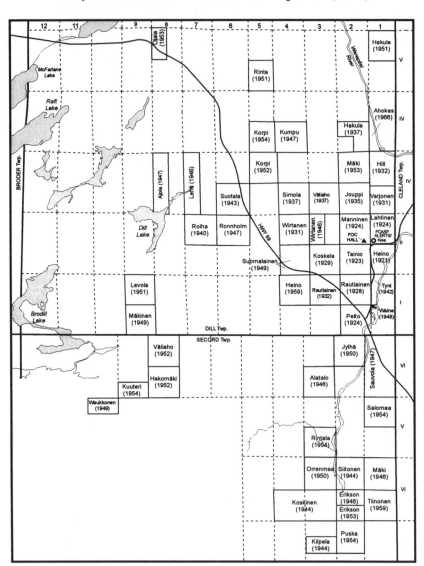

Source: Sudbury Land Registry Office.

Map 14
Early Finnish Settlement in the Wanup Area (East)

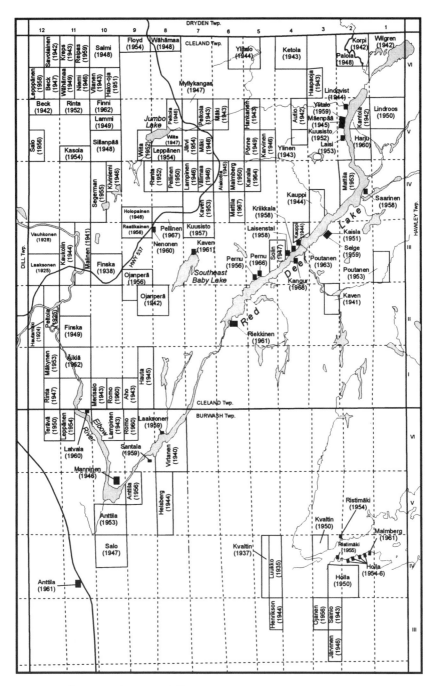

Source: Sudbury Land Registry Office.

By the middle 1930s there were an estimated two hundred Finns in the area, and the emergence of Wanup as yet another Finnish rural enclave had become an established fact.[109] William Kangassalo, a long-term resident of the Wanup area, has sketched an interesting portrayal of the area at the time (map 15). Four families and three single men, however, left the area with hopes of securing a better future in Russian Karelia. At the Dill and Cleland Public School in 1936, the ongoing Finnish presence was reflected by the fact that 80 percent of the students were Finns.[110] The Finnish character of the area remained strong up to the turn of the 1950s. At this stage, 70 percent of the students in the Wanup Public School still had Finnish backgrounds.[111] Beginning in the 1960s, however, the cultural landscape underwent change. In 1965 the local school was brought under the jurisdiction of the Sudbury Board of Education and a new elementary school opened in 1969. In order to accommodate students from the Burwash Industrial Farm, the school was expanded and the ethnic mix became more diversified. The influx of students from Burwash lasted until 1974, when the correctional farm was closed.

Map 15
An Early Sketch of the Wanup Area

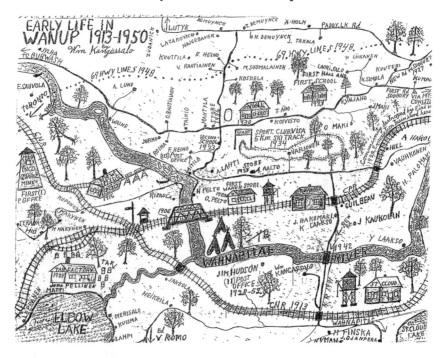

Source: William Kangassalo (1995).

It was farming that served as the main economic attraction for the Wanup settlers. According to one account,

> The early pioneers saw nothing beautiful in this valley. The lumber companies had taken the virgin timber and the area was polluted as earlier the Mond Nickel Company had roasted nickel by burning wood and sulfur near Sudbury. Later the smoke from Coniston Smelter drifted south down the River causing damage to anything that was green. To the average eye, the scenery was not beautiful—but then everyone was poor and the land was cheap and still suitable for farming. So it was to Wanup they came.[112]

Between 1935 and 1945 there were as many as sixteen active dairy farms. Dairy farming declined rapidly after World War II, at which time farmers shifted to the raising of cattle. Trapping was another source of employment. During the construction of the CPR line, two Finns, David Rautjärvi (Lake) and his son Raine, worked for the railway company; later, others found jobs on railway section gangs. The Canadian Copper Company's quartz quarry in Dill Township provided jobs from 1910 until its closure in 1924.[113] The quartz was shipped from here to the company's smelter in Copper Cliff. Some Finns, among them Kusti Varjonen, acquired work at the nearby mica and feldspar mines that employed up to sixty men and operated from 1922 until 1936. The output from these mines was shipped to New York and used for the making of porcelain dishes. Another source of jobs was a local sawmill that remained operational until World War I.

In the 1920s a tar factory was built by John and Matti Pellinen and Dr. Heikki Koljonen near Elbow Lake. This factory made tar using sawmill boilers and local stumps left behind from previous logging operations; the tar was then shipped south to Toronto via the railway.[114] During the 1930s families turned to blueberry picking, and hundreds of blueberry boxes could be found stacked at the railway ready for the Toronto market. As road connections improved, many farmers turned to mining for employment. To serve local needs, general stores were established. The first, operated by Lisi Pelto, was located near the Wanup station. Ruusa and August Aalto ran a second store on their own property. A *Raatajien Kauppa* (Pioneer Store), supported by the Finnish Organization of Canada, appeared on the scene for a short time; it was situated on Hjalmar Manninen's farm between 1931 and 1932. Frank Heino also ran a general store from the mid-1920s until 1935 when the *Wanupin Työläisten ja Farmarien Osuuskauppa* (Farmers' and Workers' Cooperative Store of Wanup) was built on Martti Mäntylä's farm.[115] The cooperative existed for twenty-five years, from 1935 to 1960, at which time it was privatized and run by Finns until 1985. It operates today as the Wanup General Store. Matti Suomalainen, another entrepreneur, was a master loghouse builder and was responsible for erecting many local farm dwellings.

The Wanup area was considered to be one of the main strongholds of Finnish socialism in the Sudbury area. A Finnish Hall, built in 1921 by

Local 9 of the Finnish Socialist Organization of Canada on Manninen's property, also served as the area's first school. It was destroyed in the great fire of 5 October 1922 as were numerous farm buildings belonging to seven Finnish families and a general store. According to *The Sudbury Star*: "[T]he fire raged up the valley of the Wahnapitae to Wanup where it died out but not before it had swept everything in its path, and at Wanup station licked up ten C.P.R. cars, the huge water tank, station property, a store and small sawmill."[116] A new school was built in 1923 and it was used for several years as a Finnish hall. The building served as a focal point for renowned leftist speakers such as Alfred Hautamäki, Sanna Kannasto and A.T. Hill.

The year 1930 was eventful. *Visa* (Curly Birch) Athletic Club was founded, a summer festival held, and a new Finnish hall erected on Manninen's farm. The property was acquired by the FOC in 1931. The hall, and its accompanying track-and-field site, served a vital cultural need during the 1930s. In 1934-35 a ski trail was added close to the Wanup Hall on the farms of Antti Lahtinen and Kusti Varjonen. The club also supported a gymnastics group and the *Jousi Orkesteri* (String Orchestra). As was the case with all of the halls owned by the Finnish Organization of Canada, Wanup Hall was closed by the federal government from 1940 to 1944. A fire gutted the building in 1946, but it was soon replaced. *Visa* continued to be active throughout the 1950s and 1960s.

In anticipation of the need for a new track facility to replace the Alerts Field at Lockerby in Sudbury, eighty-two acres of land were purchased from Antti Lahtinen in 1960 by the Alerts and *Visa* Clubs. Between 1965 and 1973 this sports field served as the site for the joint FOC/FCASF festivals. Due to old age and declining use, Wanup Hall was torn down and replaced, with the assistance of a Wintario grant, by a new building known as the Wanup Community Centre in 1983.[117] The cultural scene was broadened in 1962 when St. Matthew's Finnish Evangelical Lutheran Church acquired the former elementary school site and refurbished it as a chapel. The chapel was formally opened on 30 October 1966.

Aside from the hall and the church, another point of interest after World War II was Nestor Puska's popular bootlegging establishment, which was situated in Secord Township. Up to one hundred local residents and many guards from the Burwash Industrial Farm could be found here on weekends enjoying liquid refreshments and dancing to the beat of a nickelodeon.[118]

The inner geography of the Wanup area was profoundly influenced by the Wahnapitei River and the two railway lines that ran through the heart of the community. While the former was important for its scenery and fishing, it was at the same time an ever-present hazard. At least sixteen residents are known to have drowned as a result of its fast-moving current. The two railway lines added an interesting dimension to everyday life as the children would regularly line up along the farm fences to wave to passengers and to catch bundles of old magazines and newspapers thrown to them by conductors.[119] As the CPR train from Toronto stopped at Wanup at 5:10 a.m. and returned from Sudbury at 11:20 p.m., the trip to and from Sudbury was done only when absolutely necessary. The breakdown of isolation from Sudbury was gradual. The Burwash-Sudbury road did not open until 1933 and a northward connection to Wahnapitae on highway 17 remained until 1938. Electricity finally arrived around 1951, thereby giving the community access to modern facilities that had hitherto been lacking.

Another sign of changing times took place in 1965 when Aalto's farm was subdivided; this event heralded the last gasp of farming activity and the arrival of the first major wave of non-Finns into the area. Since then the Finnish character of the area, while still distinctive, has exhibited a slow decline. Nevertheless, the Finnish influence remains significant as indicated by the holding of the FOC/FCASF Reunion Festival in 1994 and the *Kesti* (Summer Celebration) in 1996 at the Wanup Community Centre. The Wanup Community Centre also has an important symbolic value for Finnish-Canadian history, as it represents the last remnant of the former FOC hall empire in Canada.

Post-World War II Trends

The distribution of Finnish settlement remained fairly consistent after World War II. Bolstered by the rapid growth of the mining industry, more than 2,000 Finns came to the Sudbury area during the 1950s, and by 1961 the Finnish population of the District of Sudbury reached its maximum peak of 7,446. The city of Sudbury and the townships of Broder, McKim and Waters served as the main destinations for these new arrivals. These postwar immigrants brought new life into existing Finnish organizations. Churches and the *Sampo* Hall in particular became beehives of activity. Due to the incorporation of the New Sudbury and Lockerby fringe areas on 1 January 1960, an additional 3,000 Finns now officially resided in the city of Sudbury. While classified as urban, however, many resided in the rural parts of Broder Township. Outside of the enlarged Sudbury, the earlier preference for rural and small community living was still in evidence. After 1961, however, the number of Finns in the area declined. While the 1996 figure of 6,885 Finns for the Sudbury CMA and its environs remains substantial, it must be remembered that one-half of this total now includes Finns of multiple ancestry.

A visual appreciation of the distribution of the Finnish population in 1980 is given in table 10 and map 16. Using the voters' lists for the 1980 federal election, all polling districts where more than 10 percent of the voters had Finnish names were identified for the Sudbury and Nickel Belt ridings. Six major and two minor clusters emerged from this spatial analysis. Major clusters included Broder (Long Lake) and Waters Townships; Beaver Lake in Lorne Township; the Wanup area encompassing Burwash, Cleland, Dill and Secord Townships; the Lockerby area; the Donovan; and Copper Cliff. Smaller zones of concentration were identified in Garson and Dowling. The data made it clear that the rural enclaves that developed in the outlying areas west, south and southeast of Sudbury after the turn of the century were still very much alive at the time.

Table 10
Population of Finnish Origin by Federal
Polling Districts (1980)

Generalized polling district	No. of Finns of voting age
Long Lake–Waters	799
Beaver Lake	306
Wanup	228
Lockerby	140
Donovan	83
Copper Cliff	52
Garson	26
Dowling	18
Other	2,061
Total	3,713

Source: Calculated from Sudbury and Nickel Belt Electoral District, *Federal Election Voters' List* (1980).

The Dowling cluster is notable as it symbolizes the small attraction that the "valley" has traditionally had for Finns. Prior to World War II, only a few Finnish farmsteads existed in these agricultural lowlands, notably around Whitewater and Vermilion Lakes. With the great expansion of mining employment after the turn of the 1950s, however, Finnish farmsteads such as those owned by Eino and Ellen Puska, Walte Puukila and W. Wahamaa in the Azilda area were subdivided and they attracted Finnish miners to the area. Others went to Levack and the nearby townsites along the northern rim of the Sudbury Basin that were built after the war. While settlement in Levack was never very large, Finns were nonetheless there in sufficient numbers to have supported an FOC hall in 1935. Other examples of the Finnish presence included the formation of the *Kisatoverit* (Playmates) Athletic Club and the operation of a sauna from 1944 until 1952. The FOC Hall was later transformed into a community centre. During the 1950s and 1960s several boarding houses were operated at various times.[120] Unlike most other communities, the Finns in Levack were not clustered, but could be found in various parts of the townsite.[121]

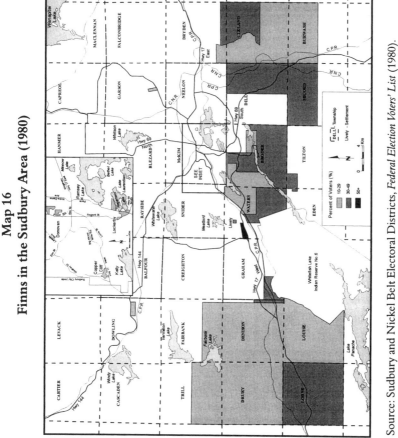

Map 16
Finns in the Sudbury Area (1980)

Source: Sudbury and Nickel Belt Electoral Districts, *Federal Election Voters' List* (1980).

In recent years there has been a reduction in the number of Finns in the Sudbury area due to fewer immigrant arrivals and the aging of the Finnish population. Since the 1980s fewer than 110 immigrants have come to Canada from Finland each year; of this meagre total, less than one-half have sought Ontario as their destination. Along with this lessening of the immigrant flow, a significant aging process has occurred; more than 20 percent of the ethnic group now consists of individuals sixty-five years of age or over. Many of these elderly Finns have moved from single-family homes in rural areas to apartments located in the Lockerby area and to the *Finlandia* Village complex. There has also been a small return migration to the old country, as some individuals have returned to Finland to spend their retirement years there.

Lake Panache Recreational Zone

After World War II a special form of Finnish settlement gained prominence at Lake Panache. Neither urban nor rural, it consisted of the many camp/cottages built by Finns that flanked the shores of Lake Panache. Panache (also known as Lake Penage) is a popular recreational body of water located southwest of Sudbury between highway 17 and the La Cloche Mountains. The development of this area as a site for cottaging, hunting, fishing and tourism arose out of its outstanding physical characteristics. After the logging era, the lake attracted American cottagers and tourist camps. The decreased isolation of the lake in the 1930s finally made it possible for Finns to acquire cottage sites. The strong influence that Finns have had at Lake Panache is indicated by the fact that they held patents at one time or another on 40 percent of the land developed from 1917 to 1989 (table 11 and map 17). It is clear, therefore, that immigrants from Finland not only had an insatiable desire for land but for summer cottages as well. The latter was especially true for the more urbanized Finns who lived in Sudbury and Copper Cliff. The Finnish pursuit of cottage sites lasted until 1967, at which time their sale was brought to an end by provincial policy.

Among the first Finns to register property on the lake were William Hotti, Jack Seppälä, Heleni Gylden and Wilf Salo. It was Hotti (1924) and, later, John Ahlqvist (1937) who pioneered the appearance of Finns on the islands of Stony Bay situated in Truman Township. In the early 1930s, Seppälä (1931) and Gylden (1932) also purchased islands along the isolated southern shore of the lake. While other cottages were in existence at the time, Wilf Salo had the distinction of having the first property patented on Fire Rangers' Bay in 1933; he was followed by C. Jacobson in 1934. In the 1930s Hotti operated the Lake Penage Log Cabin Camp on Fire Rangers' Bay, although the operation was not formally registered until 1945.[122] By the late 1930s other Finns, G. Kulmala (1933), John Gylden (1934), John

Järvi (1936), N. Jacobson (1937), Alex Salo (1938) and Taisto Sirkka (1938), among others, began to erect cottage sites along the north shore in Dieppe Township. John Gylden also ran a tourist operation on the site of present-day Pinehill Resort. In 1941 J. Laamanen became the first Finn to register property along the south shore of the Espanola stretch. Others preferred to remain along the north shore or in Stony Bay.[123] According to one pioneer camper, the 1930s and early 1940s marked "the first real development of Lake Panache by working-class Finns."[124] The spread of Finns during the interwar period was paralleled by a waning of the former American influence on the lake.

Table 11
Patented Land Parcels by Finns in
the Lake Panache Area (1917-89)

Township	Total	Finnish	Percentage Finnish
Dieppe	283	123	43.5
Truman	109	34	31.2
Caen	42	24	57.1
Foster	17	0	0.0
Goschen	8	1	12.5
Bevin	4	1	25.0
Total	463	183	39.5

Source: Calculated from Oiva Saarinen, *History of the Recreational Use of Lake Panache* (Sudbury: Laurentian University, 1990), appendix 2.

After World War II Finnish cottages sprouted everywhere on the lake, even in Caen Township. One of the best-known cottage sites was owned by Richard and Lempi Johnson. It developed as a popular summer destination for guests from Finland and the United States (biography 5). On Frank's Island, W. Helin, the developer of the flatfish lure, briefly ran a tourist operation.[125] Both marinas in Fire Rangers' Bay then came under Finnish ownership during the 1960s and 1970s. In 1966 Taisto and Tauno Lundgren and Kauko Sutinen bought the William Gemmell Marina; in 1971 Sutinen became the sole owner. In 1980 Sutinen sold his operations to Penage Bay Marina, run by Louis Dozzi. The second marina, owned first by William Whitehead and later by William Blanchard, was purchased by Voitto and Judy Erola in 1971. The marina was known as Erola's Panache Landing until its sale to Dozzi in 1976. Meanwhile, a number of Finns after 1959 started to lease cottage tracts within Whitefish Lake Indian Reserve No. 6.

Map 17
Finnish Recreational Properties at Lake Panache (1917-89)

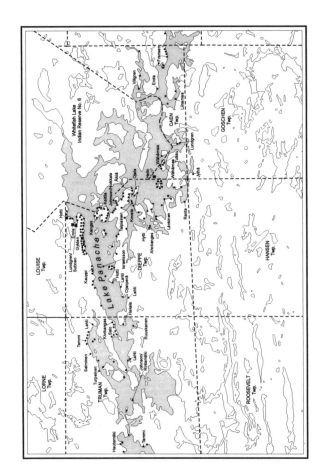

Note: The names listed here are for reference purposes only.
Source: Derived from Oiva Saarinen, *History of the Recreational Use of Lake Panache.*

Lempi Johnson (1901-98) (see biography 5) is shown here displaying a sample of her furs (c. 1960s). Established in 1942, Johnson's Furs remained as a fixture in downtown Sudbury until 1967. (Lempi Johnson, private collection)

John Ahlqvist (1881-1940) served as one of the leaders of the communist movement in Canada (see biography 6). He was also a dedicated member of the Finnish Organization of Canada. (Finnish Canadian Historical Society)

Aku Päiviö (1879-1956) was perhaps the most influential literary figure associated with the Finnish leftist movement in North America (see biography 7). He is shown here (c. 1940s) relaxing in front of his home at Tilton Lake near Sudbury. (Jules Päiviö, private collection)

Bruno Tenhunen (1898-1985) was a strong supporter of social democracy and a founder of *Vapaa Sana* in 1931 (see biography 8). He is shown here (c. 1950s) standing on the right of the second row with other *Vapaa Sana* representatives. (*Vapaa Sana* Press Limited)

Biography 5
Lempi Johnson: The Fur Lady

Lempi Johnson was born Lempi Dagmar in 1901 at Valkajärvi, Finland.[126] Her father and mother had Russian and Swedish origins respectively. Lempi had one older brother (Raine) and a sister (Sievä). In 1910 her father David and Raine left for Canada and Maria remained in Finland with the two daughters as a "North American widow." Little was heard from Canada for the next twelve years. The family in Finland moved to Copper Cliff in 1918 when the Finnish Civil War started. Lempi started a part-time career in singing and changed her name to Lempi Lake. She registered at *Suomi* College in Hancock, Michigan, in the fall of 1919, and in the following year taught a summer course in religion and the Finnish language. Returning to Sudbury, she worked for the *Vapaus* newspaper between 1920 and 1922.

Around this time she met Richard Johnson, a native of Finland and a well-known local figure in sports and outdoor activities. He was also part-owner of the first taxicab firm in Sudbury known as Luoma and Johnson. Lempi and Richard were married in 1922 at St. Andrew's Church. Lempi worked for Stafford's Goods Store for the next eleven years and acquired experience in the retailing of clothing and furs. She held various concerts, including several at New York's largest Finnish Hall in 1929, and thirty-one throughout Finland around the turn of the 1930s. After managing the Star Restaurant located on Elm Street, she worked temporarily with the *Vapaa Sana* newspaper.

Lempi's association with furs began when she was hired by Herman and Company to sell furs in Northern Ontario and Quebec. She later became a salesperson at Coldenson's fur store. In 1942 she purchased the store on Durham Street and changed its name to Johnson's Furs. Richard sold his taxi business and joined with Lempi in operating her new store. A throat operation in 1944 brought her singing career to an end, but between 1945 and 1956 she became well known to the public as an announcer for the Finnish hour heard on CKSO radio every Saturday. In the 1950s her shop became the destination for Finnish immigrants who needed help in getting employment or other forms of assistance. It was known throughout the Finnish community that if all else failed, then Lempi's was the place to go. She served as a gracious host for numerous singing and theatrical groups from Finland. A twenty-fifth wedding anniversary celebration was held for the couple at *Voima* Hall on Long Lake in 1947 with four hundred and fifty in attendance. In 1953 Richard was killed in an automobile accident.

After twenty-five years in the fur business Lempi retired in 1967. She then resided in California and Florida during the winter months, returning to her cottage every summer. During the summer months, Lempi's picnics at Lake Panache became an established part of the Finnish entertainment scene. A special tribute was held in Sudbury to honour Lempi in June of 1983. In 1992 she received the highest praise possible from the government of Finland when she was awarded the White Rose during Finland's seventy-fifth celebration of its independence. Lempi was a member of St. Matthew's Evangelical Lutheran Church, the Finnish Canadian Historical Society and Bluewater Lodge No. 59 of the Ladies of Kaleva. In 1995 she suffered the loss of her close companion of many years, Vic Hoikkala. Lempi passed away in 1998.

While the Finnish impact remains considerable on Lake Panache, aging and the resale of properties to others has brought about a diminished influence in recent years. Nevertheless, the sight of Finns trout or bass fishing in the summer, ice fishing in the winter and attending the ritual of the Saturday sauna, still serve as constant reminders of the lake's rich Finnish legacy.

Florida as a Winter Destination

The aging of the Finnish population in the Sudbury area has also brought with it another distinctive pattern of settlement: the emergence of Florida as a major winter holiday and retirement destination. Its influence has become such that an "attendance gap" has now become the norm for Finnish clubs and organizations during the winter months. The Lake Worth–Lantana area is the major node of attraction in Florida, catering to at least 15,000 Finns in the 1990s. This area became well known following its rise as a Finntown for American Finns during the late 1930s.[127] By the 1950s the area supported two large halls, a Lutheran congregation and a radio program in Finnish. Oscar Tapper is thought to have been the first Finn from the Sudbury area to travel to Florida in 1947-48. His purchase of a property two years later inspired Karl Lehto to do likewise. In 1959 these two pioneers paved the way for individuals like Lempi Johnson and Vic Hoikkala, who acquired winter retreats in Winter Haven and Lake Worth. During the 1960s and 1970s, Lake Worth became popular for working-class Finns who could by then afford to travel during the winter months. For these early "snowbirds," Florida served as a short-term holiday destination based on rental accommodation.

In the 1980s and 1990s Finnish retirees from both the Sudbury area and Finland began to purchase condominiums and trailers and their winter sojourns became longer. Florida also emerged as an alternative holiday destination to the Canary Islands for Finland's winter tourist trade. Other Finns were drawn to business opportunities, especially motel ownership. Some, however, still prefer to rent their accommodation during the winter months. The western coast of Florida, with its numerous golf courses and excellent fishing on the Gulf coast, has likewise evolved as a secondary holiday and retirement centre.

CHAPTER III

The Great Divide

One of the most enduring themes pertaining to Finnish settlement in the Sudbury area and elsewhere in North America centres around its uniquely institutional character. As Krats has affirmed, "the study of Finnish immigrant institutions has become a dominant feature of that group's historiography."[1] It is indisputable that Finns were active joiners, as reflected by the formation of such organizations as fraternal groups, halls, political bodies, co-operatives, churches and sports clubs.[2] Figures 5 and 6 illustrate aspects of the diverse institutional character as it applies to the Sudbury area. Within this "associative spirit" framework, however, the ethnic community came to reflect the presence of a *suuri hajaanus* (great split) between its leftist and conservative factions; thus, the collective umbrella evolved along two parallel streams with little interaction between the two. In some instances, internal divisions occurred within each of the factions. The beginnings of the great divide began late in the nineteenth century, reached its zenith around World War I and the Great Depression, and has subsided only in recent times. Another interesting question that has often been posed regarding the institutional nature of the Finnish-Canadian population pertains to its effect on the "Canadianization" process. Did Finnish institutions function as agents of assimilation or should they be viewed as having ghettoizing tendencies?[3]

Why did the Finnish-Canadian community develop in this fashion? Part of the answer rests with historical timing. In comparison with the United States, where Finnish settlement occurred earlier and involved individuals with church-oriented leanings, immigration to Canada took place later and included more people of a socialist/communist bent. Marginalized, discriminated against and rejected by Canadian society as "dangerous

---

Notes to Chapter III are on pp. 285-92.

foreigners," Finnish leftists reacted by forming an ethnic infrastructure supportive of their language, political and cultural needs. Following the arrival of a more conservative immigrant tide in the 1920s, a rival institutional branch developed that was supportive of rightist causes.

Figure 5
Finnish Institutional Framework in the Sudbury Area (1)

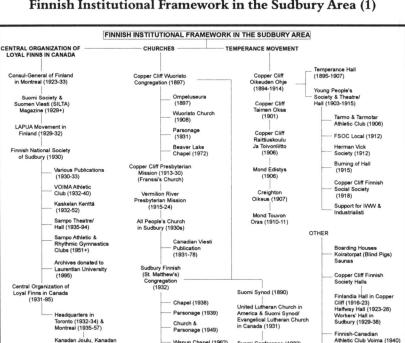

Source: Author.

The organizational framework was also forged out of geographical influences that came from different countries. Exogenous, or carry-over, effects from Finland, Russia/Soviet Union and the United States combined to introduce a climate of divisiveness within the Finnish-Canadian commu-

Figure 6
Finnish Institutional Framework in the Sudbury Area (2)

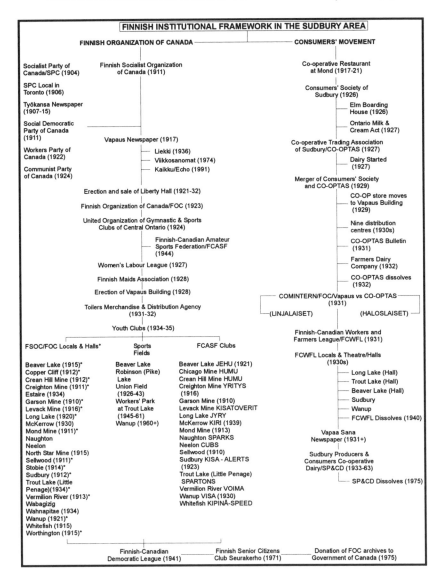

Source: Author.

nity. In this connection, Jalava has proposed a worldview explanation that emphasizes the importance of ideology as an international phenomenon rooted in events that took place in Finland and in Russia prior to the Great Depression.[4] While this geographical perspective is relevant, it must be

broadened to give equal consideration to the United States as another external influence shaping the institutional mix in Canada. Over time, these
spatial influences combined with one another to fashion an ethnic setting
that, in attempting to satisfy the assimilation needs of the immigrants, also
culminated in the formation of an unbreachable gulf within the Finnish
community. Sillanpää goes so far as to suggest that the Sudbury area was
crucial for this development as it served as the "centre for much of the
political activity which caused the Finnish-Canadian population to divide
into two opposing factions."[5] These exogenous perspectives contrast with
the stances taken by Kratz and Laine, who assert that endogenous or local
conditions rather than ideology per se were equally or more important in
fashioning the structural mosaic.[6]

While it is true that many Finns simply wanted to become Canadians,
and did not seek active membership in any Finnish organization, the reality
of everyday life was such that few managed to avoid being caught in the
web of the great divide. Through workplace associations, residential linkages, friendships and acquaintances, readership habits or casual visits to a
hall or a church, most managed to fall one way or another under the taint of
being either a "Red" or a "White."

The Legacy of Finland

The legacy of Finland was profound. Among the many cultural influences
transferred from Finland to the Sudbury area were the following: respect
for the principle of hard work; a strong village culture; a deep-rooted anticlericalism; support for socialist and Marxist ideology; co-operative endeavour; the women's liberation movement; Red and White tendencies after
1918 and the conservative thrusts of the 1920s and 1950s.

The Finnish immigrants who came to North America brought with
them a common trait—the recognition that life was a constant struggle for
survival and that betterment could only come through hard work on the part
of every individual. This legacy was inherited from a homeland where crops
were often obliterated by early frosts, where starvation, disease and war were
common and where economic opportunities, especially in western Finland,
were limited. These immigrants thus brought with them a tradition of work,
and they expected nothing less in Canada. At the same time, however, they
demanded dignified, humane treatment as a reward for this working spirit.[7]
This sense of individual worth was reinforced by the fact that, unlike some
European countries, feudalism had never become established in Finland.

Many immigrants also came from regions which had a form of village
culture that stressed associations, cliques and friendships rather than close
family ties.[8] As Sofia Pontio in Sudbury recalled:

> I have always been an organization person. Even as a small girl I was involved in the activities of the workers' hall. It became a part of my blood. After moving to Helsinki, I continued my association with various workers' associations. It was then only natural that I should be involved here. All people need some form of interest.[9]

Village solidarity often prevailed over family ties. This tradition was significant as it helps to account not only for the institutional character of the Finnish population in Canada but also as a reason why Finns sought to establish themselves in rural enclaves or working-class neighbourhoods. As well, it partially explains why the phenomenon of "chain migration" proved to be so effective in attracting migrants from selected areas in Finland.

Another imported characteristic was the sharp cleavage between the Lutheran Church and the working-class population. Following the rise of Lutheranism as a state church in the seventeenth century, an orthodoxy developed, centring around the preaching of rigid Lutheranism and the mandatory teaching of the catechism in the school system.[10] Prior to 1865, the state church was responsible for education and all members of a congregation had to read the catechism and write in order to be confirmed. Without confirmation, a Finn was ineligible to marry or to obtain an exit permit from the country.[11] This Lutheran orthodoxy and its requirement for literacy had lasting effects, which ultimately were felt throughout North America. Following the separation of Finland from Sweden in 1809 and its incorporation as a Grand Duchy of the Russian Empire, the church served as the dominant force within the country, especially in the western parts of the country known as Ostrobothnia.

As the nineteenth century progressed, Lutheranism came under attack. One outcome was the rise of revivalist movements such as Laestadianism; another was the creation of a rift between the church and activists in the growing labour and socialist movement. This polarization grew out of the narrow interpretation given to Holy Scripture by the Lutheran Church. While declaring the Bible to be the only foundation for a better world, the clergy nonetheless shifted the moral responsibility over social issues and individual betterment to state authorities and to private enterprise.[12] Fearing atheism, the clerical hierarchy repudiated socialism, using the justification that unhappy conditions in this world would eventually be compensated by the promise of a better life in the hereafter.

While this point of view had adherents in rural Finland, it held little credence for the working-class population in the urban centres of southern Finland. Rejecting the church, industrial workers in the 1880s and 1890s sought a secularized and more politicized form of religion linked to trade unionism, socialism and the co-operative movement. The Finnish General Strike of 1905 was significant, as it advanced the socialist position from a "bread-and-butter" labour stance to that of a "class struggle" between the working classes and the capitalist system. For socialists, it was now imperative to see on whose side the Lutheran Church stood. The answer came quickly, for such ideas were branded by clerics as being wild doctrines and atheistic. Another incident that did not endear the church to the working and landless classes was Bishop Gustaf Johansson's assertions in 1891 and later that mass migration from Finland was morally bad and reflected a weakening of the national spirit.[13] The church thus supported the proverb *oma maa mansikka, muu maa mustikka,* which equated the more favoured strawberry with one's own country and the less desirable blueberry with a foreign land. Relationships between the working class and the church were strained further in 1902 when the archbishop of Finland declared that a Christian could not at the same time espouse social democracy. By the turn of the century, therefore, many immigrants who came to North America did so as "godless" Finns who had abandoned their state religion. Adding insult to injury, the state church then proved unwilling to send trained mission workers to North America.

By the end of the nineteenth century, working-class ideas founded on the principles of socialism and Marxism had found a responsive audience among the peasants and new industrial workers. Of great importance was the rise of a large class of landless rural workers consisting of male labourers and women servants. By 1901 some 77 percent of rural households saw little hope of ever acquiring land.[14] Urban centres and the industrial economy proved incapable of absorbing this uprooted labour from the countryside. In response to these conditions, various working-class associations came into being. The first unions were founded in 1883, and by 1894 a working-class press had appeared. The labour movement became receptive to socialist ideology, and in 1899 a Social Democratic Party was created. Within a decade it emerged as the largest political party in the country. The socialist flame spread rapidly, and many social democrats became explicitly Marxist. After the strike in 1905, however, many of these Finns emigrated. Already radicalized, they showed little hesitation in bringing with them an ideological commitment to the fashioning of a new economic and political order in North America.

The social reform movement in Finland gave rise to a related influence—the adoption of the co-operative as an agricultural and industrial form of entrepreneurial endeavour. In rural areas, producers' societies, co-operative banks and parish shops had already appeared by the 1860s and 1870s. These fledgling operations were gradually complemented by dairy companies, trading associations and, in urban areas, consumers' restaurants and housing societies. In 1899 the movement advanced when a central organization known as *Pellervo Seura* (Pellervo Society) was formed; this was followed in 1901 by the passage of the country's first co-operative act. Co-operative ideology gained rapid acceptance, and a large number of banks, wholesale societies and farming associations allied with the working-class movement came into being.[15] Co-operation was therefore a well-known concept for those immigrants who left for overseas after the turn of the century.

The women's liberation movement was another carry-over influence. Finnish women were always in the vanguard of the reform movement. Buoyed by a tradition of self-sufficiency inherited from a rural lifestyle where men were often absent from home, Finnish women did not hesitate to fight for freedom of their own identity and actions, and for full social participation.[16] At the same time they were among the foremost critics of the Lutheran Church. Starting in 1884, several groups that fought for the improvement of civil rights, educational equality and voting privileges were founded. Other areas of concern included the temperance movement, youth organizations, self-education in literature, the arts, theatre and sports activities. One-quarter of the females in Finland quickly laid claim to be members of both a workers' organization and a women's-rights group. Prominent writers such as Minna Canth spoke out boldly for women and prepared sensational dramas for performance on the stage. These actions bore fruit in 1906, when Finnish women became the first in Europe to receive the right to vote and the first in the world to have women elected to parliament.[17] Thus, when Finnish women emigrated from Finland, they did so as "defiant sisters," buoyed by a spirit of optimism and independence. This tradition of emancipation has continued to the present day. In 1991, for instance, women held a third of the parliamentary seats in Finland.

The bitter Civil War of 1918 left another powerful legacy. Using the outbreak of the Russian revolution as a political opportunity, parliament declared Finland to be an independent nation on 6 December 1917. Independence, however, was soon marred by an internal war that broke out between the socialist Finns (Red Guard), who favoured close ties with the newly created Soviet Socialist Republic, and the conservative Finns (White Guard). The victory of the White Guard was followed by the persecution of those who had fought for the leftist side. The resulting enmity scarred those involved forever and many Red Finns opted to leave the country. Having already faced the life-and-death struggle of the Civil War, and remaining firm in their convictions, they showed little hesitation in bringing their ideological fervour to North America.

The final carry-over effect was the conservative movement of the 1920s and the rightist leanings of the immigrants who arrived in the 1950s.

During the 1920s Finland was ruled by former Whites who proved intoler-
ant of any form of left-wing activity. These conservatives harassed social
democrats, declared the Communist Party of Finland to be illegal in 1923
and supported the anti-communist Lapuan Movement after 1929. As many
of the radicals had already left Finland, emigrants who left Finland in the
late 1920s tended to be somewhat more supportive of rightist causes. These
conservative arrivals were appalled by the existing radicalism of Finnish-
Canadian communities. Concerned with this negative image, and worried
about the difficulty in securing employment, the newer Finns served as the
vanguard for the rise of a anti-radical movement in Canada. This conservative thrust was carried on by the immigrants of the 1950s, who also showed
little sympathy for leftist ideology linked to communism or the USSR.

The Influence of Russia/Soviet Union

Russia's first impact among the Finns in Canada was indirect, and it came
about through its policy of "Russification" introduced in Finland around
the turn of the century. After 1809 Finland had managed to retain a high
degree of internal freedom as an autonomous Grand Duchy within the
Russian Empire. When Tzar Nicholas II implemented restrictive legislation
in 1899 to curb freedom in Finland, however, the once loyal Grand Duchy
became rebellious and the Tzar's hated governor-general, Nikolai Bobrikov,
was assassinated in 1904. The timing was fortuitous, as the Russo-Japanese
War that broke out in 1905 allowed Finland to stage a successful general
strike and to establish itself as one of the most democratic countries in the
world. When Russia recovered from the turmoil of war, Russification policies in Finland were renewed. The resulting political climate and the fear of
being conscripted into the Tzar's army radicalized the workingmen's associations in Finland and fostered the rise of a full-fledged Marxist movement. The atmosphere was such, however, that many Marxist Finns went
to North America, where they proved to be eager advocates for reform.
Despite the signing of a peace treaty in 1920 at which time the Soviet
Union formally recognized Finnish independence, relations between the
two countries remained uneasy as Finland began its move to the right. The
ongoing political uncertainty between Finland and the Soviet Union and
the outbreak of war between the two countries during World War II were
factors underlying the high levels of emigration to Canada in the 1920s and
the 1950s.

The second influence in Canada involved the ill-fated Bolshevization
policies introduced in the 1920s. Through these policies, Lenin sought to
extend his country's global influence via the formation of the Third International, known popularly as the Comintern. The Comintern, originally

established in 1919 to assert communist leadership of the world socialist movement, provided guidelines for socialist Finns and the Communist Party of Canada (CPC) to spur the revolution of the Canadian working class.[18] Under Stalin, however, the revolutionary movement was replaced after 1935 by a revamped "Popular Front" strategy that opposed the proletarian revolution, encouraged alliances with social democrats, espoused anti-fascism and promoted the Soviet Union as a countermodel to Germany. These policies, dutifully reflected on the pages of *Vapaus*, eventually wrought major divisions within the Finnish-Canadian communist movement.

The United States Factor

Many of the spread effects from Finland and Russia/Soviet Union were felt first in the United States; aside from early religious developments, much of the institutional development in Canada found its earlier expression in the United States. Given the open border that existed between the two countries before 1924, and the ease with which Finns were still able to cross the boundary in the late 1920s via the "underground,"[19] it is not surprising that historical trends in the United States were often replicated in Canada. Kostiainen has gone so far as to conclude that the "Finnish history in Canada resembles that of the United States since the same striking kind of development is seen in organizational and labour history."[20]

The church was the earliest Finnish institution to develop in the United States. This was natural, given the fact that the first migratory flow consisted largely of conservative farmers. Bolstered by this newly found freedom, diversity and pluralism became the keynotes of Finnish-American church life. Four major religious groups were formed on American soil. The first Finnish Lutheran Church was built by Finnish Laestadians in 1873 in Calumet, Michigan. Internal schisms, a shortage of ministers, bickering over theological issues, the scattering of the Finnish population over wide distances and church practices combined to inhibit the development of a unified church movement. The emergence of the Lutheran Church as a national force began in the 1890s, when two other Lutheran bodies were created: the *Suomi* Synod, or Finnish Evangelical Lutheran Church of America, patterned after the state church in Finland (1890), and the Finnish American National Evangelical Church (1898). The latter, founded as a protest against the *Suomi* Synod's authoritarianism, was a strong supporter of congregational polity and the use of lay clergy.[21] Not to be outdone, in 1928 the Laestadians also formed their own national body, known as the Finnish Apostolic Lutheran Church of America.

While the *Suomi* Synod accepted responsibility for Finns in Canada, its missionary effort north of the border remained weak. While tangible successes were made in New Finland, Saskatchewan (1893), Copper Cliff (1897) and Sault Ste. Marie (1905), the paucity of support from the *Suomi* Synod in the United States and the state church in Finland left a vacuum in Canada that was quickly exploited by socialists and other religious denominations. The fourth church to sprout was the Free Church Finnish Congregationalists, or the Evangelical Mission Society. Started in 1891, this church virtually disappeared by World War II. As early as the 1920s, Finnish churches in the United States began to experience language problems within their congregations. While the immigrant generation wanted the church to function solely in Finnish, many of the second and later generations preferred the use of English. This language schism, however, did not begin to appear in Canada until much later.

The temperance society evolved as another part of the cultural fabric. Due to loneliness, harsh employment conditions and a sense of alienation, and lacking the social constraints of family, relatives and the church that had prevailed in the old country, Finns often turned to bootleggers and alcohol for solace. Thus, it was the *kapakka* (saloon) culture that often represented the first stage of social development in many Finnish communities. This attachment to liquor frequently led to problems related to alcoholism; in turn, the barroom setting provided the stage for many fights among the Finnish *puukkojunkkarit* (toughs carrying sheath knives) that gave these Finns a notorious reputation.

The temperance movement developed in response to this situation. As temperance was considered at the time to be religious in nature, the Lutheran Church was sought for assistance in dealing with drunkenness.[22] The movement dates from 1885, when *Pohjantähti* (North Star) was formed in Hancock, Michigan.[23] Synod Lutherans then created the Finnish National Temperance Brotherhood in 1888, and by 1895 some 105 societies had been founded, of which five were found in Canada.[24] Finns viewed temperance as a fraternal, social, cultural and educational movement as well as a crusade against the evils of drink. The movement gave rise to the *nyrkkilehti*, a handwritten newsletter containing idealistic essays, lofty poems and translations of Finnish literature.[25] The influence of the temperance movement was such that it often rivalled the church until the 1910s; thereafter, the movement declined for a variety of reasons—internal bickering, the introduction of prohibition in 1919, opposition by socialists and the lack of interest shown by native-born Finns. Organized temperance groups in Canada developed mainly as offshoots of these religious-based American societies.

The differing character of immigration after the 1890s wrought major changes. Newcomers now came from urban areas in Finland with a strong commitment to the class struggle and the labour movement. F.J. Syrjälä, Moses Hahl, A.F. Tanner and Martin Hendrickson, former leaders in the labour movement in Finland, played leading roles in promoting the labour movement in North America. Less swayed by religion, they viewed temperance societies as being suspect because of their ties to the Synod—for them, drunkenness was the result of capitalist policies that could only be rectified by socialist measures. It had also become clear by this time that most North American Finns had abandoned their original intention to return to Finland. A different attitude, therefore, began to emerge among the working class regarding their economic fate. Triggered by poor North American working conditions, many felt compelled to join workers' associations. In 1890 the first association, *Imatra*, was formed in Brooklyn, New York. A Finnish local formed in 1899 in Rockport, Massachusetts, then became the first to join the Socialist Party of America (SPA).

After the turn of the century, a movement began to create similar institutions at the national level. In 1903 two central organizations known as the Finnish American Labor League *Imatra* and the Finnish American Labor League were formed. The former sought to develop the labour movement on an ethnic basis whereas the latter leaned more towards international socialism and supported the SPA. The *Imatra* League grew to consist of thirty-two associations in the United States and one that was formed at Thunder Bay in Canada in 1903.[26] Spurred by the arrival of intellectual "gentlemen from Helsinki," such as A.B. Mäkelä, Taavi Tainio and John Viita, in 1906 American Finns established the Finnish Socialist Federation (FSF), which became the first foreign-language federation to join the SPA. It was now clear that the Finns were attracted to socialism in much greater numbers than was the case for other ethnic groups from eastern and southern Europe. The FSF flourished and locals were formed in nearly every Finnish community. Its success spurred the Canadian socialist leader J.W. Ahlqvist (biography6) to use it as a model for the creation of a similar organization in Canada.[27]

The exceptional literacy of the Finnish immigrant made it possible for the socialist movement to use newspapers as a propaganda and promotional tool for attracting men and women into a national American network. Finnish newspapers were effectively used as a vehicle of communication as early as 1876. By the turn of the century, more than sixty Finnish newspapers existed in the United States. Among the socialist newspapers were *Työmies* (Worker) founded in 1903, *Raivaaja* (Pioneer) created in 1905 and *Toveri* (Comrade) formed in 1907. Each newspaper had side publications as well, such as *Toveritar* (Woman Comrade), a women's newspaper started in 1911.[28] All had a large readership in Canada. One out of four *Toveritar*

Biography 6

John Verner Ahlqvist: Grand Old Man
of the Finnish Communist Movement

John Ahlqvist was born in Tornio, Finland, in 1881. By trade he was a tailor. As a young man he became interested both in the temperance and workers' movements in Finland. He then married and migrated to Canada with his wife in 1903. After his arrival in Canada, he developed an interest in the Canadian socialist movement. He was a member of both the Finnish Socialist Organization of Canada and the Finnish Organization of Canada from their inception in 1911. When a permanent office of the FSOC was established in Toronto in 1914, Ahlqvist served as its first director. He travelled widely in support of the socialist movement and played a key role in the founding of the *Vapaus* newspaper and in the growth of the FOC. In 1918-21 he was a member of the Independent Labour Party of Ontario. Because of his association with the FSOC and *Vapaus*, he was arrested in Sudbury in 1919 for being in possession of prohibited literature. After this clash with authority, Ahlqvist moved to Toronto and became responsible for collecting money in Canada for the Refugees from Finland Fund. The donations were then transmitted to the Soviet representative in the United States. In 1918 he wrote a letter (reproduced in part at the end of this chapter) to the federal government that stands as one of the earliest and best defences in Canada of the merits of multiculturalism.

Once made, Ahlqvist's contact with the international communist movement was never broken. He attended the famous clandestine meeting in a Guelph barn that marked the founding of the Communist Party as an underground group in May 1921. He later served as the chief Finnish representative at the conference, which culminated in the formation of the Workers' Party of Canada (WPC) in February 1922. Throughout the 1920s, Ahlqvist served as the linchpin between the Finnish Organization of Canada and the Communist Party of Canada, and much of the success achieved by the communists among the Finnish population stemmed from his efforts. Ahlqvist's easygoing personality enabled him to retain the confidence of the Finnish membership without diminishing his strong belief in the revolutionary movement. He was suspended temporarily from the Communist Party in November 1929 on the grounds that he had resorted to splitting tactics within the Finnish membership. His exclusion was of short duration; he returned to the party in 1930 and thereafter remained an active loyal member. After his health began to fail, he moved from Toronto to his rural retreat at Little Lake Panache in Louise Township, where he remained until his death in June 1940. He left behind his wife, Ida, and four children—Signe, Sally, Mary and John.

readers in the 1920s, for example, was a Canadian and the newspaper covered newsworthy items for 122 communities in Canada.[29] The number of Finnish newspapers and periodicals grew over time and by the 1930s their number had risen to over three hundred. This large number can be attributed to the high degree of factionalism associated with the Finnish community and the related belief that each faction held the key to truth.

Prior to World War I, the Finnish-American labour movement acquired a reddish tinge as Finns assumed leadership in the 1907 Mesabi iron strike in Minnesota and Michigan and the 1913-14 strike in the Copper Country of Michigan. One effect of these failed strikes was the appearance of blacklisting and the formation of an espionage network by the mining companies, which forced Finns to take up farming or to seek jobs elsewhere.[30] Many migrated to Thunder Bay and Sudbury in Ontario where they became transplanted supporters of radicalism. It was at this juncture that the ideological struggle within the American Finnish community became narrowed to a battle between revolutionary Marxism and traditional Lutheranism. The unsuccessful strikes had the additional effect in 1914 of weaning Finns from the Finnish Socialist Federation towards the IWW union. Those who espoused the radical unionism of the IWW left the socialist ranks to form their own newspaper *Sosialisti* (Socialist). Later known in 1917 as the *Industrialisti* (Industrialist), this newspaper had a large readership in Canada and many of its articles were drawn from the Sudbury area. This paper continued to publish until 1975.[31]

Another schism appeared among the leftists following the Russian Revolution and the rise of the Worker's Party of America (WPA) as a legal communist party in 1921. By 1922 Finnish-American workers found themselves divided into three factions: the IWWs, the socialists and the communists.[32] In the 1920s the IWW Finns opposed communism, maintained their own halls and ran a Work People's College in Duluth. Finnish communists proved to be the most active. They emerged as the largest ethnic group within the Worker's Party, with 41 percent of the membership in 1924; as well, they established "Committees of Examination of Recent Arrivals from Finland" in sixty-eight localities after 1921 to determine an immigrant's relationship to the Finnish Civil War.[33] Similar committees were also formed in Canada. Finnish-American communists soon found themselves at odds with the parent body. When the WPA attempted in 1923 to Bolshevize the American communist movement by eliminating ethnic groupings, Finns balked as they preferred the former structure. There was likewise the concern that the Comintern would try to assume control of their halls and co-operative enterprises. Resistance to change was so strong that the Comintern sent Yrjö Sirola from Moscow to settle the differences between the Finnish-American communists and the WPA. Through Sirola's efforts, the Finns yielded and the FSF was replaced by another Finnish organization called the Finnish Workers' Federation of the United States (FWF). These steps did little to resolve the situation, and in 1928-30 a large number of Finns were expelled from the FWF and the WPA. Opposition again became so widespread that Kullervo Manner and Aino Kuusinen (wife of Otto Kuusinen) were imported from Moscow as advisors, with the former operating mainly on the Canadian side and the latter in the United States. While these measures had some impact, they were offset by the rupture that occurred within the co-operative movement.

As in Finland, socialists in the United States endorsed the co-operative movement as an economic instrument of reform. Alanen has made the observation that "one of the most legible stamps of Finnish-American influence has been in the development of consumers' cooperatives."[34] First started in 1878, co-operatives soon became widespread in Michigan, Minnesota and Wisconsin. Their endorsement by the FSF in 1906, and the spawning of new co-operatives after the 1907 Mesabi strike, gave added impetus to the movement. In 1917 the Central Co-operative Exchange in Superior, Wisconsin (renamed in 1931 as the Central Co-operative Wholesale) was formed. New areas of co-operative activity were then established in wholesaling, retailing, the restaurant trade, credit supply and apartment construction. Unlike other forms of endeavour, support for the co-operative movement was widespread throughout the entire Finnish community.

Socialists and communists worked together throughout the 1920s in the same organizations. Around the turn of the 1930s, however, the movement became a battlefield between those who viewed co-operatives as economic agencies of reform and leftists who viewed them as political instruments of the WPA. The latter lost the battle and went on to create their own co-operative body known as The Workers' and Farmers' Cooperative Unity Alliance of Superior, which supported leftist causes such as re-emigration to Soviet Karelia, demonstrations and marches during the Great Depression and aiding the Republican side in the Spanish Civil War. While the Unity Alliance lasted only until 1939, the Co-operative Wholesale went on to enjoy considerable economic success up to World War II. These events, which marked an important watershed in Finnish-American history, were later echoed in Canada.

The final American experience of relevance for Canada was the rise of the conservative countermovement. This movement was initiated after the first signs of labour unrest appeared in 1906-1907 in Michigan and Minnesota. Churchmen took the lead in organizing against the socialists and in purging their ethnic reputation as being reactionaries. While these measures had little initial success, the long-term effect was more significant, as it heralded the start of a process that came to divide Finnish-American communities permanently and irreconcilably.[35] When Finnish socialists were again held responsible for the outbreak of strikes in Michigan and Minnesota between 1913 and 1917, conservatives in Hancock (home of *Suomi* College, the Finnish Lutheran Press and *Amerikan Suometar*) and Calumet (which had a large Finnish business and professional focus) supported a group called the Citizens' Alliance and founded the American Finnish Anti-Socialist League. Following the outbreak of World War I, many Finns refused to be conscripted into the American military forces. This opposition to compulsory service by leftists had its origins in the efforts of the Tzar to enlist Finns into the Russian army. Another loyalty movement subsequently emerged in Duluth, Minnesota, and support for the war effort was seen by conservative Finns and other Americans as the litmus test for loyalty. Rather than face this test, hundreds (thousands, according to J. Wiita) of Finns moved to Canada.[36] The loyalty movement receded into oblivion by the end of World War I as second-generation Finns eschewed their ethnic identity and became "Americanized."[37] The loyalty movement in the United States foreshadowed a similar crusade by conservative Finns in Canada in the 1920s and 1930s.

While many of the events that took place in the United States were indeed replicated in Canada, Kostiainen's conclusion that the Canadian setting serves as a simple mirror of the United States experience must be viewed with caution. While such an assessment has validity up to the early 1920s when the border was virtually meaningless, major differences became evident as early as the 1930s. Even then, it was clear that contrasts existed between the two countries. Differences in the early timing of migration, for instance, led to an institutional mix that favoured the church and conservatives in the United States. When leftist reformers arrived on the North American scene after the turn of the century, acceptance of their ideologies proved to be stronger in Canada due to Canadians' greater tolerance for social reform movements. The lack of a comparable melting pot, or Americanization philosophy, and the introduction of multicultural policies in Canada also gave encouragement to Finns north of the border to maintain their ethnic character. Finally, the shift in immigration that favoured Canada over the United States in the late 1920s, 1950s and 1960s was significant. After World War II, emigration to Canada was double the level noted for the United States. As a consequence, the relative proportion of Finns in Canada who were born in Finland was more than three times higher than that in the United States. This difference has provided the foundation for the maintenance of a more vigorous Finnish culture in Canada that has lasted to the present day.

Domestic Factors

While the institutional character of Finnish settlement in Canada was profoundly influenced by the geographical influences described above, local factors related to the deplorable state of the mining and forest industry in Ontario, the weakness of the Lutheran Church and the lack of government support for both workers' rights and the union movement served as domestic pushes that spawned radicalism and divisiveness. An important supporting element at the outset was the creation of a powerful press that promoted ideologies associated with both the radical and conservative factions (table 12). While the impact of the press was felt in all Finnish communities, including Toronto and Montreal, it was especially strong for those Finns who lived and worked in the industrial centres of Thunder Bay and Sudbury, and in the dozens of mining and lumbering communities scattered throughout the north. In the Sudbury area, the foundation for the development of these tendencies was first laid in Copper Cliff.

Table 12
Finnish Newspapers and Magazines in Canada (since 1897)

Newspapers

Aika (Sointula 1901-1904)	*Uutiset* (Toronto 1931-37)
Canadan Uutiset (Port Arthur/ Thunder Bay 1915+)	*Työkansa* (Port Arthur 1907-15)
Isien Usko (Winnipeg/Sault Ste. Marie 1935-38+)	*Uusi Länsi* (Vancouver 1966-71)
	Vapaa Sana (Sudbury/Toronto 1931+)
Länsirannikon Uutiset	*Vapaus* (Sudbury 1917-74)
Toronton Viikko-Uutiset/Viikko	*Viikkosanomat* (Toronto 1974-91)

Magazines

Aikamme (1977-?)	(Sudbury 1937-74?)
Airue (Port Arthur 1910-13)	*Canadan Viesti* (Winnipeg/Vancouver 1931-78)
Ajan Kaiku (Port Arthur 1939)	
Ajan Sana (1949-58)	*Club Finlandia Newsletter* (Calgary)
Almanakka (1930)	*Evankelis Luterilaisten Sanomat* (Kirkland Lake 1936)
Ampiainen (Winnipeg 1932-36)	
Canada Skandinaven	*Evankelis Luterilaisten Sanomat* (Sault Ste. Marie 1937)
Canadan Suomalainen (Sudbury 1964)	*Finnish Kommunisti* (1918-25)
Canadan Suomalaisten Kansallis-ja-Edistys Seurojen Joulujulkaisu (1931)	*Isänmaan Ääni* (Kirkland Lake 1939)
Canadan Suomalaisten Urheilukirja (Toronto 1938)	*Joulu* (Sudbury 1940-73?)
	Kaiku/Echo (Toronto 1991+)
	Kalevan Kansan Sointuja (1903)
Canadan Suomalaisten Taskukalenteri	*Kanadan Joulu* (Montreal 1935-38)

Kanadan Suomalainen (Montreal 1936)

Kanadan Suomalainen (Toronto)

Kevään Airut (Copper Cliff 1953)

Kevät (Port Arthur 1935-39?)

Kevät (Sudbury 1935-36)

Kevät Valo (Port Arthur 1911)

Kirkon Palvelija (Copper Cliff 1934-?)

Leuan Joulu (Thunder Bay 1914)

Liekki (Sudbury 1935-74)

Lähetysystävä (1909-11?)

Länsi-Kanadan Sosialisti (Vancouver 1913)

Länsirannikon Uutiset (Surrey 1975-?)

Maa-ja Metsätyöläinen (Sudbury 1930-32)

Meikäläinen (Toronto 1997+)

Message of Brotherhood (Vancouver)

Messenger (Vancouver)

Metsätyöläinen (Sudbury 1926-29, 1933-35)

Montrealin Suomalainen (Montreal 1993)

Murtava Voima (Port Arthur 1908)

New Voice (Sudbury 1959)

Nuori Kanada (Toronto 1925-30)

Nuorten Sana (Sudbury 1952)

Pankkiviesti (Toronto 1970+)

Punainen Työläinen (Sudbury 1929)

Pääsiäislehti (Port Arthur 1921)

Seurakuntaviesti (Sudbury)

Siirtolainen (Port Arthur 1934)

Soihtu (Sudbury 1935-36)

Spartak (Toronto 1933)

Suomalainen Evangelis-Luterilainen Seurakunta (Kirkland Lake)

The Sudbury Worker (Sudbury 1929)

Taistelun Viiri (Sudbury 1933-36)

Tiedonantaja (Toronto 1940)

Toivo (Toronto 1902-1904)

Torvi (Montreal 1933)

Totuuden Todistaja (Vancouver 1925+)

Totuus (Toronto 1897-1904)

Tyttöjen ja Ukkojen Kevät (Sudbury 1935-36)

Työkansan Nuoli (Port Arthur 1909-10)

Työlaisurheilijain Joulu (Toronto 1930-31)

Työn Vappu (Sudbury 1934-37)

Työtön Työläinen (Toronto 1931-34?)

Työtön Työläinen (Vancouver 1929-31?)

Työttömien Äänenkannattaja (Ottawa 1931?)

Uusi Totuus (Toronto 1906-1909)

Vancouver Finlandia Club

Tiedottaa (Vancouver 1975)

Vapauden Soihtu (Sudbury 1919-22)

Vapauden Viiri (Sudbury 1937-39)

Vappu (Sudbury 1964-68?)

Veljespiirimme Sana (Copper Cliff)

Vesan Kronikka (Copper Cliff 1948)

Väkäleuan Kalenteri (Port Arthur 1907-15?)

Väkäleuka (Port Arthur 1908-15)

Yritys-Spark (Toronto 1951-52)

Source: *Vapaa Sana*, 31 October 1996, 15; Arja Pilli, *The Finnish-Language Press in Canada, 1901-1939* (Turku: Institute of Migration, 1982).

Early Factionalism in Copper Cliff

The first Finnish settlers to the Sudbury area came from Ostrobothnia in the 1880s, and they were largely sympathetic to religion. Everyone supported attempts by temperance societies and the church to combat the evils that plagued the Canadian resource frontier. Following the trend set in the

United States, the first temperance society founded in Canada was *Lännen Rusko Raittiusseura* (Western Glow Temperance Society) at North Wellington, British Columbia, in 1890. It was established to counter the "bad Russian Finn" image that the ethnic group held in the English-speaking community.[38] Branch 80 of the American-based Finnish National Temperance Brotherhood, called *Oikeuden Ohje Raittiusseura* (Golden Rule Temperance Society) followed in 1894 at Copper Cliff. This was not only the first Finnish community organization in the Sudbury area, but very nearly in all of Canada—only two congregations and Sault Ste. Marie's Temperence Society were older. The Society promptly built a hall on Balsam Street in 1895.[39] Its need had been firmly established by the state of contemporary conditions: "[L]ife there [in Copper Cliff] was rough and primitive. Drinking was common, often culminating in fights and even in murders. . . . One can understand from this that the social and intellectual life in the Finnish community was in a state of flux."[40] Open to men and women, the Society fought for abstinence from alcohol and advocated the self-betterment of its members by setting up a library, a subscription service for newspapers and magazines from Finland, the levying of fines for swearing and card playing, and the formation of a benevolent circle to provide death insurance. The latter was important for those men who died or who were injured while in the workplace, as these victims and their families received little or no compensation from the Canadian Copper Company's Accident Fund or from the provincial justice system. By 1897 the Society had 143 members. The literacy of the immigrant Finns permitted the temperance movement to rely heavily on the written word. Thus libraries, newspapers and magazines evolved as important means of communication among its members.

The group at the beginning was closely allied with the *Wuoristo* Finnish Evangelical Lutheran Church of Copper Cliff. Religious activity in the townsite started in 1889, when a worship service was held at the home of Alex Ranta. This may have been the first Finnish worship service in all of Canada.[41] A congregation under the umbrella of the Finnish Evangelical Lutheran Church of America was then organized in 1897 under the leadership of Dr. J. Hoikka, a pastor from the *Suomi* Synod in the United States. From its inception until 1932, the *Wuoristo* Church served as a lonely beacon of the Lutheran faith surrounded by largely unsympathetic Finns. The *Wuoristo* congregation held its first services in the Temperance Society Hall. As a resident minister was not available until 1915, the influence of the congregation remained less than the temperance society. In these formative years, the church congregation was served by interim pastors such as John Wargelin, Jacob Mänttä and Matti Luttinen.[42] By the turn of the century, the church had a membership of almost one hundred.

The pattern of institutional divisiveness, as already manifested in the United States, was repeated in Copper Cliff. The newer urban immigrants were younger and unmarried, and they harboured scepticism towards the church and the temperance movement, with their resistance towards card playing and dancing; for them, socialism and workers' rights held the most promise for redressing the ills in the local environment, especially as they related to existing conditions in the mining industry. Socialist agitators had two strategic objectives. The first was to provoke the religious community by interfering with church services, and the second was to gain control of the temperance hall. Quick to perceive the fundamental role that the hall played for Finns in the domestic setting, socialists understood that their takeover would provide them with a powerful base in the community. The success of these tactics was acknowledged by Rev. Wargelin during his stay in Northern Ontario:

> Socialism was quite prevalent in most of the Finnish communities during the first decade of the twentieth century. It was brought over from Finland by the refugees that left the country during the Bobrikoff days of oppression. Many of them were fanatical in their belief and wanted to give expression to it. They disturbed public meetings or became members of temperance societies in order to take over the property of these organizations. In many cases they were successful.[43]

By 1902 a socialist faction headed by John Wirta had developed a strong power base within the Temperance Society, and it sought to change the direction of the Society. A split developed, resulting in the formation by the more free-thinking members in 1903 of an alternative group called *Copper Cliffin Nuorisoseura* (Young People's Society of Copper Cliff). The society became so influential that even the famous socialist Matti Kurikka was drawn to Copper Cliff to drum up support for his utopian community of Sointula in British Columbia; because of his political leanings, however, he was denied access to the temperance hall. The Young People's Society countered this opposition by constructing a prestigious building known as Finland Hall, which quickly gained local acclaim:

> To the Copper Cliff Young Men's Society (an organization of Finlanders) we are indebted for one of the finest opera halls in New Ontario. . . . The dimensions of the hall is 50 by 74 and 18 feet high with a capacity of seating 400 people; a good sized stage is erected, leading off from which are commodious green rooms. At the rear of the hall a large gallery extends from both sides of the building under which are smoking and store rooms. A polished hardwood floor forecasts many terpischorean scenes. We cannot help but congratulate our Finnish friends on their commendable enterprise in erecting such a handsome building among such sordid surroundings. We have no better foreign element today.[44]

The hall on Temperance Street became an international destination for socialist speakers and suffragettes. Serving as a theatre, libary, gymnasium, school and dance hall, the facility proved effective in attracting local Finns to socialist ideas. In 1906 the society formed *Tarmo* (Energy) and *Tarmotar* (Female Energy), the first of many Finnish athletic clubs to be established in the Sudbury area.

Anticlericalism evolved as an integral part of the Society's philosophy. Both the church and Temperance Society were seen as allies of the Canadian Copper Company, which owned most of the land in the community. The situation with respect to the CCC in 1910 has been described as follows:

> The Canadian Copper Company owns the land in the whole town of Copper Cliff and, consequently, the company is able to control arbitrarily all residents in Copper Cliff. . . . Finnish socialist speakers in the town have been prevented from speaking on many occasions. There exist the following societies: Young People's Society, the Temperance Society belonging to the Brotherhood and the Congregation affiliated with the Synod. The two last mentioned [societies] have lately, particularly in the fall of 1909, created much bad blood among the local Finns: as some of the most "dense" have acted as spies and snoops for the Canadian Copper Company among its Finnish employees.[45]

Alarmed by the strength of this grouping, the *Wuoristo* congregation and the Temperance Society banded together to build a new church on Collins Drive in 1908. The Temperance Society raffled off its building in 1907 and shifted its meetings to the church. However, apathy and inactivity came to plague the Temperance Society, and by 1914 its activities ceased, thus marking the formal passage of the temperance movement in the Sudbury area and the shifting of its work to the church. Despite the demise of the Society, however, vestiges of the temperance movement still remained in the Sudbury area, as evidenced by the prohibition of alcohol sales at *Sampo* Hall until the late 1950s.

The turmoil within the Finnish community did not go unnoticed by the Canadian Copper Company. For several years the company had kept a close eye on the socialist activities of the Young People's Society. When the Society voted to join the Social Democratic Party of Canada (SDPC) as the Finnish Socialist Organization of Canada Copper Cliff Local 31 in 1912, the CCC took steps to deal with the new situation. Thus began the three-year cause célèbre associated with the Finland Hall. Herman Vick, a former chairman of the Society, and from 1906 until 1913 a constable for the town of Copper Cliff, formed his own Herman Vick Society and managed, through a judgment of the court rendered in the *Vick vs. Toivonen et al.* case in 1913, to prevent the assets of the Society from being transferred to the SDPC.[46] In another election held in 1914 and affirmed by the court in

1915, the socialist faction managed to regain control of the organization.[47] Following an Ontario Supreme Court decision in the case *Wirta vs. Vick*, which affirmed the original 1912 victory by the socialists, the hall was destroyed by fire under suspicious circumstances in March 1915.[48]

After the fire, the CCC refused to transfer the land lease to the Young People's Society. The property then became the site of the Copper Cliff Dairy. A new Finland Hall was built by the socialists in 1916 on privately owned land on Main Street in the East Smelter neighbourhood outside of the town limits. After left-wing organizations were declared unlawful by the federal government in 1918, the Young People's Society prudently changed its name to the Copper Cliff Finnish Social Society.[49] The goals of the new local were also changed:

> to educate, improve and develop the Finnish population in the munici-
> pality of the town of Copper Cliff, and the surrounding district, by the
> maintenance of a library, and reading room, the engagement of the
> teacher of the English language and the holding of lectures, concerts,
> vocal and instrumental, theatrical performances, and gymnastic exercises,
> and to acquire and own buildings and other property necessary for the
> accomplishment of the above objects.[50]

Mirroring developments in the United States, a rift emerged between the new Copper Cliff group and its FSOC counterpart in Sudbury. The *jouppilaiset*, who had gained control of the Copper Cliff society, leaned more towards the doctrines of the One Big Union (OBU) and the IWW, which advocated direct working-class action through strikes and control of factories. This contrasted with the stance of the Sudbury local, which favoured political rather than workplace action against capitalism.[51] When the Social Society's hall was purchased by Inco for slag-dumping purposes in 1923, the organization erected another hall between Copper Cliff and Sudbury. Known as the Halfway Hall, it was destroyed by fire in 1928. Another hall was then erected on Alder Street in Sudbury.[52] Often referred to as the IWW or Workers' Hall, it remained in existence until 1938, when it was sold to the Slovak National Society.

The rivalry between the socialists, the temperance movement and youth groups was repeated in other mining camps. Beginning in 1908, youth groups, temperance societies and socialist locals were founded in the mining communities of Garson, Crean Hill, Creighton Mine and Victoria Mine. The local in Garson was formed following a visit from the well-known socialist speaker Sanna Kannasto. By 1910 all of these groups had become focal points for internal dissension because of the socialist leanings of their members.[53]

The divisions within the Finnish religious community were compounded by the successful inroads made by the Presbyterian Church. When it was formed, the *Wuoristo* congregation was the third in Canada and first in

Ontario to become part of the U.S.-based *Suomi* Synod. The *Suomi* Synod recognized the authority of Finland's state church, The Finnish Evangelical Lutheran Church. Already faced with a great shortage of ministers in the United States, the Synod's home mission effort in Canada remained ineffective. Ministers who served in Northern Ontario were called upon to care for multiple parishes covering wide distances.[54] The spiritual leadership within the community was sporadic at best. The void did not go unnoticed by the Presbyterian Church of Canada, which decided to bring a Finnish-speaking minister, Rev. Arvi Heinonen, to the Sudbury area to recruit converts. Heinonen proved to be a controversial figure. Due to his ability to draw converts, he quickly became the object of criticism, not only from the FOC and *Vapaus*, but from other Finns as well. Even the normally taciturn Rev. Pikkusaari was moved to call him "an adventurer and impostor of an extraordinary calibre . . . [and an] excellent flatterer and a totally unprincipled fellow."[55] The attraction of the Presbyterian Church for Finns was noteworthy. It can be surmised that this church provided religious Finns with a freer form of North American worship that, while still Finnish, lacked many of the dogmatic elements of the Lutheran faith.

Shift of Radicalism to Sudbury

In the 1920s the geographical focus of radicalism in the Sudbury area changed, and Sudbury became the centre for collective activity. It was in this decade that the left-wing movement rapidly gained strength in the Sudbury area.[56] This ascendency was aided by events in Russia, the spread of socialist/communist ideology in Canada and in the United States, the formation of the *Vapaus* newspaper and the weakness of the church. Activities linked to the FOC and *Vapaus* dominated much of the local Finnish scene. Between 1929 and World War II, however, this domination was gradually undermined by the Karelian exodus and internal crises; these events, in turn, allowed conservative forces such as the church and the national society to emerge as loyalist forms of Finnish organizations. By World War II the tide had clearly turned. The immigration of the 1950s marked the final collapse of both the FOC and the *Vapaus* as political forces and left both of these organizations as social and recreational rumps.

Socialism and the Labour Movement

The socialist movement in Sudbury followed the trends established elsewhere in the United States. By the turn of the century radical tendencies had appeared in Copper Cliff and in other Finnish-Canadian communities, such as Sointula, Thunder Bay and Toronto. Ross asserts that developments in these areas followed the American experience closely:

[I]t should be understood that the Finnish communities of the United States and Canada were closely linked, for the Finnish immigrants the boundary was not significant; socialist leaders moved back and forth across the border...; Wiita, who spent the war period in Canada, says that Finnish American radicals were so numerous in the Thunder Bay area that they took over and operated the bankrupt Finn Labor Hall.[57]

In 1904 the Socialist Party of Canada (SPC) was formed. It held the Marxist view that attempts to reform the capitalist system were useless and that change could only be brought about through revolution and militant political action. The leftist-leaning Finnish Society of Toronto, which had been formed in 1902, became the first language branch of the SPC in 1906. As many Finns were not citizens and did not have the right to vote, a rift developed between the Anglo-Saxon leadership and the Finns regarding the effectiveness of the SPC strategy; consequently, the latter proceeded to form the Social Democratic Party of Canada in 1911. The socialist Finnish newspaper *Työkansa* (Working People), created in Thunder Bay in 1907, was adopted as its official organ. The SDPC was thus founded out of frustration with the more doctrinaire and revolutionary SPC. The SDPC held the view that the class struggle was not inevitable and that a peaceful and non-revolutionary road to socialism was possible through the trade union movement. Even at this early stage, therefore, a major split had developed between the revolutionary (radical reds, or "impossibilists") and evolutionary wings (social democratic yellows, or "opportunists") of the left-wing movement in Canada.

With the active support of members from the Sudbury area, Finns formed their own Finnish Socialist Organization of Canada in 1911 as a national language section federated with the parent body of the SDPC. Founding locals affiliated with the FSOC in the Sudbury area included Sellwood, Garson mine, Copper Cliff, Creighton mine and Mond mine. Others joined in the next three years: Crean Hill, Sudbury, Vermilion River, North Star mine, Whitefish, Worthington, Beaver Lake, Levack and Stobie. One early stalwart of this growing radicalism among the Finns in the Sudbury area was John Ahlqvist. Like its American counterpart (FSF) formed in 1906, the FSOC was never a Finnish tail attached to a Canadian dog. Finns, along with Ukrainians, had a profound influence over the SDPC.

The outbreak of war brought Finnish radical organizations such as the FSOC under increased government surveillance. One outcome was the banning under the War Measures Act of 1914 of American socialist newspapers such as *Työmies*, *Raivaaja* and *Toveri*. Wartime restrictions and internal financial difficulties also led in 1915 to the failure of the *Työkansa* newspaper in Thunder Bay. The literary void had two major repercussions for the Finnish press in Canada. First, it led to the establishment of *Canadan Uutiset*

(Canada News) in Thunder Bay in 1915 as Canada's first non-socialist Finnish newspaper. The second was the launching of *Vapaus* some two and a half years later as the new official organ of the FSOC.

The surveillance of the radical movement was assisted by the Finnish clergy who served as *kätyrit* (informants) for companies and the federal government.[58] Rev. Edwin Kyllönen from Sudbury and Kirkland Lake, for example, prepared reports for the Royal Canadian Mounted Police (RCMP: known as the Royal North-West Mounted Police between 1904 and 1919) and for the American Consulate at North Bay in Ontario. Kyllönen proved to be a treasure house of information concerning the Red Finns in Northern Ontario:

> I . . . found that information of some value could be obtained from Reverend Edwin A. Kyllonen, a so-called White Finn who is Pastor of the Finnish United Church at Kirkland Lake, Ontario, and had asked him through a mutual friend to obtain all the information he could concerning the organization, purposes and activities of the Communist Party in Canada.[59]

These surveillance activities, known to radical Finns, served to strengthen the anticlerical attitudes inherited from Finland.

Anticlericalism was vigorously supported by socialist women. This was reflected most strongly through their ideological aversion to having marriages sanctioned by the church. It is not surprising, therefore, that common-law relationships were frequent in leftist areas. Finnish socialists would simply hold a party at home or in the local hall and formalize the union by an announcement in the newspaper. These free unions were popular during the 1920s. In *Vapaus*, for example, fifty-one bold announcements appeared declaring such unions between 1921 and 1925; another 112 were published less visibly under the local news section from 1921 to 1930. As Sofia Pontio from Sudbury explained: "I was never legally married. I felt that I would have been deceiving myself if I got married in the church when I didn't believe in it. . . . Anyway, free marriages then were so very common in Sudbury."[60] Similar ads were used to advertise the break-up of these arrangements. Common-law relationships were sometimes used by mining companies to fire workers on the moral grounds that they were "living in sin." This information was regularly given to them by Finnish pastors who abhorred the practice of free marriage. In 1929 information regarding this practice was passed on to *The Sudbury Star* by Rev. T.D. Jones from the All People's Mission and Rev. E. Kyllönen. The newspaper's headline boldly proclaimed that "Finns Marry and Part by 'Ad' in Paper."[61] Unfortunately for the newspaper, one of the declarations had previously been sanctioned by the church. Despite a quick apology on the following day, the couple was later awarded damages in a libel action.[62]

The practice of free marriage had unfortunate legal consequences for Finnish miners as it made a tremendous difference to women if their common-law spouses died. The issue was brought to the front pages of the press after the 1928 Hollinger mine disaster in Timmins, when the widows and orphans of eight Finnish victims were refused assistance by the Workmen's Compensation Board because they were not legally married.[63] The above disaster notwithstanding, such marriages continued well into the 1950s, at which time the Lutheran clergy in Sudbury still considered the matter to be "scandalous."

Vapaus, *the FOC and Communism*

The first issue of *Vapaus* came off the press in Sudbury on 6 November 1917. Owned and supervised by the FSOC, the distribution of the newspaper was entrusted to a large network of workers affiliated with various locals. The timing was auspicious, coinciding with the Russian Revolution of 1917, which acted as a powerful catalyst for the spread of communist ideology. The paper supported the aims of the SDPC, labour groups such as the OBU and working-class issues, and reported fully on the Russian Revolution. Under the editorial leadership of Yrjö Mäkelä, Heikki Juntunen, Henry Puro (John Wiita), A.B. Mäkelä (Kaapro Jääskeläinen) of Sointula fame, Onni Saari, Arvo Vaara, Sulo G. Neil, Bruno Tenhunen, J. Kokkonen and A. Hill, the newspaper paved the way for the emergence of Sudbury as the dominant centre of Finnish left-wing activity in Canada between World Wars I and II.[64] The paper alienated itself at the outset both from the Finnish religious community and the local Anglo-Canadian establishment.

With the outbreak of war in 1914, the Finnish Socialist Organization of Canada came under increasing government scrutiny; this later included its newspaper, *Vapaus*. Amid growing fears of trade union militancy and Bolshevik subversion, the federal government passed the War Measures Act of 1914 to stem the rise of the radical movement in Canada. The act gave the federal government sweeping emergency powers to pass decrees without accountability to parliament or to existing laws. After the 1917 Russian Revolution and a wave of industrial strikes in Canada, the government passed Order-in-Council PC 2381 on 25 September 1918, which suspended *Vapaus* and other foreign-language newspapers as "enemy-language" publications. The operations of *Vapaus* were affected as well by the passage of Order-in-Council PC 2384, which forced the FSOC, as a consequence of its links with the now-unlawful SDPC, to cease its operations. On 20 October 1918, after Finland requested German aid during its Civil War, the premises of *Vapaus* were raided by the Canadian Secret Service; literature was taken and several arrests were made.[65] It was clear that the Canadian government preferred to interpret the development of radicalism in the country as being influenced by "dangerous aliens" rather than as a genuine response of workers to Canadian conditions.[66] The effect of labelling ethnic organizations as radical, however, only served to drive these groups further to the left.

The regulations regarding the FSOC and *Vapaus* were repealed in April of 1919; the newspaper reappeared on the streets on 23 April under the editorship of Henry Puro, an active socialist and journalist who had fled to Canada from the United States to avoid military conscription. To conform with the repeal guidelines of the Canadian government, the FSOC officially agreed to break its ties with the SDPC, to conduct its business in English and to function as a cultural rather than political institution. *Vapaus*, nevertheless, continued to draw the attention of the Royal North-West Mounted Police for its publication of Marxist slogans and the spreading of Bolshevist propaganda.[67] Meanwhile, the FSOC was permitted to resume its operations in December 1918.

A major step was taken in 1919 when the Liberty Hall Company was created. Its first mission was to acquire a new site for *Vapaus* and the Sudbury FSOC local. The company subsequently purchased a property on Lorne Street, east of the present-day court complex, on which a building was erected in 1920 and enlarged three years later. The selection of this site on the fringe of downtown Sudbury provided the most visible expression of the shift of Finnish communal life from Copper Cliff to Sudbury. It likewise paved the way for the downtown orientation of other leftist organizations and homes for individuals linked to the FSOC. Undeterred by its early promises to the federal government, the FSOC and *Vapaus* continued to drift leftward. The newspaper entered a new stage following the formation of an underground Communist party and its legalized counterpart known as the WPC in 1921. The FSOC with some 2,200 members became affiliated with the WPC as its Finnish socialist section in 1922.[68] During this period the WPC worked under the strict control of the Communist Party.[69] The two parties existed side by side for three years until the Orders-in-Council lapsed in 1923. In 1924 the WPC legally became the Communist Party of Canada and the underground organization was dissolved. In the meantime, support for the OBU faded.

The guiding principles of *Vapaus* and its editors became those of the Communist Party. The barrier of language, the tendency for Finns to cluster together and the problems of settling down in a new country enabled the FSOC and *Vapaus* to exploit the frustrations, loneliness and bitterness felt by much of the Finnish working class; at the same time, however, this communist orientation caused some Finns to leave the Party,[70] As a reflection of its large membership, the FSOC was given special status as a language federation within the CPC, and its leaders were entitled to their own representatives on the Central Executive Committee, or Politbureau.

Left-wing activity throughout the 1920s was bolstered by the arrival of more immigrants from Finland, the expansion of *Vapaus* from a bi-weekly to a daily newspaper, and the growing popularity of Liberty Hall as a strategic centre for political and cultural activities. To bolster its ideological image, the newspaper was broadened to include the creative writings of Aku Päiviö (biography 7); as well, occasional publications such as *Vapauden Soihtu* (The Torch of Liberty) in 1921 were issued.[71] While this new publication was short-lived, it nonetheless started a trend for *Vapaus* to become a clearing house for socialist and FSOC/FOC publications of all kinds.

The Comintern and the Bolshevization Controversy

Finnish left-wing activity in Canada was strongly influenced by Lenin's formation of the Third Communist International in 1919, which laid claim to communist leadership of the world socialist movement. At its second congress held in 1920, delegates approved "Twenty One" Conditions for membership that firmly differentiated between the socialist parties of the centre and the communist parties of the far left. The formation of the Comintern, however, led to several fears on the part of leftist Finns in Sudbury. Not only was there concern with the issue of direct control and shaping of the CPC and the FSOC from Moscow rather than from local delegates, there was also the threat that the considerable assets of the FSOC would eventually be taken over by the Communist Party and the Comintern. To avoid the latter possibility, in October 1923 the FSOC transformed itself into a new body known as the Finnish Organization of Canada in order to keep its assets from falling into the hands of another body.[72]

After Lenin's death in 1924, the Comintern was controlled by Stalin who bolshevized the international communist movement along the lines of the Bolshevik Party. The concept constituted a thinly veiled attempt to shift away from ethnic and language federations towards party cells established on a workplace basis. This mass organization party line, adopted in the CPC's constitution in 1925, caused considerable consternation in Sudbury. Up to this time, Finns had enjoyed a measure of autonomy because they had joined the CPC en bloc from the FSOC. The existing structure of the Communist Party by language and geography suited the Finns just fine. When the CPC began to implement Stalin's bolshevization policy in 1924, the Finnish radical movement fully understood Tim Buck's assessment of the issue:

Biography 7
Aku Päiviö: Marxist Poet

Aku Päiviö's legacy was closely interwoven with that of the radical movement. The one Finnish writer from Sudbury of truly international stature, he was a staunch defender of Marxist socialism who felt that all writing should be aimed at the education of the working man. He saw education rather than class warfare as the road to enlightenment and the rise of a utopian socialist state. His works, both poetry and prose, are listed at length in Kolehmainen's bibliography *The Finns in America*[73] and extensively reviewed in Palmgren's *Joukkosydän: Vanhan Työväenliikkeemme Kaunokirjallisuus* (The Heart of the Masses: Literary Writings of the Former Workers' Movement).[74] Palmgren regards him as being the most influential fiction writer to emerge out of the North American Finnish working-class movement.

Aku was born in 1879 at Kärsämäki, Finland. Originally known as Jaakola Koponen, he completed elementary school and then went directly into the labour force where he obtained employment in the Oulu and Tornio areas. After changing his name to Aku Päiviö, he left for the United States in 1902, where he worked as the editor of the conservative *Amerikan Uutiset* (American News), *Päivän Uutiset* (Daily News) and *Kansan Lehti* (National Newspaper) publications in Calumet and Ironwood, Michigan. He then became attracted to the American socialist movement. In 1905 he served as editor of the *Raivaaja* newspaper in Fitchburg, Massachusetts. Here he met and married Ida Hänninen. He moved to Alppila in the Thunder Bay area in 1912 where he homesteaded for the next seventeen years. Aku and Ida had six children. Unable to make a living with the sale of his poetry and plays, he came to Sudbury in 1929 at the invitation of the *Vapaus* newspaper, where he served as an editor. In 1939 he became the editor of the special literary and woman's section known as *Liekki* (The Flame). Started in 1936, *Liekki* was unique in the annals of the Finnish press in North America as it served as an outlet for light short stories and poems with an entertainment rather than political thrust. He lived with his family on a farm on the edge of Tilton Lake on the outskirts of Sudbury.

His work was prodigious, including hundreds of poems, three novels and six plays, of which three were for children. While these works were for the most part based on North American experiences relating to poverty, harsh working conditions and slave-like rules, many of their underlying themes made references to the Finnish setting. He was especially adept at writing poems commemorating special events, such as the strike in Michigan's Copper Country in 1913, the tenth anniversary of the founding of the Cobalt FOC local in 1917, the Port Arthur and Fort William summer festival of 1919 and the opening of Liberty Hall in Sudbury in 1921. Numerous anthologies of his poetry have been published: *Ovella* (At the Door) in 1907, *Ajan Laulu* (Song of the Times) in 1910, *Kostaja* (The Revengers) in 1911, *Kokoelma Runoja* (Collected Poems) in 1912, *Hornin Orjat* (The Slaves of Horni) in 1913 and *Kuohuvat Virrat* (Stormy Streams) in 1914. Of his three novels,

Sara Kivistö (1913), which tells the sad tale of a woman in Finland and America, is the best known. He wrote a number of plays, one of which was a musical entitled *Murrosaikana* (Changing Times) in 1911. On his seventieth birthday in 1949, Aku was honoured by a special thirty-six-page edition of *Liekki*.[75] He died in 1956.

Two of his six children, Jules and Allan, became well known in the Sudbury area. Allan developed into one of Canada's best bodybuilders in the late 1940s and Jules went on to have a distinguished teaching career at Ryerson Polytechnic University. As a former member of the International Brigade, Jules was one of the prime movers in having a historical plaque erected at the provincial legislature in Toronto dedicated to the Mackenzie-Papineau Battalion. In 1996 he was invited to Spain and granted Spanish citizenship.[76]

Transformation of the party from what it is, to a party rooted in the factories, mines and ships, means much more than the mere physical reorganization. It presupposes a complete change in the whole basis of its work. It means transferring the principal sphere of party activity "and influence" from the branch meetings in the party hall—to the shops. . . . It provides, in fact, the Communist base in the struggle for power.[77]

The FOC thus became transformed into two formally distinct organizations: a Finnish Section of the CPC with no more representatives on the Central Executive Committee, and a new FOC as an independent cultural and educational institution. It was the latter that allowed the Finns in Canada to keep their own counsel and to escape the total control of the Comintern.[78] The bolshevization controversy resulted in more Finns leaving the CPC. As Avery concluded, "to many . . . Finnish workers in Canada, cultural assimilation was too high a price to pay even for the proletarian revolution."[79] With the exception of Onni Saari's editorial criticisms of communism and Marxist dogma in 1924 (for which he was dismissed), the controversy remained muted at the local level.[80] While each CPC convention dutifully voted to abolish the language federations, little was actually done to fully implement this strategy.

The FOC entered another period of bitter local conflict in 1928 following the Comintern's call for measures to promote anti-religious and anti-monarchical views, and to make preparations for a world-wide revolutionary movement by the working class. *Vapaus* took the anti-monarchical message to heart and made derogatory statements regarding the health of His Majesty King George V that drew the ire of *The Sudbury Star* and the United Church and resulted in its editor, Arvo Vaara, being fined $1,000 and imprisoned for six months.[81] This ill-advised article aroused an emotional wave of anti-communist feeling in Sudbury which took on ethnic overtones since the Finns were the most prominent group in the local communist movement.

Vapaus reacted to this criticism by declaring Vaara to be a class-war prisoner. In response, campaigns were initiated by the English- and French-speaking community and the White Finns against the Sudbury FOC local for breaking the Lord's Day Act by holding concerts; calls were also made by the Canadian Legion to suppress the publication of the newspaper. The controversy even drew the attention of provincial and federal politicians who claimed that communist activity in New Ontario (Northern Ontario) needed to "be squelched at its first manifestation."[82] Undeterred by this opposition, *Vapaus* and local FOC supporters began an active campaign to "conquer the streets" for the Communist Party. The first of these events was held in Bell Park on International Red Day, 1 August 1929.

Using growing unemployment as a rallying cry, the FOC spearheaded the Comintern's wish for revolutionary action by supporting more than two dozen demonstrations in the next three years, including May Day parades and another major International Red Day demonstration on 1 August 1932. Some of the leaders in the 1932 May Day demonstration in Sudbury consisted of people who had acquired training in the USSR as official agitators for the FOC.[83] This show of strength gave rise to fears by local officials who established volunteer guards to assist the police in breaking up demonstrations and, in 1931, called upon the Dominion Government to deport "all undesirables and Communists."[84] By this time, however, other events had taken place that laid the seeds for the demise of the FOC as a political force in Sudbury and Canada.

The Finnish Crisis

While the above events were taking place in Sudbury, another crisis was brewing within the CPC and the Comintern. In 1928-29 the Comintern demanded that ethnic organizations be finally brought under the direct control of the Communist Party and that all traces of social democracy within the party were to be eliminated. This order had important consequences for the Finns, as they constituted more than one-half of the membership of the CPC. The conversion of the CPC from a federation of language groups into a centralized Bolshevik party continued to be opposed by the FOC and *Vapaus*. This opposition grew in strength when the CPC and the Comintern made it clear that they were seeking control over the FOC's financial assets, which now included several successful Finnish co-operative enterprises. This controversy, known as the Finnish Crisis, developed out of the different opinions of the Sudbury local of the FOC and the CPC, regarding which body had the supreme authority over the management of *Vapaus* and the FOC.

Sudbury Finns reacted to the call for bolshevism in the fall of 1929 by affirming FOC control over *Vapaus* and appointing Arvo Vaara rather than

Sulo Neil as the editor of the newspaper, against the wishes of the CPC. Thus it was the Sudbury Finns who led the Canadian revolt against the Comintern leadership.[85] This reactionary stance was of such importance that it was given considerable prominence in the CPC's official history:

> Very strong resistance to the new party leadership, for example, came from some leaders of the Finnish language section. In November 1929, John Wirta, John Ahlqvist and Arvo Vaara . . . were suspended from party membership for refusing to carry out the party's decisions. They were quickly isolated as all the branches of the Finnish Organization of Canada except the Sudbury branch, where these three people were based, came out in support of the new party leadership. The Finnish Organization then transformed itself from an autonomous language section of the Communist Party into an independent progressive organization. The Communist Party was now based solely on individual membership.[86]

One account in *Vapaus* reflects how this intense internal debate was followed locally in places such as Long Lake.[87] For their insubordination, A. Vaara, J. Wirta, B. Tenhunen and J. Ahlqvist were temporarily suspended from the CPC. According to an article in *Vapaa Sana*, more than sixty persons were expelled, causing one FOC supporter to lament with tears in his eyes that the movement, by this action, succeeded only in losing many of its best and hardest-working members.[88] The growing role played by Tenhunen in this conflict was noted in the *Worker*:

> Tenhunen . . . who has consistently opposed the line of the Party in connection with Red Day and the struggle against Police Terrorism, and who is, perhaps, the most out and out expression of social democratic ideology in a developed form among the right wing splitters, called for the expulsion of all members who supported the line of the Political Bureau of the Party from the Finnish Organization of Canada.[89]

The conflict disturbed relations not only between the CPC and the FOC, but also between the FOC and its member locals in the Sudbury area. The Communist Party reacted to this dispute by shifting its support to Finnish newspapers published in the United States. Following a meeting of CPC and FOC representatives before the Comintern in Moscow, a truce was worked out which saw Vaara transferred to party duties and the appointment of Bruno Tenhunen as the new editor of *Vapaus* (biography 8). Tenhunen, however, continued to criticize the CPC leadership and, following his refusal to recant, was dismissed from the newspaper and replaced by A. Mäkelä and, for a brief time, A. Vaara.[90] Tenhunen again became mired in controversy in October 1930 when he opposed the party line that called for Finnish miners allied with the Mine Workers Union of Canada to initiate a suicidal strike at Inco's Frood mine. When the Frood mine workers voted overwhelmingly against strike action, Tenhunen was expelled from the party.

Biography 8
Bruno Tenhunen: The Voice of Social Democracy

Born in Viipuri, Finland, in 1898, Bruno Tenhunen moved with his family to the United States in 1902. Nine years later, the family returned to Finland. Tenhunen became active in the Finnish socialist movement at a young age. In 1920 he was elected a member of Kuopio City Council. He married Tynne Kokkinen and later had one son. Tenhunen was arrested in 1923 because of his illegal association with a left-wing socialist party. In 1924 he was elected to the Finnish parliament as a representative of a new left-wing organization called the Socialist Workers' and Smallholders' Electoral Federation. He, along with a number of his fellow left-wing socialist representatives, were then tried and convicted of treason and expelled from parliament. This became a major constitutional incident in Finland as members of parliament were normally protected from arrest for stating their political views. Tenhunen was released in 1926 and in the following year he moved to Canada. After working in Montreal, Toronto and Alberta, he moved to Sudbury where he wrote for *Vapaus*. In 1930 he aroused considerable controversy as the editor of the newspaper because of his strong views regarding its editorial policy. He felt that the newspaper's policy should be controlled by the Finnish Organization of Canada itself and not by the Communist Party of Canada. He concluded that the CPC represented a clandestine organization that was unable to adjust to socialist ideas. Following a failed attempt to resolve the issue in Moscow, a meeting was held in Toronto to deal with the deepening split. Despite heavy pressure from the communist-leaning supporters of the FOC and a trio of heavyweights from Russia, Tenhunen refused to recant his position and he was expelled from the FOC. Tenhunen thereafter emerged in the FOC literature as the main culprit responsible for the fostering of internal conflict and anti-party propaganda within the organization.

After his dismissal from the newspaper, Tenhunen founded the *Vapaa Sana* (Free Press) newspaper and *Canadan Suomalaisten Työväen ja Farmariliitto* (Finnish-Canadian Workers' and Farmers' Federation, or FCWFF). At *Vapaa Sana* he served as a co-editor along with Reynold Pehkonen. The newspaper emerged as a strong supporter of the CCF Party. When, for financial reasons, the publication was transferred to Toronto from Sudbury in 1934, Tenhunen left for Timmins where he obtained employment with the Consumers Co-operative Society founded in 1931 by FOC dissidents and non-leftist Finns. He left Timmins for Webster's Corners in British Columbia, where he was employed in a co-operative store from 1937-41. He returned to Sudbury and became assistant manager for one of the Bertrand Brothers stores. He was a founder of *Canadan Suomalainen Historiaseura* (Finnish Canadian Historical Society) in 1944-45 and became the society's first president. In 1949 he returned to *Vapaa Sana*, where he worked as an assistant editor until 1966. He was influential in the promotion of ethnic press organizations. In 1951 he was elected president of the Ethnic Press Association of Ontario, a position he maintained for ten years. He later became president of the Canada Ethnic Press

Federation that he helped found in 1958, and established it as a federal lobby group for immigrant interests. He retired in Sudbury in 1967 and was later awarded both the Pearson Medal and Medal of Canada. He died in 1985.

These events exposed the deep differences within the FOC. As a later editorial in *Vapaus* observed:

> About five months after the last convention [1929], when the question came up within the Finnish Organization of fulfilling the recommendation of changing it into a mass-organization, the leading opportunistic element ... attempted to lead the Organization back to the socialist-democratic course from Communistic ideology, and from a fighting line into opposition to the Communist Party and the Comintern.[91]

The Comintern tried to diffuse the situation by issuing a document that opposed these "opportunistic" elements within the FOC. The attempt, however, was rejected in Sudbury. The battle lines were now drawn for a major confrontation.

Split with the Co-operative Movement

The ideological conflict within the Finnish-Canadian community shifted to the co-operative movement in 1930-31. The split within the radical movement found its most powerful expression in the battle over the role of co-operatives between the CPC and the FOC. The co-operative movement, as early as 1910, had started to make significant inroads in places such as Thunder Bay, Timmins and Sudbury. Of the thirteen flourishing co-operative enterprises in Ontario in 1930, seven were Finnish-based.[92] The involvement of the FOC with co-operative enterprises in Sudbury can be traced back to 1926 when the *Sudburyn Kuluttajain Yhdistys* (Sudbury Consumers' Society) was established as a boarding house and restaurant for single men at the Elm House building. A small co-operative store was added later. In 1927 a milk co-operative, known as Co-optas, was formed and a dairy erected on Spruce Street. This enterprise proved to be so successful that it acquired the assets of the Sudbury Consumers' Society in 1929; distribution branches for the collection of milk were established in the Finnish farming areas of Long Lake, Whitefish, Victoria Mine, Beaver Lake, Wanup and Vermilion River. When the new *Vapaus* building on Elm Street opened in December 1929, the main store of Co-optas also located there.

The success of this venture brought forward the ideological question of the role of the co-operative movement within the CPC. While some advocated that the co-operatives should be under the control of the communists, others favoured the importance of neutrality. Led by R. Pehkonen,

B. Tenhunen and other *yhtenäisyysväki* (Uniters) who had resigned or been expelled from the FOC, control over Co-optas was won by the neutral faction, and the process of breaking away from the FOC and the CPC began. Barred from using *Vapaus* for its publicity, in 1931 the Uniters formed a new political organ for farmers and workers known as the FCWFF, and founded *Vapaa Sana*. The intent was to establish a rival organization similar to that of the FOC.[93] Individuals who followed the Pehkonen and Tenhunen stance were called *Haloslaiset* (a reference to those who espoused the George Halonen philosophy for the co-operative movement in the United States), whereas those who continued to follow the Comintern line were called *Linjalaiset*. Differences between these two factions were so passionate it was alleged that they led to Finns murdering one another.[94] In the meantime, a similar battle had been taking place in Timmins where, after the communist takeover in 1930 of the *Työläisten Osuusliike* (The Workers' Cooperative), a non-political *Kuluttajain Osuusliike* (Consumers Co-operative Society) was founded in the following year.

While the decision to create an opposition newspaper to *Vapaus* proved to be successful, the same was not the case for the FCWFF, and it was eventually disbanded in 1940 due to its weak organizational strength; some of its locals, however, managed to remain in existence until the 1960s.[95] Meanwhile, Co-optas dairy went into receivership in 1932. Due to poor management practices, and the altering of the constitution to prevent control from falling into the hands of the FOC or communists, support for the co-operative from Finnish farmers declined to such an extent that the operation was unable to make money.[96] The FOC then formed its own *Raatajien Kulutustarpeiden Jakeluliike* (Toilers Merchandise Distribution Agency); however, this strategy was not successful. The Co-optas dairy was sold to private interests and temporarily run as the Farmers' Dairy Company until 1934, at which time the operations were transferred to *Sudburyn Tuottajain ja Kuluttajain Osuusmeijeri* (The Sudbury Producers and Consumers Co-operative Dairy Limited). From 1934 until the 1960s, it functioned successfully as a commercial venture and, for a time, also as a credit union.[97]

The role of Co-optas was historically significant as it reflected a failed attempt on the part of the FOC to use the co-operative movement as an economic instrument against capitalism; its rise and fall serves to illustrate the powerful split that existed within the left-wing Finns between its social democratic and radical factions. It also marked another step in the transformation of the FOC from a political to a cultural organization. This transition was hastened by four other events in the early 1930s that further sapped the strength of the organization: the communist trials in Ontario in 1931 and the underlying threat of deportation, the emigration of its strongest followers to Karelia, the loss of Liberty Hall and the effective surveillance of the organization by the federal government.

Communist Trials and Deportation

The 1930s began on an ominous note for the left-wing movement. Concerned about the growth of radicalism in Ontario, the province initiated successful court proceedings against a number of communists in 1931. As a result of the imprisonment of eight persons in the case of *King vs. Buck et al.*, the trials in Toronto did much to create the impression that the FOC itself was illegal and violent, a matter of no small concern to an ethnic group that prided itself on being law-abiding.

The trial received extensive coverage in the Sudbury press and did much to link the FOC firmly with the threat of communist subversion. *The Sudbury Star* boldly proclaimed the following in 1931: "Editor of Vapaus Selected by Moscow"; "Vapaus Told Must Accord 'Reds' Support"; and "Reds Sentenced to Five Years, Judge Suggests Deportation." The newspaper concluded that as a result of the trial, communist activity in Canada was given a death blow.[98] In his sentencing statement, the judge upheld the charge that A.T. Hill and seven others were guilty of being members of an unlawful association and of being parties to a seditious conspiracy under Section 98 of the Criminal Code. He recommended that deportation be considered under Special Section 41 of the Immigration Act and authorized the seizure of all Communist Party property in Canada. Members of the FOC and the CPC were undoubtedly influenced by the judge's assertion that "we have the addresses of every Communist member in the party in Canada and the material seized will be sent to each province affected, so that every government will be able to prosecute should they so desire."[99] An appeal court decision in 1932 legally established the precedent that the only evidence needed for deportation was to prove that an immigrant was a member of some communist organization.[100]

The threat of deportation emerged as an ominous feature of Finnish life during the Great Depression:

> By the early 1930s, many Finns still did not have citizenship, and others were refused when they applied, so any contact with the authorities could prove dangerous. Political persecution could take place even if no laws were broken; translators for companies hiring Finns were often anti-radical informers. Protesting poor working conditions or the lack of work could have grave consequences. The political climate in Finland was not friendly to radicals; there might be a danger to liberty or perhaps to life for those deported.[101]

The belief was therefore widespread that political persecution could now take place even if no laws were broken. After the Communist Party was declared an illegal organization in 1931, it was only necessary for the government to show that a person was a member of the Party to be deported. Radical Finns could be shipped to an unfriendly Finland on other grounds as well, such as happened to those who took part in unlawful assemblies at Timmins and Port Arthur, or who participated in relief strikes or demonstrations. To show its seriousness in this regard, the Canadian government deported 1,006 Finns between 1930 and 1935 under a variety of guises; in 1932 Martin Parker (Pohjansalo), Arvo Vaara and John Stahlberg were also declared to be dangerous and deported to Finland.[102] While it is true that relatively few Finns were actually deported because of communist offenses, the potential threat of deportation remained. To lessen the likelihood of deportation, many Finns minimized or totally avoided any involvement with the FOC. Others reacted by emigrating to Soviet Karelia.

Karelia-Fever

Finnish radicalism in the Sudbury area was affected by what has come to be known as *Karjalan kuume* (Karelia-fever), the migration of FOC and communist supporters from Finland, Canada and the United States to Soviet Karelia. While Finns from Canada had migrated to Karelia during the 1920s, it was not until after 1930 that *Vapaus* actively began to promote the first five-year plan for the Karelian Autonomous Soviet Republic. As this plan was founded on the exploitation of the huge forest resources of Soviet Karelia, manpower was sought from Finland, the United States and Canada via recruitment agencies known as the Karelian Work Unit and Technical Aid to Soviet Karelia. Kero estimates that 10,000 Finns from the United States and Canada were swept up in the "fever."[103]

In 1930 Karelian Technical Aid Offices were opened in New York and Toronto. Large scale recruiting in Canada began in 1930 and ended officially by 1935. The FOC sent John Wirta to investigate the situation in 1931 and upon his return he was one of the few who had the courage to state that "if a man has a job he is better here [in Canada] than in Russia, but if he is unemployed and half starving, as so many are, then I would advise him to go to Russia."[104] High unemployment levels encouraged many forest and construction workers to leave Canada in order to participate in this great socialist experiment. Another stimulus was the threat of deportation of radicals from Canada back to an unfriendly and increasingly pro-White Finland; faced with this choice, many activists chose the Karelian option. Others were encouraged not so much by the socialist experiment itself, but rather by the dream of establishing Karelia as an autonomous Finnish-based homeland within the Soviet Union.[105]

Finns in Canada were initially reluctant to participate in the Soviet project; however, propaganda presented regularly in *Vapaus* made them ripe candidates for recruitment. While it is true that the newspaper did eventually bring out many of the hardships involved with resettlement, as reflected in its fifteenth anniversary edition in 1935 celebrating the founding of the Karelian republic, it was obvious that *Vapaus* and the FOC viewed the experiment as an important step towards the development of a new socialist society.[106] The concept of living in a worker's paradise where equality, the promise of good retirement benefits and excellent educational opportunities for their children appealed to those unhappy with their lot in Canada. The experience of Finns leaving Canada en masse for Soviet Karelia must certainly be considered a unique event in the annals of Canadian emigration. Hannes Sula served as the local representative of the first Work Unit sent in 1930 to teach Karelians about forest cutting operations.

The number of Finns who went to Karelia from Canada is uncertain; estimates range from a low of 2,500 to a high of 5,000. One source calculates that 40 percent of the North American migration came from Canada.[107] This range is significant when compared with the official 2,500 membership of the FOC in Canada in 1931. If the 1931 census figures are used as a guide, the Karelian emigration accounted for at least 5 percent of all the Finns in Canada. Up to one hundred Finns may have left Sudbury to go to Karelia. Among the stalwarts who left or who were deported to Karelia were Martin Parker, John Passi, J. Stahlberg, Arvo Vaara, Impi Vauhkonen and John Wirta. In Sudbury, the outflow comprised 40 percent of the FOC local membership.[108] There can be no doubt that Karelia-fever resulted in a devastating blow for the Sudbury FOC and that a tactical error had been made in fostering the exodus to Karelia.

Many who participated in the exodus eventually returned to Finland or North America. For some, however, the experience proved to be worthwhile. Such was the case with John Passi from Louise Township near Sudbury. Passi left for Karelia in November of 1931 and remained there as a lumber truck driver until July 1933. According to Passi, "while the work was certainly hard at times, the experiment served as a valiant attempt on the part of a new government to develop a forested region using workers from the United States and Canada."[109] Passi claims that he was well treated, paid satisfactorily and given a month of holidays each year. On his trips to Leningrad and Moscow, he was accorded favourable treatment, as were other Canadian workers because of their work ethnic and productivity.[110] When he explained to the Soviet authorities in 1933 that he had to return to Canada to assist his mother on the farm, there was no difficulty in leaving the country. He does acknowledge, however, that the situation changed substantially after 1933. An interesting aspect associated with his return to Canada was the cool reception accorded to him by many Beaver Lake residents who remained sympathetic to the Karelian experiment. According to other accounts, such reactions were common in North America as those who chose to return were regarded as weaklings and renegades.[111] For this reason, many returnees remained silent regarding any negative experiences they may have endured.

Another Karelian story involved Otto Kratz, who left Sudbury with his wife Hilja and son Kauko in 1932. An outstanding high school student, Kauko graduated in geology at Leningrad University and eventually became a professor at the Leningrad Geological Institute. He rose to great heights in the scientific world and became a member of the USSR Academy of Sciences. His visits with geologists in Finland brought him international acclaim and he served as a Finnish role model within the USSR. He returned for a brief visit to Sudbury in 1967.[112]

The experience of most emigrants to Karelia from Canada, however, was far less positive. Beginning in 1935, Stalin reversed Lenin's New Economic Policy (1921-29) and initiated an open campaign against all Finns and any form of Finnish nationalism, including newspapers, schools and radio stations. With no basis in fact, he charged that Finns were planning a counterrevolution in Karelia in an effort to rejoin Finland. Branded as traitors of the fatherland, Finns from the Sudbury area became victims of the purges. Some simply disappeared (Richard Ketola), were subjected to illegal arrests (Iivari Ketola) or became victims of Stalinism in one form or another (Wäinö Ketola, Leo-Niilo Kuula, John Mäkynen and Antti-Jussi Pohjansalo).[113] Not only did thousands of rank-and-file Finns become prey to the purges, but Stalinism also devoured the Finnish leaders who had previously espoused communism in North America. The wives and children of those purged were often resettled elsewhere in the Soviet Union. Some emigrants astute enough to retain their Canadian passports managed to return to Canada. According to one estimate, at least 20 percent chose this option. While the FOC and *Vapaus* in Canada remained largely silent regarding the latter turn of events in Karelia, they reacted vigorously to criticisms voiced by the church and the national societies. In one *Vapaus* article, the newspaper claimed that these groups were "servants of capitalism," and that their allegations of hunger and death in the Soviet Union were only foolish talk.[114]

Those who willingly or unwillingly acquired Soviet citizenship had to await the appearance of *glasnost* in the late 1980s before being able to return permanently to their former country. As part of the thawing process that took place in Russia during the 1990s, all of the victims of Stalinism were officially rehabilitated. This rehabilitation notwithstanding, most of the Karelian survivors from North America now admit that they "curse the day that we came here."[115]

Sale of Liberty Hall

The third event undermining the influence of the FOC was the sale of Liberty Hall on Lorne Street. Despite heavy use by its members, employment conditions were such that the Sudbury FOC local was unable to meet its mortgage and tax obligations. These difficulties were brought about by the expenses incurred in the upgrading of the hall in 1929-30, the breakaway of FOC members to the Tenhunen social democratic faction and the migration of others to Soviet Karelia. The hall was sold to the Independent Order of Odd Fellows on 16 December 1932. According to one assessment: "[T]he loss of the hall was a severe blow to the functioning of the local. . . . [I]t is certainly evident that the effectiveness of the Sudbury FOC local would have been more extensive, powerful and diversified, if we could have had a hall for our own use."[116] The loss of the hall removed the main presence of the FOC in downtown Sudbury and its passage was mourned on the editorial page of *Vapaus*.[117] Following the sale of Liberty Hall, many FOC members gravitated to the nearby Ukrainian Hall or to the Finnish Workers' Hall located on Alder Street until a new Finnish Hall was erected on Spruce Street in 1938.

Government Surveillance

The final influence that contributed to the weakening of the FOC was the close scrutiny given left-wing activities by the Liberal and Conservative administrations in Ottawa. This surveillance often went beyond investigative tactics to include restricting the radius of suspected individuals when necessary, and supporting those persons and organizations opposed to the Finnish radical factions.[118] Such spying started as early as 1918 when government and police officials expressed concern with the growth of the radical left. As a result of these fears, the Royal North-West Mounted Police (and after 1919 the Royal Canadian Mounted Police) initiated surveillance of suspected groupings. Of great importance were the RCMP security bulletins circulated regularly within the federal cabinet to senior civil servants, and within the RCMP itself. The major focus of the bulletins from the start was on immigrants such as Russians, Ukrainians and Finns who had associations with labour and the left. The CPC and FOC and unions such as the IWW and OBU provided the RCMP Intelligence Section with its main preoccupation.[119] Information was gathered from a variety of sources, including undercover detectives, secret agencies and volunteer informants from the Finnish community. Speeches, meetings and the content of *Vapaus* were tracked on a continuous basis. Special attention was accorded to agitators such as Sanna Kannasto. Even the American government became involved in such activities in the Sudbury area via its consular office in North Bay. These investigative actions on the part of the RCMP continued well beyond World War II and even included the surveillance of the Finnish Canadian Centennial Committee in 1967.

Among the early reports pertaining to the Sudbury area was a listing of the chief Finnish agitators in Canada. Those mentioned with some association from the Sudbury area included John Ahlqvist, John Ahola, Knutti Harju, Jacob Jarvis, Henry Juntunen, Emile Johnston, Dr. H. Koljonen, Peter Katainen, Wario Lehti, Walter Luoma, David Manninen and John Wirta. These individuals were charged with having objectionable literature in their possession as a result of raids made in October 1918.[120] Another report in 1920 described the links between the Finns and the union movement:

> From a reliable source we are informed that the O.B.U. Convention at Sudbury on 6th-9th September, was a failure due to internal dissension based on suspicion that the Finns were trying to obtain control of the O.B.U. for furtherance of I.W.W. or Socialistic schemes of such a Radical complexion as to conflict with the policy laid down for O.B.U., which recognizes that any extreme Radicalism is likely to result in legislation which will interfere with O.B.U. growth. This informant says:-
>
> "The Finns are the most dangerous part of the O.B.U. in this district, they have associations within themselves of a revolutionary nature and are only using the O.B.U. for their own purposes: I am convinced that they are in close touch with European Bolshevists and that they know better than to confide in their O.B.U. confreres, unless they happen to be Finns. It is well known that the most secret O.B.U. matters leak out sooner or later; but a good deal goes on among the Finns that is closely associated with European politics."[121]

Another concern of the federal government during the 1920s were the *tutkijakomiteat* (investigation committees) established by various FSOC/FOC locals to determine the political suitability of new immigrants. These committees were a North American phenomenon; it has been estimated, for example, that forty to fifty investigation bodies also existed in the United States around the same period.[122] According to one report submitted to the American consulate in North Bay by Rev. Edwin A. Kyllönen:

> [F]rom 1921 to 1926 the Finnish arm of the Communist Party in Canada maintained what is called [an] inquisition board. This board had a local board in each communist center. The purpose of the board was to summon before it every newcomer from Finland to ascertain whether or not he should be considered as a "Red Finn." The first thing the board did was to ask the newly-arrived whether he had a certificate from the com-

munists in Finland. If unable to give satisfactory references the board proceeded to write to Finland concerning the man. Those found upon investigation to be connected in any way with the "White Finns" were told that they must make a public apology in *Vapaus* (Liberty), a communist newspaper published in Sudbury, before he should be allowed to be free from cognizance of the board. Failing to apologize he was persecuted by notices sent wherever he should go for communist neighbors to do their worst by him.

The last of the many cases of this kind in Kirkland Lake occurred in 1929 when a newly-arrived young "White Finn" was asked to go to a certain hotel room where he was told some one wanted to see him. When he entered the room he found six men awaiting him. They constituted the local inquisition board at Kirkland Lake. The door was closed and locked behind the victim and he was questioned for a period of two hours. The board accused him of having been a party to this, that or the other thing in Finland, in order to force him to confess having committed some crime. To use a common expression they wanted to get something on him to terrorize him into joining the Communist Party in Canada or if he would not join then to keep him silent concerning the inquiry. In effect the inquisition board was a sinister instrument of terrorism for "White Finns" throughout Canada.[123]

Reception committees were common in the Sudbury area. A review in *Vapaus* in 1921 reveals that investigation committees were openly active in Worthington, Copper Cliff, Sudbury and Long Lake. These committees determined whether or not a new arrival should be classified either as a "red comrade" or as a *lahtari* ("white butcher"). Depending on the result, the committee would either grant a Red Pass or encourage the immigrant to settle elsewhere.[124] The findings of these investigations, sometimes accompanied by the appropriate confessions, were often published in *Vapaus*.[125] According to Kyllönen, some of those who refused to recant may have been murdered, especially if they were young men without families, relatives or friends in the area. This allegation, however, has been strongly rejected by some members of the Finnish community.[126] The above notwithstanding, there have been assertions made in the United States that "white butchers" there were routinely killed in the forests by accidents involving falling trees.[127] Due to complaints made to the Canadian authorities, these boards disappeared by the turn of the 1930s. Nevertheless, the tradition of reviewing applicants for suitable membership was still carried on in a less formal fashion by many Finnish organizations, including the Loyal Finns in Canada.[128]

Kyllönen continued to serve as an informant in the 1930s. In a report to the American consulate in 1932, he listed some of the active communists in the Sudbury area:

I am enclosing some names . . . which you may run across sometime or other in your capacity as U.S. Consul: Matti Tenhunen. Formerly on the staff of *"Vapaus,"* Sudbury, Ont.; Arvo Vaara. Former Editor of *"Vapaus,"* who was convicted for slander on King George V; Dr. H. Koljonen. Claimed by some to have been, in years past now, the "brains" behind the Finnish Organization of Canada, and its Communist activity; J.W. Ahlquist. Manager of *"Vapaus,"* Sudbury; J. Jarvis. More secretly active communist. Has a general agency in that city; U. Ronni. Secretary of Finnish Organization of Canada Athletic Association; J. Wirta. Communist Agitator. Made a trip to Soviet Russia, summer 1931, in official capacity; H. Ellmen, Sudbury, Ont.[129]

Reports such as these were used by the mining industry to blacklist Finns with known associations with the FOC or *Vapaus*. For this reason, many Finns sympathetic to left-wing causes did not become members of the FOC and stopped subscribing to *Vapaus*, knowing that their mail could be used as evidence leading to the loss of employment or the threat of deportation.

The combined influence of the above events—the threat of deportation and the trials of 1931, the Karelian exodus, the sale of Liberty Hall, and the effectiveness of governmental spying techniques—was such that the political thrust of the FOC gradually shifted towards cultural and recreational pursuits. Laine has outlined the nature of this change:

[B]y emphasizing cultural activities to an even greater extent . . . the FOC tried to retain the loyalty of its members and even to attract new ones. Sports, theatre and music were made an integral part of the FOC's program to entertain, to educate and to raise the morale and dignity of the Finnish Canadian working man. . . . *Vapaus* was incorporated in 1935 as the *Vapaus* Publishing Company Limited, not only to shield the FOC from the threat of exorbitant judgments in libel actions, but also to facilitate *Vapaus'* undertaking of ambitious, new publishing ventures such as the publication of the literary weekly, *Liekki*.[130]

This new role was acknowledged by the FOC itself. In 1933 its secretary was quoted as saying that the "Finnish Organization is an educational and cultural organization in the class fight."[131] It was clear at the ideological level that the CPC's emphasis on the use of class relationships as a divisive force in Canada had proven to be an obsolete, ineffective tool. Avakumovic agrees with this assessment:

[T]he history of the CPC is the story of a small number of men and women who operated mostly on the fringe rather than in the mainstream of Canadian politics. Handicapped by the ethnic origin of much of its rank-and-file and by the social background of many of its leaders . . . the Communists advocated policies which most of the time the majority of Canadians found abhorrent, incomprehensible or at best irrelevant to Canadian needs.[132]

William Eklund (1906-85) (see biography 9) is shown here in 1967 with Edwin Suksi, holding Finland's Fiftieth Anniversary of Independence medal, which was awarded the *Vapaus* Publishing Company. (Finnish Canadian Historical Society)

Rev. Lauri Pikkusaari (1911-65) was the multitalented minister of the *Wuoristo*-Copper Cliff Finnish Evangelical Lutheran Church (see biography 10). He was also a driving force behind the formation of the Finnish Canadian Historical Society. (Finnish Canadian Historical Society)

Oliver Korpela (see biography 11) is shown here (fourth from the left) at "Lancaster" Field near Island Lake in Northern Ontario (c. 1950s). His donation of land led to the construction of the Sudbury Finnish Rest Home facility in the city of Sudbury. (Oliver Korpela, private collection)

Sulo and Bertha Heino (see biography 12) are shown here in the backyard of their Long Lake home (1977). After World War II, Sulo and Bertha were well-known figures in the Sudbury restaurant trade. (Sulo and Bertha Heino, private collection)

In a number of frank assessments made in *Vapaus* in 1937, it was stated that the FOC's future was also in jeopardy because of its failure to attract Canadian-born Finns. It was conceded that young Finns in Canada lacked commitment to revolutionary theories, and that concerns linked to the Russian Revolution, communist ideology and the class struggle were less relevant to them than their everyday concerns. Other reasons advanced were the introduction of the radio, a lessened reliance on *Vapaus* as a news outlet, workplace terrorism in the mining industry, the attraction of other political organizations and unions and a lifestyle that was more social and entertainment oriented.[133] This situation was not unique to Canada, however, as the leftist movement in the United States had faced a similar problem in the 1920s. To accommodate these concerns, *Vapaus* briefly introduced a youth section in its newspaper written in the English language. None of these efforts succeeded, and by World War II it was clear that the FOC as a political force was no longer attractive for younger Finns.

Under the editorships of A.T. Hill, Paul Frederickson and, after 1934, William Eklund (biography 9), the newly incorporated *Vapaus* continued to pursue aspects of CPC and Comintern ideology. In contrast to the situation in the early 1930s, the newspaper abandoned its revolutionary policies; instead, following the Comintern line, it supported the new Popular Front policy that called for strategic alliances with social democrats, a negative stance against Germany, a favourable attitude towards the Soviet Union and support for the anti-fascist Republicans in the Spanish Civil War of 1936-39. Jules Päiviö typified the strong reaction felt by many FOC members towards the war in Spain. Inspired by his father, he grew up in Thunder Bay with a strong sense of social consciousness. After graduating from Sudbury Mining and Technical School in 1936, he was disturbed by the events in Spain. Despite the Foreign Enlistment Act passed by the Canadian government, which made it a criminal offense to fight in Spain, Jules, along with another 180 Finns from Canada, joined the ranks of the 45,000 volunteers who constituted the International Brigades. These Finns were among the 1,250 Canadians who formed the Mackenzie-Papineau Battalion known as the "MacPaps." More than a dozen volunteers came from the Sudbury area. Captured in April 1938, he was saved from death by a turn of fate and, after a year of captivity, he returned to Sudbury.

For Finnish radicals, the Popular Front transformation was a bitter pill to swallow. What support remained for the FOC and the CPC declined further when hostilities erupted between Finland and the Soviet Union in 1939. Aided by a high level of public support for Finland in its fight against the Soviet Union, the Canadian government squashed the political ambitions of FOC and CPC during the war years. For all practical purposes, World War II brought with it the end of radicalism as an organized force

Biography 9
William Eklund: The Voice of the FOC

William Eklund was born in 1906 in Pori, Finland. His formal education was limited to six years of public school and some vocational schooling. He was a metal worker by trade. After completing his compulsory military service, he discovered that he was blacklisted from getting employment in Finland. Disillusioned, he emigrated to Canada in September 1928, where he became a tireless worker in the Canadian labour movement.

First hired as a summer vacation substitute in 1937, Eklund rose through the ranks and became the editor-in-chief of *Vapaus* for thirty-seven years from the autumn of 1939 to January 1975. His tenure was interrupted only by his active service in the Canadian Armed Forces during World War II. While serving as editor-in-chief, he wrote many articles concerning Canada. Among them were accounts of the Riel Rebellion, the realities of Canada as a two-nation state, the problem of national unity, the position of Canadian ethnic groups, the Canadian government and the judicial system, social services and the development of war veterans' pension legislation. He collaborated with Pekka Mertanen in writing a defence for the reinstatement of the illegal FOC. This defence, which appeared in the book *The Illegal Finnish Organization of Canada*, was published in 1942. In 1946 he edited the *Canadan Sotilaiden Muistoalbumi* (Memorial Album of Finnish Canadian Soldiers), which received much popular acclaim. In 1951 Eklund translated *Sunshine Sketches of a Little Town* by the Canadian author Stephen Leacock into Finnish.

Eklund wrote and edited the anniversary issues and historical overviews of *Vapaus* and *Liekki* for the years 1947, 1949, 1957, 1967 and 1972. He also edited the *Kevät* (Spring) and *Joulu* (Christmas) publications. For over thirty years, he was responsible for the popular *Taskukalenteri* (Pocket Calender), containing information for immigrant workers concerning the availability of Canadian social services. After retiring in January 1975, Eklund continued his journalistic and literary endeavours. He was a member of the FOC Archives Committee and was instrumental in having the records of the FOC and the *Vapaus* Publishing Company donated to the Public Archives of Canada in 1975. In 1983 he wrote a history of the Finnish Organization of Canada, entitled *Canadan Rakentajia: Canadan Suomalaisen Järjestön Historia vv. 1911-1971*, which also appeared in English as *Builders of Canada: History of the Finnish Organization of Canada 1911-1971* in 1987.[134] His most enduring memory was the strong sense of co-operation shared by all of the Finnish groups in Canada during the World War II period and the 1967 Centennial celebrations. Eklund passed away in 1985. He was survived by his wife Aliina (Pesonen) Oja and one stepson, Oliver.

within the Finnish-Canadian community; however, as Sillanpää has demonstrated, support continued to be given by leftist and working-class Finns to the union movement and pro-labour parties in municipal, provincial and federal elections.[135]

Conservative Countermovement

While the events between 1917 and 1929 favoured the development of left-wing activities, the situation changed in the 1930s as conservative forces began their ascendency. The foundations for this surge were laid in the previous decade, as the influx of arrivals from Finland included a large contingent of the White Guard, most of whom were absorbed into the conservative faction of the community. Despite their numbers, however, they were unable at the start to compete with the zeal, dedication and organization of the leftist movement. The situation improved somewhat during and after the Great Depression, when the leftist movement entered a period that *Vapaus* called the "crisis" years.[136] By the end of the 1930s, the forces of the Finnish State, nationalistic societies, religious groupings and *Vapaa Sana*, and the weakened state of the left-wing movement, had combined with one another to completely revamp the institutional setting.

Finnish State

After independence was attained in 1917, Finland undertook a policy of fostering patriotism and conservativism among the *ulkosuomalaiset* (outlander) Finns in Canada and the United States. To this end, the Finnish government in 1920 appointed its first consul in Thunder Bay. A consulate was then established in Montreal that later was upgraded to the status of a consulate-general in 1925. Akseli Rauanheimo, the consul and consul-general of Finland in Montreal from 1923 to 1933, served to champion the government's aims in Canada; he can arguably be regarded as being the "father" of the conservative countermovement. Since Montreal was the major port of entry for incoming immigrants, Rauanheimo promoted the establishment of various institutions to challenge the primacy of existing Red organizations.[137] Honorary vice-consuls likewise appeared at Copper Cliff (Tuomas Franssi in 1926 and Herbert Johnson in 1931). Canadians were inspired by other influences from Finland as well, such as the formation of *Suomi Seura* (Finland Society) in 1927, its magazines *Suomen Viesti* (Message from Finland) and *Suomen Silta* (Finland Bridge), and the right-wing *Lapuan liike* (Lapua Movement). Conservative Finns in Canada used these external thrusts as the base for countering the strength of the radical movement. Other steps taken were Canadian-based, and they included the establishment of national societies, the strengthening of the church and the formation of the *Vapaa Sana* newspaper.

Finnish National Society of Sudbury and the Central
Organization of Loyal Finns in Canada

A rallying focus for the conservative Finns was the national society. Concerned with the difficulty of obtaining employment, the negative image of radical Finns and the threat by the Canadian government that they should be deported, a number of Finns sought to change this situation through the formation of loyalist groups known as national societies, and the creation of another central body similar to that of the FOC. The changing political mood in Finland, and the well-publicized divisions within the FOC, were other factors that encouraged this new orientation.[138] By the late 1920s, a number of independent national societies had been formed in Canada such as *Turisti* (Tourist) in Port Arthur (1926), *Suomi Seura* (Finnish Society) in Montreal (1927) and *Valistus-ja Edistysseura* (Enlightenment and Progress) in Vancouver (1928). Other groups were formed in 1930, among them a national society in Sudbury.

Spearheaded by Rev. Felix Mayblom, the decision to establish *Sudburyn Kansallisseura* (The Finnish National Society of Sudbury) was made at a meeting held at the Wesley Hall on 23 May 1930. This meeting attracted considerable attention in *The Sudbury Star* under the heading "Finns Organize to Fight Communism." The newspaper gave the following account of this historic meeting:

> With the announced object of completely disassociating themselves from the "Red" element and their doctrines, and at the same time reaffirming their allegiance to the British flag and Canadian ideals, the "white" Finns of Sudbury and District held a meeting at Wesley Hall last Friday and laid plans for the formation of an organization which, in effect, will be anti-communistic in its aims. . . . [T]he conference unanimously adopted the following resolution—This conference expresses its regret regarding the troublesome and destructive action of the class of Finnish people who have allied themselves with the communistic movement. We, the conference, do not approve of the ideas, the method nor of the philosophy of life of the said movement and therefore do not desire to be connected with it in any way.[139]

In June the first official meeting of the Society was held at which time 110 members signed up. The FNSS encouraged all Finns to respect Canadian laws, avoid alcohol, support nationalism and promote Finnish culture in Canada.[140] There was, however, a practical slant to this loyalty stance, as many conservative Finns had experienced difficulty in gaining employment because of the suspicion that they could be "Reds." The Society also supported a strong temperance stance prohibiting drinking, which lasted into the late 1950s. The first meetings were held in the basement of the United Church; on occasion, some were held elsewhere, such as the August Svensk farm in Louise Township. Between 1932 and 1935, regular meetings were held at the Orange Hall on Cedar Street.

On 3 May 1931, the Society became linked with the Central Organization of Loyal Finns in Canada (COLFC). The Loyal Finns had been formed in Toronto on 11 February 1931 to provide cohesion for the existing national societies. The aims of the organization were to combat the influence of the FOC, to change the radical image of Finns and to increase employment opportunities for its members.[141] An elaborate organizational structure was also proposed similar to that of the FOC. Finns who passed the membership requirements were then given a letter of introduction to be given to prospective employers as proof of his or her good character and religious spirit.

By 1936, however, the Loyal Finns could claim the support of only eighteen affiliated societies and five hundred members. Of this total, half were from Montreal, which had by then emerged as the headquarters for the organization. In the absence of a clear-cut program other than its opposition to communism, COLFC found it difficult from Montreal to create the strong bonds necessary to unite its locals scattered throughout the country; consequently, it never did attain the strength of the FOC that in the 1920s could claim nearly one hundred locals and halls. The societies nevertheless retained some measure of influence because of the recognition they received from the governments of Canada and Finland, and from publicity offered through the Finland Society.

The FNSS started in active fashion, publishing its own newsletters such as *Oottako Kuullu?* (Have You Heard?) and *Oras* (Sprout). A study circle, a women's and theatre group and a library were created as well. A sporting club, *Voima*, was formed in 1932 and it members constructed an athletic field known as *Kaskelan Kenttä* (Kaskela's Sports Field) at Bruce and Dell Streets on land leased from the city. The club then experienced a number of problems and it ceased to operate in 1940. In the early 1930s, free meals were provided by the Society for unemployed Finns with the assistance of food and money donations from area farmers and its employed members.

In 1935 the FNSS was forced to look elsewhere for a meeting place. Consideration was given to purchasing the Finnish Workers' Hall on Alder Street but this was not successful. A joint meeting was subsequently held between the Society and St. Matthew's congregation, at which time it was agreed that they would jointly purchase a lot and build a hall on Antwerp Avenue in the Donovan. Reino Mannila's recommendation that the new building be named *Sampo* was approved; on 8 December 1935, *Sampo* Hall was officially opened. The facility brought with it a burst of energy that included the formation of a choir and an expansion of its library. These developments led the Society in 1937 to acquire more land for parking purposes and to expand the original building. Financial assistance was given by Inco for these purposes. Activity was so brisk at the hall that COLFC was considered to be a model for other societies in Canada.[142] Bolstered by the concept *oma tupa, oma lupa* (own home, own boss), and a renewed interest in theatrical activities, membership grew substantially. By 1938 the FNSS had emerged as the largest local in COLFC. The Society also gained approval from the non-Finnish community through its support for the Royal Visit to Sudbury in 1939.

The Fighting Church

Until the late 1920s, organized religious life for the Finns in the Sudbury area remained in a state of disarray, due in part to the poor support from the *Suomi* Synod centred in Hancock, Michigan. In Canada, there were only four Lutheran churches and the *Suomi* Synod was supported by a mere 4 percent of the Finnish population. When Antti Karhu left the Copper Cliff church in 1922, there was not one Lutheran minister left in the country. The root cause of this situation was exposed by Rev. John Wargelin:

> In 1912 I received a letter from the Copper Cliff, Ontario congregation which belonged to my first parish. They were without a pastor and certain sects were making inroads into their congregation They wanted to know if I could extend my visits there once a month. . . . But those early years when there was a great shortage of ministers and home mission work was unorganized in the Synod, the pastors were called upon to care for large multiple parishes. The large Copper Cliff-Sudbury areas had thousands of Finns without any Lutheran pastor.[143]

In the 1930s the religious setting underwent change. At the *Wuoristo* Lutheran Church in Copper Cliff, the congregation reaped the benefits of more lengthy ministerial tenures (table 13). Major changes introduced by the *Suomi* Synod in the United States assisted Sudbury Lutherans in countering the inroads made by the Presbyterian (after 1925 the United) Church in Canada. Indeed, by the late 1920s, the United Church had succeeded to such an extent that it had nine Finnish ministers and seven Finnish congregations in Canada. By 1928 the *Suomi* Synod felt itself so powerless that it gave the United Lutheran Church in America (ULCA) free reign to administer the Finnish churches in Canada. In 1931 an agreement was reached between ULCA, the *Suomi* Synod and the Finnish Lutheran Churches in Canada to transfer all charge over the churches in Canada to the ULCA, thereby initiating a new period in the history of the Finnish Lutheran Church in Canada.[144] As part of the agreement, the churches in Ontario joined the Evangelical Lutheran Synod of Canada. In 1932 all the Finnish-Canadian member churches of the ULCA were given permission to form their own synod, known as the Finnish Evangelical Lutheran Conference in

Canada (*Suomi* Conference after 1962). These developments wrought major changes to the church scene. Between 1931 and 1935, new congregations were brought into the ULCA at Kirkland Lake, Timmins-South Porcupine, Toronto, Windsor, Montreal, Sylvan Lake, Manyberries, New Finland, Vancouver and Sudbury.

It was in response to the above events that the religious setting in Sudbury experienced a remarkable metamorphosis between 1928 and 1932. The United Church of Canada initiated this process in 1930 by starting the publication of the religious magazine *Canadan Viesti* (Canadian Messenger), and reasserted its Finnish mission effort by appointing Rev. Thomas D. Jones and his Finnish-speaking assistant, Felix R. Mayblom, as missionaries for Sudbury and Copper Cliff. Rev. Jones promptly began a public tirade against *Vapaus* and other local left-wing elements. This crusade was undoubtedly caused by the refusal of many leftists to be married in the church or to receive the rites of the church at burial ceremonies.[145] The All People's Mission in the Donovan on the corner of Antwerp and Jean Streets was dedicated in January 1930 as the focal point for the Finnish missionary effort in Sudbury, and Jones's position was taken over by Mayblom. Alarmed by these actions, the *Suomi* Synod appointed Frans J. Koski and Vilho J. Hänninen to the St. Timothy congregation in Copper Cliff. The appointment of these Finnish ministers set the stage for the formation of a Finnish church in Sudbury.

Table 13
Ministers of St. Timothy's Evangelical Lutheran Church
(1896-1998)

J.J. Hoikka	1896-1901	Frans Koski	1940-43
John Wargelin	1906-1907	Lauri Pikkusaari	1943-49
Jacob Mänttä	1908-1909	Juho Ojanto	1950-52
John Wargelin	1910-12	Lauri Pikkusaari	1952-58
Matti Luttinen	1913-15	Toivo Häkkinen	1958-62
Otto Mäki	1915-16	Pentti Palonen	1963
J.T.R. Hartman	1916-18	Niilo Tuomenoksa	1964
Antti Karhu	1920-22	Toivo Häkkinen	1964
Matti Luttinen	1923	Pentti Murto	1965-69
Otto E. Mäki	1924-26	Yrjö Raivio	1970-77
Anton Korhonen	1926-28	Matti Pekkarinen	1979-81
Missionary pastors	1929	Yrjö Raivio	1981-83
Frans Koski	1930-31	Harry Laaksonen	1983-88
Vilho J. Hänninen	1931-36	Yrjö Raivio	1988-89
Edwin A. Kyllönen	1936-40	Shirley Ruller	1989+

Source: St. Timothy's Evangelical Lutheran Church, *Annual Reports* (1989-95).

The glaring lack of a Lutheran congregation in Sudbury finally prompted the Lutheran Synod of Canada into taking action. Pastors Vilho J. Hänninen from Copper Cliff and John Saarinen from Toronto met with Hannes Kaskela in 1932 to lay the foundations for a new congregation. An organizational meeting was held on 29 November 1932 at the Cedar Hall, at which time the *Sudburyn Suomalainen Evankelis-Luterilainen Seurakunta* (Sudbury Finnish Evangelical Lutheran Church) was formed. Services were initally held in the Cedar and *Sampo* Halls. The congregation benefited from the fact that the All People's Mission in the Donovan lacked a Finnish-speaking minister following the resignations of Felix Mayblom and Edwin B.A. Kyllönen in 1932-33. Rev. Hänninen from St. Timothy's congregation served as the first part-time minister (table 14). Following Kyllönen's shift of allegiance to the Finnish Evangelical Lutheran Church, he was placed in charge of both the Sudbury area churches in 1937-39. In 1938 a church property was purchased by the Donovan congregation from the city of Sudbury on Tedman Avenue. A year later a parsonage was acquired on the same street.

The congregation celebrated the arrival of its first full-time minister, Rev. Matti Lepistö, in 1938, by changing the name of the congregation to *Pyhän Matteuksen Suomalainen Evankelis-Luterilainen Seurakunta* (St. Matthew's Finnish Evangelical Lutheran Church).[146] John Heino served as the second resident pastor in 1942. Both Lepisto and Heino resided at the Tedman parsonage. The religious effort of the young congregation was bolstered in 1935 by the appearance of the magazine *Isien Usko* (The Faith of our Fathers). Published by the Finnish Evangelical Lutheran Conference in Canada, the magazine raised the awareness of its congregations and promoted the spiritual life of their members.

Table 14
Ministers of St. Matthew's Evangelical Lutheran Church
(1932-98)

Vilho Hänninen	1932-36	Markku Suokonautio	1971-75
Edvin Kyllönen	1937-39	Jukka Joensuu	1976-79
Matti Lepistö	1939-41	Lari Junkkari	1980-85
Johan Heino	1942-46	Markku Rautiainen	1986-91
Armas Korhonen	1946-60	Markku Sarento	1991-93
Pellervo Heinilä	1964-66	Markku Rautiainen	1993-96
William Sumner	1967-71	Kari Valanne	1996-

Source: St. Matthew's Evangelical Lutheran Church, *Annual Reports* (1982-97).

Meanwhile, Finnish Pentecostals appeared on the religious scene. The Finnish Pentecostal movement in North America began with the formation of a congregation in New York in 1925. The religion spread from the United States into Canada and new congregations appeared in Toronto (1930), Montreal (1932) and Thunder Bay (1933). Other congregations permanently established in Northern Ontario included Sudbury (1936), Sault Ste. Marie (1939) and South Porcupine (1946). The Finnish pentecostal movement at its height included thirty-two congregations; by the 1990s, however, this number had been reduced to ten.[147]

Pentecostal missionaries first appeared in the Sudbury area in the 1930s. Tyyne Nykänen spent three weeks in the Louise and Lorne Townships area, where her missionary work was hindered because farmers considered her to be a "bourgeois stool pigeon." She was followed by Esther Greus, who also received a cool welcome:

> In the fall of 1933 God called me to Sudbury. . . . After obtaining a few addresses from some religious folk, my train arrived in Sudbury early in the morning. . . . I walked around for more than half a day, but no Finns paid attention to me, after learning that I was an evangelist. . . . On the day of the first service, the preacher was ready, his wife at the organ, and we waited eagerly for the first Finnish arrivals. Only one man showed up and he was a bit drunk. We held a service for him, and he went on his knees and cried, but we were not sure if this was because of the sermon or because he was intoxicated.[148]

Greus was later accompanied by Aino Koistinen in 1935, at which time meetings were held at their small home on Bessie Street. Through their efforts the *Sudburyn Siion Helluntaiseurakunta* (Sudbury Finnish Pentecostal) congregation was formed in 1936. A larger property was later acquired in 1936 on the corner of Haig and Whittaker Streets, where the Caruso Club now stands. When Greus left for India in 1938, the young congregation remained without a formal leader for six years. In 1944 Väinö Suokas became the new minister. During his stay, which lasted more than five years, he initiated many improvements to the church building before returning to the United States.

All of the above Finnish churches were similar in one respect—they actively promoted the concept of *Suomalaisuus* (Finnishness). Church services, Sunday schools and confirmation classes were generally held in Finnish; as a result, second-generation Finns who were members of a church before World War II often retained a good command of the language.

Vapaa Sana

The final opposition to Finnish radicalism came in the form of the *Vapaa Sana* newspaper. The launching of the paper evolved out of the schism in 1929 between the Finnish Organization of Canada and the Communist

Party of Canada and the ideological conflict in 1930-31 between these organizations and the co-operative movement.[149] The first issue, which appeared on 22 December 1931, followed a weekly bulletin known as *CO-OPTAS* that had been created earlier in the year.[150] The newspaper proclaimed that its policies were supportive of the co-operative movement and the FCWFF. While it was headquartered in Sudbury, *Vapaa Sana* remained committed to a non-revolutionary form of socialism; in 1933 it also expressed interest in the Co-operative Commonwealth Federation (CCF) Party. Started on Lisgar Street where the present downtown post office now sits, the newspaper moved to another site near the corner of Frood and Elm Streets.[151] At the beginning, the enterprise was not so much a commercial undertaking as an ideological reply to the left. Unable to pay the Nickel City Press for its publishing costs, the newspaper moved to Toronto in 1934, where it became more commercial and less socialist.[152] This is made clear in its statement of aims:

> *Vapaa Sana* has up to now been the sole free-minded paper in Finnish on this continent published on behalf of the productive working masses, and it will continue to be so. Its aim will be to closely follow the strivings of the population proper of this country in politics, the economy, in the co-operatives, and elsewhere, while at the same time reporting the activities of the Finnish Uniters in these fields. *Vapaa Sana* intends to remain a paper of the masses, the messenger of those who study social affairs in their entirety from the perspective of the interests of the productive workers, not merely of some minor groupings.[153]

Close ties with the FCWFF were loosened, and with the aid of the Finnish Social Club in Toronto and the Timmins Consumers Co-operative in 1936, the publication was transformed into a shareholding company known as *Vapaa Sana* Press Ltd. Following the acquisition of the Toronto-based *Viikko Uutiset* (Weekly News) in 1937, the newspaper broadened its readership by publishing articles and reports from Finnish churches and national societies. During the 1930s many of the staff consisted of employees who had left or been banished from *Vapaus* and the FOC; these included editors R. Pehkonen and B. Tenhunen and business managers K.G. Asiala and Onni Saari. By 1939-40 the links between *Vapaa Sana* and the FCWFF had disappeared, and the newspaper proclaimed itself to be independent. The FCWFF had in any event been inactive, and in 1940 it was replaced by the *Kanadan Suomalainen Kansanvallan Liitto* (Finnish Canadian League for Democracy), which also had a short life.[154] By the end of the decade, the circulation of *Vapaa Sana* had overtaken that of *Canadan Uutiset* published in Thunder Bay.

World War II and Its Aftermath

The Winter War between Finland and the USSR in 1939-40, Finland's declaration of war against the Soviet Union in 1941, the Continuation War of
1941-44, the armistice between Finland and the Soviet Union in 1944 and
the Treaty of Peace signed by Finland with the victorious allies in 1947 (of
which Canada was a co-signer), all had profound consequences for the local
Finnish community. While individual Finns rallied for the Canadian war
effort, *Vapaus* and the FOC were suppressed, as patriotic forces supportive
of Finland gained prominence. After the war, a brief accommodation of
interests was forged between the various factions through the Canada-
Finland Aid Society. This co-operative experiment proved to be short-lived,
and by the late 1940s the Great Divide had returned. The ongoing persistence of a split was given tangible expression with the formation by conservatives of the Finnish Canadian Historical Society in 1944, and the inability
of the Finland Week participants in 1967 to bring about a permanent coalition of interests. It thus remained until the late 1980s before progress was
made in resolving existing differences.

Throughout the postwar period, the interests of the Finnish state were
served in the area by Kauko Mäki, Teuvo Eloranta and Hannu Piironen.
Appointed as vice-consul in 1950, Mäki was named consul in 1957. He was
succeeded by Teuvo Eloranta in 1985. Since 1991 this position has been
filled by Hannu Piironen.

Finnish-Canadian War Effort

The World War II effort was noteworthy in that it provided solid evidence
that the Canadianization of the Finnish community had finally started.
During World War I, immigrant Finnish Canadians of enlistment age, who
harboured memories of forced conscription into the Russian army, and who
still bore the emotional scars of Finland's Civil War, often destroyed their
naturalization papers to avoid Canadian military service.[155] Following the
outbreak of World War II, however, Finns in Canada enlisted with a
stronger sense of Canadian patriotism. No more vivid example of the
Finnish-Canadian contribution to the war effort can be found than
Eklund's remarkable seventy-page *Muistoalbumi* (Memorial Album), which
contains nearly eight hundred photographs and biographical profiles of
Finnish Canadians who served in the Canadian Armed Forces.[156] Another
illustration was the enlistment of thirty-five members (including two
women who enlisted in the Wrens) from St. Timothy's Finnish Lutheran
congregation.[157] In her memoirs, Nelma Sillanpää also provides a detailed
accounting of the many different fronts in Europe where Finnish-Canadian
soldiers such as Paul Sillanpää participated.[158] On the home front, civilian

Finns belonging to all factions actively participated in Canadian Red Cross activities and the Victory Loan campaign. In this connection, the role of Finnish women was particularly remarkable.

While many Finns enlisted in the Canadian Armed Forces, not all of them saw foreign combat. Those who had close relatives in Finland were sometimes classified as enemy aliens; others, whose background was "tinged with red," often found themselves in unusual situations. Postings for these individuals were available only in Canada. Such was the case with Sulo Heino, who was trained as a paratrooper, but was never sent overseas. This proved to be fortunate as most of his battalion died in combat while fighting in Europe. Jules Päiviö was likewise restricted to teaching duties at Petawawa where his role as an instructor was secretly scrutinized by army personnel posing as students.[159] Leftist associations even led to job barriers after the war, as exemplified by Sulo Heino, who was denied employment as a caterer on the Dew Line while his wife Bertha was accepted.[160]

One Finn who saw extensive action in Europe was Oliver Korpela. Despite having only a grade 10 education, he acquired a commission as a pilot officer and was sent to England with the Royal Canadian Air Force (RCAF). After being arrested for fighting with an RCAF officer, he prudently joined the Royal Air Force in 1943. During a bombing mission he was shot down in the Netherlands. Aided by the Dutch underground, he posed as a wandering cripple and deaf mute tailor known as John Bos. He experienced a number of harrowing experiences, including measuring a German SS officer for a uniform. The resistance helped Korpela to get across German lines as the Allied forces were liberating the southern part of the Netherlands. In the chaos of troop movements, he accidentally climbed aboard a truck carrying German prisoners of war to Eindhoven, where by chance several Canadian divisions were based. That was when Oliver started talking again. He returned to Canada in 1945.[161]

Left-Wing Suppression

The invasion of Finland by the Soviet Union had a strong negative effect on the fortunes of the FOC. In 1939, for example, *The Sudbury Star* trumpeted the following report:

> [H]undreds of once 'pinkish' Finns in the Sudbury District are turning away from Communism and are wholeheartedly supporting any movement which might aid in ousting the Red menace from Finland. While it is difficult to estimate the numbers who have recently tossed Stalin and his doctrines overboard, it is reliably estimated that Loyal Finns in Sudbury outnumber the Reds by three to one.[162]

The fact that the Soviet invasion involved the takeover of the Petsamo nickel deposits run by Inco gave an added local impetus to these sentiments. Feelings ran so high in the Sudbury area that thirty-four men left Sudbury to join the Finnish fighting forces against the Russians.[163] One member of the FNSS, Toivo Kaipia, died while fighting in Finland.[164]

On 4 June 1940, the Canadian government passed an Order-in-Council affecting sixteen organizations that deprived the FOC and its seventy locals of their legal status; *Vapaus* was not affected by the decree.[165] Over two hundred communists were interned in Canada, among them A.T. Hill, who had been the national secretary of the FOC, an editor of *Vapaus* and an organizer for the Ontario lumber workers. Finland's declaration of war against the Soviet Union crystallized feelings of local Finns and other Canadians against the FOC and *Vapaus*. The FOC responded by forming a propaganda organization known as the *Suomalais-Canadalainen Demokraattinen Liitto* (Finnish Canadian Democratic League) in December 1941. The League supported conscription into the Canadian Armed Forces, the Victory Loan Campaign and came out in favour of Finland's effort against Nazism and all forms of fascism.[166] No mention, however, was made regarding the Soviet aggression against Finland. The Order-in-Council against the FOC was lifted on 14 October 1944.

Canada-Finland Assistance

While the Canadianization of the Finnish population was apparent by World War II, there still remained considerable emotional support for the plight of the "old country." Many local efforts were thus put into place to aid Finland in its war effort. Assistance was sent to Finland by groups such as the Sudbury District Finnish War Aid Association. Spearheaded by the Finnish consul Herbert Johnson, Antti Heiskanen and Karl Lehto, the Association was formed at *Sampo* Hall on 26 November 1939 at which time representatives from various conservative groupings agreed to assist Finland through the Canadian Red Cross Society.[167] Among the fund-raising events were coffee parties, bingos, Finnish ski patrol demonstrations, *kruunuhäät* (royal weddings) and theatrical performances.[168] *Sampo* Hall was booked virtually every day for this purpose throughout 1940. A summer picnic sponsored by the Association at Lake Ramsey in July 1940 proved to be so successful that it evolved into an annual summer festival tradition that has continued to the present.[169] In December 1939, the FOC also started its own campaign to help Finland through the Canadian Red Cross and published an appeal for donations in *Vapaus*.

Finland's declaration of war against the Soviet Union in June 1940 and its alliance with Germany made it for a time an enemy country of Canada. Government-sponsored assistance through public bodies such as Ontario

Finnish Aid stopped; however, the war aid effort at the private level went on as before. The FNSS, for example, established a *Kummikerho* (Godmother Club) that assumed care for two adopted children from Finland in 1941 and the War Aid Association continued the summer festivals. The Sewing Circle of the Democratic League likewise provided aid to various groups, including the Canadian Aid to Russia Fund.[170]

Following the 1944 armistice signed between Finland and the USSR, Canada passed the War Charities Act in 1946, which again permitted public assistance to be given to Finland. The legislation, however, required that such permission would be granted only to a single organization. This dictate forced the two main central bodies in Canada, FOC and the COLFC, to combine their efforts under the umbrella of *Suomi-Apu Yhdistys* (Canada-Finland Aid Society). The first meeting of the Aid Society held at *Sampo* Hall on 30 March 1946 was remarkable as it represented the first time that all Finnish organizations had banded together in a co-operative effort. According to one account:

> An estimated 122 organizations, societies, churches, clubs and groups sent representatives. The left wing organizations sent 61 representatives from the FOC locals, the Finnish Canadian Amateur Sports Federation, and women's clubs. In addition, one representative was sent by the Labour Progressive Party. The right wing organizations sent 47 representatives from the Nationalist societies, Finland Aid groups, churches, women's groups, and sports organizations. In addition, there were representatives of various persuasions from six co-operatives. The seven remaining representatives came from various minority groups.[171]

The Society functioned successfully for two years and reached its goal of raising $100,000. Attempts made by the FOC in 1947 to use this body as a foundation for future co-operation among all Finnish Canadians, however, floundered, and it was to remain another twenty years before a renewed effort at unity would be undertaken. Despite this setback, support for the homeland continued; between 1945 and 1949, for instance, some 240,000 packages were sent to Finland from Canada.

Finnish Canadian Historical Society

Another indicator of the persistence of the Great Divide was the formation of the Finnish Canadian Historical Society. The initiative for this new organization came from the Montreal branch of the Loyal Finns in Canada. Representatives from church groups, branches of the Loyal Finns of Canada, the *Voima* Athletic Club, the Finnish Social Club of Toronto, the Sudbury Finnish War Aid Association and *Vapaa Sana* held a meeting at *Sampo* Hall in Sudbury on 2 July 1944, at which time the Finnish United Historical Society of Canada was formed. The Society expressed the importance of gathering information regarding the activities of non-communist Finns, the development of an archives and the publication of a historical book on Finns in Canada.[172] At a meeting held in Long Lake in 1945, the name of the organization was changed to the Finnish Canadian Historical Society.

The Society fell heir to the records dealing with the campaigns to raise funds and material assistance for Finland during the Winter War; this served as the core of archival material for its own collection. The collection brought about the need for a custodian and a storage place for these holdings. Rev. Lauri Pikkusaari served as the first archivist, and the basement in the manse of St. Timothy's Church in Copper Cliff was used as the site for the archives until they were transferred to the nearby home of Elli Tulisalo. They remained there until they were donated to the Multicultural History Society of Ontario in 1979.

A number of branch affiliates were established in other parts of Ontario and Canada. Annual celebrations were held and medals awarded to honour early Finnish pioneers such as Kusti Hautamäki, Onni Rossi and Einari Jouppi. Among the publications issued by the society were a twenty-year retrospective in 1963 called *Canadan Suomalainen* (Finnish Canadian) and a history entitled *Kanadan Suomalaisten Historia I* and *II*. Since the 1980s the main focus of the society has been on the collection and preservation of old photographs.

Growth and Consolidation of the Church

The postwar years provided fertile ground for the growth and consolidation of the Finnish churches. At St. Matthew's Church, Rev. Armas Korhonen arrived in 1946; this event marked the beginning of a fourteen-year tenure as the congregation's longest-serving pastor. A new church and parsonage on the corner of Bloor and Mackenzie were inaugurated in 1949, and the previous properties on Tedman Avenue were sold. Bolstered by the migration wave of the 1950s, the congregation experienced a great increase in activity. Between 1965 and 1971, the church was served by pastors Pellervo Heinilä and William Sumner. In 1966 a former elementary school was acquired and refurbished as a rural chapel in the Wanup area. Meanwhile, the congregation was affected in 1963 by the incorporation of *Suomi* Synod into the newly formed Lutheran Church in America (a union of the ULCA, the Augusta Synod and the American Evangelical Lutheran Church). Spurred by demands from Finnish Lutherans in Canada, the previous work of the *Suomi* Synod was delegated to a body known as *Suomi Konferenssi* (Finnish Conference), whose mission it was to ensure that Finnish immigrants throughout North America would continue to have worship services in the Finnish language.[173]

St. Matthew's council, as late as 1970, considered the church to be "100 per cent Finnish-speaking."[174] With the arrival of newer and younger pastors in the 1970s, however, the congregation started the transition towards bilingual services. By the turn of the 1980s, attendance at the English-speaking services was on the rise, with weekly attendances hovering between thirty-five and forty. Since 1980 the church has had four pastors: Lari Junkkari, Markku Rautiainen (on two occasions), Markku Sarento and Kari Valanne. During their tenures, numerous improvements were made to the church, and innovative forms of religious expression were introduced.

In 1986 the congregation became part of the Evangelical Lutheran Church in Canada (ELCIC), a merger of the Lutheran Church of America and the Evangelical Lutheran Church of Canada; three years later, the congregation dropped the word "Finnish" from the official name of the church. To reflect the new organizational setting, the former *Suomi* Conference was split into two separate bodies—the Finnish (*Suomi*) Special Interest Conference of the ELCIC, consisting of thirteen congregations, and the Finnish (*Suomi*) Special Interest Conference of the Evangelical Lutheran Church in America. The two *Suomi* Conferences, however, work closely together to publish the monthly publication *Isien Usko* and the Finnish (*Suomi*) Special Interest Conference Yearbook.

St. Matthew's remains as the largest Finnish congregation in the Sudbury area, with more than 950 members. Services are held in both languages; as well, there are two choirs (Finnish Choir and Luther Bells) and two women's groups (Ladies Aid, or *Naistenpiiri*, and the Evangelical Lutheran Women). A variety of programs exist for the youth, including Sunday School (known since 1997 as Cool Kids' Corner), a confirmation and children's camp at Hannah Lake and a teens' group. Outreach services are held in the Wanup Chapel and in the town of Onaping Falls. While the pattern of Finnish dominance continues, there has been in recent years an increase in attendance at English services. By the mid-1990s, English attendance at Sunday church services accounted for 40 percent of the total.[175] These trends prompted a plea by Rev. Markku Rautiainen in 1996 for St. Matthew's to implement a Canadianization strategy leading towards the formation of a primarily English-speaking congregation.[176]

The postwar years also witnessed the strengthening of the *Wuoristo* congregation in Copper Cliff under the vigorous leadership of Rev. Lauri Pikkusaari (biography 10). A new parsonage was erected on Finland Street in 1957 to replace the former one on Poplar (now Collins Drive), originally completed in 1931. In line with the increased English-speaking orientation of the church, the name of the congregation was renamed St. Timothy's Lutheran Church in 1962. Following the departure of Pikkusaari in 1959, the church had several ministers, most serving for short periods of time.

Biography 10
Rev. Lauri Pikkusaari: Church Historian and Archivist

Born in Lapua, Finland, in 1911, Pikkusaari studied music at the Universities of Helsinki and Chicago. He married Olga Johanna Alastalo—an elementary schoolteacher and musician—in 1936. He graduated in theology from the University of Helsinki in 1937 and was ordained at Turku in the same year. He arrived in Canada in 1938 and served as a minister in the Timmins-South Porcupine area until 1943. During this interval, he and Olga had two children: Elina and Erkki. In 1943 he became the minister of the *Wuoristo* Copper Cliff Finnish Evangelical Lutheran Church in Copper Cliff. Pikkusaari served the Copper Cliff congregation for twelve years until 1958, interrupted briefly by a stint as pastor in the Kirkland Lake area. While in Copper Cliff, he established himself as a prolific writer, musician and composer. He also initiated many structural changes such as the addition of a new belfry and the construction of a parsonage on Finland Street, and instituted English-language programs and promoted church services at Creighton Mine and in Waters Township. In addition to writing poetry and musical compositions, he directed the choir.

Pikkusaari was an amateur historian and archivist in the fullest sense of those terms. He made up for any lack of historical and archival training with his love of the work and the use of his experience as a member of the Geneology Association in Helsinki. The extent of his inborn historical talent is documented in the 1948 jubilee publication entitled *Copper Cliffin Suomalaiset ja Copper Cliffin Suomalainen Evankelis-Luterilainen Wuoristo-Seurakunta* (The Copper Cliff Finns and the Copper Cliff Evangelical Lutheran *Wuoristo* Congregation) that he wrote for the fiftieth anniversary of St. Timothy's Church, a book which still serves as an excellent regional history of the Finns. He wrote a pamphlet commemorating the sixtieth anniversary of the *Wuoristo* congregation and served as the first archivist for the Finnish Canadian Historical Society. After leaving Copper Cliff, he went to Pelkie, Michigan, where he led three congregations. Pikkusaari passed away in 1965 while serving as a pastor at Ogeman, Wisconsin.

The longest serving was Rev. Yrjö Raivio. As part of the church's outreach program, monthly services were started in 1962 at the Beaver Lake Lutheran Chapel, which was constructed in 1957. An enlarged chapel was dedicated in 1972. The transition towards an English-speaking congregation was given tangible expression by the disappearance in 1985 of the *Ompeluseura* (Copper Cliff Ladies Aid), the rebirth of the Maria Club as the ELW (Evangelical Lutheran Women) in 1986 and the hiring in 1989 of Rev. Shirley Ruller as an English-speaking minister. Another major change was the disbanding in 1992 of the Martha Club, which was first started in 1932.[177] By the middle of the 1990s, more than 80 percent of worship attendance was in the English language; as well, both the ELW and St.

Timothy's choir now function largely in English. Finnish services are provided once a month using the minister from St. Matthew's Lutheran Church in Sudbury.[178] While the congregation celebrated its centenary in 1997, there remains some concern for its future due to the small size of the congregation (less than three hundred), financial problems and declining Sunday school attendance.

The Finnish Pentecostal Church in Sudbury also flourished. In the early 1950s, Eeva Kestilä, Selma Ylinen and Anna Pönni served as short-term leaders. The congregation expanded following Veikko Kyllönen's arrival from Finland in 1953. Supported by immigrants, he began a weekly radio program and started an annual summer conference for youth (1955). A summer property was purchased on St. Charles Lake in 1958. By this time the need for a new church building was evident and in 1958 the congregation purchased the former Liberty Hall on Lorne Street. After Kyllönen's departure in 1963, he was replaced by Matti Hämäläinen and Eero Pyykkönen.

In 1966 the former Haig and Whittaker Street site was sold to Societa Caruso and the existing property on Paris Street was purchased two years later. A new church, built largely with volunteer labour, was dedicated in the following year. The congregation has since been served by Aimo Selin, Taimo Maijalahti and Paavo Korpela. The congregation is well known for its youth work and for the excellence of its choir and musical performances. It also continues to offer religious programming on television. The church currently has a membership of about 150, a figure that constitutes 15 percent of the total number of Finnish Pentecostals in Canada. Links between the North American congregations have been established through *Todistaja* (Witness), a publication of the Pentecostal Churches in Canada and the United States.

Centennial Year and Finland Week

In 1967 a centennial year project was undertaken by the Knights and Ladies of Kaleva to unite the Finnish factions in the Sudbury area. Under the leadership of Keijo Kaitila and Oliver Laine, who served as the chairman and secretary of the committee respectively, some twenty Finnish clubs, congregations and associations were brought together for a centennial project under the umbrella of the Finnish Canadian Centennial Committee (Sudbury). This represented the first occasion since the Finland-Canada Aid effort of 1946 that local Finns had agreed to work co-operatively. The committee's work culminated in the holding of a highly successful *Suomi-Viikko* (Finland Week) between June 18 and 24, 1967. Nine major events were organized, including a church service, track-and-field competition, two theatrical performances, an arts and crafts show, a gymnastics performance, concert, bonfire and centennial dance. For many individuals, this brief interlude of co-operation marked one of the highlights in the history of the Sudbury Finnish community. While an attempt was made to continue the work of the group on a permanent basis, it was unsuccessful, as certain groups within the Finnish community were still unwilling to bridge existing differences.

Decline of FOC, COLFC and Vapaus

After the 1967 centennial year, the two central organizations, FOC and COLFC, rapidly declined in significance as attitudes inherited from Finland mellowed due to aging and the passing of the old guard. The change to a non-immigrant composition was also important; second- and third-generation Finns showed little interest in perpetuating former divisions and in joining many of the traditional organizations. This attitude was reflected in the demise of the two central organizations and their locals, the sale of the Finnish, *Sampo* and *Voima* Halls in Sudbury and the transformation of *Vapaus* from a newspaper to that of a volunteer monthly publication. Another contributing factor was the formation of a non-political central organization known as the Finnish Canadian Cultural Federation in 1971.

The most important post-centennial development has been the decline of the left-wing movement within the Finnish community. Whereas the FOC once had locals in about one hundred places in Canada, this number has now been reduced to three—locals only remain in Toronto, Sudbury and Wanup. The two locals in the Sudbury area exist in name only, since most of the senior members have shifted their allegiance to *Seurakerho* (The Finnish Senior Citizens' Club of Sudbury), founded in 1971. This Club has a membership of almost one hundred, of which half regularly attend weekly meetings. Many of its members reside at the Sudbury Finnish Rest Home. Meetings are held at the Jubilee Hall on Applegrove Street (the former site of the Finnish Hall) and club activities include card playing, bingos, singing, gymnastics and raffles. A popular event is the sponsoring of bus tours to other parts of Canada and the United States.[179]

Despite the small number of locals, a determined FOC national executive continues to exist. Its aims are to assist and support the newsletter *Kaiku/Echo*, to promote senior citizens' activities and to expand relationships with all other Finnish-Canadian organizations.[180] The executive also makes recommendations concerning the location of the Reunion Summer Festivals that were reestablished in 1995. Another almost-defunct body is the Finnish Canadian Amateur Sports Federation, which still has a steering committee in Toronto. FCASF continues to be represented by the Alerts-*Kisa* Athletic Club in Sudbury which owns property in the Wanup area. For the executive, the Wanup Hall remains an important symbol:

The Wanup Hall remains a symbol of the tenacity of its members who, in spite of the many difficulties involved with its upkeep, continue to proudly maintain this as the last of the great FOC Finnish Halls in Canada. We are proud of our members; of our Hall; and it is our responsibility to continue to assist in its maintenance for as long as it is in our power to do so.[181]

A similar trend occurred for the Central Organization of the Loyal Finns in Canada and the Finnish National Society of Sudbury. For many years COLFC functioned only as a paper organization, and its executive was the same as that of the Sudbury local. By the 1990s, only two locals in Sudbury and Thunder Bay remained. While a seniors' group known as *Ystävien Ympyrä* (Friendship Circle) was associated with *Sampo* Hall in 1975, it has since faded away. In 1995 the central organization COLFC was officially disbanded, thus bringing to a formal end the main central body of the Finnish conservative movement. For financial reasons, the FNSS sold *Sampo* Hall to the Sudbury *Suomi* Lions Club in 1992. The Lions Club, however, was unable to run the hall profitably and it was given back to the Society which, in turn, resold it to a church group in 1994. The Society continues to exist as a charitable organization providing financial assistance for projects of interest to the local Finnish community.

From a readership of almost 5,000 during its heyday, *Vapaus* slowly began to lose its readership, due to the aging of its supporters and the political orientation of the newer immigrants. Because of financial difficulties, *Vapaus* and *Liekki* were combined in 1974 into a weekly known as *Viikkosanomat* (Weekly News). In 1975 the operations of the *Vapaus* Publishing Company were moved to Toronto and the *Vapaus* building in Sudbury was sold. Under the editorial leadership of Veli Kentala, Helen Tarvainen, Vappu Tyyskä, Irma Laakso Milnes and Matti Mäkelä, *Viikkosanomat* published until 11 March 1991, when it was replaced by *Kaiku/Echo*, a monthly publication that first appeared in April of 1991, produced by second-generation volunteers.[182] Its contents are bilingual and the paper caters both to the original pioneers and to the children of the Finnish-Canadian left. With a subscription list that topped six hundred in 1996, the publication retains a link with the FOC and its first local, known as the Finnish Society of Toronto.[183] The remaining two Finnish newspapers in Ontario—*Vapaa Sana* and *Canadan Uutiset*—continue as weekly newspapers. With declining subscription levels, however, both of these weeklies are seeking ways of broadening their readership to include second- and third-generation Finns. It is unlikely, however, that the existing market can continue to support two newspapers on a permanent basis.

Finnish Canadian Cultural Federation

An important event occurred in Windsor on 3 July 1971, when *Kanadan Suomalainen Kulttuuriliitto* (The Finnish Canadian Cultural Federation, or FCCF) was formed.[184] Discussions concerning the need for a new central body in Canada had already taken place at the 1968, 1969 and 1970 Grand Festivals. A consensus was finally reached in 1971 that the Central Committee of the Finnish Canadian Grand Festival (FCGF), formed earlier in 1961, needed to be revamped and enlarged so that it could serve as a new national federation for all Finnish Canadians. Since 1971, the federation has emerged as the dominant umbrella organization for Finns in Canada. Its mandate has been to carry on the tradition of the Grand Festivals at various locations throughout Canada, bringing the views of the Finnish ethnic community to the attention of Canadian authorities, liaising with the Finnish government on issues such as the portability of Finnish pensions to Canada and promoting Finnish-language instruction in Canada.

While ostensibly neutral, membership in the federation for a long time consisted only of groups of a neutral or conservative character. In the 1990s the question of admitting membership to the FOC faction became topical. The reality of such participation at the local level had, in fact, already been established at the 1989 Grand Festival held in Sudbury, at which time the Finnish Senior Citizens' Club (*Seurakerho*) of Sudbury gave a gymnastics performance. This was a watershed event, as it represented the first time that a group associated with the FOC had been invited to give a formal performance at a Grand Festival. The FOC National Executive then made a formal request in 1994 to the federation that it be permitted to join as a member group. This petition was rejected on the basis that membership in the FCCF was not open to other central organizations. The situation was resolved in 1995 when a decision was reached that locals or groups associated with the FOC, but not the parent body itself, could join the federation and participate in the annual festivals.[185]

In 1996 the FCCF celebrated its twenty-fifth anniversary at the Grand Festival held in Timmins, Ontario. As the central body for more than fifty organizations throughout Canada, it could now claim to be truly representative of the Finnish-Canadian community. To celebrate this role, it has spearheaded efforts to organize a festival in the year 2000, to be jointly held with FinnFest USA, its counterpart in the United States.[186] Conceived in 1982, FinnFest USA has sponsored national festivals since 1983. While many festivals had previously been held in the United States, they were mainly of a local or regional nature only.[187] While the Finn Grand Fest celebration will be held in Toronto, the event is intended to also commemorate the memory of the Finnish scientist/explorer Pehr Kalm through the erection of a plaque in his honor at Niagara Falls. This first event of the next millennium is significant as it may well herald the beginning of a new and perhaps permanent relationship between Canadian and American Finns.

Despite the success of the FCCF, a number of concerns have arisen regarding its effectiveness; at the annual meeting held in Sault Ste. Marie in 1997, for example, measures were approved to raise the future profile of the FCCF, to improve links with its member bodies and to increase the attendance of Finnish-Canadian youth at the annual festivals.[188] With respect to the latter, one youthful participant made the following observation:

> Young people are neither interested nor inspired by the grand festivals. . . . The issue is not simply a question of language, but also of our roots . . . but, at the same time, the language issue will not go away. . . . I only have a hazy view of the future. . . . What is clear, however, is that the festivals in their present shape will not long endure. . . . Certain changes are obviously needed.[189]

Finnish Institutions and the Canadianization Process

One important question remains to be answered. What effect did the extensive nature of Finnish institutional development in the Sudbury area have on the Canadianization of immigrant newcomers? Past studies in North America have focused on two aspects of the role that ethnic institutions have had in terms of language and assimilation effects. While some researchers assert that such institutions played a ghettoizing role by emphasizing language and old country customs, others have maintained the opposite, claiming that they served as the first pathways to Canadianization.[190] For the latter proponents, the institutional mix was positive, as it served as a nursery for the cultivation of "two patriotisms."

Finnish institutions in Canada officially espoused the merits of cultural pluralism. While they continued to function in the Finnish language, most organizations nonetheless had statements of intent and articles of incorporation that supported the principle of assimilation. In 1923, for example, the FOC's constitution approved as one of its objectives "to assimilate the Finnish-speaking people of Canada with the native population by instilling in their minds the benefits of Canadian citizenship, by the teaching of the English language, by disseminating true information about the laws, customs, traditions, history and current events in Canada and by a lawful and intelligent use of the rights and duties of Canadian citizenship."[191] Not to be outdone, the Loyal Finns, too, proclaimed in its 1931 constitution that the purpose of the society was "to unite the Finns in a patriotic and educational way, to raise their intellectual and economic standard, to maintain contacts with the old homeland, to make Finland and the Finns known to

Canadians, and to acquaint the Finns with Canada and Canadians and that way prepare good and loyal citizens for Canada."[192]

There were aspects of Finnish individual and organizational behaviour prior to World War II that did not at first blush reflect this intent. Leftist Finns, for example, sought independent status in national political organizations and fought vigorously against full integration. Ahlqvist, however, suggested that these apparent ghettoizing effects actually had an opposite effect. In a classic letter written to the deputy minister of Justice in 1918, he put forward an eloquent defence on behalf of the FOC and *Vapaus* against legislation declaring certain foreign-language organizations unlawful. He made the proposition that the retention of the Finnish language and the residential segregation of the Finns actually fostered the assimilation process:

> From the point of view of narrow nationalism it is of course unfortunate that any part of the population in any country is using a language other than the historic and official language of the country. The Dominion of Canada, however, ... must make the best of the natural impediment which the presence of a foreign-speaking population presents. Such elimination of these impediments ... does not lie in preventing the foreign speaking people from employing their native language. ... An opportunity to develop such interests is the greatest incentive to the immigrant not only in bringing him to the country but, what is most important, in making him stay in the country, partake in the development of the national resource and as far as possible, assimilate himself with the native population, leaving all thoughts of a return to the land from which he came.
>
> A prohibition to use their native tongue in collective enterprises of an economic or intellectual character is, at least to the Finns, analogous with taking away from them the most essential means of enjoying those advantages of civic life, which have brought them to the country, and which make them stay here, gradually making them fullfledged Canadians, not only in respect to their interests and activities but in their language as well. The logical result of a prohibition will be not only a cessation of further immigration, but, as indications already show, a movement to leave the country in great numbers,—and, as we will endeavour to show ... the interests of the Dominion would require a retention of the industrious, clean mannered and efficient Finnish immigrant.
>
> Narrow nationalism regards as a calamity the fact that foreign speaking people in Canada segregate in colonies and in these colonies develop activities in their own language, Such segregation and such activities are regarded as an obstacle to assimilation and Canadization [*sic*]. ... [W]e, however, beg to make the rejoinder that foreign segregation and activities in a foreign tongue are not a *cause* but a *result* of the inability to use the official language of the country. The alternative is not *an elimination of foreign segregation* nor activities in the English language among the native population, but a *continuance of segregation.*[193]

Wilson believes that this letter represents one of the best and earliest defences in Canada of the merits of cultural pluralism or multiculturalism. At the same time, the letter can be used to support the argument that the Finnish language and segregation served as effective long-term melting-pot mechanisms, assisting immigrants in making the necessary adjustments to their new homeland.

Since the leftist organizations had less interest in traditions binding them to Finland, it is arguable that they were more effective at assimilation than their conservative counterparts, who continued to foster old country customs and usages. For the latter groupings, their close association with the state of Finland and *Suomi* Synod/*Suomi* Conferences had the effect of maintaining these ties at a higher level. This is especially true for the church; as Glad has asserted, Finnish congregations do not seem to follow the traditional path of North Americanization or Canadianization.[194] Unlike the situation in the United States, where language divisions began to appear in the Lutheran Church as early as the 1920s, the same situation did not occur in Canada until the 1960s. Part of the reason for this tighter linkage lies in the fact that the Lutheran Church in Finland has supported strong ties by sending pastors to Canada. This frequent exchange has given the Finnish congregations a natural bridge to the homeland and its culture.

The above notwithstanding, the fact that the institutional infrastructure was so extensive had the practical effect of lessening the need for Finns to fully integrate themselves with Canadian society. Given the extensive network of halls, newspapers, businesses and churches, Finns found it easy to pursue their everyday activities in the Finnish language. Thus, while purporting to be agents of assimilation, the widespread influence of these institutions within the community may actually have had an opposite effect. The geographical dispersal of the Finns was also significant. As Maunula has demonstrated with respect to the Thunder Bay area, the fact that many Finns continued to reside in urban and rural enclaves until the 1980s mitigated the need for them to interact with the larger non-Finnish community.[195] This isolation probably contributed more to their slowness in learning the English language and in becoming Canadian citizens than did any overt decision to remain "Finnish." Laine has suggested that there was yet another factor hindering the assimilation process—the formidable cultural barriers that were erected to prevent the Finns from entering Canadian society:

> [C]onditions were such that the early Finnish-Canadian community (including its Canadian-born members) was left with no alternative but to accept its innate Finnishness as the fundamental quality of its being. Therefore, it was no matter of choice for this community but one of necessity to create its own cultural environment in which its members could participate as complete human beings.[196]

CHAPTER IV

Finns in the Workplace

Finns were no exception to the immigrant axiom that they came to Canada as working people. For them, normal channels of capital accumulation, through inheritance of money and property, land ownership and credit resources, were cut off by the act of immigration to a new homeland. When Finns arrived in Canada they understood explicitly that survival rested in their own hands. Survival, in turn, meant a job. The need to work also represented the fulfilment of the Protestant work ethic or the necessary means by which they could return to Finland with money in their pockets.[1]

Prior to World War II, the Finnish role in the workplace was largely blue collar, and was linked mainly to jobs in transportation, mining, construction, forestry, agriculture and domestic service. Some of the more enterprising Finns operated as craftsmen serving the internal needs of the immigrant group; others managed to make the economic jump to businesses that made them part of the community merchant class. Only a select few attained what could be called professional status.

The workplace changed considerably after World War II. While the immigrant wave of the 1950s sustained the earlier trend favouring blue-collar occupations, a number of second- and third-generation Finns demonstrated upward economic mobility through entry into the white-collar labour force, especially in the health, education and government sectors. In the latter occupations, they succeeded in attaining positions of regional leadership and prominence. Upward mobility was spurred, in part, by the greater emphasis given to schooling by their immigrant parents, who saw education as being the key to enhanced economic status. This emphasis on education notwithstanding, many younger Finns still shied away from

Notes to Chapter IV are on pp. 292-96.

post-secondary opportunities in the 1950s and 1960s with the knowledge that blue-collar jobs were plentiful and well paid.

Labour Force (1883-1945)

From the 1880s to World War II, Finns in the labour force consisted largely of farmers and unskilled workers in the resource industries. This was a natural occurrence, as most came from rural areas with limited skills in the trades. Three traits could be associated with these blue-collar Finns. The first was the development of a solid reputation as being hardworking, reliable and efficient workers. Secondly, Finns helped to forge a philosophy of class consciousness underpinned by a strong belief in workers' rights and the union movement. A third distinguishing feature was the high degree of female participation both in the workplace and as volunteer workers within the leftist movement.

Due to the scattered distribution of the Finnish population, small businesses sprouted in every rural enclave and urban Finntown for the provision of goods and services to the ethnic community. In the more urbanized areas of Sudbury and Copper Cliff, some flourished to such an extent that they became well known in the non-Finnish community. Others sought economic advancement through post-secondary education and entry into professions such as nursing and engineering.

Transportation

The first Finnish workers in the Sudbury area were those temporarily headquartered at the Sudbury Junction and engaged in the construction of the CPR main line in 1883-84. Because of their favourable reputation as workers, the CPR hired other Finns as the main line moved westward towards Manitoba. In 1902 one Settlement Branch official observed that on "the Can. Pac. Ry. mainline, west from Sudbury as far as Port Arthur, the majority of the section hands consist of Finlanders, who have remained on the road since its construction."[2] On the 126-mile rail line from Cartier to Chapleau there were so many Finns that of the twenty-five sections in the division, there were thirteen totally Finnish, meaning that in each of these sections there was a Finnish boss, section foreman and workmen. This identification with railway employment was a carry-over from Finland, where a large program of railway line construction had been initiated during the latter part of the 1800s. Even after the turn of the century, Finns continued to provide an important source of labour for railway construction jobs in the region of Sudbury.

The lot of the Finns in railway construction was not easy. The work was hard and often dangerous. The company held absolute power and the construction manager was also the Justice of the Peace. There was no union and the workers could be discharged, taken to court and sentenced by one man, the construction manager. With no place to go on Saturday night and no other place to spend their money except in the company store and the mail-order service, it is not surprising that Finns abandoned these railway construction jobs for alternative employment opportunities elsewhere.

Mining and Construction

Copper Cliff emerged as the first place of permanent employment for Finnish immigrants. The first group of Finns who arrived there in 1885 consisted of eleven men, of whom four immediately acquired employment as unskilled workers with the Canadian Copper Company. The circumstances surrounding their arrival has been described by Thomas Jacobson:

> There were 11 of us who took "ship" with a hotel keeper in New York in order to obtain employment. We were supposed to get to construct the railway on the Sault line, on the stretch between Algoma and Sault Ste. Marie. As we arrived by boat from Collingwood to Algoma, there was no work going on. There was nothing to be done but to start walking along the already constructed railroad toward Sudbury, where jobs were available. We arrived on Midsummer Day in 1885 in Copper Cliff. Four of us got work right away including myself. At that time the copper company employed no more than two men and a foreman. When we were added to the pay roll there were a total of seven the majority of whom were Finns. Later on new men were hired, and they came from New York and later from Montreal. I was the youngest of the bunch, a mere 19-year-old lad. I am also the first Finn at Inco, and the fourth to be employed by Inco.[3]

Finns were later hired by the Canadian Copper Company at its Evans, Stobie, Crean Hill, Vermilion and Creighton mines. Following its incorporation in 1902, Mond Nickel Company also became a major employer of Finns at its Victoria, Worthington, Kirkwood, Garson and Levack mines. Finns were hired at these sites both as miners and construction labourers.

In the early years of the mining industry, Finns assumed a dominant role in drilling and blasting jobs, and comprised an important part of the overall mine personnel. They constituted the majority of the front-end miners known as drill runners and drill helpers.[4] Drill runners were responsible for opening drifts and stopes, whereas drill helpers assisted in the transport or operation of a pneumatic drill mounted on a tripod. Boring holes into the walls of the stope, the men used either gelignite or dynamite to blast quantities of ore from the section being worked. Once the ceiling of the stope was broken, they enlarged the hole thus constructed. At the Mond Nickel Company in 1911, for example, 66 percent of the drill runners and 62 percent of the drill helpers were Finns.[5] Other areas of mining employment included carpentry, shoring and the mechanical fields. Finns were especially sought after as timbermen for the developmental phases of mining. John Passi states that these Finnish workers constituted rovers who went from mine to mine and from company to company as the need arose.[6]

From articles published in the *Inco Triangle*, it is clear that the work habits of the Finns drew the admiration of Inco officials. They were referred to as being a band of "skilled, hard-driving miners who specialized in shaft sinking and who developed a tradition in the Nickel Belt for speed and efficiency in this kind of work."[7] Over the years, numerous references were made regarding the reliability and dedication of the Finnish workers. In various reminiscences, Emil Kiviaho was referred to during his forty-seven years of service as being a "machine doctor," an "inventor," a "living legend" and an employee who never lost a shift at Creighton mine, despite travelling seventeen miles to and from the mine on skis during the winter months.[8] On their retirements, similar tributes were made to other Finns, such as Matti Sirka who was called "dependable and efficient"; Kosti Tulisalo as "an able and steady tradesman"; Charlie Saari as a "steady workman"; Nestor Matson with a "fine record of Garson service"; Pete Akkanen as "one of the finest men who ever worked in the Copper Cliff Smelter plant"; John Suoranta as "solid"; and Gus Bontinen as having performed "valuable service."[9]

Employment in the mining industry, however, was uncertain and hazardous. In the early days of mining, there were many fatal accidents due to falling rocks from cracks and fissures that were difficult to see, as the sole source of light was from the candle in the miner's cap. Accidents involving explosives were common. As Finns preferred underground rather than surface metallurgical operations, they were highly prone to such incidents. From 1890 to 1939, 189 Finns died in mining accidents in Ontario.[10] In the Sudbury area alone, fifty-three Finns were killed while working in mines between 1886 and 1930.[11] According to one study for 1912-13, 24 percent of all accidents with the CCC involved Finns.[12] For drill runners and helpers, the comparable figure was more than 60 percent. The annual reports of the Ontario Bureau of Mines provide numerous examples of such mishaps. The 1902 report, for instance, noted the following:

> Another fatal accident . . . occurred on 3rd April in the Canadian Copper Company No. 2 mine, when two Finlanders named Emil Sarminen and John Kuski were killed. The men were working under the brow of the stope at the entrance of a drift when a piece of ore weighing about two tons fell upon them from a height of 10 or 12 feet and instantly crushed them to death. It is stated that the ground at this point was scaled the day before the accident and again on the morning of the day the fall took place, and that all the men working in the pit were satisfied there was no

danger. The surface of the ore which fell showed some frost, indicating that there was a seam into which the frost had penetrated, and that as the frost came out the block of ore was loosened. An inquest was held by Dr. Struthers. The jury simply found that the men accidentally came to their death by being crushed under falling ground, without attempting to place the responsibility for the occurrence upon any one.[13]

Two other accounts involving the CCC were found in the Bureau's 1907 annual report:

On 20th June a Finlander laborer named Rusta Stanros (or Stenaras) while attempting to get on the foot-board of a locomotive which was backing up after having been connected with two cars loaded with rock, missed his footing, fell on the rails and was immediately killed. At the company's request Coroner Oliver held an inquest. The jury returned a verdict of death through misadventure. . . .

In the course of making some alterations in the hoisting apparatus at No. 2 mine, two Finlanders named Matti Vaysi (also written Warri) and Frank Salo, the former a trammer and latter a drill runner, were killed. . . . Coroner Oliver decided that an inquest was required, and accordingly a jury was empanelled, which after hearing the evidence, rendered the following verdict: "We, the jury, find that Matti Vaysi and Frank Salo came to their death through an accident, the clamp giving way and the cable slipping through and throwing them on the skip track. The cable was covered with grease, and no doubt the weight of the rope overcame the pressure of the clamp, but the jury's verdict did not place censure upon any one.[14]

Nor was the Mond Nickel Company immune to similar tragedies. The Bureau's 1912 annual report noted that "at the Garson mine, January 29th, Otto Heinanen, machine-runner, was killed falling into the chute of No. 32 stope."[15] Equally important were the large number of serious, but non-fatal, accidents that resulted in men being crippled for life and unable to work any longer for the mining companies.

Lumbering

Another sector where Finns were active was in the lumbering industry. The fact that they came to Canada familiar with wood operations in Finland provided them with an advantage over other ethnic workers. Many worked in lumber camps in the winter to achieve a living standard they could not derive from agriculture alone. Rural Finns readily found forestry employment on the outer fringes of the Sudbury area at places such as Nairn Centre, Spragge-Mississaga and Lake Panache. During the 1920s there were twenty large operating companies in and around Sudbury; at Webbwood and Massey alone, 2,000 men were employed annually in logging, sawmilling, river driving and towing.

Biography 11
Oliver Korpela: The Woodsman

Oliver Korpela was born on 18 June 1920 in Nemegos, located some thirty kilometres east of Chapleau on the CPR line. His grandfather (John) and father (Kalle) came here from Finland in 1905 and 1909 respectively. His grandfather worked in the lumbering industry as a logging contractor (jobber), cutting and delivering logs to be sawn into mining timbers and railway ties, while his grandmother ran the boarding house where the lumberjacks stayed. After John died, Kalle ran a number of lumber camps. Until he went to school at the age of eight, the only languages Oliver heard spoken by the twenty or so families who lived at Nemegos were French, Finnish and Cree. He had many exciting experiences as a youngster involving hunting, fishing, trapping, canoeing, skiing and swimming. In 1931 the family moved to Sudbury. During the 1930s he attended Central, Alexander and Minnow Lake Public Schools. He acquired one year of high school before returning to the lumber camps.

At the lumber camps he became familiar with scaling, bookkeeping and retail selling in the small camp store. During World War II, he enlisted as an administrative clerk at Trenton, Ontario. Despite his limited high school education, he was chosen for pilot training and posted to Cap de la Madeleine in Quebec and Centralia in Ontario. He graduated as a pilot officer and was posted to England where, after an evening of drinking, he was almost court marshalled for knocking out an RCAF officer. He then reenlisted in the RAF Bomber Command and was posted to Skellingthorpe. In September 1944 he was shot down in the Netherlands. Aided by the Dutch underground, and disguised as a mute Dutch tailor, he eluded capture by the Germans until the country was liberated by the British.

Following his return to Canada in 1945, he worked for the Kormak Lumber Company (named after his father and Oscar Mäki), which had been incorporated the previous year. Frank Korpela, a junior partner of the firm, later formed Wesmak in 1953. Oliver worked as a scaler, operated the company's two sawmills at Kormak and Nemegos, ran a number of lumber camps and did some charter flying on a part-time basis. The Kormak company was among the first to do extensive timber cruising from the air. After the great Mississauga fire of 1948, two mills were erected at Flame Lake to make ties.

Using Finnish immigrants for his bush crews, Oliver started Island Lake Lumber Company in 1950. After the death of his father and Oscar Mäki around the turn of the 1960s, Oliver became president of the Kormak, Island Lake and Wesmak operations; these were subsequently amalgamated under the umbrella of Wesmak Lumber Company Ltd. In 1966 he acquired, in partnership with Cliff Fielding, the Biglow Lumber Company located at Devon, Ontario. He eventually became the sole owner and operated the mill until it burned down. Wesmak merged with Chapleau Lumber Company Ltd. in 1981 to form Chapleau Forest Products Ltd. A unique energy plant was constructed in 1986 that produced electricity using waste from the three sawmills in Chapleau.

When Oliver learned of the local interest in erecting a Finnish seniors' facility in Sudbury, he promised to donate land in the Minnow Lake area for the project. This promise was fulfilled in 1983 when he gave twenty-seven acres of rural land off Fourth Avenue to the Sudbury Finnish Rest Home Society. This generous gift set the stage for the eventual construction of a multi-staged Finnish seniors' complex.

In 1995 he sold his interests in Chapleau Forest Products Ltd.

Employment in the lumber camps was easy to obtain as "the Finns proved to be as good and as sought after as French Canadians."[16] Woods managers ranked Finns among the best producers and cutters in the logging camps. While not as energetic as the French Canadians, Finns were considered to be more steady and consistent. Studies also showed that Finns were better at cleaning up their cutting area, which facilitated subsequent steps in the logging process, and that they kept their camps tidier. On the other hand, operators complained that Finns used too much butter and sugar, and cost 15 percent more to feed than French Canadians.[17]

Starting as lumberjacks, Finns often progressed to pulpwood cutting. Some pulpwood operations in Northern Ontario became virtually 100 percent Finnish.[18] The extent to which lumbering affected the Sudbury area can be ascertained from the lament of a *Vapaus* correspondent that winter activities among the Vermilion River Finns were infrequent as "virtually all the farmers had gone to lumber camps."[19] The opportunities afforded by lumbering and pulpwood cutting operations provided economic stability during the winter months for Finnish rural enclaves such as Lorne Township. Sudbury benefited from this activity as it was the major source of supply for employment agencies seeking wood workers. Among the rising young entrepreneurs who provided employment for Finns was Oliver Korpela (biography 11).

As was the case in the mining industry, jobs in forestry involved work that was backbreaking, exhausting and dangerous. The use of axes, horses and saws and the threat from falling trees inevitably led to high carnage in the bush. Finnish bush workers were also forced to handle and pile eight-foot bolts. As one cutter recalls, "I nearly killed myself making eight-foot piles. . . . Many of those logs had ten-inch diameter tops, I found myself crying, it was such strenuous work."[20] River driving, which included the need for jam breaking and dynamiting, also exacted a high toll. The following poem, penned by a Finnish immigrant who cut pulpwood in the Shield country, serves as a poignant reminder of the dangers of logging:

Kalle Koski's Last Testament

It happened on a job like this:

A gang was hauling logs.
The chain broke with a clang.
We came down the hill at breakneck speed;
The load burst apart with a crash.
Others fled.
Kalle Koski tripped on a chunk of snow:
The luckless fellow was pinned beneath the logs.
They rushed to his side
and took away the log
that had felled the frightened Kalle.
Johnson—the boss—examined the wounds.
"Men, this is death.
His spine has been badly injured."
"Let me rest in peace," uttered a deathly pale Kalle Koski.
The expression on his face is earnest; he is
speechless. He was very fond of the dying man.
"You were my best friend," said Kalle Koski.
"Our roads part: I remain here."
"This is my last request:
Look for my picture—You remember the one—
Somewhere . . . it might be in my wallet.
Take it, along with my love, to my fiancé
My gold watch—that is yours.
Tear open my shirt:
I hid my dollars in a pocket.
Send them to my old mother in Perho.
Write to her saying
I remembered her, and my childhood."
Then his head suddenly jerked:
He had passed through the gates of the House of Death.
So ended the journey of one wanderer—Kalle Koski.
Born in Perho, Died Now.
In the forest, beneath the skies of Canada.[21]

Farming

One of the main ambitions for Finns was to become a part- or full-time farmer. Before migrating to Canada, many had been crofters, that is, they belonged to the landless class; for them, the acquisition of rural land became a deep-rooted obsession. This is revealed by the place names on maps that Finns in Canada gave their farming areas such as *Intola* (Enthusiasm), *Tarmola* (Energy) and *Toimela* (Accomplishment). The attraction of agriculture was rooted in part by their dreams of an ideal society. While industrial jobs were seen as tedious and dangerous, the countryside was the place where they could regain their souls and replicate agricultural life as it had been in Finland.[22] Kalle Sillanpää, for example, came to the Beaver Lake area even though, as the oldest son of a farmer, he stood to gain by remaining in Finland. He was successful in this pursuit. When his father died, he owned five times more land in the Beaver Lake area than he would have been entitled to in Finland.[23]

As noted earlier, by the time the Finns arrived in the Sudbury area, much of the best agricultural land had already been settled by French Canadians or withdrawn from public sale. Only the more peripheral land in the Beaver Lake, Vermilion, Whitefish, Waters Township, Long Lake and Wanup districts remained. Thus, it was left to the empty-handed Finns to mine the stumps and stones of these marginal lands for root crops, pasture, dairy and beef herds.[24] For these farmers, owning land was worth all the hardships they had to endure. With reference to Beaver Lake, one pioneering settler recalled the following: "[E]veryone was poor, everyone was empty handed. Those with empty hands cannot go to the better lands, rather they come where land can be gotten . . . for fifty cents an acre. . . . They were not able to go and buy good land, the good lands were all previously taken."[25] While the original intention of the typical immigrant may have been to return to the homeland, the acquisition of a farm usually bound the settler permanently to the Sudbury area. At the beginning, farming served as a supplementary form of income on top of wages from mining or forestry. When enough land had been cleared, and with wives and children now handling many of the chores, only then did full-time farming become a viable option.

The migration wave of the 1920s brought to the Sudbury area more Finns who went directly into farming. As *The Sudbury Star* observed:

> Large numbers of immigrants have passed through Sudbury during the past few weeks. Many of these were Finlanders and over 100 of them stopped off at Sudbury and other points in the district. . . . A few of the Finns found work in the mines but the majority have gone out to the farming districts and have found work with friends on the Finnish settlements . . . with the hope of building up homesteads for themselves.[26]

The year 1924 was noteworthy. In this year Finns accounted for 40 percent of all land applications in the district. Some of these requests involved lands in "free grant" townships such as Broder, Neelon, Garson and Dill, while others were associated with the "sale" townships that included Cleland, Dryden, Louise, Lorne and Waters. In free grant townships, each applicant was entitled to 160 acres free of all charges on fulfilling certain conditions. These requirements included residing on the property for six months of each year, the erection of a habitable dwelling measuring at least sixteen feet by twenty feet and the clearing of a minimum of two acres of land each year. If the settler had fifteen acres under cultivation after three years, and was a British subject, a deed would be granted. In the sale townships, land was sold at fifty cents an acre and the buyer had to assume the same conditions as required under the free grant program.[27]

It did not take long for the Finnish farmer to acquire a solid reputation in line with his counterparts in the mining and forestry industries. As early as 1892, the *Sudbury Journal* wrote the following about the first Finnish farmer in the Sudbury area who left for Manitoba after selling a mining claim in Denison Township: "Mikki Myllymäkki [*sic*], the Finlander . . . is a superior man in every way, and will be greatly missed from here, but Manitoba will get an honest, industrious, self-reliant, good settler."[28] In another article in *The Sudbury Star*, it was concluded that John Salo managed after 1905 to make a prosperous farm out of land that had previously been "regarded as hopeless."[29] By the 1920s the basic character of the Finnish farmer had become well established:

> A few years ago the greater number of the Finlanders in this part of the country were engaged in the mines but when the period of depression came and mine forces were cut to the limit these were thrown on their own resources and it was then that they proved themselves good settlers. In a district where farming was not known as one of the successful operations, many of them settled, and by hard labour built up small farms. They farmed, hunted, trapped and fished. They made a living and the Finnish settlements at Long Lake, along the Vermilion River, and out near Worthington are the results. At these points the Finnish settler is running his farm and making money at it. He has built up a little community and each is independent. Each settlement has its own baker, shoemaker and its own tannery. One of the admirable characteristics of the Finnish settlers in this district is that they never grumble. They never admit that they have trouble. They seem to smile it away.[30]

In 1932 *The Sudbury Star* continued this favourable treatment. The newspaper praised the fact that many farmers in Dryden and Cleland Townships displayed the spirit of the early pioneers by hewing out homes in these rural areas rather than accepting relief. The fact that they were squatters on land that was officially closed because of sulphur fumes and timber limits seemed of little consequence. As the supervisor of Settlements stated, "all credit to these squatters. They have no legal right to the land they are on, but it is doubtful if the government will put them off."[31] Fortunately for these squatters, the province and the federal government introduced an assistance scheme in 1932 that permitted them to legally acquire eighty-acre homesteads in fifteen local areas, including Dryden, Cleland,

Dill, Broder and Waters Townships. An integral feature of this program was the explicit encouragement by government officials for land seekers to settle in groups where they would be among their own people.[32] This aspect of the scheme worked well in Dryden Township, where farms south of highway 17 were taken by Finns and those to the north by French-speaking settlers.

Farming by Finns reached its height in the 1930s when high unemployment levels and the threat of deportation encouraged many of them to retreat to the land. While dairy farming predominated, many farms depended as well on beef herds, root crops and the raising of chickens and pigs. While farming was sufficient to provide daily sustenance for the family, the continuing unemployment in urban areas and the weak economy resulted in little monetary flow. As one Finnish farmer in the Long Lake area recalled, "there simply was no such thing as cash at the time."[33] Frequent calls were made to government officials by Finnish farmers to improve the lot of farming.[34] After the turn of the 1940s, the marginal nature of these cleared lands, new legislative requirements for dairy farming, the lack of enthusiasm shown by immigrant children for farming and the good wages offered by the mining industry resulted in a slow but continual decline of farming by the Finnish population.

Workers' Rights and the Labour Movement

The Finnish working-class immigrants who came to the Sudbury area in the early 1900s were offended by the prevailing economic status quo, which made them easy subjects of capitalist exploitation. They showed little hesitation in fostering organized resistance in the form of workers' organizations and the union movement. Unlike the earlier Finns who had seemed so quiescent and malleable, those who arrived later were ardent advocates of unions and socialism.[35] Whether they came from Finland or the United States, workers in the mining and forestry industries began to express dissatisfaction regarding safety conditions, wages, lack of employment security, fringe benefits and the eighty-four-hour work week. Particularly irksome to them was the fact that employment could be brought to an end by the whim of a boss or senior administrator, especially where involvement in union activities was suspected. For those Finns who came from the mining areas of Minnesota and Michigan, this corporate tactic sometimes resulted in yet another round of blacklisting of their names and termination of employment. A few workers reacted to this threat by changing their names to English equivalents. For others, however, it was socialism and the labour movement that held the most promise for redressing the concerns in the Northern Ontario environment.

Support for radicalism was stimulated by the presence of articulate and highly motivated Finnish leftists from Finland and the United States. These individuals were highly dedicated representatives of workers' rights whose oratory proved capable of swaying the working class towards the labour movement.[36] Even *The Sudbury Star* was moved on one occasion to state the following regarding John Wirta, one of the leftist leaders in the area:

> Mr. Wirta speaks in a quiet, restrained voice, with none of the unrestrained language or fanatical fervour one hears from Communist soap boxes. He gives one the impression, despite his lack of English and his rough exterior, that he is a student who has read deeply and thoughtfully, that his convictions have come as a result of study, and not by emotional excitement.[37]

Finnish working-class radicalism in Sudbury expressed itself most strongly in the mining industry, where the eighty-four-hour work week and dangerous conditions were the norm. Hazardous conditions in the mines, and the feeling among the workers that coroners' investigations always absolved the mining companies of negligence in the deaths of miners, encouraged Finns to turn to socialism and unionism as a match to corporate power.[38] The first strikes at the Canadian Copper Company in 1899, 1903 and 1904 were led by Italians; it was not until 1909 that Finnish activism started at the Mond mine in Garson. When the mine supervisor demanded that a Finn by the name of Gus Viitasaari pay for a damaged tool, he was fired for his refusal to do so. Despite the lack of a union, the next shift went on strike demanding that he be rehired and not forced to pay for the drill. The Mond Company reluctantly agreed to this first show of strength among the Finns.[39] From this point on, the trail of the Finnish mine worker could be seen in every subsequent major strike.

Another step towards reform took place in 1911 with the founding of the Finnish Socialist Organization of Canada. The FSOC worked closely with the WFM, a Colorado-based radical union formed in the United States in 1893 that fought strenuously for better mine regulation, the eight-hour day, workmen's compensation and trade union rights.[40] This union was the first to appear on the scene in Northern Ontario; it organized locals at Cobalt, Elk Lake, Gowganda, Porcupine, Silver Centre and Swastika/Kirkland Lake between 1906 and 1910. John Ajola, a local Finn, acted as the secretary-treasurer of the first WFM local in Garson, which was organized in 1913. Another WFM local was formed in Sudbury in the same year. From these starting points, union activity spread to the Mond mines at Stobie, Gertrude and Worthington and the CCC's mines at Creighton, Crean Hill and Copper Cliff. John Penttinen recalls some of the early influences that led to union activity:

Because the circumstances were not to our liking, we started to think about what we had to do in order to improve conditions a little. So we decided first to found a Finnish socialist local. But this caused some difficulty because only a few had enough courage to join the local. They said that if "the nickel company gets to know that we belong to a socialist local, we will be without a job." Despite everything we continued to hold meetings. . . . Then we started dealing with the issue of the eight hour work day. Meetings were held in all Sudbury area mines on account of the demand for an eight hour work day. Representatives were elected from different mines to attend a meeting at the Sudbury Town Hall. The chairman of the meeting was the Ontario Minister of Mines. Although the meeting led to no fast or specific results, it gave the initial push to the struggle for the eight hour day.

However, an even stronger push in the fight for the eight hour day came from the miners' union that was founded in different parts of Ontario. So we also founded the Western Federation of Miners local No. 182 in Garson. Later on a union local was also founded in Sudbury. . . . We were not allowed to operate in peace for long before the nickel company started to cause difficulties and to hamper activities and the strengthening of the union. They started to dismiss Finnish workers and replaced them with others. . . . After the union membership lists had, through a vile crime, passed into the hands of the anti-union employers, persecution and blacklisting followed, leading to the cessation of Western Federation of Miners' activities in the Sudbury area.[41]

The pursuit of unionism by Finns at the Mond Nickel Company worried the management of the CCC. According to one official, it was important "to watch certain of our employees as they are liable to get filled with the idea that they are of very considerable importance."[42] To offset the growth of unionism, the CCC, following the trend set by its industrial counterparts in the United States, hired a detective agency to spy on union activity. The company was so adamant in this regard that it promised to close entire properties should unionism succeed at any of its operations. Raids were undertaken at the offices of the Sudbury and Garson locals in 1915 and membership lists were used to blacklist union members, the majority of whom were Finnish miners. The existence of blacklisting was made public at the hearings of the Royal Commission on Industrial Relations held in Sudbury on 17 May 1919 where the following testimony was given: "I know that immediately a man takes an active part in labour organization he is discharged from his position. . . . Finlanders, mostly. Bright people, intelligent people, were especially persecuted in this regard. When there is slack time, they are the first to be laid off."[43]

By 1916 the fledgling union movement had been crushed. The WFM disbanded and was reorganized as the International Union of Mine, Mill and Smelter Workers (IUMMSW). Politicians exploited the "Red scare" issue to discredit the FSOC and to isolate it from the mainstream of the labour movement. Finnish miners thus had to bide their time and place their trust in the future. Despite its failures, the WFM did help to win some reforms, such as the enactment of the eight-hour day for underground workers and the institution in 1915 of Workmen's Compensation for the casualties of the mining industry.[44]

The 1920s remained a bleak time for the miners' movement. For many years the CPC, FSOC/FOC and the Mine Workers' Union of Canada were the only groups active in the miners' movement. Union rivalries involving the OBU and IWW, and internal differences within the Finnish community likewise hindered Finnish efforts at working-class reform. As *The Sudbury Star* noted,

> [T]here are as many different forms of radicalism in the labor world, as there are denominations in religion. A Socialist is not necessarily an Anarchist, an Anarchist is not necessarily a Bolshevist, a Bolshevist is not necessarily a Laborite, a Laborite is not necessarily a Red, a Red is not necessarily a Communist. . . . Similarly . . . the Red Finns and the White Finns don't mix. With opposition from those of their own countrymen who are opposed to Red doctrine and with but a small numerical strength, the Communists . . . have little chance to do any actual harm.[45]

Also important was the ability of the Canadian Copper Company to offset union activity through the use of corporate power. This was achieved in many ways. First, effective use was made of the company's monopoly. With more than 110,000 acres of prime mineral lands and strong financial backing from Ohio interests, the company was able, in the 1890s, to acquire a monopoly over Sudbury nickel and copper production. Aside from Canada's two railways, the company stood as a giant within the national economy. The power of the CCC was strengthened in 1902 when it became a subsidiary of the International Nickel Company controlled by the United States Steel Corporation. The company was so influential that Nelles concluded that "in mining, it would seem that the regulated group experienced greater success in bringing the regulator under control than the other way around."[46]

By 1913 the Sudbury area had the giant's share of the world's nickel supply, with 90 percent of proven reserves of nickel and more than 70 percent of annual output. Attempts made by the federal and provincial governments to regulate workers' conditions within the industry were easily thwarted. There was the added significance of the incorporation of Copper Cliff as a company town in 1901. This allowed the CCC to control both the town council and its police force. As Nicholson has observed, "the incorporation of the Town of Copper Cliff in 1901 . . . heralded an age of corporate control that was complex, ruthless and complete."[47] As the CCC owned 75 percent of the town's buildings before World War I, it had power over housing and the ability to evict tenants deemed undesirable.[48] The company rarely used this option, though, preferring instead to use other methods to lessen employee discontent. The case involving the socialist leader John Wirta is instructive. When Wirta offered his boarding house for sale in 1914, the CCC concluded that the simplest way of getting rid of him would be to purchase his boarding house and sublet it to more desirable tenants. The difficulty facing these early miners has been outlined as follows:

> If a miner who worked at the Canadian Copper Company in 1910 wished to organize a strike, he found the company ready to dismiss him, the police and local militia ready to fight him, and the courts ready to convict him. If, on the other hand, he wanted merely to secure a more substantial amount of money in compensation for miners who had been killed in the job, he might find the coroner's jury difficult to convene and harder to convince of the company's negligence, the courts unwilling to convict and the provincial government ignorant and indecisive.[49]

A third tactic used to intimidate workers and to lessen solidarity was the fostering of ethnic rivalries within its labour force. In 1903, for example, some Italians were replaced by a party of Finns with the intent of flaming discontent between the two groups. A similar incident occurred in the following year, which resulted in four Finns being attacked and one hospitalized. The CCC did not hesitate to encourage rivalry within the Finnish community itself. Being self-contained, well organized and by far the most radical of the local ethnic groups, the Finnish community had long been a thorn in the side of CCC management. When the socialists acquired control of the Young People's Temperance Society in 1912, CCC officials provided the temperance people with another hall owned by the Company. According to one official, "the idea of having two factions nearly equally divided among them is a good idea, and we should encourage it."[50]

Finally, the incorporation of Copper Cliff gave the CCC considerable control over the results of coroners' investigations and compensation for accidents before 1915. Up to this time, prosecutions of the mining companies by the provincial government were rare. While the Ontario Bureau of Mines' 1912 report noted that there were 43 deaths and 341 serious accidents at the various mines and workplaces regulated by the Mining Act of Ontario, investigations resulted in the prosecution of four workmen and the fining of only one company for $100. As blandly stated in the Bureau's 1913 report, "the majority of non-fatal accidents were due to carelessness and incompetence of the injured workers."[51] With judgments such as these serving as the norm, mining companies found it easy to fire their workers and to limit compensation awards. Such was the case with John Passi, who was fired for his "carelessness" at Frood mine, after having an accident in 1931.[52]

These tragedies were compounded by the fact that the men who died or who were injured frequently had wives and children who had to fend for themselves or rely on assistance from the Finnish community. Through the CCC's Accident Association, the company was empowered to adjudicate the merit of all claims. If workers tried to seek additional compensation from the courts, they faced great difficulties because of the narrow interpretation of the laws and the willingness of the CCC to fully challenge all claims in the courts. By the mid-1930s, the situation improved somewhat for the union movement. In the organizing drive that led to the formation of the International Union of Mine, Mill and Smelter Workers' Local 239 at Sudbury in 1936, Neil Mäkelä served as the editor of the first Sudbury district union paper known as the *Union News*;[53] another IUMMSW local covering Falconbridge mine workers was chartered in 1937. These locals did not last long. Through the use of spies and intimidation tactics, the mining companies again succeeded in eliminating the union threat. Both unions were dissolved in 1938-39.

The situation changed dramatically after the bitter strike involving eight gold mines in Kirkland Lake in 1941-42; this strike was solidly supported by Finnish miners and the Finnish co-operative movement. Public support for union reform in Ontario by then could not be stopped. In one of the greatest ironies associated with Canadian mining history, the subsequent movement of miners from Kirkland Lake to other industrial centres such as Sudbury did more to encourage the spread of industrial unionism than to defeat it.[54] Sudbury Mine Mill Local 598 was formed in 1942, and the first issue of its weekly paper, known as the *Sudbury Beacon*, came off the presses of the *Vapaus* Publishing Company. Concerned about major gains made by the CCF Party, workers' shortages and the need to maintain mining production for World War II needs, the province passed the Ontario Collective Bargaining Act in 1943. Federal government recognition of the need for reform was given through the enactment of Order-in-Council PC1003 in 1944, which guaranteed the right of workers to choose the union they wanted, and directed employers to bargain in good faith with unions. These initiatives proved to be potent forces clearing the way for a new era of unionism in Canada. When Mine-Mill was certified as the bargaining agent for both Inco and Falconbridge workers in 1944, Finnish workers finally realized the full satisfaction due them for their past efforts.

Finnish radicalism also made its presence felt in the forestry industry. In this connection, Bradwin remarked in his classic *The Bunkhouse Man* that the Finns were "easily the most eager to acquire a working knowledge of English," were "given to the expression of radical ideas" and appeared "loathe to abide the slower constitutional methods" of social and economic reform.[55] Both the FOC and *Vapaus* were vigorous advocates of the forestry union movement. Early attempts to unionize this sector were foiled because of the ready supply of labour, the seasonality of the industry, the practice of jumping from one job to another and employer resistance. The fact, however, that so many of their countrymen had found work in the forest industry made this industry an obvious target for Finnish leftists. One of the first organizers was A.T. Hill, a union recruiter with the IWW, who had some success in promoting a Wobbly-sponsored union movement in the Thunder Bay area and along the Algoma Central Railway. In 1919 the Lumber and Camp Workers' Industrial Union (LCWIU) was formed as an affiliate of the Canadian-based OBU, and *Le Travailleur/The Worker* was created as the union's newspaper. *Vapaus*, for a time, gave its hearty endorsement to this new union. Due to high levels of unemployment, and a split between the OBU and the LCWIU, however, unionizing ground to a halt in 1920-21. From this split onwards, neither the OBU nor the LCWIU flourished in the forest industry.

The increasingly radical orientation of the FOC and *Vapaus* of the 1920s brought about a reassessment of their support for the labour movement. After the failure of early union drives, the task of rebuilding the labour movement in the Ontario forest industry was taken up almost entirely by Finnish immigrants who provided the leadership and the majority of union members.[56] Many of these lumber workers were influenced more by local conditions than by the efforts of union organizers. As one Finn observed in 1926:

> More than anything, the conditions among which the [Finnish] immigrants live here contribute to swell the lines of the Communists. . . . They are often cheated at their working places of the wages which they have supposed were due to them. . . . The living conditions at the camps are often very miserable.[57]

This view is supported by Repo, who concluded that "it was their Canadian experience as industrial workers that intensified their class-consciousness and provided the impetus to create working-class institutions in Canada."[58]

Part of the organizational framework for this rebuilding phase took place in Sudbury. Two rival bush worker unions appeared within the Finnish-Canadian left. One of the unions evolved from the members who remained within the OBU. Influenced by IWW's publication *Industrialisti*, many OBU bush workers opted to join the IWW's Lumber Workers Industrial Union (LWIU). The success of the LWIU could be attributed in part to the presence of Finnish-speaking Wobbly leaders who had fled the United States and come to the Sudbury district. One of the major supporters of the IWW movement was Einari W. Jouppi from Sudbury. Following a vote among union workers in the Sudbury area, local OBU bush workers in 1923 affiliated with the IWW. By 1925, however, the OBU was only a rump, its older rival having won the day.

Not content with either the OBU or the IWW, the communists within the Finnish left, among them A.T. Hill, launched, in 1924, their own union in Sault Ste. Marie: the Lumber Workers Industrial Union of Canada (LWIUC). Kalle Salo recalls how this union came into being.

> When I arrived in Canada in late 1923 and found a job in Ontario in an Algoma Line lumber camp, I immediately noticed that the workers in the Eastern Canada forest and lumber industries were almost totally unorganized. . . . I moved to the Northern Ontario pulp wood camps in the spring of 1924. While working in these camps, I met organizers of the lumber workers for the first time. A conference organized with the help of the Finnish Organization of Canada was held in Sault Ste. Marie for those members who were interested in organizing the lumber workers. The conference, known as the first convention of the Lumber Workers Industrial Union, made provisional plans for the unionization of lumber workers. It was indeed necessary to start building a union in this trade after the previous union had been destroyed when the OBU was dissolved. An overall attack against wages had begun. Wages had already fallen to almost half of what they had been two or three years ago. It was the Finns who started the Lumber Workers Industrial Union in Eastern Canada.[59]

The first two national secretaries of the new union were Finns: Alfred Hautamäki and Kalle Salo. The following year saw the launching of its magazine *Metsätyöläinen* (The Lumber Worker) which came off the *Vapaus* press between 1926 and 1935. This magazine, for a time under the direction of Hannes Sula from Sudbury, proved to be a powerful propaganda tool for leftist Finnish lumber workers.[60] Among the LWIUC organizers was Edwin Suksi who came to Thunder Bay from Finland in 1924. He remembered:

> It was tough. There's not much friendliness. You have to walk from the railroad 28 or 30 miles in through the bush, and when you got there you get a very cold reception from the camp foreman if he was there. One time, I walked into the camp at one o'clock and had to leave by evening.[61]

Suksi left the LWIUC for the *Vapaus* Publishing Company in 1935, where he served as the business manager until his retirement in 1971.[62] Other Finnish organizers were not so fortunate. Viljo Rosvall and John Voutilainen, two organizers for LWIUC, were found dead near Port Arthur after trying to organize one hundred men at the camp of "Reverend" Mäki, a Finn subcontractor. While the inquest concluded that the two organizers

died from accidental drownings, many believed that they had been murdered. Rosvall and Voutilainen subsequently emerged as martyrs for the
lumber workers' organizing struggles, and as heroic victims of the class war
by Finnish-Canadian leftists.[63]

In 1927 the LWIUC aggressively promoted unionism in northeastern
Ontario; these efforts gained some success at the White and Plaunt operations
found along the CNR line north of Sudbury. While disputes existed among
the Finnish workers, between the Wobblies and Communists and Whites and
Reds, the majority nonetheless banded together during strikes through
United Front Strike Committees. One interesting aspect of the struggle in
the forest was the appearance of differences between working-class Finns and
Finnish subcontractors who worked for the large timber companies.

The LWIUC emerged as the major union within the Ontario logging
industry in the late 1920s. Following the inclusion of agricultural workers,
and its affiliation with the left-wing Workers' Unity League in 1930, the
union remained dominant in the north. For a time its headquarters was
situated in Sudbury. A new era arrived in 1936 when the union joined the
Lumber and Sawmill Workers' Union (LSWU), an affiliate of the American
Federation of Labor.[64] Despite the fact that an LSWU local had been
formed in Sudbury, the leadership role of the Sudbury Finns diminished
thereafter.[65] As was the case with the mining industry, Finns in the lumbering sector shifted their attention towards supporting left-wing political
parties rather than functioning as leaders within the labour movement.
After World War II, reliance on the ballot box thus emerged as the favoured
tool among the Finns for labour reforms:

> One obvious observation to be made is the strong support for left-wing
> candidates in some Finnish polling divisions through most of this period
> [1930-72]. Voters in these areas were among the first to give substantial
> support to leftist candidates in the District. Many Finns were pioneers in
> the trade union and co-operative movements and this transferred natu-
> rally to political action.[66]

The use of political power, however, reflected a significant long-term
change for the Finnish radical movement. Whereas ethnic variables such as
attitudes towards the Lutheran Church and other conservative bodies, and
the general experiences of Finnish immigrants, had previously been the
core elements shaping radicalism, the same was no longer true after the
1970s. By this time, it was identification with the working class rather than
Finnish ethnicity per se that distinguished the support Finns gave to the
New Democratic Party (NDP). As more and more Finns moved into the
middle class after World War II, the inevitable result was a weakening of
support for the NDP and a greater conformity to regional voting patterns.[67]

Gender Equality in the Labour Force

Another carry-over influence that shaped the local work setting was the emancipation movement. As women who came from Finland were often single, familiar with hard work and highly literate, they showed little hesitation in becoming part of the labour force. This situation contrasted sharply with the experience in other ethnic groups, where wage labour was considered to be improper for women. Often Finnish women first entered the workforce as informal volunteers for existing institutions, political parties and workers' organizations. In the formal labour force, the most common form of employment for single females was as domestic servants, laundry women or cooks; some proved to be remarkably entrepreneurial, especially when it came to the running of restaurants, boarding houses and bootlegging establishments. Finnish women in the Sudbury area were, from the outset, active participants in the reform movement. Lindström-Best characterizes these early pioneers as being "defiant sisters":

> [T]he strategies and survival techniques created by Finnish women were often coloured by defiance. This defiance could be directed against the old country and its conditions, against their own bodies, against the traditional Lutheran religion, or against Canadian society and ultimately against its legal and political systems.[68]

This rebellious attitude was supported by *Toveritar*, the radical organ of Finnish working women of America which appeared between 1911 and 1930. Embodying a mixture of militant socialism, spirited feminism and grass-roots journalism, this publication had a strong readership at Beaver Lake, Copper Cliff, Creighton mine, Frood mine, Levack mine, Nairn Centre, Quartz, Sudbury, Victoria Mine, Wanup, Whistle mine, Whitefish and Worthington. A reader of *Vapaus* known as "Mummu," for instance, recalls how this newspaper became a "good friend" after her arrival in Garson in 1912.[69] Inspired by its content, women aggressively promoted their involvement in institutional development of all kinds. Some emerged as strong workers for the socialist movement and helped to found the Sudbury local of the FSOC in 1912.[70] Eklund has stated that it is impossible to picture the development of the FSOC/FOC without women, who often constituted one-half of the membership and who "were extremely active and productive."[71] This was especially true in the rural areas where women ran locals in the absence of their spouses who were working elsewhere. Women members of the FOC generally participated in the FOC organization as equals with the male members. For other women, the road to the workplace started with sewing circles allied with churches or socialist groupings. Finnish women instinctively sought a separate identity from men, feeling comfortable in each other's company. For religious women, the Lutheran Church in Canada, in contrast to the patriarchal setting in Finland, offered them new and important roles. In addition to serving as Sunday school teachers, they established *naistenpiirit* or *ompeluseurat* (sewing circles). These circles were crucial for the raising of funds for the young immigrant church.

While the practices of the sewing circles varied slightly from community to community, they generally followed the same format. Funds were raised through membership fees, bazaars and coffee evenings to purchase items required by the church. They also filled an important social role by allowing women to share their experiences with one another. One such group was the Copper Cliff sewing circle at St. Timothy's Church, which was founded in 1897 by Greta Koski. In 1932 a Martha Club was formed for women who preferred to communicate in the English language. Another sewing circle was created at St. Matthew's Church in 1937. The importance of these circles, now known as Ladies' Aid, has continued to the present. After World War II women raised their sights and sought positions on church councils. It has now become the norm for the Lutheran Church in recent years to have councils consisting equally of men and women; St. Timothy's Church now has the distinction of having a female pastor, Rev. Shirley Ruller.

Sewing circles of like character developed in the FOC locals, where funds were needed for the construction of halls, the purchase of books and musical instruments and aid to strikers. Another aim was to foster equality by educating women to be socialist speakers, debators, writers and agitators. This thrust was heightened in 1927 and 1928 by the impact of one woman, Sanna Kannasto. Kannasto was an influential speaker who, in 1908, became the first paid political organizer for the Finnish socialists. She provided such a powerful role model that Canadian officials viewed her as one of the most dangerous radicals in the country, and the RCMP even sought to deport her. She was tireless in her coaxing of women to join socialist organizations and to form their own women's groups. Prominent among these was *Canadan Työläisnaisten Liitto* (The Canadian Working Women's Federation), founded to attract salaried workers into the union movement. One of her dedicated followers was Taimi Davies (Pitkänen) who rose through the ranks of the Young Communist League and, following a period of training in the Soviet Union, served as an activist in Sudbury in 1932.[72]

As a result of Kannasto's visit, a Sudbury local of the Federation was formed towards the end of 1927 with twenty-seven members.[73] Shortly thereafter, eleven other locals were established and a regional secretariat formed.[74] At the end of the first year of activity, there were 304 members in all of the regional locals. These locals were active supporters of workers' rights and the union movement; many distributed handwritten, or "fist," pamphlets, offered speaking courses, ran summer camps for children and provided aid to those arrested by the authorities.[75] Encouraged by the rise of domestic servants' unions elsewhere in Canada, the Federation even had two "servants" locals. In 1931 the "Tenhunen" factor had caused a rift within the organization, especially in the Sudbury local. Nevertheless, membership in this local still managed to grow to seventy by 1933. When the Finnish Organization of Canada decided to form its own women's clubs in 1937, however, interest in the League waned and it eventually went out of existence. After the FOC halls were banned by the federal government during World War II, it was the female members who remained strong throughout the closure period, often giving support to its members on strike.

These organizational efforts bore fruit as Finnish women in the Sudbury area did not encounter many of the problems found elsewhere, such as Toronto, where domestics faced the problem of having to pay a fee for a position:

> This is a question which is causing considerable concern to the officials who are charged with the responsibility of eliminating the unlicensed persons who make a practice of preying upon the uninformed by charging fees for the finding of positions. As is well known, this practice was carried on by many Finnish rooming-house owners, who were quite active in soliciting employment, principally through advertisements in the daily papers, and in return for this service collected fees from the individual so assisted. . . . [T]he personnel of the Women's Department of the Employment Service does not include one conversant with the Finnish or other foreign languages. The wily rooming-house owners are well aware of this condition, and utilize the knowledge to their own personal gain and to the disadvantage of the worker.[76]

Finnish women were active as wage earners in the formal workplace, and their experience as voluntary workers with churches and socialist groups served them in good stead. Within the FOC, many advanced to administrative positions, serving as editors, typesetters and printers for *Vapaus*; three of the editors of *Liekki*, for example, were female. The cooperative movement provided employment opportunities as well. It was in domestic service, however, where Finnish women excelled. It was the only category, aside from farm work, within which single women from Finland during the 1920s were allowed to enter Canada.[77] The reputation gained by Finnish women in this occupation was such that they were rarely out of work. Finnish maids were proud of their reputation as reliable and hardworking employees. The following riddle by Arvo Lindewall in *Toveritar* illustrates the point:

I am not beautiful,
Yet, I am the most wanted woman.
I am not rich,
Yet I am worth my weight in gold.
I might be dull, stupid,
Dirty and mean,
Yet, all the doors are open for me.
I am a welcome guest
All of the elite compete for me.
I am a maid.[78]

Maids were especially sought after in large communities such as Montreal, Toronto and Winnipeg. In many circles, having a Finnish maid was a status symbol. While such employment was limited in the Sudbury area, it nonetheless remained important. Domestic work had the advantage of aiding females in the assimilation process, a situation that contrasted sharply with the experience of Finnish men who worked in isolated resource areas.[79] A maids' organization was established in Sudbury in 1928 to ensure a minimum wage level and to promote insurance schemes for the sick and unemployed.

Jobs also existed for women in the lumber camps, where good cooks were well paid and highly esteemed by the men. Nelma Sillanpää, however, recalls that the work done by her mother was long, hard and exhausting:

> [W]e went to a summer camp near Hoyle. . . . Mother had to cook for seventy-five men there. She had a woman helper, a handy man and two chore boys. . . . The black flies were dreadful! We had cheesecloth netting around our beds so that we were able to sleep. It was hot! Our beds were in the corner of the cook camp. My mother worked seven days a week in that heat around a huge wood-burning stove.[80]

If months of endless work at a remote lumber camp were not attractive, Finnish women easily found work in restaurants or in boarding houses. This employment was common in Sudbury due to the large number of single men who worked in mining and lumbering.

Many restaurants were owned and/or operated by enterprising Finnish women who took pride in their good food, clean premises and discipline. By 1931 there were numerous Finnish-run restaurants in Sudbury, such as the Canadian Cafe, Elgin Lunch, Finlanders' Cafe, National Lunch, Saima Cafe, New Ontario Cafe and North Cafe. Hilja Pulkki and Ida Tuuri were two well-known female restaurant operators around this time. Bertha Heino started her career in the restaurant trade and she later established, along with her husband, North Cafe and Heino's Grill (biography 12). These commercial ventures provided women with jobs such as waitressing, dishwashing, cook's helpers or cleaners.

Biography 12
Sulo and Bertha Heino: The Restaurateurs

Sulo and Bertha Heino's history has been closely intertwined with the restaurant trade. Sulo was born in Elimäki, Finland, in 1922. In the following year his family migrated to Sault Ste. Marie, Canada. Both of his parents worked in the bush camps north of the Sault. As a youngster he worked for a time as a baker at Ankila's Bakery. Following his schooling, he enlisted in the army in 1942, where he became both a chef and paratrooper at Camp Borden, Ontario, and Fort Benny, Georgia, in the United States. Due to his Finnish heritage, however, he was designated as an enemy alien when Finland allied with Germany and attacked Russia; thus, he was not allowed to fight on the European front. This was fortunate as most of his fellow paratroopers were subsequently killed in Europe. Upon his return to civilian life in 1946, he went to the Reagan bush camp on the CPR line near White River where he was employed as a pulp cutter, cook and jobber for Abitibi Lumber. It was here that he first came into contact with Bertha Hill. Born in Sudbury in 1927, Bertha was raised in Wanup and started working as a teenager. During World War II, she was employed at the Scandinavian Lunch cafe in Toronto where she became interested in the restaurant trade. She briefly returned to Wanup. From 1946 to 1952, she served as a cook at the Reagan bush camp where she met and married Sulo in 1947.

Sulo and Bertha first appeared on the restaurant scene in Sudbury in 1952 when they took over the North Cafe, formerly run by Hilja and Kusti Pulkki and Väinö Siitonen. It was situated on Lisgar Street across from the well-known Queen's Hotel. The restaurant, as was the case for Slim's Lunch and the Northern Cafe on nearby Borgia Street, developed a reputation for cleanliness and the serving of good Finnish food. The main items on the menu consisted of large portions of *mojakka* (Finnish stew), *suolakala* (salted salmon), *puuro* (porridge) and *soppa* (soup). Lunch pails were prepared for miners on shift work. For many single Finnish men, the cafe served as a part-time home. Among the other customers were those with vouchers from the Salvation Army. Situated in the heart of the Borgia district, the cafe, however, had constant problems dealing with drunks and unsavoury characters.

The Heinos sold the North Cafe in 1955 and purchased Wimpy's Grill situated on the corner of Beech and Elgin Streets. It was renamed Heino's Grill and transformed into another *mojakka sappa* (stew grill) catering to workers. Among their customers were newly arrived immigrants from Finland with vouchers from the city that enabled them to buy meals until they found employment. As many as two hundred lunch pails a day were prepared. Each Christmas, they prepared a huge meal for 85 to 130 persons sent by the Salvation Army. The Heinos acquired Consumers' Restaurant on Elm Street from Bill and Pearl Kivinen in 1955, and changed its name to the Uptown Restaurant. This restaurant proved to be a losing proposition and it was sold.

After 1959 Sulo and Bertha ran a private catering business that operated out of their home on Long Lake. Sulo later became an automobile and truck salesman for McLeod (later Cambrian) Motors in 1962. He spent over thirty years in the car and heavy truck sales business until his retirement in 1994. During the 1960s and 1970s, Sulo and Bertha catered to numerous stags and weddings, served food at beerfests held at the Sudbury Arena and worked regularly at the Wanup and Workers' Park Halls. Sulo was an active member and fund-raising supporter of the Broder-Dill Snowmobiler's Association, Associated Canadian Travellers, Automotive Transportation Superintendents Association and the Sudbury *Suomi* Lions Club. In 1992-93 Sulo received the Lion of the Year Award from the Sudbury *Suomi* Lions Club. Sulo and Bertha had two children; Charles was born in 1948 and Michael in 1949. Sulo passed away in 1997.

Lodging and boarding houses provided another source of employment. For the owners, these establishments provided a means of income that required no knowledge of the English language, little capital and few specialized skills. The resulting income made it possible for them to pursue their individual dreams, be it the purchase of a farm, a commercial venture or a return visit to Finland. Boarding houses permitted female spouses to engage in gainful employment while their men were working in the mines or forests. For young female immigrants, who came with reputations as being honest, clean and hardworking, these enterprises provided them with employment and the opportunity to meet men of similar age. Many marriages in the Sudbury area were founded on relationships that began in these *poikatalot*. Boarding house entrepreneurs frequently met incoming trains to search out young females as prospective employees. When sufficient money was raised, boarding and rooming houses were often sold to newcomers. For boarders, the homes served as a haven of stability that gave them a semblance of family life and the opportunity to communicate in their native tongue.

Prior to World War II more than twenty families operated such houses in Copper Cliff alone. The boarding-house tradition was started by Herman and Greta Koski. Many others followed this path of upward economic mobility.[81] During a period of Finnish settlement in Copper Cliff in 1928, one boarding house even served meals for up to 140 men, and other rooming houses were so crowded that boarders often slept on floors.

In the 1920s and 1930s rooming/boarding houses spread to Sudbury. In the year 1929 alone, there were four women who received licences in Sudbury for lodging or boarding houses.[82] These houses were especially popular in the Donovan district, where Fannie Puska along with B. Hänninen, L. Neva, S. Rautanen and Joseph Talso ran well-known enterprises. Others could be found elsewhere in the city, such as those run by Emile Johnson (near the old CNR Station on Samuel Street) and Justiina Ritari (Spruce

Street).[83] Ritari's boarding house also served as a regular meeting place for the Sudbury *Kisa*-Alerts athletic club. Aspects of Sudbury's boarding-house living style at the time are vividly depicted in Antti Tuuri's historical novel *Uusi Jerusalem* (New Jerusalem).[84] Other Finnish women looked for faster ways of making money and more lucrative business opportunities. Many of them were widowed, single parents or simply in need of income; consequently, they were not afraid to break or bend the law to achieve their goals. Bootlegging establishments (known as blind pigs or doghouses) run by women flourished in resource towns such as Sudbury and Copper Cliff. Sulo Äijö has given the following account of their significance:

> The doghouses in Thunder Bay, Sudbury and Toronto were almost all run by women, older women in their forties and fifties, some married. They were strong and big "mammas." There were at least forty illegal Finnish taverns in "Artturi" [Port Arthur] and "Viljami" [Fort William], another 20 in Sudbury and in Toronto there were two dozen just within a walking distance from Widmer Street.[85]

Despite the fact that Finnish organizations, churches, mining companies and the press waged endless battles against this form of illegal activity, blind pigs flourished. Their popularity can be attributed to the desire by young Finns for a homelike atmosphere, the opportunity to get out of rooming/boarding houses or to get away from an unhappy marriage. A high degree of mutual trust existed between female bootleggers and their customers with respect to credit and the handling of paycheques. An indication of the popularity of these establishments is given by J.T., who made beer deliveries with his horse and buggy in Sudbury: "I delivered more beer to the bootleggers than to the licensed joints. The brewery often paid whatever fines the bootleggers collected and they also helped bribe the police, who in turn gave protection to the women who ran the doghouses."[86] The popularity of the blind pigs was enhanced by their flexibility. As many of the male Finns were miners who worked on varying shifts, it was not uncommon for these establishments to have liquor and striptease performances available even in the morning hours.

What is exceptional about this form of tavern culture is the fact that in Finnish communities women dominated the business, setting the standards, prices and their own code of operating ethics. Some opened their homes to customers, while others ran more sophisticated businesses with a variety of entertainment, food and drink. Adele Mäki's home in Lockerby, for example, served as a *"tippakauppa* with finesse," where patrons came by invitation only for a few drinks and to hear the latest music direct from Finland.[87] Others such as Iisakki and Ida Mannisto, who lived on the corner of Lorne and Spruce Streets, also sold the occasional bottle of homebrew.

Sandra Mäki in Lockerby provided more extensive "roadhouse" forms of entertainment for local residents, miners and lumberjacks.

Bootlegging establishments abounded in the Donovan. On Melvin Street, *Lahti Maija* served beer and homebrew for young Finnish immigrants in need of evening solace. The fact that she was the wife of Herman Vick, the first policeman in Copper Cliff, only added to her reputation. Another bootlegger, Martha Hill, ran a similar operation on Eva Street. Due to a leg injury which caused her to limp, she was referred to as *polkupyörä Martha* (bicycle Martha). The Wanup-Estaire area, too, had a noteworthy concentration of bootlegging establishments. In 1937 there were at least fifteen such operations, many of which were allegedly run by "God-fearing folk."[88] After World War II, Nester Puska ran a lively roadhouse that was patronized by dozens of persons, many of them guards from the Burwash Industrial Farm.

While the prostitution trade served as another example of the entrepreneurial spirit of Finnish women, it was not sufficiently prevalent to arouse much controversy within the Finnish-Canadian media or the religious community. Given the large number of single and young males in the community, it was inevitable that prostitution would accompany drinking in some of the bootlegging establishments, especially those found outside of the city of Sudbury in the Lockerby and Long Lake areas. Within socialist circles, Finnish prostitutes were treated sympathetically, and any form of criticism usually focused on the circumstances rather than the individual.[89] Some prostitutes were well known throughout the Finnish community: *Juoppo Sulvi* (Drunkard Sulvi) and *Musta Ruusu* (Black Rose), who was also known as *Tampereen Ruusu* (Rose from Tampere).

White-Collar Pursuits

While the majority of the Finns were engaged in farming or in blue-collar pursuits, a substantial number entered the petite bourgeoisie, or white-collar working class. One of the first reflections of this trend was in dairy production. This was a natural occurrence, given the large number of Finnish dairy farmers in the area. John Salo started a small dairy in Copper Cliff in 1910 and ran it until 1924 when he joined with other dairy farmers from Waters Township, including Henry Pynttäri (Nelson), Elias Kallio and John Harju, to establish Copper Cliff Dairy. In 1935 Frank Anderson built another dairy at the Creighton Mine townsite. It was later acquired by Copper Cliff Dairy, which continued, however, to supply milk to Anderson's former plant until 1958. Beginning in 1948, the history of Copper Cliff Dairy became closely intertwined with that of Bill Johnson (biography 13).

Bill Johnson: Mr. Copper Cliff Dairy

Bill Johnson was born on 15 May 1920 at Creighton Mine, Ontario. His parents, Matti and Mari Johnson, came from Finland and settled in Michigan, where his grandfather worked in the iron mines. The family left Michigan and came to Copper Cliff in 1897 before moving to Creighton Mine. He attended elementary school at Creighton Mine, where at least one-half of the students were of Finnish origin. His father worked at Creighton mine until he obtained a job at the Workers' Co-operative in Timmins in 1927. The family then acquired a farm in Lorne Township. Bill attended Beaver Lake Public School until 1929 when the family moved to Timmins. In 1930 they returned to Beaver Lake where Bill completed one year of high school. At the age of fifteen he worked on the farm and ran a trapline. Like other Finns in the Beaver Lake area, he held odd summer jobs, including one at the High Falls power project and another with the Nordale Construction Company. By World War II he had acquired a reputation of being an excellent theatrical performer; he was also active in summer and winter sports.

In 1941 he enlisted in the Canadian Army. Following his basic training at North Bay where he emerged as a corporal, he moved to Petawawa, Ontario, and Vernon, British Columbia, and was promoted to sergeant. At Sussex, New Brunswick, he was a battle drill instructor. This training helped him to maintain his conditioning for competitive cross-country skiing. Following his discharge from the army in 1945, he returned to Beaver Lake and worked at several jobs, including one with Palm Dairies. Bill competed in many ski meets for the *Jehu* Athletic Club at Beaver Lake, and in 1946 he won a silver medal for cross-country skiing at the Canadian Championships. He tried out for the Canadian Olympic team in 1947 but narrowly lost to another competitor. Following his marriage to Martha Ranta in the same year, he enrolled in dairying at Guelph Agricultural College. After graduating in 1948, he obtained employment at City Dairy.

He was hired as manager of Copper Cliff Dairy in 1948. During the evenings Bill was actively involved in the theatre at the Finnish Hall on Spruce Street. This involvement lasted until 1954, when he was advised by a top Inco official that it would be advisable for him to stop his visible association with the FOC. He abandoned competitive skiing and gained a new interest in flying. In 1962 he obtained Stationary Engineer qualifications and, to improve his accounting skills, attended classes at the Sudbury Business College. Bolstered by these qualifications, he rose through the ranks to become the general manager, vice-president and later part-owner of the dairy. Copper Cliff Dairy was sold to Ault Foods in 1981 and Bill retired in 1982.

His many achievements include a five-year stint as chairman of the Sunnyside Public School Board and service as a board member of the Ontario Milk Distributors Association. He served as president of the following organizations: Northern Ontario Dairyman's Association, Copper Cliff Rod and Gun Club, Ontario Milk Foundation and the Sudbury, Copper Cliff and Levack Milk Distributors' Association. Since his retirement he has travelled extensively with his wife, attending virtually every summer Olympic event. They continue to live at their residence on Long Lake in Broder Township, and much of their leisure time is spent at their island cottage on Lake Panache, which they purchased in 1972. He and his wife, Martha, have three children, Ken, Vicki and Cindy.

Shown here is Bill Johnson (c. 1950s). He is widely known throughout the Finnish community for his theatrical and sporting interests (see biography 13). Beginning in 1948, his name became synonymous with that of Copper Cliff Dairy. (Bill Johnson, private collection)

Two other large Finnish dairies were established in Sudbury. The first was a workers' co-operative known as Co-optas in 1927. It began by acquiring the equipment of a smaller Finnish dairy operated by E.J. Ojala. Due to economic problems, brought on in part by a boycott of some Finnish farmers, its dairy on Spruce Street was sold in 1932 to the Farmers' Dairy Ltd., and later, in 1934, to the Sudbury Producers and Consumers Co-operative. This co-operative produced milk until the 1960s, at which time its equipment was sold to Palm Dairies Ltd. The second enterprise was City Dairy. Owned by Nickel Belt Trading Company and run by Karl Nurmi, Oscar Luoma, Jussi Ajola, John Lehtelä and Ilmari Järnefelt, it was built in 1935 on Antwerp Street in the Donovan. It remained in existence until the turn of the 1950s. These dairy operations provided many people such as Elvi Duncan with jobs of a clerical and administrative nature.

In the meantime, other Finnish-based enterprises flourished in and around Sudbury. While Karl Lehto was the best-known merchant throughout the interwar period, others such as Arne Ritari, Lempi Johnson, Toivo Pajala and Karl Nurmi achieved considerable success. Arne Ritari started an insurance and travel agency in 1934 and ran it until his retirement in 1975. His office at the corner of Cedar and Elgin Streets was a fixture in the Finnish presence downtown. Another successful downtown business was Johnson's Furs on Durham Street, run by Lempi Johnson for twenty-five years between 1942 and 1967. Toivo Pajala and his brother took over the Northern Ski Factory on Edna Street, which had been established by Emil Pernu in 1925, and ran it until 1945. Bought by C. Fielding, it was proclaimed in 1947 as "Canada's Largest Ski Factory." Pajala later established another ski operation known as Pajala Ski Company on Long Lake Road, which was sold to interests in the United States in 1951. In 1916 Karl and Arvi Nurmi started Finnish Bottling Works, which developed into one of the largest Finnish businesses in North America. The operation moved from Victoria to Regent Street in 1918 where it remained for fifty years under the name of Star Bottling Works. In 1968 the plant moved to Lorne Street, after which time it was sold.

The Korpela family operations were another success story. Starting in 1917, Karl Korpela and his son Oliver established lumbering and sawmilling enterprises in the Chapleau area. Their plants provided employment for hundreds of Finnish immigrants throughout the interwar period and during the 1950s. The *Vapaus* Publishing Company provided white-collared opportunities as well for individuals such as Kaarina Ritari, Rauha Mäki and Edwin Suksi.

A sampling of Finnish businesses that were established in the Sudbury area before World War II is given in table 15. This listing, derived mainly from paid advertisements found in various Finnish publications, indicates that more than one hundred Finnish commercial ventures existed in the area. Most of these enterprises were associated with serving the everyday needs of the Finnish population: restaurants and cafes, bakeries, tailoring needs, men's wear, saunas, taxis, shoe repairs, etc. Other enterprises, such as Star Bottling Works and Koivula Bakery, had markets that extended beyond the local ethnic community.

Some Finns became professionals. These included: two medical doctors, Dr. Heikki Koljonen, who resided in Sudbury from 1915 until 1938 and for a short time in the late 1940s, and Dr. W. Markkanen, who practised briefly around World War II; ministers from the Copper Cliff Presbyterian

Mission, St. Timothy's, St. Matthew's and Finnish Pentecostal congregations; and the vice-consuls for Finland (T. Franssi 1926-31 and H.E. Johnson 1932-39). Finnish employees also made their influence felt in technical areas, such as Inco's engineering and geological divisions and in the surveying field.[90] Nursing and teaching provided the main employment opportunities for Finnish women. Many Finnish women teachers worked at Chicago Mine, Copper Cliff, Grassy Lake, Kelly Lake, Wahnapitae and Waters Township, where much of the student population was Finnish in origin.[91] For some individuals, *Suomi* College at Hancock, Michigan, served as the post-secondary route for entry into the professions.[92]

Table 15
Selected Finnish Enterprises/Professions in the
Sudbury Area before 1945

A. Aalto's General Store	Finlandia Cafe
Aho's Barber Shop	T.J. Franssi Store
Alavo's (Penna's) Sauna	Fulin and Laine Grocery
Albion Aurat (Ploughs)	J. Halonen, chiropractor
J. Allan Jewellery Store	F. Heino's Store
Anni's Hairdressing	Heiskanen Jewellers
Arcade (M. Hamari) Beauty Salon	Helvi's Ladies' Wear
Balmoral Annex Hotel	L. Hotti Auto Repair
Balmoral Beauty Salon	C.G. Jacobson Store
Bessie Street Sauna	A. Jakkola's Sauna
Bohm's Garage	M. Jalonen Barber Shop
Burton Grocery	Jacob Jarvis Agency
Canadian Cafe	Jansson's Sauna
City Dairy	Johnson's Furs
Cliff Taxi	Emil Johnson Boarding House
Cliffbury Garage	Herbert Johnson Store
Club Lunch	Julius Barber Shop
Consumer's Restaurant	Wm. Kallio Hardware
Copper Cliff Dairy	Kangas (Miners') Men's Wear
Creighton Tailors	Kari Pharmacy
Durham Cafe	Kati's Beauty Parlor
Eagle Cafe and Boarding House	H. Kaukanen Tailor
Elgin Lunch	Dr. Kaukinen, dentist
Eloranta and Oksanen Grocery	G. Kivinen Supply
J.A. Erickson Agency and Real	Koivula Bakery
Estate	E. Kolari Jewellery Store
A.W. Este Tobacco and Games Store	Dr. Heikki Koljonen
Finnish (Purity) Bakery	K. Korjonen Tailors
Finlander's Cafe	Koski Brothers Store

Herman Koski's Store
Art Lahti's Store
J. Lahti and Sons Coal and Wood
L. Laine Ski Distributor
Lake Penage Log Cabin Camp
Karl Lehto's Men's Wear
J. Lievonen Tailoring
Lind Taxi
Lindberg Taxi
Lindgren's Store
Luoma and Johnson Taxi
Lähde's Sewing
E. Länsi's Barber Shop
Albert Mantere Tailoring
P. Manninen's Sauna
I. Mannisto Cleaners
Maple Leaf Cafe
Dr. W. Markkanen
Mary's Ladies Wear
Melody (M. Hamari) Music Shop
Melvin Groceries
Miller Mäki Law Firm
L. Mäkela, seamstress
Mäki Shoe Repairs
O. Mäki and Sons Groceries
Heikki Mäkinen's General Store
National Lunch
New Baking Company
New Cliffbury Garage
New Ontario Cafe
Niemi Studio
North Cafe
North End Bakery
Northern Ski Company
Northern (O. Koivula) Tailors

K. Nyberg Barber Shop
E.J. Ojala Meat Supply
Paju's Restaurant
Paju's Sauna
Pulkki's Pool Room
Paavo Ruohonen Travel Agency
Piispanen's Men's Wear
Ritari Travel and Insurance
Rose (K. Eklund) Hairdressing
Saima Cafe
I. Salo's Barber Shop
Salminen's General Store
Slim's Lunch
Eino Smith's Barber Shop
Snow White Restaurant
South End Cafe
Star (Finnish) Bottling Works
Star Restaurant
Sudbury Billiard Parlor
Sudbury Finnish Cafe
Sudbury Footwear (E. Latvala and
    H. Mäki)
Sudbury P and C Dairy
Sudbury (Seppälä) Steam Baths
Sudbury Boat and Wood Factory
Sundholm's Watch Repair
Valkeapää Groceries
Vapaus Publishing Company
Verner's Men's Wear
Vuori Construction
Waltonen's Masseurs
Wanup Co-operative Store
Ylönen's Hairdressing
I. Ylönen, therapist

Source: Compiled from various publications.

Post-World War II Employment

By the 1950s Finns who had come to Sudbury as part of the first immigration wave were starting to retire from the labour force. They were replaced by the tide of new immigrants and second- and third-generation Finns. In contrast to the situation before World War II, these postwar groups showed little inclination to enter the agricultural labour force. They no longer identified happiness with the *Onnela* (Happy Land Farm). While both Inco and Falconbridge continued to serve as major sources of employment, others found jobs at the booming settlement of Elliot Lake, often working there during the week and returning to their permanent homes in Sudbury for the weekends. Both immigrant and native Finns continued the tradition of establishing small and medium-sized companies of all kinds. Spurred by their parents, increasing numbers of second- and third-generation Finns left for colleges and universities elsewhere, and returned to Sudbury as white-collar professionals. Many of these graduates emerged as successful Finnish entrepreneurs and respected community leaders. A selective listing of some of the enterprises/professions that have existed in the Sudbury area after World War II is given in table 16. While some were founded earlier, well over one hundred new enterprises and professional occupations were created in the postwar period.

Table 16
Selected Finnish Enterprises/Professions in the
Sudbury Area after 1945

Accordian Ambassador	El-Equip Inc.
Akela Airways	Teuvo Eloranta, lawyer
Alavo Sauna	Erkila Excavating
Alan Arkilander, lawyer	Erola Panache Landing
A Moment for You	K. Erola, physician
Anna's Art Studio	FCT Group Engineering
Anndesign	Finmark Construction
Ash-Core Golf Course	Finn Aluminium
Heikki Auvinen, lawyer	Finnish Book and Music Store
Balmoral Beauty Salon	Finnish Sauna Sales and Service
Bertha's Catering	Mr. Grocer (Paris Street)
Brown's Concrete	Guy's Place
Canadian Tire Stores (Downtown	Hardrock Mine Developers
and Sudbury South)	Mike Heino Auto Supply
Ceming Investments	Heino's Grill
Comrock Construction	Heiskanen Jewellers
Co-op Shoe Repair	Helvi's Catering
Copper Cliff Boarding House	Helvi's Flower House
Copper Cliff Dairy	Jack Hill Luggage and Gifts
Countryside Estate Realty	J. Holub, physician
Cranehill Mining	Hyytiainen Fuels
Cranehill Siding	House of Finland
Alan Dumencu, chiropractor	John R. Hämäläinen Engineering
Egan Laine Real Estate	Jacobson Store

Johnson's Furs
K. Kaitila, chiropractor
Kanerva Brothers
Kangas Men's Wear
Kari Pharmacy
K.E. Kaukinen, dentist
Kauko Heino, mining consultant
Kauppi Construction
Kingsway Transmission
The Kitchen Store
Emil Kiviaho Real Estate and
    Insurance
Gary Kivinen, physician
G. Kivinen Supply
R.A. Kolari Realty
Koski's Radio and TV
KSM Heating Maintenance
Kähkönen Construction
Sonja Kähkönen, chiropractor
Leo Laakso Electrical
Laamanen Construction and BLM
    Service Group
Laari Construction
J.H. Lahti Real Estate
Laine Agencies
Lampinen Fine Art and Custom
    Framing
Jorma Larton, accountant
Leinala's Bakery
Leppa's Dressmaking
R.J. Lindquist, accountant
Lockerby Auto Service
Long Lake Auto Repair
Loon Construction
Eric Lovin Photography
Lundgren Fuel Service
ME Construction
MK Custom Metal
F. Mackenzie, chiropractor
Michael Majalahti, graphic artist
Mark Mahonen, chiropractor
Marita's Finnish Goods and Gifts
Marttila Sewing Centre and
    School
Maxim's and Maxim's II

Mike's Aluminum
Miriam's Beauty Salon
Miller Mäki Lawyers (Kauko and
    Thomas Mäki)
Matti Mottonen, lawyer
Mullola Machining
Mylly's Janitor Service
Jamie Mäki, optometrist
John Mäki Motors
John Mäki, physician
Niemi Studio
Tom Niemi Sales
Nordic Energy Systems
Nordic Ski Hills
North Cafe
North End Bakery
Northern Cafe
Northern Communication
    Services
O.J. Construction
Olav's Auto Body Supply
Omar Aviation
Paris IDA Pharmacy
Parr Home Improvements
William Passi, lawyer
Patrakka Construction
Pelkola Real Estate
Auvo Peltola, broker
Peltola Agencies
Penn Systems
Perttula Excavation
R. Perämäki, ophthalmologist
Hannu Piironen, lawyer
Pinehill Cottages
Pinehill Lumber
Presley's Corner Store
Ramakko's Tackle World
Anna-Liisa Raatikainen (ALR)
    Bookkeeping and Translation
Rayvor Construction
Ratko Pumps
Regency Hairstyling
Regent Marine
Regional Conservatory of Music
    (Karl Pukara Music Studio)

Rintala Construction
John Rintala Trucking
Ritari Travel & Insurance
Saari's Flowers & Gifts
Santala General Store
C.W. Savela, dentist
Scandia Upholstery
Scandinavian Foods
Scandinavian Security
Selton Contractors and Engineers
The Shop
Don Sirkka, optometrist
Sirkka Summer Camps
Lasse Skogberg Real Estate
Slim's Lunch
Soucie-Salo Safety Supply
Spectrum 2000 Communications
   Group
Standard Variety Store
Star Bottling Works
Steel Communications
Sudbury Mining Contractors
Sudbury Footwear
Sudbury Service Station
Sutinen/Lundgren Landing
Tamrock Canada

Telstar Hydraulics
A. Tenhunen, psychiatrist
L. Tenhunen, physician
T. Tenhunen, anaesthetist
Thrifty Transit Service and Car
   Rental
Toby's Bodyshop
Glen Toikka, accountant
Uniglobe Travel
Uptown Restaurant
Valrita's Hair Salon
Paul Villgren Inc. (Sling-Choker,
   Ground Control, Toojacks, etc.)
A.J. Väliaho, physician
Walden Animal Clinic (Rod
   Jouppi, veterinarian)
Walden Electric
Walden Grower and Garden Cen-
   tre
Wanup Pit Sand and Gravel
Waters Hotel
Water Ways
Wesmak (Kormak and Island Lake)
   Lumber Companies
Whitewater Camp
Wierre's Confectionery

Source: Compiled from various publications.

   The majority of Finns in the 1950s sought employment with mining firms in Sudbury and in Elliot Lake. Due to the strong international demand for nickel and uranium, the mining industry in these areas underwent unprecedented expansion, and thousands of workers were hired. Building on the solid reputation established by their earlier counterparts, new immigrants such as Pentti Talpiainen and Pentti Laurikainen found little difficulty in being hired by companies such as Inco, Falconbridge, Denison Mines and Rio Algom. Second-generation Finns, as well, abandoned farming life for the higher incomes provided by mining and construction. Finns were particularly attracted to private mining companies such as MacIsaac Mining and Tunnelling, Redpath and Dravo, where long hours and the bonus system offered the promise of large annual salaries. Veikko Kivikangas was typical of many of those immigrants who followed this route. After coming to Sudbury from Finland in 1956, he worked in Elliot Lake for four years, residing in the company's bunkhouse during the week and returning on weekends to his home in Sudbury. After working briefly with Falconbridge Nickel Mines and Dravo, he was then hired by MacIsaac, where he remained until his retirement in the 1980s.[93]

It was through the "contracting-out" process that these smaller, non-unionized firms were able to obtain lucrative contracts from larger companies, especially for development work linked to the opening of new mines. For these companies, the Finnish work ethic and ability to perform tasks independent of close supervision proved to be key assets. Beginning in the mid-1960s, for instance, MacIsaac Mining and Tunnelling hired Finns for development work at the Worthington, MacLennan, Totten and Lockerby mine sites and at Pickle Lake and Cobalt in Ontario, and at Campbell River on Vancouver Island. MacIsaac found it efficient to hire working teams of up to twenty-five persons consisting entirely of Finnish workers. In development work, non-Finns were preferred for the breaking-shift phase, with the Finns specializing in the timber-shift phase.[94]

In construction, numerous companies—Acme, Kähkönen, Laamanen (biography 14), Laari, Loon, ME, Mansikka, Rayvor, Neil Smith, Harrison, Carmen, Cecil and Cliff Fielding—provided unlimited employment opportunities for Finnish carpenters. One immigrant whose life has centred around construction is Pentti Laine. After coming to Canada in 1956, he formed an aluminum and construction business in Orillia before coming to the Sudbury area in the 1980s. One of his most notable achievements was to serve as the project foreman for the multimillion-dollar Eaton estate in southern Ontario.[95] Lumbering operations such as those operated north of Sudbury by W.B. Plaunt, Oscar Mäki and Oliver Korpela continued to offer good job prospects. Unlike the situation with earlier immigrants, however, it proved more difficult to entice newer Finns into the woods. Employment shortages in the woods were so severe in 1956 that Oliver Korpela was forced to charter two planes from Finland to bring in over two hundred Finns for his Kormak, Island Lake and Wesmak Companies.[96]

While Finns were still attracted to work in the mining, lumbering and construction fields owned by non-Finns, there was a growing tendency for both new immigrants and native-born Finns to open their own businesses and to seek independent professional careers. Many Finnish enterprises in the immediate postwar period involved construction. Viljo Kähkönen, for example, started his business in the late 1950s, using immigrant Finnish labour. He was often contacted by government officials to hire new immigrants; as these workers were well qualified, the arrangement proved to be of benefit to all concerned. His workers were popular with Inco and Falconbridge officials. In one inspection of newly constructed houses in the Creighton townsite, for example, one Inco engineer was astounded to find a

Biography 14
Risto Laamanen: Community Booster

Risto Laamanen came to Canada in 1950 as a two-year-old child. His family first went to Timmins where Risto's grandfather was employed at the time. After working briefly with Kormak Lumber, the family moved to Sudbury in 1952, at which time his father, Elias, started a construction firm. Risto obtained his elementary schooling at Val Caron Public School and later attended both Capreol and Sudbury High Schools. During the summer months, he gained valuable technical experience working with his father in construction. He attended Cambrian College and graduated from the Civil Engineering Technology program in 1970. After working with Rayvor Construction for several years, he joined with his dad and formed Laamanen Construction Ltd. He then married Aino Kinnunen, who came from Oshawa, Ontario.

The company grew rapidly in the 1970s, developing a specialty in industrial contracting and services and related design-built construction. The firm also became an authorized pre-engineered building dealer. The company headquarters, repair/metal fabrication shop and carpentry/millwork facility are located on Fielding Road in Lively. Over the years the company's staff has ranged from fifty to three hundred employees. In 1988 Risto joined with Stan Bharti to form the BLM Service Group. Since its inception, this group of companies has provided engineering services, contracting services and specialized products to the mining industry through a variety of firms, including Bharti Engineering Associates, Dynatec Engineering 1994 Inc., BLM Mining Services Inc., BLM Mincom Inc. and Pearson, Hofman & Associates. The Service Group, which has 250 employees, has grown rapidly since its formation, and now boasts an impressive client list from all over the world. In 1994 the BLM Service Group became linked with William Resources Ltd., a large multinational corporation headquartered in the United States, and Risto now sits on this company's Board of Directors.

In addition to these achievements, Risto has maintained a high leadership profile in the Sudbury community. Between 1976 and 1982 he was on the Board of Cambrian College and, since 1983, has served as the chairman of the Cambrian Foundation. He has forged strong links with Science North, serving as a Board member since 1992 and as its chairman in 1996. He is also the chairman of the Rusty Blakie Heritage Aviation Group. Over the years he has been a constant supporter of the Finnish community. Risto and Aino have four children: Melissa, Karli, Kristopher and Sarah.

Finnish worker painting the interior of one of the homes using both hands at the same time! When construction was still a summertime activity in the 1960s, Kähkönen had forty to fifty Finns on the payroll; later, when winter construction became more widespread, the number of employees grew to almost three hundred. Kähkönen's company served an important "roll-over" function, providing short-term employment for immigrants until they were hired by either Inco or Falconbridge. He sold his business in 1979.[97]

Risto Laamanen is a successful entrepreneur who established Laamanen Construction in the 1970s and is now a co-owner of the BLM Service Group (see biography 14). He has maintained strong links with the Finnish community, Cambrian College and Science North. (Risto Laamanen, private collection)

Paul Villgren (biography 15), Roy Äyräntö and Ron Kanerva are other success stories. After emigrating to Canada in 1952, Äyräntö grew up on his family's farm in southern Ontario. During the winter, his father worked for Oliver Korpela at Island Lake while he attended high school in Sudbury. He went on to acquire a Bachelor of Science degree from the University of Waterloo and an MBA from the University of Manitoba. He began his association with Canadian Tire in 1977. After serving as a dealer in Port-aux-Basques, Newfoundland, and at Weston in Ontario, he acquired the downtown Sudbury franchise in 1992. In 1995 he opened a large Canadian Tire store in the southern part of the city.[98] Another large operation, The Shop, opened in 1975 with some fifty-five employees; it is one of the world's largest snowmobile dealers. The roots of this business can be traced back to 1936, when Ron Kanerva's father and grandfather first began to experiment with snow machines.[99]

Biography 15

Paul Villgren: Entrepreneur of the Year

Paul Villgren was born in Finland and came to Canada at the age of five. After graduating from the Haileybury School of Mines in 1967, he worked locally for both Inco and Falconbridge in their engineering offices. He then became a mining equipment and supplies salesman with the Timmins-based Hugh J. O'Neill Company for another five and a half years. Noticing a niche in the market for wire rope and slings, Villgren investigated the possibility of opening his own company to exploit this opportunity. On 1 January 1975, he formed Sling-Choker Manufacturing, in partnership with another local entrepreneur. The company began with a specialty in rigging supplies—slings for the mining industry and chokers for forest plants. Stressing the use of rigging products for enhanced safety and efficiency, he became a supplier for Inco and Falconbridge. As the mining companies moved towards continuous operations, Villgren initiated a two-shift system in his Algonquin Road plant to give the companies immediate service. Two and a half years later, he became the sole owner. His concept of developing or acquiring new firms in short-term partnerships with other entrepreneurs was a pattern that he was to follow in future years.

In 1977 he created Ground Control (Sudbury) on Kelly Lake Road for the wholesaling of underground stabilization products. Shortly thereafter, the company moved into the direct manufacturing phase. Ground Control then started the manufacture of products for mine roof support, including bolts, wire mesh, rebars and grout. A year later, Paul Villgren, Inc. was created as an umbrella firm for the above two operations. Faced with the threat of an impending strike against Inco in 1978, Villgren realized that sole reliance on the mining industry was too narrow; consequently, he developed an expanded marketing strategy and acquired the Lob Blasting Mat Company in Sturgeon Falls, which specialized in the recycling of automobile tires into construction blasting mats. Another marketing strategy involved the expansion of Sling-Choker manufacturing operations in places such as Elliot Lake, Sault Ste. Marie, Manitouwadge, Timmins, Val d'Or, Noranda and Hamilton.

Villgren's diversification strategy included the acquisition of three other enterprises: Rezplast Manufacturing for fibreglass products required by the pulp and paper industry; Wilatt Conveyors for frame and rollers for industrial conveyor belts; and Soucie-Salo Safety Inc., featuring a wide variety of safety products. By 1995 he had a string of sixteen companies with some 176 employees in Ontario, Quebec and Michigan, and market sales totalling almost $50 million. Another key to his ongoing success was the introduction of a profit-sharing scheme. In 1995 he was selected by *Northern Life* as Northern Ontario's Entrepreneur of the Year.

In 1995 Paul Villgren was selected as Northern Ontario's Entrepreneur of the Year (see biography 15). He has widespread business interests located in Ontario, Quebec and Michigan. (Paul Villgren, private collection)

As well as being a successful businesswoman, Maija Ceming has been actively involved with the Finnish community (see biography 16). She is shown above serving in her capacity as president of the Sudbury *Suomi* Lions Club in 1992. (Sudbury *Suomi* Lions Club)

Women became prominent entrepreneurs as well. They specialized in a number of areas such as hairstyling, the confectionery and gift trade, art and floral design and catering. The bakery tradition has likewise been continued by Marjaana Laakso at Leinala's Bakery/Scandinavian Foods. Others have taken on more unusual occupations. Maija Ceming, for example, is co-owner of a large number of apartment buildings in Sudbury and Lively (biography 16). Aira Lindroos has acquired a solid reputation for her expertise in the installation of energy systems, including sauna heaters. For twenty-two years, Ellen Kerr (nee Ruismäki) served as clerk for the city of Sudbury; in 1997 she assisted the United Nations in overseeing the first free municipal elections in Bosnia.[100]

For others, upward mobility began through entry into white-collar fields such as education, health, law, accountancy, financial services and government. In education, Finns continued the tradition of teaching in rural elementary schools associated with the Finnish farming and mining areas and later within Sudbury itself. Finns also made their mark at the secondary level.[101] One of these teachers, Sandra Korpela, had the distinction of winning a council seat in the 1978 Sudbury civic election.[102] Finns have also exerted their influence at Laurentian University and Cambrian College as administrators, professors, librarians and teachers.[103] Others obtained university positions elsewhere. After obtaining a degree in architecture from the University of Toronto in 1952, Jules Päiviö eventually became chairman of the Department of Architecture at Ryerson Polytechnic University.

As can be seen from table 16, many Finns have been attracted to the health sector as nurses, medical doctors, dentists, chiropractors, optometrists and pharmacists. Related health specializations included ophthalmology, veterinary and medical administration. Other occupations taken up by the Finnish community include accountancy, government administration, investment, the legal profession and real estate.

Starting in the late 1980s, another process of workplace transition began. It was associated with the retirement of the immigration wave of the 1950s, and included a growing number of second- and third-generation Finns. Many workers retired from Inco and Falconbridge Ltd., and from the working ranks of education, health and government. While these retirements led to a considerable diminution of the Finnish presence in the labour force, they also provided the basis for increased participation in volunteer activities associated with groups such as the Sudbury Finnish Rest Home Society, the Sudbury *Suomi* Lions Club, the Knights and Ladies of Kaleva and the Sudbury Finnish Male Choir.

Biography 16
Maija Ceming: Finnish Ambassador/Entrepreneur

Maija Ceming was born on 3 November 1944 in Lahti, Finland. Both of her parents, Maire (nee Heimonen) and Martti Eskola were also born in Lahti. The Eskola family came to Canada in 1957 and went directly to Foleyet, Ontario, where their sponsors resided. Martti worked for a time in Foleyet before moving on to Sudbury in 1958. The timing was auspicious, as it was the year of the strike against Inco. Martti held a variety of jobs before he established his own company, known as ME Construction. Maija's two brothers, Matti and Mikko, worked with their father as apprentices. The family lived on Elgin Street and Howey Drive before moving to Mäki Avenue in 1969. Maija attended Prince Charles Public School and completed her secondary education at Sheridan Technical School.

During and after her schooling, Maija held a variety of jobs with the Eaton's department store, Lawrence Drug Store, UNAPCO, Ritari Travel and Insurance, Sykes Insurance Company and Sun Life Insurance of Canada. With the latter company, she was the only licensed female agent at the time. She married Jack Ceming, a high-school teacher, in 1970. The couple subsequently purchased the Eskola home on Mäki Avenue. When Jason was born in 1973, this led to an interesting situation with Sun Life Insurance of Canada as the company had only vague policies for dealing with the kind of benefits that Maija thought the contingency warranted. The issue was ultimately resolved and Maija derived considerable satisfaction for the small role she played in helping to feminize the corporate workplace. A daughter, Tanja, was born in 1977.

In the early 1970s, the couple took two steps that eventually led them towards a business career. First, they purchased a sixplex on Mäki Avenue and, second, they acquired part-time employment as superintendents for Lakeshore Manor Apartments. It was the latter course of action that encouraged them to become apartment owners. Bolstered by Maija's entrepreneurial enthusiasm and Jack's long-term vision of becoming self-employed, they decided in 1976 to buy the Parkview Apartments on Paris Street. Almost a decade passed before they acquired the Lively Apartments on Coronation Street in nearby Lively, Ontario. Other acquisitions followed—The Banyan Apartments on Paris Street in 1988, the Northridge Apartments on LaSalle Boulevard and the Beverly Apartments on Beverly Drive in 1991, Cityview Gardens on Ste. Anne Road in 1993 and Regency Park on Regent Street in 1994. With 630 units now in their ownership, they are among the largest apartment owners in the Sudbury area.

Following her arrival in Sudbury in 1958, Maija became active in rhythmic gymnastics. In 1959 she joined the gymnastics group associated with the Finnish National Society of Sudbury. By 1961 she had expanded her talents into coaching. While the gymnasts retained their affiliation with their Finnish heritage through the adoption of the name *Sampo* Rhythmic Gymnastics Club, they eventually acquired independent status as a non-profit organization in the 1970s. Throughout this period, she served as the main driving force behind the growth of the sport.

Instructional classes were held both at *Sampo* Hall and in school gymnasiums in the city under use-share agreements. The club currently has 150 members, many of them now non-Finnish.

Maija became involved with the sport at the provincial and national levels, as well. Between 1969 and 1987, she served as regional chairperson for the Ontario (Rhythmic) Gymnastics Federation (OGF). Maija became an official judge in 1967 and obtained her national coaching credentials in 1976. Over the years, the *Sampo* Rhythmic Gymnastics Club has served as goodwill ambassadors for Sudbury, not only in Finland and elsewhere in Canada, but also in in the World Gymneastradas held in cities such as Amsterdam and Berlin.

Maija has consistently had a deep involvement with the Finnish community. In 1972 she became an executive member of the Finnish National Society of Sudbury, a position that she has retained to the present. From 1986 until its demise in 1989 she served as a member of the Mayor's Finnish Liaison Committee. In 1989 she became a charter member of the Sudbury *Suomi* Lions Club and was its president in 1992-93. She has likewise served on many committees associated with the Grand Festivals held in Sudbury. Another sign of her ongoing interest in Finnish culture is the large and attractive log sauna imported from Finland that she had constructed on the family's summer retreat at Manitoulin Island. Along with these activities as a parent, ambassador and entrepreneur, Maija managed to complete a Bachelor of Arts degree from Laurentian University between 1980 and 1996.

CHAPTER V

Finnish Cultural Contributions to the Sudbury Area

Aclear indicator of the "associative spirit" within the Finnish community was the creation of a strong subculture linked to the physical, artistic and intellectual well-being of the immigrant group. This subculture served as a haven against a hostile new environment, and eased the painful transition of being uprooted from the old homeland. The most notable manifestation of this creative spirit could be found in the promotion of sports, the summer festival tradition and the performing arts. While the organizational aspects of this cultural enthusiasm evolved largely within the framework of the Great Divide, some characteristics, such as the sauna and symbolic ethnicity, remained rooted at the personal and family level. Bolstered by the presence of halls and a highly developed infrastructure, the subculture remained durable up to World War II. After the 1960s, the organized sports tradition declined rapidly. With the aging of the Finnish immigrant population, the remaining elements of the cultural fabric underwent change, and attention began to be directed to new interests, such as fraternal lodges, service clubs, seniors' facilities and language retention through the heritage-language school movement. The latter was important as it reflected growing concerns regarding the survival of the Finnish language among the non-immigrant population.

Sports

One of the most enduring traits associated with the Finns in Canada was their passion for amateur sport. According to one sports historian, "the Finnish Canadians were the best organized and most athletically gifted of the worker sports participants in Canada."[1] Michael Ondaatje's sketch of the athletic exuberance of the Finnish Canadians in his novel *In the Skin of a*

Notes to Chapter V are on pp. 296-298.

Lion also describes their real-life passion for the out-of-doors, their endless energy and their ability to transform almost any setting into an arena of athletic drama.[2] This passion was largely a carry-over from the old country. Started as gymnastics and athletic clubs for the middle and upper class in Finland, the philosophy of physical well-being spread to the workers' movement, which sought a commitment to a new lifestyle based on a holistic approach towards work, education, culture and sports. By 1906 sporting groups had been formed at Thunder Bay, Toronto and Copper Cliff. Interest in long-distance running, wrestling and gymnastics among the Finns was spurred by the great success of Finnish athletes during and after the 1912 Stockholm Olympics. During the 1920s, the Finns could boast that they "ran their way onto the map of the world."[3] Equally important was the support given by European bodies, such as the Workers' Sports League (*TUL*) in Finland, the Workers' Olympics sponsored by the Socialist Workers' Sports International and the Young Communist International (YCI). The first and second wave of immigrants who came to Sudbury brought with them this lifestyle concept and the satisfaction of Olympic success.

After these athletic clubs began to accept non-Finnish speaking members in the 1920s, the clubs, more than any other form of cultural activity, served as an effective means of assimilating Finns into the Canadian mainstream.[4] The sporting tradition was carried over by the third wave of migration in the 1950s; by then, however, the Finnish contribution to organized sports waned, due to the development of secondary schools, a shift of interest among the youth to North American sports, such as football, basketball and hockey, and the triumph of capitalist sport as exemplified by the rise of the National Hockey League.

Athletic Clubs

Finnish sporting activities began under the umbrella of the athletic clubs that were tied to the numerous halls. The majority of these halls were founded by the Finnish Organization of Canada, which proclaimed the need for a strong moral and material commitment to sports as a necessary adjunct to socialism. Later, other clubs developed that were neutral or allied with the national societies. It is important to note, however, that regardless of their political leanings, the sporting clubs maintained a high degree of administrative and "mental" independence from the two central organizations, FOC and COLFC. This was especially true for the FOC-oriented clubs. *Voima*, linked at first to the Finnish National Society of Sudbury, acquired independent status in 1940. While the *Sampo* Athletic Club was formed in 1951 as part of the FNSS, its everyday activities were nevertheless run separately from those of the society's executive.

The first sports clubs in the area, *Tarmo* (Energy) and *Tarmotar* (Woman's Energy), were established in Copper Cliff in 1906. Others came into being between 1909 and 1911 at the Creighton, Garson, Sellwood, Crean Hill and Mond mine sites. The three most dominant clubs were the *Jehu* Club at Beaver Lake (1921), *Kisa* in Sudbury (1923) and *Visa* at Wanup (1930). One important feature associated with all of these clubs was the symbolism of the names chosen to reflect their spiritual aims. They included the following: *Jehu* (Leader) for Beaver Lake, *Tarmo* (Energy) and *Vesa* (Sprout) for Copper Cliff, *Humu* (Bustler) for Chicago Mine, *Yritys* (Endeavour) for Creighton, *Kisatoverit* (Game Comrades) for Levack, *Jyry* (Boisterous) and *Voima* (Power) for Long Lake, *Kipinä* (Spark) for Naughton, *Kisa* (Alerts) and *Visa* (Curly Birch) for Wanup.[5]

The first attempt to create a form of co-ordinated athletic activity in the area was spearheaded by the Beaver Lake *Jehu* Club. *Jehu* was formed originally as an independent sports club with no affiliation to any federation, and the intention originally was to maintain it as such. In 1923, however, its members were barred from participating in meets because of this stand of neutrality. After considerable debate, *Jehu* joined the FOC. Once this decision was made, *Jehu* led the way in forming the Central Ontario Gymnastic and Athletic Clubs Co-ordinating Organization in 1924. So much interest was expressed in the organization that a national body known as the Finnish-Canadian Workers' Sports Federation (FCWSF) was formed in 1925 at the Creighton FOC Hall. FCWSF was closely associated with, but never formally affiliated with, the FOC. The first secretary was Hannes Sula, who was also the editor of *Vapaus*. Competition was initially restricted to sports clubs sponsored by locals of the FOC. One participant recounted a family that had been "run out of Beaver Lake" because the father had travelled through Amsterdam to watch the bourgeois Olympics of 1928 on his way back from Finland.[6] Close ties were also kept with the *Suomen Työväen Urheiluliitto* (Labour Sports Federation) in Finland and the Workers' Sports Association of Canada (WSAC) formed in 1928. In 1932 the headquarters of the Workers' Sports Federation was moved from Sudbury to Toronto. Following an unsuccessful attempt to create a multi-ethnic sports organization in 1932, and conflicts regarding the bolshevization of WSAC, the FCWSF returned to its roots in 1937, and was renamed in 1944 as the *Suomalais-Canadalainen Amatööri-Urheiluliitto* (Finnish-Canadian Amateur Sports Federation, or FCASF). The federation at its height included some seventy-seven clubs from all parts of Canada, of which one-quarter could be found in the Sudbury area.[7] It was FCASF that started the tradition in 1930 of holding an annual federation sports festival.

Voima Athletic Club did not have any left-wing association. Originally established in 1932 by the FNSS, it built a track facility in the Donovan known as Kaskela's athletic field. By the end of the decade, however, the club had ceased to function. During the discussions that led to the formation of the Sudbury District War Aid Association, interest was expressed in resurrecting the club. A new *Voima* Athletic Club was thus created in 1940 as a neutral association with a membership based solely on criteria of good character. For the first few years, *Sampo* Hall in Sudbury was used for winter sporting activities; summer events took place at the Farmers' Hall property at Long Lake. During the war years, use was also made of the FOC Hall at Long Lake. In 1944 *Voima* purchased the Farmers' Hall. The club was run as a trusteeship until 1952 when it was incorporated as FCAA *Voima* (Finnish Canadian Amateur Athletic Club *Voima*). *Voima* has since been led by the following presidents: Jack Seppälä, Antti Heiskanen, Paavo Ruohonen, Eero Pessala, Simo Kälviäinen, Leo Raaska, Ray Korkiala, Oiva Tuomi and Harold Huhtanen. Membership over the years varied from 60 to over 350, many of whom are now of non-Finnish origin. The efforts of the club since 1940 have concentrated on the promotion of provincial, federal and international cross-country ski competitions; in 1954, 1956, 1967, 1976 and 1979 it served as host to either the Canadian Senior or Junior Cross-Country Championships. In the 1970s events such as the Inco, *Voima* and Pepsi Loppets, the *Voima* Citizen Race and the *Voima* International were sponsored. Other forms of sport and recreation promoted by the club included *pesäpallo* (Finnish baseball), wrestling, gymnastics, folk dancing, track-and-field events and shooting. In 1997-98 the hall and property were sold to Cliff Fielding with the provision that *Voima* could lease the facility on a year-to-year basis.[8]

Sampo Athletic Club, formed in 1951, grew rapidly because of the new influx of immigrants. Its members went on to achieve sporting honours in track-and-field events, skiing, boxing, weightlifting and wrestling. Large contingents of youthful men and women from the club performed regularly at summer festivals held in places such as Timmins, Sault Ste. Marie and Thunder Bay. In 1957 the club hosted the Canadian National Cross-Country Championships. For the newly arrived immigrants, *Sampo* Hall and its athletic club served as a "home away from home" until the end of the 1960s. After the hall was rebuilt in 1959, interest in rhythmic gymnastics and folk dancing grew rapidly. By the 1970s, however, younger Finnish Canadians had lost interest in the hall's sporting activities, and the *Sampo* Athletic Club faded from the scene.

These sports clubs were important as they were responsible for the majority of the athletic fields that were constructed in the Sudbury area. In many communities, Finns blasted rock and cleared trees and stumps to level out athletic fields and running tracks. Even if they had only a small clearing or a corduroy road, they raced, threw the javelin and performed mass drills. In the early years of the century, these fields were owned or leased by the FOC organization and affiliated with the FCASF. In Sudbury, *Kisa* AC used a property owned by the FOC on the shore of Pike (now Robinson) Lake for its outdoor track-and-field events. This facility proved to be unsuitable so, in 1926, the club built a 250-metre cinder track known as *Union Kenttä* (Union Athletic Field) on Victoria Street. This was a strong volunteer effort as many workers were required to blast rocks and stumps, carve the hillsides and fill the lowlands. Due to mounting taxes and real estate pressures, the field was sold in 1943. Another property was then bought in the Lockerby area. Known as Alerts Field, it opened in 1945. Boasting an Olympic cinder track, a pavilion and a grandstand with a seating capacity of 640, it was considered to be one of the best facilities of its kind in Ontario. In 1961 municipal taxes again forced this field to be sold. The Sudbury Alerts and Wanup *Visa* clubs then joined forces to build a 400-metre cinder track on property acquired from Antti Lahtinen in Wanup. Meanwhile, the Finnish National Society's sporting field continued to be used from 1932 until 1952, at which time it became the site of the Queen Elizabeth II Public School.[9] Smaller sports fields were constructed as well in virtually all of the outlying communities.

One feature integral to the sporting scene was the equal role assumed by women. It was clear that Finnish women in Canada were much more actively involved in organized sport than their sisters from other English-speaking countries.[10] In all the sporting clubs, membership was open to females, and they frequently held important administrative positions. Aside from wrestling, all competitions, whether they consisted of track-and-field events, gymnastics or skiing, always included separate events for men and women. Neither were the children forgotten, as special efforts were made to get them involved with sports at an early age. While it was the traditional European sports, notably wrestling, cross-country skiing, track and field and gymnastics that prevailed, hockey was also played; for instance, in 1934 the Sudbury *Kisa*, Naughton Sparks and Long Lake *Jyry* all had competitive teams.

Wrestling/Bodybuilding

The early history of wrestling in the Sudbury area is closely tied to Karl Lehto. After his arrival, public awareness of the sport, as discerned from the newspaper coverage of the time, was heightened considerably.[11] The handsome and muscular Lehto established a reputation as a clean fighter who had never been known to lose a match in the USA or Canada. Lehto developed into something of a local cult hero. Despite defeating George Walker, the Canadian wrestling champion in the light heavyweight category, he refused to accept the crown that he had won. He retired from wrestling and put his efforts into his clothing store and promoting the sport. One of his protégés during the 1920s was Wilf Salo, who appeared in many of the FOC halls when wrestling was at its height. Over the next few decades, amateur wrestling remained confined to the various halls scattered throughout the Sudbury district. Outside of the Finnish community, interest in wrestling shifted to professional wrestlers such as Whipper Billy Watson.

In the 1950s two wrestling champions emerged, both associated with the *Sampo* Athletic Club. They wrestled in the classical, or Greco-Roman, style, which was popular among the Finns because of its spectacular over-the-head throws. Antti Filppula in 1955 reached the pinnacle of amateur wrestling in the nation by taking the Canadian championship. When Matti Jutila arrived in Sudbury from Finland in 1956, he had already established himself as Finland's second-best wrestler. Beginning in 1957, he won ten Canadian titles in Greco-Roman and freestyle wrestling. From 1961 to 1970 he won numerous awards, including a silver medal at the 1962 British Empire Games in Perth, Australia, top honours at the North American championship in New York in 1963 and a silver medal at the 1963 Pan-American Games in São Paulo, Brazil. For these latter efforts, he was selected Sudbury's Athlete of the Year.[12] Jutila's career peaked in 1964 when he gained a berth at the Tokyo Olympics. He did not win a medal but managed nonetheless to defeat the reigning world champion. His last achievement was the winning of the Canadian Open Wresting Championship in his class in 1970. Other members of *Sampo* who distinguished themselves in wrestling in the 1950s and 1960s were Pentti Jutila and Veikko Saric.

Allan Päiviö, the son of Aku Päiviö, likewise brought fame to the Sudbury area when he placed second in the Canadian weight-lifting championships of 1947. This was followed by his crowning as "Mr. Canada of 1948."[13]

Cross-Country Skiing

Finns brought to the Sudbury area their natural love for cross-country skiing, and established themselves as the dominant influence guiding the development of this sport. Prior to the Great Depression, skiing was done mostly at the local level, involving competitions among clubs. In the 1930s the situation changed. With high levels of unemployment and plenty of leisure time, more Finns had time to ski at a rigorous and competitive level. If they were working miners, they often practised at night with the aid of their miners' lamps. An indication of this enthusiasm is demonstrated in the following account:

> In 1932, four *Jehu* AC skiers went to a ski meet in Timmins. They were Toivo Torvi, Hj. Laamanen, Urho Wirta and Niilo Myllynen, who first managed to get a ride from Beaver Lake to Sudbury. From there they took the train to Westree, skied nine miles east to the Hydro line, and then skied along the line to Timmins. On the way up it took them two nights and three days. On the return trip they really travelled and were back in Westree in two days. (They slept at linemen's cabins along the way). . . . The distance each way was about 120 miles. The same trip was duplicated in 1939 by *Jehu* AC skiers Kalle Saari, Olavi Salminen and Gunnar Ronka, accompanied by Lauri Huuki of Sudbury Kisa AC.[14]

Finnish skiers from the Sudbury area left a strong national imprint as Canadian skiing champions (table 17). While many of the better skiers such as Paul Jansson and Lauri Huuki originally came from sports clubs associated with the FOC, the trend changed in the 1950s as *Voima, Sampo* and the Nickel Teen clubs began to produce winners as well. By this time newly arrived skiers from Finland, such as Arvo Äyräntö, Antero Rauhanen and Matti Mäki, dominated. Rauhanen, in particular, posted achievements in men's senior cross-country racing that will unlikely be equalled again. Mäki was successful at several provincial, national and international meets during the early 1970s. Mention should also be made of the efforts of Ellis Hazen, a local high school teacher, who in 1940 assumed the task of developing a club, known as the Nickel Teen Ski Club, solely for junior age skiers. Many young Finns became affiliated with the Nickel Teen Ski Club and represented Sudbury at various meets throughout the country until Hazen's death in 1978.

Table 17
Finnish-Canadian Skiing Champions from the Sudbury Area

Canadian National Cross-Country Championships

Men's Senior Cross-Country
1936 Aate (Arnold) Back, Alerts AC (18 km)
1947 Lauri Huuki, Alerts AC (18 km)
1948 Lauri Huuki, Alerts AC (18 km)
1954 Arvo Äyräntö, *Voima* AC (18 km)
1956 Arvo Äyräntö, *Voima* AC (30 km)
1957 Arvo Äyräntö, *Voima* AC (15 and 30 km)
1958 Antero Rauhanen, *Sampo* AC (15 km)
1959 Antero Rauhanen, *Sampo* AC (15 km and 4×10 relay)
      Arvo Äyräntö, *Voima* AC (30 km)
1960 Antero Rauhanen, *Sampo* AC (15,30 km and 3×10 relay)
      Matti Jutila and Kauko Riihiaho, *Sampo* AC (3×10 km relay)

Table 17 (continued)

1961   Antero Rauhanen, *Sampo* AC (15 and 30 km)
1963   Antero Rauhanen, *Sampo* AC (15 and 30 km)
1965   Antero Rauhanen, *Sampo* AC (30 km)
1966   Antero Rauhanen, Estonian Toronto AC (15 km and 4×10 km relay)
1967   Antero Rauhanen, Estonian Toronto AC
            (15, 30 km and 4×10 km relay)
1968   Eric Salkeld, *Voima* AC (4×10 km relay)
1969   Eric Salkeld, *Voima* AC (50 km and 3×10 km relay)

Women's Senior Cross-Country
1956   Mary Juoksu, *Voima* AC (7 km)
1957   Mary Juoksu, *Voima* AC (7 km)

Junior Men's Cross-Country
1978   Perry Säkki, *Voima* AC (5 and 7.5 km)
1979   Perry Säkki, Ari Niemi, *Voima* AC (3×7.5 km relay)
1980   Perry Säkki, Ari Niemi, *Voima* AC (3×7.5 km relay)
1981   Perry Säkki, Laurentian University (*Voima* AC)
            (15 km and 3×7.5 km relay)

Other National and International Championships

Men's Senior Cross-Country
1941   Paul Jansson, Sudbury Ski Club/Alerts AC
            (International Ski Classic at Duluth, USA)

Men's Intermediate Cross-Country
1959   Eino Marttila, Beaver Lake *Jehu* AC

Men's Junior Cross-Country
1951   Altti Liimanaa, Nickel-Teen (Alerts AC)
1952   Altti Liinamaa, Nickel-Teen (Alerts AC)
1953   Jorma Tervo, *Voima* AC
1954   Jorma Tervo, *Voima* AC
1957   Karl Krats, Beaver Lake *Jehu* AC
1958   Karl Krats, Beaver Lake *Jehu* AC
1959   Lauri Valiaho, *Sampo* AC
1964   Jack Krats, Nickel-Teen (Beaver Lake *Jehu* AC)

Girl's Junior Cross-Country
1960   Shirley Rönkä, Beaver Lake *Jehu* AC

Junior Nordic Combined (Cross-Country, Downhill, Slalom and Jumping)
1952   Arne Mäki, Nickel-Teen (Alerts AC)

Boy's Junior Nordic Combined
1952   Arne Mäki, Nickel-Teen (Sudbury Alerts AC)

Men's Nordic Combined
1956   Aulis Kangas, *Sampo* AC

Sources: Jim Tester, ed., *Sports Pioneers*; Frank Pagnuccio, *Home Grown Heroes*; Cross Country Canada, *Cross-Country Guide 85* (Ottawa, 1986), pp. 50-63.

While interest in competitive skiing within the Finnish community has virtually disappeared, the cross-country skiing tradition was maintained up to 1998 by the *Voima* sports club through its sponsoring of *loppet* competitions for the general public at its Long Lake *Suomiranta* Hall.

Track and Field

Finns have exhibited a long-standing love of track-and-field sports. The success of Finnish athletes was largely due to the infrastructural support provided by the halls, their athletic organizations and superb track-and-field facilities. The development of these sports remained very much a Finnish enterprise until the early 1960s. The participation of Finns in track-and-field events took place at two levels. For most club members, local competitions and summer festivals represented an opportunity to become physically fit, associate with other athletes and to engage in friendly rivalries with other Finns. Competition was generally limited to athletes belonging to the same sporting organization; cross-participation occurred infrequently. While local competitions were major events within the Finnish community, they did not attract much attention in the local press. Among the first competitions to be held was one that took place along the shore of Vermilion River on May Day in 1917. This pioneering event was followed by the formation of the Beaver Lake *Jehu* Athletic Club in 1921, which eventually became the strongest rural club in the history of amateur sports in Canada. Known as the first club in Canada to have an Olympic track, it maintained a strong tradition in track-and-field sports that spanned the next fifty-eight years.[15] Another strong club was Sudbury *Kisa* formed in 1923. During the 1920s as many as ten track-and-field meets were held each summer. With the formation of Wanup *Visa* in 1930, and the beginning of the FCASF summer sports festivals in the same year, the competitive setting was enhanced considerably. Up to the 1950s, track-and-field events sponsored by Finnish clubs provided an important competitive outlet for non-Finns who had no other venues for their athletic endeavours.

Gymnastics

Gymnastics was another popular sport, performed both at individual and group levels. A gymnastics club was formed at Copper Cliff as early as 1906. Other clubs were then formed elsewhere. During the winter months, the halls in the area were filled with women who performed intricate routines and men who strove to attain the highest possible pyramid formations. The gymnastic pyramid had great symbolic value as it was used to depict the importance of working-class solidarity in the class struggle. Performances in the halls featured gymnasts proudly wearing the outfits and colours of their respective clubs. The sport was blessed with having coaches of the highest calibre, such as Lahja Tanner, Jack Hymander, Helmi (Pearl) Kivinen and Elvi Duncan. The mass performances that took place during the summer festivals were real crowd pleasers. After World War II, the gymnastic tradition slowly disappeared from the scene, and it now remains as one of the recreational activities of the Finnish Senior Citizens' Club of Sudbury that was formed in 1971. Rhythmic gymnastics, however, has been carried on. Under the banner of *Sammon Tytöt* (*Sampo* Girls), and the strong leadership of Maija Ceming, this sport flourished at *Sampo* Hall. The *Sampo* Girls continue to perform this activity, and they have participated regularly in the Grand Festivals and in competitions held throughout North America and Europe.

The Summer Festival Tradition

The most celebrated of the Finnish customs has been the summer festival. It brings together thousands of participants and spectators for several days of music, sports, theatrical presentations, gymnastic displays, concerts and dancing. Finns felt it very important to attend these festivals, and they frequently travelled by freight trains or drove many hours bundled up in open trucks along long and lonely stretches of single lane highways. Until the 1980s, these celebrations were primarily Finnish-Canadian events, with little input from Finland. One highlight is the holding of a parade, or "Grand March," involving all of the participants and their club banners. Over the years, the Sudbury community has been one of the strongest supporters of the festival tradition in Canada. It was FCASF that held the first sports festival in Sudbury in 1930. With the outbreak of World War II, these festivals came to a halt because of the wartime restrictions on the FOC and its allied organizations.

Another summer festival event then emerged known as *Canadan Suomalaisten Laulu-Urheilu-ja Osuustoimintajuhlat* (The Finnish Canadian Song, Sports and Co-operatives Festival). This celebration was first organized by Sudbury Finns in 1940 at Lake Ramsey. Intended as a fund-raising event to aid Finland in its war effort against the USSR, it proved to be so successful that another five summer festivals were held in the Sudbury area. After World War II, the tradition continued in places outside of Sudbury with profits being directed to Finnish-Canadian communities rather than to Finland. The name of the festival was later changed to the *Kanadan Suomalaisten Suur-juhlat* (Finnish Canadian Grand Festival, or FCCG) in 1959.[16] Meanwhile, FCASF was given permission by the federal government to reestablish its summer festival at Toronto in 1944. In 1957 the FOC, which had been holding separate annual music festivals since 1938, joined forces with the FCASF, as it had become evident by this time that the leftist movement could no longer support two annual events. The first joint Sport and Cultural Festival was held in Sudbury in this year. In 1961 the Grand Festival format also underwent organizational change as a central committee was established to assist local communities in the continuance of the annual festival.

The practice of having two annual festivals continued until 1973 when the Sports and Cultural Festivals came to an end. Thus, in 1974, the Grand Festival was the sole event of its kind in Canada. Beginning in 1994, however, the FOC and FCASF reestablished what were called "Reunion" Festivals. The first festival was held at the Wanup Hall; it was sponsored by the Sudbury and Wanup FOC locals, the Alerts and *Visa* Athletic Clubs and the Finnish Senior Citizens' Club of Sudbury.

The sports and cultural focus of the Grand Festival underwent change in the 1980s. While the role of sports diminished, the cultural emphasis was broadened to include fashion shows, groups from Finland, guest lecturers and the marketing of Finnish goods. While these festivals have continued to be successful, there is concern with the lack of interest shown by younger Finns unable to converse fluently in the Finnish language.[17] It is clear that the future success of this event will be determined largely by the willingness of the Grand Festival and Finnish Canadian Cultural Federation representatives to adopt a more English-oriented format as has occurred, for example, with the FinnFest USA festivals.

The Sudbury area has served as the most important site for festivals in Canada (table 18). Of the forty-two festivals sponsored by the FCASF/FOC between 1930 and 1997, fifteen were held in the Sudbury area, more than any other community. Similarly, sixteen of the fifty-eight festivals sponsored under the umbrella of the FCGF involved Sudbury, again more than any other community. Sudbury has thus been the site for almost a third of the one hundred Finnish festivals held in Canada.

Table 18
Annual Summer Music and Sports (Grand) Festivals
in Canada (1930-97)

Sponsored by Finnish-Canadian Amateur Sports Federation/ Finnish Organization of Canada	Year	Sponsored by Finnish Canadian Grand Festival/Finnish Canadian Cultural Federation
Sudbury	1930	
Beaver Lake	1931	
Toronto	1933	
Toronto	1935	
Toronto	1936	

Table 18 (continued)

Sponsored by Finnish–Canadian Amateur Sports Federation/ Finnish Organization of Canada	Year	Sponsored by Finnish Canadian Grand Festival/Finnish Canadian Cultural Federation
Toronto	1937	
Beaver Lake	1938	
Timmins	1939	
	1940	Sudbury
	1941	Sudbury
	1942	Sudbury
	1943	Sudbury
Toronto	1944	Sudbury
Sudbury	1945	Sudbury
South Porcupine	1946	Sudbury
Toronto	1947	Port Arthur
Kirkland Lake	1948	Toronto
Sudbury	1949	Sault Ste. Marie
South Porcupine	1950	Timmins
Toronto	1951	Sudbury
Port Arthur	1952	Port Arthur
Sudbury	1953	Sudbury
Toronto	1954	Sault Ste. Marie
South Porcupine	1955	Toronto
Sudbury	1956	Montreal
Sudbury[a]	1957	Windsor
Port Arthur	1958	Port Arthur
Toronto	1959	Timmins
South Porcupine	1960	Sudbury
Sudbury	1961	Sault Ste. Marie
Port Arthur	1962	Toronto
Toronto	1963	Port Arthur
South Porcupine	1964	Sudbury
Sudbury/Wanup	1965	Timmins
Port Arthur	1966	Sault Ste. Marie
Toronto	1967	Montreal
Sudbury/Wanup	1968	Toronto
Port Arthur	1969	Port Arthur
Toronto	1970	Sudbury
Sudbury/Wanup	1971	Windsor
Thunder Bay	1972	Sault Ste. Marie
Sudbury/Wanup	1973	Vancouver
	1974	Toronto
	1975	Thunder Bay
	1976	Montreal
	1977	Sudbury
	1978	Sault Ste. Marie
	1979	Toronto

Table 18 (continued)

Sponsored by Finnish-Canadian Amateur Sports Federation/ Finnish Organization of Canada	Year	Sponsored by Finnish Canadian Grand Festival/Finnish Canadian Cultural Federation
	1980	Vancouver
	1981	Thunder Bay
	1982	Timmins
	1983	Calgary
	1984	Sudbury
	1985	Sault Ste. Marie
	1986	Vancouver
	1987	Toronto
	1988	Thunder Bay
	1989	Sudbury
	1990	Timmins
	1991	Sault Ste. Marie
	1992	Vancouver
	1993	Toronto
Wanup[b]	1994	Thunder Bay
Toronto	1995	Sudbury
Wanup	1996	Timmins
Toronto	1997	Sault Ste. Marie

a First combined Music and Sports Festival. Starting with Toronto in 1938, the FOC held annual music festivals in different communities until 1957, when they were merged with the sports festivals organized by the FCASF.

b Start of Reunion, Summer Festival, *Kesäkestit* and Jubilee gatherings.

Sources: Jim Tester, ed., *Sports Pioneers*, p. 225; Finnish-Canadian Grand Festival Committee, *Finnish-Canadian Grand Festival Sudbury, Ontario 1995* (Sudbury, 1995), p. 19.

Performing Arts

Finnish-Canadian culture in the Sudbury area has been closely interwoven with the performing arts. Over the years, the cultural scene was enriched by a plethora of artistic pursuits involving bands and orchestras, theatrical performances and choral singing. While much of this cultural orientation came from traditions established in Finland, the nature of the infrastructure in Canada gave added impetus. These activities complemented sports and the role of the annual festivals as adaptation mechanisms for immigrants in their new homeland. Appearing first as part of the leftist culture, interest in the performing arts spread throughout the Finnish community. Celebrations such as *Vappu* (May Day) *Kalevala* Day, *Juhannus* (Midsummer Festival) and *Itsenäisyyspäivä* (Finland's Independence Day) gave ample opportunity for performing artists to appear regularly on the stage.

Brass bands and orchestras featuring the use of the accordion appeared as backdrops for dances, weddings, the presentation of musicals and theatrical performances. An orchestra known as *Vuoriston Kaiku* (Mountain Echo) existed before 1908 in association with the Copper Cliff Temperance Association. Each hall had its favourite group of musicians. In the Long Lake area, Vern Kinnonen and Aimo Mäkinen for years provided lively music at the Farmers' Hall. They were later followed by the Northern Lads. Arvo Tuuri, Taito Ristimäki and Väinö Manninen played regularly during the interwar years at halls in Creighton and Beaver Lake. Manninen served as the mentor for Leo Niemi, who later played as a regular at the Finnish Hall in Sudbury. Leo Niemi started as a soloist, but later organized a band featuring the popular singer Eric Kinos. He is also a master technician, rebuilding and tuning accordions for players all over North America.[18] Other regular performers at the Finnish Hall included Karl Niemi, Taisto Länsi and the Melody Orchestra. The Wanup scene was musically activated by people such as Arvid Salonen, Eino Ahokas and Risti Hako-Oja. Other musicians who became popular after the 1950s included the Saari Brothers, Hannu Lambert, Eero Jutila and the Rhythm Boys and Karl Pukara.[19]

Karl Pukara is especially well known in the Sudbury area. He started his professional career in 1946 at *Sampo* Hall, and in 1957 became a musical instructor at the Prom School of Music. He worked there until 1964, when he opened a private music school known as the Karl Pukara Music Studio. Two of his noteworthy achievements included the formation of the Karl Pukara Senior Accordion Orchestra, which he led between 1957 and 1987, and his guidance of Iona Reed to a world championship in 1962.[20] Throughout his career, Pukara taught more than 5,000 to play accordion and piano and performed at more than 3,000 concerts, dances and parties. According to him, "music to a Finlander isn't just music, but a way of life . . . it's in our blood and in our souls."[21] In 1996 a gala reunion attended by six hundred people was held in his honour at Laurentian University. His death in 1998 was a great loss to the Finnish cultural community.

Choral singing has continued as a mainstay of the cultural setting to the present day. Aided by accomplished and devoted directors, choirs of all kinds sprouted everywhere. The first choir to appear was *Leivo* (Skylark), formed as part of the Temperance Society in Copper Cliff in 1900.[22] Another choir was soon formed in the Copper Cliff Finnish Church. Choirs were strong in the FOC locals, where singing was used as a "medium for expressing joy and despair, longing and desire" and a "rich variety of inner feelings."[23] Such was the case with the mixed *Sävel* (Melody) choir from the Sudbury FOC local. *Voima* Athletic Club also had a choir consisting of up to sixty members that participated regularly in the

Kiwanis Music Festival. Within Finnish churches, choirs flourished. The choral tradition still remains very active at both St. Matthew's Evangelical Lutheran and the Finnish Pentecostal Churches. Among the more recent arrivals on the music stage can be included the singing groups *Annin Pojat* and Octovox. The most widely known choral group is the *Sudburyn Laulu-miehet* (Sudbury Finnish Male Choir). Formed in 1960, it has had a membership ranging between thirty-seven and fifty-five. The choir has gained a well-deserved reputation for its presentation of Finnish music and for its versatility in performing songs from other cultures. Its directors have included Timo Kotilehti, Erkki Hietänen, Aksel Palgi, Ella Lillo, Antti Saari and Marlene (Salo) Sovran.[24] Each year the choir presents an annual concert and performs at churches, festivals, Christmas programs and multicultural events. It has also given performances in the United States and Finland.[25] Over the years, the choir has been financially assisted by a Ladies' Auxiliary through bake sales and the publication of a Finnish cook book.

Theatre has been another impressive feature of the performing arts. It was here where the creativity of the Finnish community found its fullest expression. Whether in the form of writing plays, directing, acting, assisting with costumes, make-up or set designs, Finns presented hundreds of plays depicting aspects of life centred around traditional Finnish and Shakespearean classics, revolutionary themes, love and romance and the hardships associated with everyday life. For the FOC, the theatre was used as an ideological tool, whereas for other Finns it was essentially a means of providing entertainment and diversion.[26] Regardless of the intent, the theatre held powerful sway in the Finnish community. On a more practical note, the theatre was also promoted as it served as a major source of income for the halls. This was especially important for the leftist movement, which required these theatre revenues for the building up of strike reserves, newspaper support and the promotion of union activity.

Theatrical presentations began shortly after the construction of the Temperance Society building in Copper Cliff in 1895. In 1903 a faction of the society, the Copper Cliff Young People's Society, gave its first performance in the hall. By 1917 numerous plays were being performed at the Copper Cliff Finnish Social Society's new hall on the site of the present-day slag dump. Plays were presented there until 1923. The centre of theatrical activities then shifted to Liberty Hall in Sudbury. Theatre was at its liveliest during the 1920s and 1930s. Activity peaked in 1929, when thirty-two full-length theatre plays and six one-act performances were presented in Liberty Hall alone. To assist its small locals, the FOC created a central registry from which theatrical or movie scripts could be rented. In 1929, for example, the registry had 732 scripts available for distribution. The drama

The Sudbury area reflects many aspects of "symbolic ethnicity." Pentti and Louise Laine's rural retreat known as "Little Karjalia," set in the midst of a birch grove near Estaire, is a good reflection of this form of Finnish symbolism, 1993. (Oiva Saarinen, private collection)

Another form of symbolic ethnicity is the use of the national costume. Edith Saarinen and Tuula Kaitila are shown here wearing national costumes from Finland, 1996. (Oiva Saarinen, private collection)

Since the 1980s, the most active force within the Finnish community has been the seniors' movement. The first phase of Finlandia Village, known as *Finlandia-Koti*, was completed in 1985. Shown above are the self-contained apartments, 1996. (Oiva Saarinen, private collection)

In 1992, the second phase of Finlandia Village, known as *Palvelukoti*, was completed. Shown above is a view of the award-winning residential care facility, 1996. (Oiva Saarinen, private collection)

Lutherans who lived in Sudbury had to await the 1930s for their own congregation to be formed. Shown above is the first parsonage of St. Matthew's Finnish Evangelical Lutheran Church on Tedman Avenue in the Donovan, c. 1939. (Archives of Ontario, F1405-15-15/MSR 2029-18)

A major Finnish landmark in the Donovan was St. Matthew's Finnish Evangelical Lutheran Church. The church is shown above during construction in 1948. (Archives of Ontario, F1405-15-15/MSR 2029-34)

Not all Finns were Lutheran. A Finnish Pentecostal church was erected in 1936 on the corner of Haig and Whittaker Streets where the Caruso Club now stands. (Archives of Ontario, A03467)

In 1968 a new site was purchased for the Finnish Pentecostal congregation. Shown here is the existing church building on Paris Street in the Lockerby area, c. 1990s. (Finnish Pentecostal Church)

The halls associated with the Copper Cliff Finnish Social Society served as lively centres of cultural activity after World War I. Shown here is the Society's "Halfway" Hall that was located midway between Sudbury and Copper Cliff, c. 1920s. (Finnish Canadian Historical Society)

The second postwar building associated with the Copper Cliff Finnish Social Society was the Workers' Hall on Alder Street, which was constructed in Sudbury in 1929. (Finnish Canadian Historical Society)

The Finnish cultural scene was greatly enhanced by the many concerts such as this one sponsored by the Sudbury District Finnish War Association in 1940 to assist Finland in its war effort. (Finnish Canadian Historical Society)

One of the fund-raising events associated with the War Aid Association was the *kruunuhäät* (mock wedding) where people would pay to dance with an honorary bride and groom. Laina Ojala, accompanied by Isaac Hirsimäki, is shown here wearing a large tiara, 1940. (Oiva Saarinen, private collection)

Laila Rintamäki is a well-known actress who performed in many Finnish plays in the 1940s and 1950s (see biography 17). She is shown here, fourth from the left in the front row, in a play entitled *Marietta*, which was performed at Beaver Lake in 1948. (Laila Rintamäki, private collection)

Wilf Salo is a colourful figure whose background has included retailing, wrestling and involvement with many community activities and fraternal organizations (see biography 18). He is best known for his portrayal of Santa Claus for more than fifty years. (Wilf Salo, private collection)

Arne Ritari (1906-97) founded Ritari Insurance and Travel Agency in the 1930s and was an "Ambassador of Goodwill" for international Lionism (see biography 19). He was also instrumental in establishing the first Lions Club in Finland. (Arne Ritari, private collection)

Judy Erola, granddaughter of Thomas Jacobson, is shown here with the author prior to receiving a Doctor of Laws degree from Laurentian University on 31 May 1996 (see biography 20). Her career has spanned both politics and the private sector. (Oiva Saarinen, private collection)

Biography 17
Laila Rintamäki: Devotee of the Theatre

Laila Rintamäki (nee Johnson) was born on 21 February 1918 at Creighton Mine, Ontario. Her mother was Mari Pesonen, who had emigrated from Finland at the age of nine to Hancock, Michigan. Mari completed her schooling at Suomi College and came to Creighton in 1913. Matti Ojala, her father, came to Copper Cliff in 1896. As was the case with many other Finns, the Ojala name was changed to Johnson. Matti and Mari met in Creighton Mine and were married in Copper Cliff in 1916. Laila also had a brother, Bill (see biography 13), who was born in 1920.

As a youngster, Laila attended Creighton Public School. Following brief sojourns in Beaver Lake and Timmins, the family moved to the Pesonen homestead at Beaver Lake where Laila completed two years of high school. She left home at the age of sixteen and found work in Sudbury as a domestic; this was followed by a short stint at Elna Marttila's boarding house in Creighton Mine. She married Onni Rintamäki in 1936. Over the years of their marriage, they followed mining jobs and moved twenty-one times to various places in Creighton Mine, Sudbury, Levack and Lockerby. They had two children, Helen (born in 1937) and Ann (1944). Laila and Onni returned to Beaver Lake in 1946, where they operated the Rintamäki General Store and ran milk deliveries to the Copper Cliff, Standard, City, Co-operative and Palm Dairies. Following the sale of their business in 1950, Onni again became a miner at Crean Hill and Levack. The couple returned to Beaver Lake in 1961 and Onni retired in 1971. After Onni's death in 1980, Laila moved to Sudbury and then to Lively, where she currently resides.

Like many of her Finnish counterparts, Laila was not content to remain solely a housewife and a mother. From her early childhood, she was drawn into the web of the Finnish hall culture of her mother and father, who were both involved in the theatre as actors and directors. As well, Mari possessed a lovely soprano voice and Matti performed as a musician. As her parents were active supporters of the FOC Hall in Creighton, Laila was always brought there where, along with other children, she participated in gym classes, attended school on Sundays, where English was taught by her mother, and became an avid devotee of the stage. She then began to memorize the roles and songs performed by adult actors. Her first singing solo was given at the age of three at the Creighton Hall; this was followed by her first stage performance in a play at Timmins in 1930. From this point on, her life was closely intertwined with that of the stage. At the Beaver Lake Hall in 1931, she played a memorable role as a young boy in a play called *Kultainen Nuuskarasia* (The Golden Snuff Box). Her first adult role was in 1935 in *Manouverit* (Manoeuvres). During World War II, she sang with the *Sampo* and *Voima* choirs. Over the span of eight years, she also performed in numerous plays at *Sampo* Hall. Many of these plays were associated with the Finnish clan competitions known as the *Heimo Juhlat*. In later years she had major roles in the musical *Mustalais Manja* (The Gypsy Manja) and the play *Marietta*.

She directed many plays for the theatrical group at Beaver Lake—*Helsingittäriä Maalla* (Helsinki Girls on the Farms), *Ristiaallokossa* (In the Cross Waves), *Auto Tyttö* (The Girl Chauffeur) and *Kuka on Perheen Pää?* (Who Is the Boss in the Family?) among them. Her involvement with the stage declined after the 1960s due to difficulties in attracting younger persons who could speak the language fluently. In the 1967 centennial year, however, she performed in the well-known Finnish play *Tukkijoella* (River Drive), presented during Finland Week at Laurentian University and later at the Finnish and *Sampo* Halls. At the present time, she is actively involved with the Ladies of Kaleva and the seniors' group, *Seurakerho*.

For Laila, the stage was important for Finnish women as it served as a medium for growing up and for experiencing life in its many forms; it also paved the way for women to express themselves effectively and to become more self-confident and poised as individuals. The stage likewise provided average Finnish women such as herself an excellent opportunity to develop their inherent Finnishness.[27] She laments the contemporary decline of the Finnish stage, feeling that it represents a lost opportunity for younger Finnish Canadians to associate with their heritage.

---

society of the Sudbury FOC local alone produced over six hundred plays between 1921 and 1970. Some thirty-two directors worked for the society in its first forty years of activity, many coming directly from Finland. The theatre was remarkably strong in the outlying areas served by the Beaver Lake, Copper Cliff, Creighton, Levack, Long Lake, Vermilion River, Wahnapitae, Wanup, Whitefish and Worthington locals of the FOC. Many plays written by playwrights from the Sudbury area, such as Aku Päiviö, Reynold Pehkonen (Hellä Kotijärvi), Einari Jouppi and John Wirta, were also presented on stages elsewhere in North America and Finland. Wirta was responsible for the formation of the Copper Cliff Young People's Society and its theatre group in 1903 which presented more than one hundred plays over a ten-year span. Wirta continued his stage work in the Sudbury area until 1932 when he left for Soviet Karelia.[28] During the 1930s the left-wing theatre experienced problems because of the Karelian exodus and the bolshevization of the stage.

Theatrical life was an integral part of other Finnish organizations as well. Beginning in 1933, a drama group known as *Elo* (Life) began at the Finnish-Canadian Workers' and Farmers' Federation Hall in Sudbury. This theatre group was formed to provide an alternative to the highly politicized plays which, at the time, stressed class issues and Marxist ideology. In contrast to the FOC locals, this group drew upon a central registry of plays provided by the IWW. A *Finlandia* Club formed within the Copper Cliff Lutheran Church between 1933 and 1935 also produced several plays under the direction of John Kontturi, who had previously been active with drama in Finland.[29]

Following the construction of *Sampo* Hall in 1935, a lively theatre group evolved there and, during the Finnish Winter War, plays were presented on a weekly basis. While most performers, such as Laila Rintamäki (biography 17), were content to serve only on the Finnish stage, others such as Aino Pirskainen and Helen Grenon moved on to become active in the Sudbury Little Theatre Guild. The theatrical tradition has been carried on in recent years via the Grand Festival. Unfortunately, the barrier of language has meant that few in the outside community came to appreciate the high quality of the Finnish theatre. There was one performer, however, who managed to gain instant recognition throughout the community for his unique acting ability—Wilf Salo for his portrayal of Santa Claus (biography 18).

Biography 18
Wilf Salo: Mr. Santa Claus

Wilf Salo was born in 1907 in Ishpeming, located on the Upper Peninsula of Michigan in the United States. His father was Viktor Lakaniemi, who subsequently changed his name to Salo. He married in the United States and had five children. Viktor came to Canada in 1912. After working briefly in Copper Cliff, the family moved to the Magpie mine site near Wawa. Following the closure of the mine, the family came to Sudbury in 1918 where Wilf attended Central and Elm Street Public Schools. In 1922 Viktor took his other children back to Finland while Wilf stayed in Sudbury.

In 1922 Wilf worked on the railway from Temiskaming to Ville Marie in Quebec. He took a course in bookkeeping from the Nickel City (Sudbury) Business College, and later became a linesman for the Temiskaming and Northern Ontario Railway at Swastika, Kirkland Lake and Timmins. This was followed by an employment stint with the British America Nickel Company at Murray Mine. When this operation closed in 1923, he found employment in the lumbering industry at Chapleau and along the CPR railway line, where he was a witness to one of the investigation committees that sought to determine the political orientation of Finnish immigrants.

Wilf returned to Sudbury in 1924 and became a taxi driver. Between 1924 and 1927 he worked as a volunteer fireman, linesman, mechanic's helper and bread deliverer for the Ontario (Weston) and Northern Bakery Companies. In 1927 he started in the retail industry as a clerk and salesman at Karl Lehto's store. Under Lehto's tutelage, he became an accomplished wrestler, appearing frequently in the Grand Theatre, the Palace Rink and many Finnish halls. After completing a course in merchandising and advertising, he obtained a position in 1929 with Silverman's Store as an advertising supervisor. He served as a floor manager at Silverman's for thirty-six years until 1965. In the same year, he established the Soucie-Salo Safety Supply Company store on Lorne Street.

In 1927 Wilf married Nellie Pernu, who worked at the *Vapaus* Publishing Company. Nellie was active in the cultural activities of the FOC, especially in sports and in the theatre at Liberty Hall. Wilf and Nellie had one child, Joyce, who gained prominence in Canada as a figure skater and skating instructor, and whose career served as the basis for the book *The Bells on Finland Street*.[30] Wilf was always involved with organizations and community activities. At an early age, he joined the Lone Scouts, Boy Scouts, Lone Indians and Nomads youth groups. He later joined the Sudbury Lions Club, became a member of the Masonic Order in 1945 and a Shriner in 1947. In 1947 he won the King of the Beards title in the Sudbury Winter Carnival Whiskerino Contest, a feat that he repeated in 1967. He served as president of the Sudbury Lions and Shriner Clubs, and was a past deputy district governor of Lions International. In 1965 he became a member of the Knights of Kaleva. Among his other achievements, he served as chairman of the Sudbury Housing Authority, Sudbury and District TB and Lung Association, Christmas Seals Campaign and Sudbury Coordinating Council of Service Clubs, honorary governor of the Canada Jaycees and honorary governor of the Memorial Hospital.

Wilf is best known, however, for serving as Sudbury's official Santa Claus for more than fifty years. For generations of Sudburians, Wilf Salo really was Santa Claus! His Santa career began as a promotional stunt for Silverman's toy department in 1934. The rest became Yuletide history. As his reputation grew, he served as Santa Claus for the Shriners, the Sudbury Lions Club and the General and Memorial Hospitals, Police and Fire Departments, Retarded Children's Association, the CNIB and Sudbury's annual Santa Claus parade. Wilf made home visits as well. He became widely known for his annual half-hour Santa program, which started on CKSO-TV in 1952. His TV Santa career lasted thirty-five years. Knowing how to say Merry Christmas in fourteen different languages separated him from all other pretenders. In 1979 he was congratulated on being the oldest continuing Santa Claus on private television in Canada. For reasons of health, he retired as Santa in 1987.

Wilf resided on the south shore of Long Lake from 1971 until 1996, when he moved into a retirement home on Walford Road. On his eighty-fifth birthday in 1992, Wilf was honoured at a gala party held at the Four Points Inn. He has been the recipient of numerous awards that bear testimony to his adage that "everyone should put something back into the community." These include the Canadian Centennial Medal (1967); Sudbury's Citizen of the Year Award (1977); the Bicentennial Certificate from the city of Sudbury in 1984; life membership in The Commercial Travellers' Association of Canada in 1985; a Fifteen-Year Volunteer Service Award from the Ontario Ministry of Citizenship and Culture, Province of Ontario in 1986; a Certificate of Recognition for Outstanding Contribution to the Spirit of Christmas from the city of Sudbury in 1992 and a commemorative medal for the hundred and twenty-fifth anniversary of the Confederation of Canada from the governor-general of Canada, Ottawa, 1993.

The Sauna

For most Canadians, it is the sauna that serves as the "root metaphor" of Finnish culture.[31] Few, however, realize the true importance of the sauna as a cultural symbol for the Finns. The history of the sauna extends back for centuries; indeed, the *Kalevala*, Finland's folk epic, has numerous references to the sauna and its utility for the making of malt, as a place for childbirth, a means of driving away evil, for spiritual nourishment, the resolution of problems and as a final resting place for the departed. Viljo Virtanen from Sudbury, for instance, claims that fourteen of his sixteen brothers and sisters in Finland were born in the sauna.[32] Among the tasks included in the *Kalevala*'s "Instructing the Bride" verses was the warming of the sauna:

> When the evening bath is wanted,
> Fetch the water and the bath-whisks,
> Have the bath-whisks warm and ready,
> Fill thou full with steam the bathroom.[33]

In treating ailments, the sauna served as a hospital and sick room. A sauna was the prescription for nearly all ills. Cuts, sprains and bruises were washed and covered with pine tar. Common colds, sore throats and lung ailments were treated by inhaling steam from hot water mixed with tar. According to one old Finnish proverb, "if the sauna and tar cannot help a man, death is near at hand." One lonely Finnish trapper in Northern Ontario remembered his mother's advice when he was suffering from chest pains, possibly pneumonia. He wrote:

> Now I am staying at home, I heat up the sauna and bathe and I inhale the vapours from heated tar into my lungs so that I can kill all the bacteria. . . . I can cure all bad coughs, it is the only way to kill the needling pain in my chest, I breathe also vapours from turpentine and again tar . . . you remember mother the way I used to do it at home.[34]

In wartime, military regulations in Finland made it mandatory for Finnish soldiers to take at least one sauna per week. The sauna has more recently served as a place for government decision-making in Finland, perhaps because of the equality inherent in nakedness.[35]

When Finns immigrated to North America, it was the sauna that became the sure sign of the Finn.[36] For Finns in North America, no matter how poor they were or how humble the building, it was the sauna that gave them stability and a link with the past that was almost as necessary as food or shelter. In rural areas such as Beaver Lake and Wanup, it became part of a circular farmstead landscape featuring a house, barn, hayshed, ice shed, milk house, woodshed, tool/implement shed, root house, outhouse and garage. Saunas were generally built out of hewn rather than round logs, and utilized moss and oakum instead of clay for insulation. Considerable technical expertise was involved in its construction, as evidenced by the use of various corner joints, such as saddle, dovetailed and locked-dovetail.[37] Another striking feature associated with the sauna was the covering of the building with homemade red iron paint. The adoption of this colour originated from Finland, where farmers used rust-red paint from the iron-ore district of central Sweden.[38] The sauna occasionally became a part of labour negotiations in northern Ontario. In at least one Finnish lumber camp, conditions were so bad that the workers refused to work until the boss agreed to build a sauna.[39]

A wary description of the sauna as viewed by non-Finns can be found in one *Sudbury Star* article:

> Sauna, in Finnish, means steam bath; and steam bath means sweating in sultry temperatures, alternating with ice cold showers and beating with birch switches. The Finnish people love it! Rather than an elaborate torture chamber, the Finns regard the Sauna as pleasant relaxation. . . . The Sauna itself is a wooden building, erected in the surroundings of a lakeside beach, a wooden grove, or on the Finnish farmland. . . . To obtain the steam, a brick stove, with an iron mantle on top is filled with stones, each the size of a man's fist. When these stones have been heated by a birch wood fire, to a redhot temperature, water is poured over them to generate steam. The bathers lie on a ledge near the roof, a ledge wide enough for a person to lie down upon. There are tiers of these benches, with the more hardy bathers braving the top perches, for the higher they go, the more intense the steam and heat.[40]

Variants known as a *savu* (smoke) sauna were sometimes built. An interesting example of this type was one built on the Henry Ellmen farm in Louise Township along the Vermilion River. According to one account:

> The steam bath has neither stove nor chimney as have the newer bath houses in the community. A fireplace of small, round stones occupies almost one-quarter of the interior of the 16-foot square log building 35 yards from the swiftly-flowing river. A steady fire is kept burning for two or three hours to heat the stones and building to a desired temperature. As there is no chimney, the smoke fills the structure and then bellows out the door or squeezes through the cracks between the logs. Sunlight bravely struggles into the dim bath house through a tiny window inadequate for the size of the building. Pails of water are placed on the stones which bring the water to a boil as the fire snaps and crackles below. The stones must be hot enough to give off steam when splashed with water before the fire is allowed to go out. It usually takes an hour for the smoke to clear away after the fire has died down. When the smoke has gone, the door is opened wide for a few minutes to let in fresh air before the bathers enter.[41]

A ritual associated with the sauna was its use by families on Saturday afternoons, prior to evening events such as dances and festivals. It was an accepted practice for Finnish families to show little concern for nudity; as the sauna became part of the general culture of the area, however, this practice gradually disappeared. Another habit associated with the sauna was the use of a *vasta* or *vihta* (birch switch) to stimulate circulation by beating the body while taking *löyly* (steam).[42] In rural areas, saunas were used on a daily basis during seeding and haying sessions to wash away the grime collected in the fields.

The sauna contributed to the Finns' reputation for cleanliness. Nurses frequently commented on the healthy respect that Finns had for the cleansing properties of soap and water as most families, however poor, possessed a sauna. It may also have been a factor contributing to the relatively low mortality rate for Finns in Canada. As Lindström-Best writes:

> The sauna was also useful during childbirth. If at all possible mothers would retreat to the sauna, usually a separate building away from the main dwelling, when their labour started. This age-old practice had several advantages. First, it isolated the mother from the rest of the family and gave her the needed peace and quiet to concentrate on the birth. Secondly, the sauna could be heated to a comfortable temperature for the mother and new-born infant, and there was always plenty of warm water available for washing. The afterbirth was easily disposed of in the sauna oven. Furthermore, the carbon present in the old-fashioned smoke sauna prevented bacterial growth. Thus, the midwives and the women giving birth had ideal sanitary conditions and privacy.[43]

In some of the isolated mining communities of Northern Ontario, the sauna played a role in courtship and marriage. One lonely miner at Nickelton near Murray mine placed the following advertisement in the *Vapaus*:

> So now the Nickelton's family sauna is ready—and all the families have their own women to wash their backs, except I the undersigned. That is why I decided to turn for help to the women. . . . The old maids and the widows of living or dead men get the first chance.[44]

On another occasion, one woman described her initial difficulties with her Slavic friend:

> On Saturday night, I took him to a sauna—well—he thought that he was in hell, and when I jumped into the icehole, he ran screaming to the house convinced that I was possessed by the devil. That ended that, you couldn't make him into a Finn and no way was I going to give up my Saturday night sauna—no, not for any man.[45]

The sauna accompanied the movement of Finns from rural to urban areas such as Copper Cliff and Sudbury. These saunas were of the more traditional type, with a stove and chimney instead of a fireplace and a higher entry door. The newer saunas were preferred because they could be heated more quickly, and there were no problems with soot covering the walls and benches. Before World War II, when the rental or ownership of small homes was the norm, public saunas were popular. Among them were the Copper Cliff Finnish Baths (Jaakkola's Sauna), Sudbury Steam Bath (Seppälä's Sauna) on Spruce Street, Alavo Steam Baths on Antwerp Street and the Workers' Park sauna at Lake Nepahwin. Others were also found on Pine (Manninen's) and Ontario Streets (Kaartinen's). The use of the sauna occasionally led to safety concerns. After two Finns died in the Copper Cliff Finnish Baths in the early 1920s from heart attack and suffocation, a coroner's inquest recommended that the operation of public baths should be looked into and regulations drawn up to eliminate existing dangers.[46]

For Finns who had cottages at Lake Panache and other lakes, the sauna evolved as a standard feature of the shoreline. One of the more distinctive saunas found at Lake Panache is the smoke sauna imported from Finland by Aulis and Shirley Kangas. Equally impressive is the majestic sauna built of round logs, also imported from Finland, by Jack and Maija Ceming on their Manitoulin Island retreat.[47] After World War II, the popularity of the sauna culture was such that it was adopted by other ethnic groups as well.

Knights and Ladies of Kaleva Organizations

In the 1960s the Knights and Ladies of Kaleva emerged as a new phenomenon on the local Finnish scene. The Kaleva movement was started by John Stone in the United States as a response to the prevailing ideological splits among the Finns. He came to the conclusion that Finnish immigrants could best help themselves through the establishment of lodges (*majas* for men and *tupas* for women) based on the Finnish epic *The Kalevala*. It was this epic that provided much of the basis for nationalism in Finland in the latter part of the nineteenth century. The first Knights of Kaleva lodge *Pellervoisen Maja No. 1* was created in Belt, Montana, in 1898.[48] A Ladies of Kaleva lodge, known as *Mielikin Tupa No. 1*, was formed in 1904 at Red Lodge, Montana. These organizations were intended to develop fraternalism, brotherhood and sisterhood among their members, and to preserve Finnish customs and kinship.[49] Later, a Grand Lodge for each (known as *Ylimaja* for the men and *Ylitupa* for the women) was created at the international level. While entry into these lodges was ostensibly open, the great majority of the members were supporters of the church or temperance movements; representation from workers' groups was generally infrequent.

By 1968 some eighty-eight lodges had been formed in the United States, Canada and Finland, with a total membership of 2,000. Representatives from these lodges meet regularly at national conventions, and they have made valuable contributions toward the preservation and promotion of the Finnish heritage. The organization has, for instance, sponsored the publication of two books, including *Epic of the North*.[50] These activities have been recorded since 1913 through an annual publication known as *Kalevainen*. Five men's lodges were eventually created in Canada: *Saaren Maja* No. 47 at Ladysmith, British Columbia (1927), *Sampo Maja* No. 51 at Thunder Bay, Ontario (1954), *Nikkeli Maja* (Nickel Lodge) No. 57 at Sudbury, Ontario (1965), *Vaahteranlehti Maja* No. 58 at Toronto (1967) and *Kulta Maja* No. 59 at Timmins, Ontario (1968). Two women's lodges were formed at Thunder Bay (*Ainikin Tupa* No. 55) and at Sudbury (*Sinijärvien Tupa* No. 59, or Bluewater Lodge). Many of the names given to the lodges are derived from the *Kalevala*, for example, *Lemminkäisen Maja*, *Väinöttären Tupa*, *Suvantolaisen Maja* and *Annikin Tupa*. While the organization remains active, it faces the problem of an aging membership and a lack of interest on the part of North American-born Finns. The Kaleva movement in the Sudbury area began on 10 October 1965 when the men's Nickel Lodge No. 57 was established. This step was followed by the formation of the women's Bluewater Lodge No. 59 on 9 October 1966. The early years of the two lodges were lively, with members giving assistance to many Finnish organizations. Major festivals such as Midsummer Day, *Kalevala* Day and Finland's Independence Day were always commemorated in some fashion. A memorable event was the role of the lodges in the formation of the Finnish-Canadian Centennial Committee (Sudbury) to help celebrate Canada's centenary and Finland's fiftieth year of independence. Another major occasion was the holding of the thirty-fourth National Convention of the Knights and Ladies of Kaleva held at Laurentian University in August 1970. During the 1970s and 1980s, the two local lodges proved to be strong supporters of the Kaleva movement as at least one member from Sudbury served as an executive member of the International Grand Lodges up to 1990. Throughout this period, membership in the two lodges has varied between thirty and fifty. The lodges have actively supported post-secondary education for Finnish-Canadian students by means of annual scholarships and bursaries. The funding for these awards has been derived from a variety of sources, including Kaleva Balls, Finnada fashion shows, teas and the sale of *tynnyri* (barrel) saunas. The first student bursary was given in 1969. Between 1969 and 1998, more than two hundred awards valued in excess of $100,000 have been given to students. These awards have come to be widely recognized throughout the Sudbury educational community.

Sudbury Finnish Rest Home Society

The most dominant cultural force since the 1980s has been the seniors' movement centred around the Sudbury Finnish Rest Home complex. This development evolved within the context of a Canada-wide rest home movement that began with the establishment of a seniors' society in Vancouver in 1958 and the opening of Canada's first Finnish seniors' home in 1963.[51] This was the second Finnish rest home to be established in North America; the first was a seniors' home constructed in Massachusetts in 1951. The pioneering effort at Vancouver was followed by the formation of *Ontarion Suomalainen Lepokotiyhdistys* (The Ontario Finnish Resthome Association) at Sault Ste. Marie in 1971. By 1991, a three-phase seniors' residence had been built there that included *Suomi-Eesti Maja*, *Kotitalo* and the *Mauno Kaihla Hoivakoti*.[52] In 1987, Toronto's Finnish-Canadian Seniors' Centre, *Suomi-Koti*, opened with rental and life-lease apartments; a nursing home facility was added in 1992. *Suomi Koti* of Thunder Bay opened its sixty-unit seniors' facility in 1988, and a seniors' residence known as *Kulta-Koti* (Golden Home) opened in Timmins in 1990. These rest home complexes in Canada now provide accommodation and services for some 1,250 individuals. To assist in the development of the Finnish-Canadian rest home movement, representatives of the various associations started to meet informally in 1993. In 1996 a major step was taken when the Finnish Association for Seniors in Canada was established at the Grand Festival held in Timmins, and Niilo Saari, chairman of the Sudbury Finnish Rest Home Society, was elected as its first president.[53]

The idea of a seniors' centre in Sudbury began to take shape around the turn of the 1980s. The first step towards the construction of a rest home for Sudbury was taken in the heat of a sauna by Oliver Korpela and Leo Raaska. In discussing this matter, Korpela stated to Raaska that if "you folks build the rest home, I will donate the land."[54] The proposal was brought to a meeting held at St. Timothy's Evangelical Lutheran Church at Copper Cliff in 1982, where it was agreed that a seniors' centre offering different levels of service, from self-contained apartments to chronic care facilities, should be erected as soon as possible.

Subsequent meetings held at *Sampo* and *Voima* Halls brought the proposal to a wider audience. On 30 May 1982 the name, constitution and bylaws of the Society were approved and a Board of Directors duly elected. A building committee, a finance committee and the Ladies of the Finnish Rest Home Society were also formed. Another major step taken was the approval of a long-range plan to erect a phased seniors' facility known as Finlandia Village that would provide three levels of care: Phase I for self-care apartments (*Finlandia Koti*); Phase II for residential care (*Palvelukoti*); and, finally, Phase III for nursing care (*Hoivakoti*). The Sudbury Finnish Rest Home was incorporated as a private non-profit corporation on 30 November 1982. Since its inception, the Society has been headed by the following presidents: Leo Raaska, Aate Ojalammi, Taisto Eilomaa, Antti Kurkimäki, Maire Laurikainen and Niilo Saari.

Mindful of Korpela's promise to provide the necessary land, planning approval was obtained for the rezoning of eleven hectares (twenty-seven acres) of rural land adjacent to Fourth Avenue. Permission was granted by the Regional Municipality of Sudbury in the fall of 1983 and the land transfer from Oliver Korpela to the Finnish Rest Home Society followed. By this time membership in the Society had grown to almost 1,000, a figure that made it one of the largest Finnish organizations of its kind in Canada. In 1984 plans for the self-care apartments were prepared by the architect Seppo Kanerva from the Toronto firm of Sedun and Kanerva. With the assistance of Nickel Belt MP and minister Judy Erola, a $4.5 million mortgage was obtained from Canada Mortgage and Housing Corporation (CMHC) to assist in the construction of ninety self-care units. *Finlandia-Koti* officially opened on 29 september 1985. The building includes sixty-seven one-bedroom and twenty-three two-bedroom apartments, with five of the units designated for the handicapped. In addition to apartments, the site accommodates a convenience store, two saunas, a gym, auditorium, laundry facilities, craft rooms and a chapel.

In line with the co-operative thrust of the Society, *Kotikerho* was formed as a tenants' association. Through activities such as teas and bake sales, bingos, film presentations and morning coffee socials, the association provides financial assistance for the purchase of furniture and equipment. An intense effort likewise goes into enhancing the surrounding landscape through the planting of colourful flower beds and a large garden plot.

With the support of its members, a decision was reached by the Board in 1986 to proceed with Phase II. Kanerva was again given the responsibility for designing this assisted-living phase. The efforts of the Society regarding Phase II were rewarded in 1990 when the Ontario government announced that it would provide close to $5 million for the construction of *Palvelukoti* as a joint venture involving the Finnish Rest Home Society, the Ministry of Housing and the Ministry of Community and Social Services. Another fund-raising program was put into place by the Board, and *Palvelukoti* was opened in May of 1992. The core of Phase II consists of a forty-six-unit, sixty-bed residential care facility in a one-storey building in a park-like setting. Within the complex there are twenty-eight one-bed and twelve two-bed apartments, with six units for the handicapped. The facility supports a two-storey administrative and multi-services centre, housing the entrance, offices, kitchen, dining room, saunas, swimming pool, therapeutic whirlpool, and several craft, counselling and meeting rooms. The building was awarded the architectural distinction of being the best new facility erected in the Sudbury area in 1992. To service the two buildings, the Society employs ten full-time and three part-time staff. The opening of Phase II was accompanied by the appointment of Eric Leinala as the executive director of the Society.

In 1993 the Society embarked on a revised Phase III plan, incorporating a twenty-unit *Rivitalo* (townhouse) project for seniors over fifty-five years of age who were members of the Society. Designed as a self-contained neighbourhood, the concept permitted individuals to purchase a townhouse with a *kotioikeus* (life-lease) form of tenure similar to that of a condominium, where a monthly maintenance fee is required. Residents are also permitted to use existing services in the Finlandia Village. The project was completed, and by 1996 all of the units were sold. In the same year the Society acquired Garson Nursing Home Ltd. It is planned that the existing building will be sold and a new eighty-bed nursing home (*Hoivakoti*) erected at Finlandia Village in 1999-2000.

Sudbury *Suomi* Lions Club

A more recent addition to the Finnish scene is the Sudbury *Suomi* Lions Club. The origins of this club can be traced back to the formation of The Mayor's Finnish Liaison Committee by Mayor Peter Wong of the city of Sudbury in May 1986. The objective of the committee was "to assist the Mayor of the City of Sudbury to promote goodwill and friendship, to encourage recreational, cultural and social activities, and to foster and develop a closer relationship between the City of Sudbury and her sister-city, Kokkola, Finland."[55] Between 1986 and 1989, the committee assisted the mayor in developing a student exchange program, provided translation services, liaised with business and industry and hosted visitors from Kokkola and Ylivieskä. The latter is the sister-city to the town of Walden, which constitutes part of the Regional Municipality of Sudbury. By this time, however, it had become clear that there was a need for a more broadly based Finnish group within the Sudbury area to assume some of these functions. The Liaison Committee passed a resolution in 1989 calling for the creation of a Finnish-based service club. The Committee disbanded and Arne Ritari was asked to undertake the task of forming a Lions Club. He was considered to be an ideal candidate for this challenge because of his links with the local Finnish community and his involvement with the Sudbury Lions Club (biography 19). He accepted the challenge of forming Canada's third Finnish Lions Club—the others being the Toronto *Suomi* Lions Club for men and the Toronto-Finlandia Lions Club for women.

The first meeting of the Sudbury *Suomi* Lions Club was held at the Northbury Hotel in November 1989 with twenty-seven members in attendance. Ray Kivinen was elected the charter president. To reflect the non-immigrant character of the majority of its members, it was agreed that the

Arne Ritari: Mr. Lion

Arne Ritari was born in 1906 at Seinäjoki, Finland. His father, Thomas Ritari, came to Copper Cliff in 1898 and was hired by the CCC at the age of eighteen. Thomas met Justiina in Copper Cliff and they were married in 1905. When Justiina became pregnant, she went back to her home in Seinäjoki where Arne was born. Both then returned to Copper Cliff. Thomas went to Creighton in 1908 and two years later moved with his family to the Moose Mountain Iron Company operations at Sellwood, where Justiina ran a boarding house. After the operations closed in 1914, he worked at the Garson, Kirkwood and Levack mine sites before moving south in 1918 to Roger's mine in Illinois.

Roger's mine closed in 1920 and the family returned to Copper Cliff. When the CCC opened its Frood operations, Thomas moved there to work and Justiina operated the company's clubhouse for company officials and single workers. The family moved back to Copper Cliff where Justiina again ran a boarding house. Arne's organizational talents were in evidence even at this early stage, as he had developed an ongoing correspondence with fifty-five other Lone Scouts of America. He also established the Nomads, a group of Lone Scouts. Thomas left for Kirkland Lake in 1921, but the family remained in Copper Cliff. Later, Justiina moved the family to Sudbury where she ran a boarding house on Spruce Street. Arne attended the Sudbury Mining and Technical School where he had the distinction of co-editing and editing the first two editions of the *Wolf Howl* in 1924-26.

Following his graduation, he became a draftsman for the Department of Lands and Forests. It was through the purchase of a life insurance policy with Sun Life Assurance that he first considered a career in insurance. Arne was hired by Sun Life in 1928 as a sub-agent, and as his talents for selling insurance became apparent, he became a full-time agent. By 1929 he was one of the top life insurance agents for Sun Life Assurance in Northern Ontario. In 1929 he then began to provide home and automobile insurance as a sub-agent with A. Fournier Ltd. In 1932 Arne married Kaarina Heinonen. Born in 1904 in Tampere, Finland, she emigrated to Sault Ste. Marie in 1916 to join her father, who was a tailor. After attending business college, she worked with the *Vapaus* Publishing Company in Sudbury. In 1934 Arne opened his own insurance agency in the Cochrane Block; two years later, he expanded into the steamship and airline travel business. It was then that the Ritaris acquired a cottage property on Clearwater Lake that became a focal point for gatherings of the Sudbury Lions and Lioness Clubs and the Knights and Ladies of Kaleva. Arne was actively involved with the Sudbury District Chamber of Commerce, serving on many committees and rising to the position of president in 1950. During World War II, he was a supporter of the Sudbury District Finnish War Aid Association, acting for a time as its treasurer. In 1949 he shifted his office to the corner of Cedar and Durham Streets; he moved again in the 1950s to the Rothschild Block at Cedar and Elgin, where he remained until his retirement in September 1975.

Arne is best known for his contribution to the promotion of international Lionism. He joined the Sudbury Lions Club in 1937, rose to the position of president in 1946-47, became zone chairman in 1949-50 and district governor in 1957-58. While promoting airline tourism between Finland and Canada in 1948-50, he introduced the concept of Lionism to Finland. The latter paid dividends in 1950, when Finland became the twenty-ninth country in the world to embrace Lionism. By 1997 Finland could boast 905 clubs with 29,900 members. In addition to his honorary title as "Godfather of Lionism" in Finland, he was the recipient of numerous awards, such as The International Association of Lions Clubs Ambassador of Good Will in 1969-70, the Melvin Jones Fellow Award in 1987-88, Finland Society's Gold Medal in 1989 and the Knight of the Order of the White Rose from the president of Finland in 1991. The Arne Ritari Foundation was also established on his behalf in Finland in 1986. Among his other distinctions is the receipt of the Canada Centennial Medal in 1967 and the designation of Life Member with the CAA-Auto Club Sudbury for his continuous membership dating from 1932. He was a key figure in establishing the Sudbury *Suomi* Lions Club, which was chartered in 1990. Arne passed away in 1996, leaving behind Kaarina and his one daughter, Carol.

---

meetings of the club would be held in English. In 1990 *Sampo* Hall became the club's official den. The Club celebrated its Charter Night on 6 April 1990, with the highlight of the evening being the induction of fifty-nine male and female members into Lions International. The Club has since been guided by the following presidents: Ron Lundgren, Maija Ceming, Oiva Saarinen, Walter Karen, Polly Rutenberg, Lasse Skogberg, Hannu Piironen and Antti Haaranen.

By 1992 the *Sudbury Suomi Lions Newsletter* editor, Reijo Viitala, saw fit to write the following historical reflection:

> Ten thousand dollars in donations in our first year of operations! Numerous donations to other worthy causes, three successful Rubber Boot Casino Nights, innovative raffle-type fund-raising activities, grass-roots fund-raising barbecues, Coke booths, Bunny sales—unselfish donation of services to three Telethons, Red Shield Appeals and a Benefit Concert! The Suomi Lions are heard to be roaring loudly by other Clubs.[56]

On 16 April 1992 an agreement was signed between the Sudbury *Suomi* Lions Club and the Finnish National Society for the purchase of *Sampo* Hall by the Lions. The main reason for the purchase was the desire by club members to retain *Sampo* Hall as a Finnish cultural landmark. It soon became clear, however, that *Sampo* Hall could no longer be run profitably; thus the hall was returned to the Society which, in turn, resold it to Grace Outreach Ministries in 1994.

A new era for the Club began in December 1994, when its members opted to have the Sudbury Finnish Rest Home as the site of their new den. A successful fifth Charter Anniversary Night was held on 18 May 1995. In addition to its obligations to Lionism, the Club has been a supporter of the Sudbury Finnish Rest Home Society.

Finnish War Veterans (Sudbury)

The migration of war veterans to Canada after the Finnish Civil War and throughout the 1920s stimulated considerable interest in the formation of a veterans' association in Canada. While discussions had taken place as early as 1933, it was 1935 before the Association of Finnish War Veterans in Canada was established in Montreal.[57] This was later followed by the formation of the Finnish War Veterans in Canada (Toronto). Encouraged by support from war veteran associations in Finland and Toronto, *Sudburyn Sotavelikerho/Asevelikerho* (The Finnish War Veterans of Sudbury) was formed in 1976 with Leo Raaska as its first president. Other associations were formed in Thunder Bay, Vancouver, Timmins and Sault Ste. Marie. By 1978 the veterans' group in Sudbury had a membership of over two hundred. The association, with the help of its women's auxiliary, has assisted needy local families and veterans and veterans' hospitals in Finland. Presidents of the Sudbury association have included Olavi Heikkilä, Eero Kotipelto and Matti Asu. In 1995-96 part of the veterans' group in Sault Ste. Marie also became affiliated with the Sudbury association. In 1996 the War Veterans of Sudbury/Sault Ste. Marie had a combined membership of 233.

While these groups had in the past met regularly at the Grand Festivals and sponsored wreath-laying ceremonies, it was not until 1982 that the idea of having an umbrella group for the seven associations in Canada was first raised. In 1984 the Finnish-Canadian War Veterans' Association finally became a reality.[58] Matti Asu from Sudbury served as the first president, from its founding in 1984 until 1990. The central association and its almost seven hundred members now receive funding from Finland, which is shared by its member associations. The most recent thrust of the group has focused on the need to replace former veterans who have passed away through the promotion of more supporting members.[59]

Finnish Language Schools

Concern for the preservation of the Finnish language reflects another aspect of postwar cultural development. Until the 1940s, little concern was shown regarding language use among second- and third-generation Finns. The need to use the Finnish spoken word with grandparents at home, at Sunday school and confirmation classes, at dances and concerts, in choirs and other organized groups, ensured a high degree of language retention among

Finnish youth. The situation changed after World War II, when the use of Finnish as a home language began to decline significantly; in many homes, the most common form of communication became *fingliskaa*, a blend of English and Finnish that has, in recent years, been popularized by Kaattari in his book *Rubberboots in the Sauna* and in articles written for the monthly *South Side Story*.[60]

This trend spurred calls for language instruction as a way of preserving the Finnish heritage. The first language school for Finnish instruction appeared in Toronto in 1960. While language instruction was given in the Sudbury area as early as 1943 by Rev. Lauri Pikkusaari and Fanny Hill, their efforts were temporary, and it was 1962 before another language school was initiated at *Sampo* Hall under the auspices of the FNSS. This school again proved to be short-lived. Resurrected in 1971 as the Sudbury Finnish Language School, courses began to be taught at Sheridan Secondary School. By 1977 language instruction had expanded to include the Wanup and White-fish elementary schools. Since then, enrolment in language courses has fluctuated between 50 and 120. Classes in Sudbury have been held in a variety of locations, including Lo-Ellen Park Secondary School, Lockerby Composite School and Jesse Hamilton Public School.

Funding for language instruction has been supported by the Canadian government, the Ministry of Education in Finland, the Ontario Ministry of Education and the Sudbury Board of Education. Credit courses have been offered at the secondary level by the Sudbury Board and, for a time, at Laurentian University. When the Canadian government's assistance program to heritage-language schools was cancelled in 1990, the Ministry of Education of Finland increased its support to compensate for the loss. By 1996 there were twelve Finnish-language schools scattered throughout Canada.[61] To enhance the professional development of Finnish-language teachers, training seminars were started in 1980; since then, three seminars have been held in Sudbury (1983, 1988 and 1996). These annual seminars have received financial support from three sources: the Canadian government through its multicultural programs, the Ontario Ministry of Education and the Finland Society. A second step taken to foster improved instruction was the formation in 1984 of the Finnish Language Teachers' Association of Canada.

Symbolic Ethnicity

For many second- and later-generation Finns, cultural markers of their innate Finnishness have been maintained not by the use of the language or through organizational participation but rather by means of more personalized expressions that can be referred to as symbolic ethnicity. This form of ethnic bonding consists of a nostalgic or emotional allegiance to the immigrant generation and to the old country, and pride in a tradition that can be felt without having to be incorporated in everyday behaviour.[62] Important here has been the use of the home and cottage as an indicator of Finnish attachment; allied to this residential expression has been the use of the motor vehicle and clothing as complementary forms of ethnic labelling.

Residences (both homes and cottages) in the Sudbury area continue to serve as strong symbolic elements of Finnish ethnicity. These elements can be linked to patriotism, handicrafts, calendar days, literature, music, food and sporting equipment. Among the more patriotic forms of symbolism are the showing of the Finnish national flag, provincial banners and coats of arms. In living and dining rooms there are items such as glass candlesticks manufactured by the Iittala Company, wood carvings of all kinds, vases by the Finnish architect Alvar Aalto, other types of glassware from the Nuutajärvi and Riihimäen Lasi companies or by the designer Tapio Wirkkala in lighted cabinets, Finnish *ryijyt* (woven rugs), *täkänät* (double woven quilts), *raanut* (decorative textiles), dinnerware and year plates from the renowned Finnish-based ceramics company, Arabia, reindeer horns from Lapland and pictures of the Finnish landscape. Symbols based on the calendar year consist of national costumes, Väinämöinen outfits from the Finnish national epic *Kalevala* and Christmas ornaments such as wooden candleholders. Finnish literature of all kinds is usually on display, for example, *The Kalevala*, a family Bible, works by famous Finnish writers such as Väinö Linna, J.L. Runeberg, Mika Waltari and Aleksis Kivi, and imported magazines and newspapers. Paintings of the ancestral home or family photographs may be hung on walls. Copper pots can frequently be found in the kitchen and *puukot* (knives) in dens. Families listen to Finnish musicians such as Katri Helena, Matti and Teppo, Jamppa Tuominen, Eino Grön, Tapani Kansa, Arja Koriseva and Aikamiehet, and local talent such as the Sudbury Finnish Male Choir; the voices and music of Erkki Kinos, Eero Jutila, Annin Pojat, Leo Niemi and Karl Pukara can also be heard in many homes.

Traditional Finnish food is another form of cultural retention, especially for holiday events, when households offer such treats as *ruisleipä* (rye bread), *pulla* (Finnish buns or coffee bread), *sokerikakku* (sugar cake), *tiikerikakku* (tiger cake), *riisipuuro* (rice pudding), *suolakala* (salt-cured salmon), *piirakat* (rice or hamburger patties), *rosolli* (beet and carrot salad), *kaalilaatikko* (cabbage casserole), *kaalikääryleet* (cabbage rolls), *lihapullat* (meatballs), *lihapiirakat* (meat pies), *sillilaatikko* (herring casserole), *mojakka* (Finnish stew) and *Karjalanpaisti* (Karelian ragout). Cross-country skis manufactured by Karhu and Peltonen and hockey equipment made by Koho can also be seen on snow trails and in community arenas.

Automobiles and clothing serve as other manifestations of Finnish attachment. These are apparent on bumper stickers that depict the Finnish flag, licence plates proclaiming *Oulu*, *Mummu*, and Happiness Is Being Finnish, and t-shirts or hats emblazoned with slogans such as *Sisu*, Finn Power, Sudbury *Suomi* Lions Club, *Suomalainen Kansallisseura* F.N.S. of Sudbury and *Suomalainen Suomen Kieli Kasvaa Kanadassa—Sudbury* (The Finnish Language Is Growing in Canada—Sudbury).

How long these forms of symbolic ethnicity can continue to exist without a firm loyalty to language or traditional institutional attachment remains an interesting question. While some scholars like Gans see this concept of Finnishness as being a limited phenomenon for the United States, Lindström has advanced a more optimistic viewpoint for the Canadian setting.[63] Given the sizable number of Finnish Canadians that still reside in the Sudbury area, the position can be advanced here that symbolic ethnicity will remain highly visible on the local scene for at least another generation.

CHAPTER VI

Conclusions and Retrospect

This study has presented some of the broad features of the "Finnish factor," as it has affected Sudbury's historical and geographical development. Many of the essential qualities of the Finnish-Canadian experience in the Sudbury area have been defined. The main virtue shown by this work is that the Finnish immigrants who came here were full of energy and ideals, and that they successfully struggled to shape their lives and environments within the context of their own ambitions. In one way or another they, along with other ethnic groups such as the Italians, Ukrainians and Poles, greatly affected Sudbury's growth pattern from the turn of the century to the present. While this investigation has sought in part to provide those of Finnish extraction with a greater sense of their personal past and heritage, it has also attempted to establish a firm position for the ethnic group within the region's historical geography.

The driving force behind the growth of the Finnish presence in Canada came in the form of three major waves of migration linked with the pre-World War I period, the 1920s and the 1950s. Finnish immigration began early in the 1870s, peaked in the 1961-71 period and then declined substantially. It can thus be concluded that the era of Finnish immigration to Canada has come to an end. Over the years, a gender change from male to female dominance occurred in the migratory flow; as well, there developed a trend for non-immigrant Finns, because of exogamous marriages, to be of mixed rather than single origins. The general distribution of Finnish settlement throughout the century has remained fairly constant, showing a preference for Ontario, British Columbia and the Prairie provinces. Within this provincial framework, Finns initially showed a predisposition toward rural and small towns, but most can now be found in larger metropolitan

Notes to Chapter VI are on pp. 298-99.

centres such as Toronto, Thunder Bay, Vancouver/Victoria and Sudbury. While the association of Finns with the Lutheran religion remains firm, intermarriage among second- and third-generation Finns has fostered allegiance with other denominations; a growing secularization trend has also emerged. Among the contemporary features shaping the ethnic environment can be included a high degree of transfer from Finnish to the everyday use of English, and an aging of the Finnish population. With respect to the former, it is clear that there has been a dramatic retreat from the use of the Finnish language and that there is little sense of "language loyalty" among the non-immigrant group of Finns. At the same time, the gradual passing away of the immigrant group of Finns has been accompanied by an erosion and change in the Finnish institutional base.

At first glance, the above analysis points to bleak prospects for the survival of the Finns as a distinctive ethnic group in Canada and particularly in the Sudbury area. The lack of new immigrants, the shift to a non-immigrant and mixed ethnic composition, the decline in the use of Finnish as a home language and the aging of the Finnish immigrant group suggest that the Finnish heritage in Canada is rapidly losing ground. There can be no doubt that the Finnish population in Canada has in many ways become an indistinguishable part of Canadian society. Some researchers have used these trends to support the existence of a crisis for Finnish cultural survival.[1] Lindström, in contrast, has come to the viewpoint that the Finnish-Canadian culture, especially in Toronto, is not dying or experiencing any serious illness; rather, it has simply changed and continues to reflect a community that is very much alive.[2] Another manifestation of vitality was the holding of the FINNFORUM II and V academic conferences in Toronto and Sudbury in 1979 and 1996 respectively. These conferences are an ongoing reflection of the academic interest in North American Finns that began in Duluth in 1974.

Some support for Lindström's more optimistic viewpoint comes from the fact that, in addition to the 39,230 single-origin Finns recorded in the 1991 census, approximately 40 percent of the 59,865 Canadians with partial links to Finnish culture were fifteen years of age or less. A significant potential thus remains for the maintenance of Finnish roots in Canada. Indeed, census data has been used by the Canadian government to support the contention that ethnic groups such as the Finns in Canada "may in fact be becoming more aware of their origins than ever before."[3] Another positive influence that should not be underestimated is the impact of those Finns coming to Canada on a "temporary" basis for educational and business purposes. There remains, therefore, fertile ground in the immediate future for the ongoing promotion of the Finnish heritage in Canada. Another signal of such an increased interest lies in the birth of the *Journal of Finnish Studies* in 1997.

On the other hand, the Finnish-American experience is instructive. As Kivisto's reviews of the development path in the United States suggest, future forms of "Finnishness" in Canada will undoubtedly be different from the culture fostered by the immigrant generation. It will likely be based on newer modes of ethnicity focusing more on "individual identity" rather than on "institutional affiliation" along with a concomitant reduction in the use of the Finnish language.[4] Lindström's optimism must also be tempered by several geographical caveats. First, it is likely that new connections between the Finnish ethnic community and geography will be forged. At the institutional level, the survival of the Finns as an ethnic minority will be attainable only for larger metropolitan centres such as Toronto, Thunder Bay, Vancouver/Victoria and Sudbury, where institutional support from universities, churches, heritage-language schools and Finnish service clubs can be found; even in these major urban nodes, however, the extent to which ethnic maintenance will be sustainable will increasingly depend upon the leadership exerted by middle- and upper-class Finnish Canadians. The survival of the Finnish culture in these larger centres may to some extent be encouraged by the establishment in 1997 of an Expatriate Parliament in Finland comprising those persons of Finnish extraction who do not reside in Finland. Sponsored by *Suomi Seura*, this new parliament has been charged with the task of furthering new networks between Finland and people of Finnish heritage in places such as Canada.[5] The fact that membership in this parliament is to be restricted to Finnish-based organizations with a membership of five hundred members or more will certainly favour representation from the larger urban centres.

For smaller communities, where the existing organizational and leadership base is weak and membership in Finnish organizations minimal or non-existent, Laine's contention that organized Finnish culture will not survive in any meaningful fashion will likely prove to be true. It may well be, however, that at the personal level the opposite may in fact occur. New modes of communication on the Internet now hold considerable promise for the survival of Finnish culture by individuals scattered across immense geographical distances. Project 34 is a case in point. It is an American Internet project spearheaded by John Laine, which has the objective of developing long-term strategies for the retention of Finnish culture by third- and fourth-generation Finns. If the potential impact of this technology is considered, alongside the current renewal of cultural particularism and the new emphasis on ethnic and religious identity, then there is hope for the retention of the culture in the minds and hearts of these Finnish-Canadian nomads. The above notwithstanding, it must be acknowledged that, for the great majority of Finnish Canadians, the new millennium will bring with it a significant attentuation of ethnicity, and that a redefining of ethnicity that will be more abstract and optional.

From a North American perspective, the Canadian immigration experience, while similar in many respects to that of the United States, offers four important contrasts. The first difference is that a generation gap exists between the two countries in terms of the migratory flow. Whereas immigration started in the United States in the 1860s and 1870s, the movement of Finns into Canada did not get under way until the late 1870s and 1880s. This has had important implications for the shaping of the institutional mix. While the church and conservative Finns were able to become well established south of the border before the turn of the century, such was not the case for Canada. When the leftists came to Canada prior to World War I, they were able to assert their ideological hegemony in a more vigorous fashion. Second, the earlier arrival of Finns in the United States permitted the Americanization process to be well under way by 1920, at which time the number of native-born Finns in the United States exceeded the number of foreign-born for the first time. This watershed event was followed by the passage of immigration laws that reduced the influx of new Finns into the United States to a trickle, and diverted the emigrant flow from Finland to places such as Canada and Australia. The espousing of an "America First" ideology in the United States was paralleled by a "retreat from Finnishness" among second-generation Finns and their progeny. Assimilation factors such as intermarriage and language shift have accelerated the integration process at an even more rapid rate.[6] The shift of the migratory flow northwards, however, had an important effect in that it helped to slow any Canadianization tendencies that may otherwise have occurred.

A third contrast evolved out of the ongoing Finnish immigration to Canada after World War II. The influx of the 1950s renewed the Finnish-Canadian community and, as was the case in the 1920s, slowed the erosion of the ethnic base. The impact of the second and third waves of the 1920s and 1950s was such that it was 1961 before native-born Finns in Canada exceeded those who were foreign-born. The fourth factor reinforcing distinctiveness from the United States was the introduction of a multicultural policy by the federal government in 1971, and later by a number of provinces, that provided financial and other resources for the support of ethnic pluralism. These policies have had a significant impact on sustaining the institutional strength of the Finns in the Sudbury area.

Finns first came to the Sudbury area as part of the great tide of European emigration that occurred in the late nineteenth century. This mass migration developed in response to push-and-pull factors. Among the push factors were poor economic circumstances, the worsening of conditions in the agrarian sector due to rural population growth and Russian political oppression. Bending under these pressures, that portion of the population not secure in land ownership—tenant farmers, crofters, cottagers, rural workers, servants, dependent lodgers—somehow managed to get together the price of a ticket to head overseas. The Civil War in Finland and its aftermath led to a second surge in emigration that lasted up to the Great Depression. Economic and political uncertainties fostered yet another exodus during the 1950s and 1960s. The pull factor was clear-cut. Beginning in the latter part of the nineteenth century, Canada underwent enormous economic expansion that offered immigrants the hope of land, farms and jobs. Economic opportunities associated with the erection of canals, the building of the CPR main line across Canada, the growth of the lumbering and mining sector, construction projects of all kinds and the distribution of free land by the federal government served as irresistible lures to those unemployed or discouraged in Finland. Letters sent home by early emigrants prompted others to come. Women who came to Canada did so directly and went mainly to the large urban centres. Men, in contrast, came to Canada by more circuitous routes, often through the United States.

The early emigrants who came to the Sudbury area exhibited what could be called farming fever. As most of them came from rural areas as landless emigrants, it is not surprising that the acquisition of land served as their main preoccupation. In order to attain this objective, many were forced temporarily into construction, mining and lumbering jobs. The scattered nature of mining employment and the fact that the best agricultural lands had already been settled by French Canadians forced these pioneering Finns into the marginal areas flanking the CPR and CNR railway lines south and west of Sudbury. This fringe development pattern encouraged the development of settlement enclaves, each featuring a high degree of cultural segregation, economic and political self-dependency and a charming landscape centred around red buildings, saunas and neatly tended farms. As was the case in the Thunder Bay area, the construction and layout features associated with these ethnic islands represented a carry-over of peasant habitations found in Finland.[7] Within these clusters, Finnish immigrants were free to make their own choices and to create their own lifestyles.

It was not until the 1920s that the Finns were attracted to Sudbury itself. By World War II three distinctive Finntowns had emerged in the downtown, Donovan and Lockerby districts. The gravitational pull of the rural enclaves and the popularity of mining communities such as Copper Cliff, Creighton and Garson, however, continued to sustain the widespread dispersal of the

Finnish population until the 1950s. By then, the farming fever of the pre-World War II era had dissipated. While second- and third-generation Finns, and the new immigrants of the 1950s, showed an increasing predisposition for urban living in the city of Sudbury, the rural lifestyle preference remained surprisingly strong up to the 1980s. In fact, it appears as though the enclaves in the Sudbury area have retained stronger vestiges of their Finnish heritage than is currently the case in the Thunder Bay area.[8] This difference, however, is unlikely to continue for long as the level of Finnishness in the Sudbury rural outposts will inevitably decline over the next few decades.

The character of Finnish life in the Sudbury area evolved within the confines of a highly developed "associative spirit." The institutional framework that emerged was complex in nature, and was moulded both by influences that originated in Finland, Russia/Soviet Union and the United States, and by the hardships of local working life in construction, mining, forestry, agriculture and domestic service. One manifestation of these dual forces was the titanic struggle for the ideological hegemony of the Finnish immigrant community. On one side, there were those who espoused radical ideologies from Europe and the United States. Spurred by their uprooting experiences from previous village and family ties, rejection of religious institutions, harsh conditions in the resource industries and a dedication to the reform of capitalism, the leftists developed a remarkable infrastructure after the turn of the century. With extraordinary energy and creativity, a dedicated group of leaders came to the fore as the intellectual apostles of socialism. In accord with the belief that it was necessary to cultivate the whole person, radical Finns erected an elaborate organizational system to provide for their cultural and economic needs. Halls, newspapers, central organizations, women's societies and groups promoting activities of all kinds were the basis for this counterculture. It was Finn Hall, however, that evolved as the dominant ethnic symbol. Within its walls, there developed a flourishing artistic life, embracing music, theatre, poetry, fiction and oratory. For these radicals, the hall represented a secularized version of the church, and its stage served as the new pulpit. On a community level, Sudbury emerged as the geographical focus for much of the intellectual and political expression of Finnish radicalism in Canada. Not to be outdone, conservative and religious Finns in the 1930s developed a similar, but much smaller, infrastructure based on halls, national societies, a central organization, a historical society and churches. The result was an institutional framework that, while effectively catering to the needs of the immigrant Finns, brought about a dual system of halls and a community divided.

Institutional divisiveness resulted in the development of polarized communities that spatially segregated the life of the residents. The nature and extent of this polarization varied from one community to another. Communal life in the rural enclaves (with the exception of Waters Township and, for a brief time, Louise Township) favoured the radical Finns, whereas the church and conservative Finns managed to gain a solid foothold only in the urban centres of Copper Cliff and Sudbury. This evolutionary pattern contrasts somewhat with the situation in the Thunder Bay area, where the church managed to exert more influence in some of the outlying Finnish communities, such as Lappe.[9]

Attempts to bring these factions together after both World War II and the centennial year of 1967 failed totally. By the late 1980s, however, the weakened state of the FOC and COLFC, the aging of the population and the shifting of the Finnish composition in favour of second- and third-generation Finns led to a waning of interest in these immigrant organizations. Melting-pot forces such as secondary schools and mixed marriages also dealt blows to the prevailing institutional mix. The sale of the Finnish, *Sampo* and *Voima* Halls in the 1980s and 1990s simply confirmed the above trends—today, they remain only as abandoned monuments to the halcyon days of the Great Divide. At the national level, the formal disbanding of COLFC in 1995 and the decision in the same year that locals and individuals associated with the FOC could join the Finnish-Canadian Cultural Federation, were highly symbolic—these two events finally heralded the movement of the Finns in Canada towards a "community united." While the emotional scars associated with the Great Divide have largely disappeared, a number of interesting questions still remain. For example, was the basis for this institutional attachment really ideological or was it simply a natural form of ethnic response? Which geographical setting played a more important role—domestic or international? How extensive was the Great Divide within the community?

A number of studies in North America have taken the view that the basis for institutional attachment was more a pragmatic and ethnic response, rather than an avowedly ideological one—associations were joined primarily for their ability to provide sports, cultural and recreational opportunities. The fact that the FOC and COLFC were supportive of radical or conservative causes was incidental. Associative Finns were thus "hall socialists or conservatives," whose membership could be attributed largely to non-ideological factors such as the closeness of a particular hall, friendships or the fact that it was simply convenient. This school of thought implies that lessons learned in the "North American school of hard knocks" did more to encourage radicalism among Finnish workers than any allegiance to socialism or communism; radicalism in Canada thus had deep domestic roots. To some extent, this argument could be extended to the conservative side as well. Aside from the dedicated church adherents, it was generally the threat of job losses associated with the Finnish red-tinge factor, rather than opposition to radicalism per se, that served as the main rallying cry for the rightists.

Ollila not only supports this proposition, but also claims that ideology came into play only as a subsequent rather than an antecedent form of rationalization. His interpretation of the American experience can be readily applied to the Canadian setting:

> Thus we have a dramatic story of continued radicalization of the Finnish worker and his labor movement. The evidence does not suggest that this radicalization was primarily the result of ideology. One of the myths that has been perpetuated by the Finnish community is that Socialism was the result of Socialist agitators who led the innocent worker astray. Rather, the movement . . . was the result of an agitated response to inhuman conditions in industrialized America. Given the confrontations with industrial capitalism and the failure of the worker to gain anything substantial from the confrontations, he simply concluded that better organization and more radical confrontation were necessary. Ideology then came as a rationalization to explain why the confrontation took place, and how the worker might succeed next time. . . . Marx was only used as an explanation and remedy for what had taken place.[10]

Others have given ideology a more prominent role. Jalava, for example, has demonstrated that the influence of socialism, Russia and communist ideology was very influential in the Sudbury area, at least until the early 1930s. This influence, however, was short-lived, and, for all practical purposes, had disappeared by World War II. The political establishment likewise favoured the ideology argument. As far as the governments of Ontario and Canada were concerned, it was politically expedient for them to blame the rise of radicalism on Russian communism or on agitators from Finland and the United States rather than to remedy the ills and failures of capitalism in Canada.

Any attempt to explain radicalism among the Finns as being either a response to domestic triggers or to political ideology imported from abroad, however, falls short of the mark. The proposition is made here that the real roots of this radicalism were indeed ideological in nature—however, the ideology was more cultural than political in nature, and it was one that rested in the general character of the Finnish immigrant rather than from any overt political commitment. As Kivisto has concluded in his assessment of radicalism in the United States, the majority of Finns who came to this continent brought with them a personalized ideology that was underlain by a solid commitment to the principles of freedom, equality and fraternity and by what Lindström-Best calls dignified human treatment.[11] As Robert-

son has demonstrated, late-nineteenth-century literature in Finland contributed significantly to the creation of such an ideology through its
fostering of the idea of the value and dignity of every individual in society.[12]
When the North American experience with capitalism or domestic servi-
tude ran counter to these principles of self-fulfilment, the Finns rebelled.
Indeed, one of the most enduring themes in the leftist literature was that
they did not come to North America simply to be *orjat* (slaves) to the
capitalistic system. While they did not ask for any special place in Canadian
society, they demanded that they should at least be treated with dignity and
respect. When this did not occur, they responded by taking the only
avenues available to them—they banded together, forming their own institutions, supporting workers' rights and the labour movement and joining
radical political parties. All of these activities served as way stations to the
attainment of their own values and ambitions.

If radicalism is considered in these more personalized terms, it provides a rationale as to why Finnish women in North America, in contrast to
many other ethnic groups, were so defiant and supportive of radical causes.
Radicalism was not confined solely to men who worked in the agricultural,
mining, forestry, construction or transportation sectors on the resource
frontier, but could also be found among women who resided in urbanized
areas. The fact that radicalism drew no gender boundaries among the immigrant Finns is a noteworthy point that has often been neglected or minimized. Lindström-Best offers an interesting perspective here. According to
her, Finnish women who came to Canada brought with them not so much
a political ideology, but rather a cultural heritage and "an iron will to
improve their material, social, and spiritual life, often by making great personal sacrifices."[13] Like their male counterparts, they, too, brought with
them a faith that valued the worth of a person within the economic system.

Another characteristic that worked to promote radicalism was the high
literacy of the Finnish immigrant. This trait made it possible for all kinds of
viewpoints to flourish within the North American Finnish community, via
an information network consisting of a handwritten ("fist") press, books,
magazines and newspapers. A. Päiviö claimed that this literature was
extremely important as it served as a window on the world for the
immigrants.[14] From this perspective, Sudbury played a key role, as it has
historically served as a major distribution centre for the Finnish media
throughout Canada.

Another question concerns the number of Finns who were caught in
the web of the Great Divide. Krats has suggested that assertions of divisiveness within the Finnish community have been exaggerated, and that the
majority of Finns chose to have little or no formal affiliation with the left,

the churches or national societies. There is some support for this viewpoint. Even at the height of its influence, the FOC could only claim the formal allegiance of some 10 percent of the Canadian-Finnish population.[15] In 1933 the two Lutheran churches in the Sudbury area only had a total membership of approximately 750, and many of these individuals could also be found in the forty-three-member total for the FNSS for the same year.[16] Comparative data for the FOC locals in the Sudbury area also indicated a membership level of less than three hundred.[17] Even if allowances are made for other family members and for the "hall" type of persons, it can be inferred that many Finns before World War II had no formal linkages with organized groups. Such a statistical interpretation, however, is misleading as many Finns supported these organizations without acquiring official membership. This was especially true for Finnish radicals, as many supporters of the FOC understandably hid their true allegiance due to fears of job loss, deportation and community reaction.

While the above conclusion that most Finns were not involved with the Great Divide is statistically appealing, an interesting question remains. If the majority of the Finns associated with the various factions had only tenuous hall relationships, history should have recorded a more rapid decline of the Great Divide after World War II. As well, a tendency should have been noticed for Canadian-born Finns to easily cross traditional lines within the ethnic community. This does not appear to have been the case. Lauri Toiviainen, the editor of *Vapaa Sana*, for instance, was able to conclude after his arrival from Finland in the middle 1960s that many Finnish Canadians were still allergic to the radical left, and that certain places within the community remained off limits well into the 1970s.[18]

This conclusion applied to Sudbury as well, as evidenced by the failure among the Finns to promote a non-political central body after 1967. It is also relevant to note that, despite Jalava's conclusion that the left wing, as early as 1932, had begun the transition from idealistic enthusiasm to silent acceptance of assimilation, he could still lament, as late as 1983, that "wistful Finns today find themselves irrevocably divided into two ideologically opposite camps. There is a feeling that reconciliation is not possible as long as even one person from that period is alive."[19]

As late as the mid-1990s, the controversy regarding the FOC's participation in the FCCF was another sign suggesting that immigrant ties to these organizations were not as weak as some have postulated. Also interesting is the fact that, despite the reduced role of the two central organizations, seniors' groups such as the Finnish Senior Citizens' Club and the Friendship Circle continued to ally themselves with their respective central organizations. Even at the Sudbury Finnish Rest Home a polite but reserved

wall remains between the conservative and the leftist factions. It can be concluded, therefore, that any previous relationship with the Great Divide,
whether formal or casual, had a branding effect that lasted up to the 1980s;
linkages, however tenuous, were taken by others as a commitment to a
particular cause.

Finnish immigrants developed an admirable reputation for their work
ethic, whether as farmers, construction workers, miners, lumbermen or
domestics. Admirable as this reputation may be, it should not overshadow
the fact that everyday life for these immigrant Finns was largely an endless
stream of working days in jobs that were low paying, dangerous and that
frequently led to loss of life. This miserable existence has been made
abundantly clear in the remarkable series of letters contained in a yet-
unpublished manuscript entitled *Syvempi kuin meri* (Deeper than the
Ocean), compiled by Saara Karttunen. In these letters written from
Sudbury to Finland between 1929 and 1933, her husband Mauno writes
poignantly about the everyday hardships and loneliness of working life in
the mines in Sudbury.[20] A review of the Finnish obituary history also makes
this point abundantly clear.

The role played by women in the work force was significant, especially
when compared with the customary role females played in other ethnic
groupings. Such work in the formal labour force was often preceded by
previous training as either paid or volunteer workers within the Finnish
institutional framework.[21] Given this background, it is not surprising that
women such as Judy Erola managed to climb into the highest corridors of
political power (biography 20). Within the labour force, Finns, out of all
proportion to their numbers, were involved in radical politics, labour struggles and the union movement. Those who promoted workers' rights and
the union movement in the Sudbury mining and forest industries were
dedicated and courageous people who faced opposition and the threat of job
loss in order to assert their personal convictions. Radforth claims that these
efforts by Finnish radicals within the lumbering industry would have been
in vain had it not been for the support given by the FOC:

> Yet, however impressive, the courage of organizers would never have
> been enough to build a union movement of lumber workers. They
> needed the support not only of bushmen in the camps but also of
> hundreds of other workers and their organizations. During strikes, the
> Finnish Organization of Canada and members of other Finnish halls
> donated much-needed funds which paid for leaflets, transporting pickets
> and the legal defence of those arrested. Strikers used the halls as meeting
> places and slept on the floors. At Finnish cooperative restaurants women
> volunteers served pickets cheap or free food, much of it donated by co-op
> stores and Finnish farmers. . . . The Finnish Organization of Canada also
> arranged concerts, and big dances to raise funds, build solidarity and

entertain strikers. The solidarity of the left-wing Finnish community gave strikers the moral and concrete support necessary to fight for their rights. . . . This solidarity . . . enabled the Lumber and Sawmill Workers' Union to transform conditions in the lumber camps after the second World War.[22]

In the same vein, Seager pays tribute to the Finnish labour pioneers who toiled in the mining industry:

Needless to say, the old dream of the labour pioneers, that the mines should belong to the people of Ontario, has yet to be realized. The fact that there *is* a miners' movement, which plays an ongoing and positive role in the workplace and in the community as well as in the larger political arena, should not, however, be overlooked. The part played by the Finnish Canadian immigrants . . . in building the movement against all odds and against formidable opposition from within and without should not be forgotten.[23]

In retrospect, it appears as though a reevaluation of the Finnish radical movement is in order. There is no doubt that the rank-and-file Finns were clearly radical for the times, and that some extreme elements in the FOC firmly espoused communist ideology. The great majority, however, were essentially concerned with workers' rights and the union movement in the mines and forests of Northern Ontario, or as domestics in metropolitan places such as Toronto and Montreal. For these leftists, radical action was the only available path to reform. Finns thus served as heroic spearheads of organized working-class reform, jeopardizing their well-being and lives by challenging the formidable capitalist system. To cast the broad shadow of "communism" over all of the activities of radical Finns, as, for example, Yrjö Raivio does in his history of the Finns in Canada, is simplistic and does great injustice to those Finns who sought, through the FOC, union activity and support for the CCF and NDP, to simply improve the lot of their everyday lives.[24] History has in fact recorded that many of the rights that these radicals fought so hard for, and for which they were heavily criticized by conservative Finns and others have now become firmly entrenched in union contracts and government legislation. Viewed from today's perspective, these reforms were not really radical. The time has come to recast the leftist/radical tradition of the Finns in Canada and in the Sudbury area as being progressive rather than radical or communist in character.

The institutional mix fostered a rich texture of cultural activities that included sports, the theatre, summer festivals, music and hall events of all kinds. While the Great Divide was partly responsible for this diverse range of activity throughout Canada, the importance of geography should not be lost. Immigrants who came to Canada suddenly found themselves scattered over wide distances in a country thirty times the size of Finland; thus, the

Biography 20
The Honourable Judy Erola: Finnish Femme Extraordinaire

Judy Erola's Finnish roots in the Sudbury area extend back to 1885, when her grandfather, Thomas Jacobson, came to the Sudbury area and was hired by the CCC. Thomas married Susanna Franssi and they had seven children, one of whom was Niilo. Niilo later married Laura Rauhala. Brought up in the town of Walden, Niilo Jacobson's daughter, Judy, first burst on the public scene as a radio and television personality. She was a founding member of Sudbury's first theatre group, and was an accomplished theatrical performer in the 1950s. In the 1970s Judy and her husband, Voitto Erola, ran Erola Panache Landing. Operating the two-hundred-bay marina gave her valuable insights into the world of private entrepreneurship. Voitto passed away in 1977.

In 1980 Judy was elected to the House of Commons as the federal member of Parliament for Nickel Belt and appointed minister of State for Mines. Two years later, she became minister responsible for the Status of Women. She expanded the criteria whereby Native women could maintain their Aboriginal status under the law. In 1983 she was appointed minister of Corporate and Consumer Affairs. After her parliamentary career, in 1987, she became the president of the Pharmaceutical Manufacturers' Association of Canada. She also served as a director of the International Federation of Pharmaceutical Manufacturers Association based in Geneva, Switzerland. Judy Erola is the first woman to be appointed to the Board of Directors of Inco Ltd. Among her other accomplishments can be included a term as the first fund-raising chair of the Canadian Institute of Child Health and selection as a co-chair and a member of the Legal Education and Action Fund (LEAF) Foundation National Endowment Campaign.

Judy, however, never forgot her roots. As a federal cabinet minister, she was a major force in the reshaping of Sudbury through the creation of Science North and the funding of Laurentian University's Centre in Mining and Mineral Exploration Research (CIMMER). Within the Finnish community, she has consistently been a major supporter of the Sudbury Finnish Rest Home Society and the Ladies of Kaleva. More recently, she has worked in concert with the Sudbury Regional Development Corporation to promote Sudbury as a centre of pharmaceutical research. In recognition of her contributions to the Sudbury area, Ms. Erola was granted an Honorary Doctorate of Laws by Laurentian University in 1996. This was her second honorary award, having previously been awarded a Doctor of Human Letters, Honoris Causa, from Mount Saint Vincent University in 1992. In 1994 she was appointed to the Board of Directors of the Canadian Medical Hall of Fame. She has written extensively concerning women's rights and affirmative action. Judy has two daughters, Laura and Kelly.

fostering of local institutions became for them a critical need. The same "discipline of geography" applied to the Sudbury area. Finns in the Beaver Lake area, for example, could be found sixty kilometres from their counterparts at Wanup. Given the lack of automobiles, and the primitive nature of the road networks that existed until World War II, Finnish rural enclaves and urban Finntowns reacted to this isolation by creating their own social networks and cultural institutions. While these initiatives essentially involved the Finns, some had considerable impact on the wider Sudbury community. This was especially true for amateur sport. Prior to World War II, most of the athletic fields and skiing and track-and-field clubs were created by the Finns. Indeed, it was not until the 1940s and 1950s that non-Finnish skiing and track-and-field organizations came into being. While aspects of the theatre, performing arts and music were remarkable for their breadth and expertise, the barrier of language minimized any transfer of appreciation to other sectors of the population. Today the best-known ethnic marker associated with the Finnish lifestyle remains the sauna.

These cultural activities were important, as they provided immigrant Finns with a sense of place and stability while they were being transformed into Canadians. For second- and third-generation Finns, however, the importance of the halls and their cultural activities were less appealing. The most visible expression of this lack of interest was the virtual disappearance of the immigrant hall by the middle 1990s. Other indicators of assimilation among Canadian-born Finns include the declining use of the Finnish language, the transformation of the church into an English or bilingual institution, the increasing use of English in publications such as *Vapaa Sana* and *Kaiku/Echo* and the appearance of English-speaking groups such as the Sudbury *Suomi* Lions Club.

These trends may lead some to conclude that the Sudbury-area Finn is becoming an endangered species. It should be remembered, however, that throughout the course of the twentieth century, Finnish Canadians have always predicted the imminent demise of their culture. Conflicts between the immigrant and later generations have regularly given rise to pessimism and gloomy pronouncements to the effect that "young people are not interested—they don't care about Finnish culture"; that "all the old leaders are dying and nobody bothers to take their place"; or that "everyone today is too busy to do anything—it's not like in the good old days."[25] These expressions of concern for the survival of the Finnish Canadian culture continue to be heard today. The issue remains important and the question can indeed be asked—what are the realistic prospects of its survival in the Sudbury area?

This study offers the basis for some optimism regarding the immediate future of the Finnish community. The Finnish community is far from being extinct. In 1996 there were almost 6,700 persons with some form of Finnish identity who resided in the Sudbury area. While it is true that these numbers have declined in absolute terms since 1961, and that the Finnish landscape in rural areas and communities such as Copper Cliff, Garson, Donovan and Lockerby has undergone considerable change, elements of vitality remain. Among these can be included the resounding success of Finlandia Village, the ongoing support for heritage-language training and the existing vibrancy of groups such as the Sudbury Finnish Male Choir, the Knights and Ladies of Kaleva, the Sudbury *Suomi* Lions Club and the Summer Festival tradition. This situation thus contrasts with that found in the United States where Finns have shown a greater propensity to divorce their association from immigrant-based Finnish organizations and culture in favour of the English-language and symbolic ethnicity.

As the new millennium takes hold, however, two additional factors will greatly influence the salience of Finnish ethnic identity in the Sudbury area. Throughout the twentieth century, immigrant-born Finns have generally assumed the lead in preserving aspects of the ethnic culture; as these immigrants are rapidly fading from the scene, the question arises as to whether or not third- and later-generation Finns will be willing to assume the new mantle of leadership. While second-generation Finns have so far risen to the task, there are signs that the third and fourth generations may not share the same degree of ethnic loyalty. The long-term persistence of Finnish ethnicity is made even more problematic because of the reduced attachment of youth to spoken Finnish. The gradual elimination of this aspect of identity adds a second level of uncertainty in forecasting any cultural future. Some institutions and organizations have already started to adapt to the language issue by increasing their reliance on the use of the English language.[26] It can, however, be argued that such a move can be taken as constituting the first major step towards the full assimilation of Finns into Canadian society and their succumbing to the easier and less-demanding route of symbolic ethnicity centred only around the celebration of Finnish holidays, the purchase of Finnish consumer goods, the use of church rites, such as baptism, confirmation, marriage and funerals in the Lutheran Church, and the use of Finnish markers in homes or on cars.

The indeterminacy of the present situation makes it essential to treat predictions about the future somewhat circumspectly. What is certain is that the Finnish community will continue to make its mark felt in the Sudbury community for at least another generation. Beyond this, it is unclear what, if anything, Finnish identity will mean.

Notes

Acknowledgments

1 Arja Pilli, *The Finnish-Language Press in Canada, 1901-1939* (Turku: Institute of Migration, 1982), p. 9.

2 A thematic guide outlining the scope of the extensive collection associated with the Finnish Canadian Archives in Ontario is contained in Edward W. Laine, *On the Archival Heritage of the Finnish Canadian Working-Class Movement*, Research Report No. 5 (Turku: Institute of Migration, 1987), and Edward W. Laine, *Archival Sources for the Study of Finnish Canadians* (Ottawa: National Archives of Canada, 1989). A guide to the Finnish Canadian Historical Society Archives, along with other Finnish photographs, manuscripts and taped interviews, can be found in Gabriele Scardellato, ed., *A Guide to the Collections of the Multicultural History Society of Ontario* (Toronto: Multicultural History Society of Ontario, 1992).

Introduction

1 Mauri Amiko Jalava, "Radicalism or a 'New Deal'?: The Unfolding World View of the Finnish Immigrants in Sudbury, 1883-1932," in Michael G. Karni et al., eds., *Finns in North America* (Turku: Institute of Migration, 1988), p. 227.

2 "Ashcroft Lauds Inco's Finns," *Inco Triangle* (Copper Cliff, ON) (June 1992), pp. 1-2.

3 Interview with Wilf Salo, Sudbury, 1985.

4 For a North American perspective on Finnish surname changes, see Pertti Virtaranta, *Amerikansuomen Sanakirja* (Turku: Institute of Migration, 1992).

5 Interview with Henry Nelson, Sudbury, 1996.

Chapter I

1 Mauri Amiko Jalava, "Pehr Kalm: First Contact (1749-1750)" (paper presented at the FINNFORUM V Conference, Sudbury, 1996).

2 Akseli Rauanheimo, *Kanadan-kirja* (Porvoo: Werner Söderström Oy, 1930), pp. 212-16.

3 Oiva W. Saarinen, "The Pattern and Impact of Finnish Settlement in Canada," *Terra* 79, 4 (1967): 113; Varpu Lindström-Best, *The Finns in Canada* (Ottawa: Canadian Historical Association, 1985), p. 6.

4 Christine Kouhi, "Labour and Finnish Immigration to Thunder Bay, 1876-1914," *The Lakehead University Review* 9, 1 (1976): 17-40.

5 Nancy Mattson Schelstraete, ed., *Life in the New Finland Woods: A History of New Finland, Saskatchewan* (Rocanville: New Finland Historical and Heritage Society, 1982), p. 6.

6 Reino Kero, "Emigration from Finland to Canada before the First World War," *The Lakehead University Review* 9, 1 (1976): 13; Reino Kero, *Suureen Länteen: Siirtolaisuus Suomesta Pohjois-Amerikkaan* (Turku: Institute of Migration, 1996), pp. 40-41; Canada, *Sessional Papers*, No. 14 (1884), pp. 23-24.

7 Mark Rasmussen, "The Geographic Impact of Finnish Settlement on the Thunder Bay Area of Northern Ontario" (M.A. thesis, University of Alberta, 1978), p. 45.

8 Public Archives of Canada, Manuscript Census (1871-91).

9 Quoted in Mattson Schelstraete, ed., *Life in the New Finland Woods*, p. 8.

10 Kero, "Emigration from Finland to Canada before the First World War," p. 14.

11 Juhani Järvinen, *From Finland to Canada: Siirtolaiselämää Sault Ste. Mariessa Vuosina 1890-1940* (Sault Ste. Marie: Sault Ste. Marie and District Finnish-Canadian Historical Society, 1993), p. 3.

12 Interview with Varpu Lindström, Toronto, 1997.

13 Keijo Virtanen, "'Counter Current': Finns in the Overseas Return Migration Movement," in Michael G. Karni, ed., *Finnish Diaspora I* (Toronto: Multicultural History Society of Ontario, 1981), p. 191.

14 Marc Metsäranta, "The Workingmen's Associations, 1903-1914," in Marc Metsäranta, ed., *Project Bay Street: Activities of Finnish-Canadians in Thunder Bay before 1915* (Thunder Bay: Thunder Bay Finnish-Canadian Historical Society, 1989), p. 18.

15 Peter V.K. Krats, "'Sudburyn Suomalaiset': Finnish Immigrant Activities in the Sudbury Area, 1883-1939" (M.A. thesis, University of Western Ontario, 1980), p. 32.

16 *The Sudbury Star*, 2 July 1932, p. 5.

17 Kero, "Emigration from Finland to Canada before the First World War," p. 14.

18 Mika Roinila, "Finland-Swedes of Canada," *Suomen Silta* 314, 3 (1997): 36-38.

19 Peter Kivisto, *Immigrant Socialists in the United States: The Case of Finns and the Left* (Toronto: Associated University Presses, 1984), p. 69.

20 It is interesting to note here that 10,536 of these Finnish immigrants in 1995 still retained their Finnish citizenship. See "Suomi Kansainvälisessä Seurassa," *Emigrantti* (Helsinki, Finland) 4 (1995): 10.

21 Varpu Lindström-Best, *Defiant Sisters: A Social History of Finnish Immigrant Women in Canada* (Toronto: Multicultural History Society of Ontario, 1988), pp. 38-39.

22 Roinila, "Finland-Swedes of Canada," p. 36.

23 Mika Roinila, "The Finns of Atlantic Canada," *Terra* 104, 1 (1992): 35-44.

24 Arnold R. Alanen, "Finns and Other Immigrant Groups in the American Upper Midwest: Interactions and Comparisons," in Michael G. Karni et al., ed., *Finns in North America* (Turku: Institute of Migration, 1988), p. 66.

25 Quoted in Krats, "'Sudburyn Suomalaiset,'" p. 27.

26 *The Sudbury Star*, 12 April 1924, p. 3.

27 Statistics Canada, *Census of Canada* (1931).

28 Mattson Schelstraete, ed., *Life in the New Finland Woods*, p. 9.

29 Alan Anderson with Brenda Niskala, "Finnish Settlements in Saskatchewan: Their Development and Perpetuation," in Michael G. Karni, ed., *Finnish Diaspora I* (Toronto: Multicultural History Society of Ontario, 1981), p. 156.

30 See, for example, J. Donald Wilson, "Matti Kurikka and A.B. Mäkelä: Socialist Thought among Finns in Canada, 1900-1932," *Canadian Ethnic Studies* 10, 2 (1978):

9-21; Paula Wild, *Sointula: Island Utopia* (Madeira Park, BC: Harbour Publishing, 1995), pp. 105-106.

31 Laine, *Archival Sources for the Study of Finnish Canadians*, pp. 7-8.

32 Rauanheimo, *Kanadan-kirja*, p. 213.

33 Varpu Lindström, "Finnish Canadian Culture in 1995: Toronto Perspectives," in Leena Rossi and Hanne Koivisto, eds., *Monta Tietä Menneisyyteen* (Turku: Turun Yliopisto, 1995), p. 91.

34 *Vapaa Sana* (Sudbury and Toronto), 4 September 1997, p. 2.

35 Ibid., 6 June 1996, p. P2.

36 Leo Glad, "Planning Strategies for an Ethnic-Finnish Lutheran Congregation in Transition to a Canadian Lutheran Congregation" (Doctor of Ministry diss., Luther Seminary, St. Paul, MN, 1995), pp. 8-9.

Chapter II

1 Oiva W. Saarinen, "Ethnicity and the Cultural Mosaic in the Sudbury Area," *Polyphony* 5, 1 (1983): 86-92.

2 See Lauri Pikkusaari, *Copper Cliffin Suomalaiset ja Copper Cliffin Suomalainen Evanke-lis-Luterilainen Wuoristo-Seurakunta* (Hancock: Suomalais-Lutherilainen Kustannus-liike, 1947), p. 38; Krats, "'Sudburyn Suomalaiset,'" p. 225; Reino Kero, *Migration from Finland to North America in the Years between the United States Civil War and the First World War* (Turku: Institute of Migration, 1974).

3 Kero, *Suureen Länteen*, p. 51.

4 Canada, *Sessional Papers*, No. 8 (1885), p. xxvi.

5 Krats, "'Sudburyn Suomalaiset,'" p. 47.

6 Quoted in Nelma Sillanpää, *Under the Northern Lights: My Memories of Life in the Finnish Community of Northern Ontario*, edited by Edward W. Laine (Ottawa: Canadian Museum of Civilization, 1994), p. 4.

7 *The Sudbury Star*, 2 July 1932, p. 5.

8 Information provided by the Anderson Farm Museum.

9 Lindström-Best, *The Finns in Canada*, p. 5.

10 Canada, *Sessional Papers*, No. 14 (1884), p. 21.

11 Pikkusaari, *Copper Cliffin Suomalaiset*, p. 34.

12 *Vapaa Sana*, 14 April 1962, p. 4.

13 Eileen Goltz, "Genesis and Growth of a Company Town: Copper Cliff, 1886-1920" (M.A. thesis, Laurentian University, 1983), p. 32.

14 Ibid., p. 72.

15 Pikkusaari, *Copper Cliffin Suomalaiset*, p. 36.

16 Quoted in Peter V. Krats, "'Suomalaiset Nikkelialueella': Finns in the Sudbury Area, 1883-1939," *Polyphony* 5, 1 (1983): 40.

17 Eileen Goltz, "Copper Cliff: The Pioneer Period," in *Industrial Communities of the Sudbury Basin: Copper Cliff, Victoria Mines, Mond and Coniston* (Sudbury: Sudbury and District Historical Society, 1986), p. 20.

18 Thomas Nicholson, "A Sordid Boon: The Business of State and the State of Labour at the Canadian Copper Company, 1890 to 1918" (M.A. thesis, Queen's University, 1991), p. 60.

19 Arnold R. Alanen, "Finns and the Corporate Mining Environment of the Lake Superior Mining Region," in Michael G. Karni, ed., *Finnish Diaspora II* (Toronto: Multicultural History Society of Ontario, 1981), p. 37.

20 Calculated from Town of Copper Cliff, *Assessment Roll, 1915*.

21 William Eklund, *Builders of Canada: History of the Finnish Organization of Canada 1911-1971* (Toronto: Finnish Organization of Toronto, 1987), p. 124.

22 Among these entrepreneurs could be included the following: tailors (Karl Korppinen, Greta Walli and Isaac Mannisto); shoemakers (Ed Hill, Matti Antilla and Jacob Walli); barbers (Raine Lake, Herman Vick and Herman Koski); sauna operators (Antti and Eino Jaakkola and Andrew Pakkala); taxi driving (Karl Manner); and photographic services (A. Niemi & Son).

23 Goltz, "Genesis and Growth of a Company Town: Copper Cliff, 1886-1920," p. 157.

24 *Vapaus* (Sudbury and Toronto), 5 May 1921, p. 4.

25 W.H. Mäkinen, "The Mond Nickel Company and the Communities of Victoria Mines and Mond," in *Industrial Communities of the Sudbury Basin: Copper Cliff, Victoria Mines, Mond and Coniston* (Sudbury: Sudbury and District Historical Society, 1986), pp. 32-41.

26 *Vapaus*, 23 April 1921, p. 4.

27 *The Sudbury Star*, 3 June 1914, p. 1.

28 Mäkinen, "The Mond Nickel Company and the Communities of Victoria Mines and Mond," p. 36.

29 Hannes Sula et al., *Suomalaiset Nikkelialueella* (Sudbury: CSJ:n Osasto No. 16, 1937), p. 58.

30 Ray Kaattari, *Voices from the Past: Garson Remembers* (Garson: Garson Historical Group, 1992), pp. 27-95.

31 Others who acquired rural holdings around World War I were Allen and Wili Harjula, Charles Matson, Onni Mäki, August Niemi, John Nerkki, J. Pontainen, Oscar Kuula, Charles Engblom, William Bontinen and Matti Lehto. Among the farms established between 1920 and 1930 were those by John Luhta, Antti Lehto, John Virta, Emil Aho, Salmon Porttila, S. Hautämäki, William Heino, O. Mäenpää and N. Koski.

32 The five boarding houses were operated by the William Bontinen, Emil Ahonen, Charles Matson, Andrew Mäkelä and John Pentinen families.

33 Kaattari, *Voices from the Past*, p. 121.

34 Inco Archives (Sudbury), Garson Real Estate Records. Among the Finns taking this option were Niilo Sippilä, Eino Nyfors, Margaret Kamula, Martin Tall, Veikko Pajunen and O. Matson.

35 Royal Ontario Nickel Commission, *Report* (Toronto: Legislative Assembly of Ontario, 1917), p. 37.

36 Inco Archives (Sudbury), Creighton Rent Rolls.

37 Anderson Farm Museum Project, *There Were No Strangers: A History of the Village of Creighton Mine* (Walden: Anderson Farm Museum, 1989), p. 56.

38 Goltz, "Genesis and Growth of a Company Town: Copper Cliff, 1886-1920," p. 152.

39 Mauri Amiko Jalava, "Radicalism or a 'New Deal?' The Unfolding World View of the Finnish Immigrants in Sudbury, 1883-1932" (M.A. thesis, Laurentian University, 1983), pp. 29-30.

40 Frederick Simpich, "Ontario, Next Door," *National Geographic* 62, 2 (August 1932): 158.

41 *Vapaus*, 20 March 1936, p. 3.

42 Sula et al., *Suomalaiset Nikkelialueella*, p. 47.

43 Peter V.K. Krats, "The Sudbury Area to the Great Depression: Regional Develop-
    ment on the Northern Resource Frontier" (Ph.D. diss., University of Western
    Ontario, 1988), pp. 194-95.

44 *Vapaus*, 17 September 1921, p. 4.

45 A sketch of Karl Lehto's sporting achievements can be found in Frank Pagnucco,
    Home-Grown Heroes: A Sports History of Sudbury (Sudbury: Miller Publishing, 1982),
    pp. 131-32.

46 Interview with Elvi Duncan, Sudbury, 1995.

47 *Kaiku/Echo* (Toronto), July/August 1997, p. 7.

48 *The Sudbury Star*, 7 February 1944, p. 1, and 23 November 1944, p. 5.

49 Oiva Saarinen with Gerry Tapper, *Sudbury* Suomi *Lions Club, Sudbury, Ontario,
    Canada, 1989-1995* (Sudbury: Sudbury *Suomi* Lions Club, 1995), p. 35.

50 Interview with Anita and Walter Mäki, Sudbury, 1995.

51 Interview with Varpu Lindström, Toronto, 1997.

52 Interview with Arnel Michel, Sudbury, 1996. To facilitate the shipment of milk, the
    dairy financed the construction of Walford Road.

53 Lennard Sillanpää, "A Political and Social History of Canadians of Finnish Descent
    in the District of Sudbury" (M.A. thesis, University of Helsinki, 1973), p. 13.

54 *The Sudbury Star*, 12 April 1924, p. 3.

55 Krats, " 'Sudburyn Suomalaiset,' " p. 35.

56 *The Sudbury Star*, 20 August 1932, pp. 1-2.

57 Ibid., 2 July 1932, p. 5.

58 The fifteen voters included Jacob Karppi, E. and A. Kallio, Elias Kangas, Herman
    Koski, Alex and Jacob Lauttamus, John Lahti, Solomon Mäkelä, J. Mattson, A. Nel-
    son, Antti Pleuna, John Ristimäki, John Salo and Jacob Salomaa (Township of
    Waters, *Voters' List, 1909*).

59 Township of Waters, *Assessment Roll, 1916*.

60 Waters Women's Institute, *The Story of Waters Township* (Walden Township: Waters
    Women's Institute, n.d.)

61 Varpu Lindström-Best and Charles Sutyla, *Terveisiä Ruusa-tädiltä: Kanadan Suoma-
    laisten Ensimmäinen Sukupolvi* (Helsinki: Suomalaisen Kirjallisuuden Seura, 1984).

62 Waters Women's Institute, *The Story of Waters Township*, n.p.

63 *Vapaus*, 26 October 1967, p. 2; see also Jim Tester, ed., *Sports Pioneers: A History of the
    Finnish-Canadian Amateur Sports Federation 1906-1986* (Sudbury: Alerts AC Historical
    Committee, 1986), p. 53.

64 Among the farmers who sold their properties were John Salo, Ernest Kallio, John
    Harju, Kusti Holmes, Edwin Salo, Fabian Mäkelä, Oscar Kulmala, John Mäenpää
    and Frank Anderson.

65 *Vapaus*, 28 October 1947, p. 54.

66 These included Aatu Kolari, Oscar Laine, John Laaksonen, John Luopa, Otto Man-
    ninen, John Pellinen, William Peterson, Konsta Ristimäki, John Salminen and Victor
    Soini, along with their families.

67 Among the farmsteads developed in the 1920s were those owned by David Helin,
    Oscar Luoma, Tom Kopsa, Oscar Tapper, Otto Salo, Onni Rossi and Theodor
    Honkasalo.

68 Oiva W. Saarinen and G.O. Tapper, "The Beaver Lake Finnish-Canadian Commu-
    nity: A Case Study of Ethnic Transition as Influenced by the Variables of Time and
    Spatial Networks, ca. 1907-1983," in Michael G. Karni et al., eds., *Finns in North
    America* (Turku: Institute of Migration, 1988), p. 168.

69 *Vapaus*, 5 May 1921, p. 4.

70 G.O. Tapper and O.W. Saarinen, eds., *Better Known as Beaver Lake: An History of Lorne Township and Surrounding Area* (Walden, ON: Walden Public Library, 1998).

71 Pat Koski and Bill Mäkinen, *Wuoristo-St. Timothy's Lutheran Church, Copper Cliff, Ontario: 100 Years, 1897-1997* (Sudbury: St. Timothy's Lutheran Church, 1997), pp. 57-64.

72 *Vapaus*, 27 February 1936, p. 6.

73 In the following year, Fred Hill, Charles and William Hotti, Irene Lindala and John Wentela also registered properties.

74 *Vapaus*, 12 May 1921, p. 4.

75 *The Sudbury Star*, 7 May 1921, p. 7.

76 *Vapaus*, 28 September 1971, Part I, p. 2.

77 Much of this information has been gleaned from Archives of Ontario (Toronto), *Rev. Arvi Iisakki Heinonen*, by Maire Punkari (1982), in Arvi Iisakki Heinonen Papers, F1405, Acc. 21210, Ser. 15-115, MSR 11554.

78 Arvi Heinonen, *Finnish Friends in Canada* (Toronto: United Church of Canada, 1930), p. 86.

79 *The Sudbury Star*, 18 June 1913, p. 1.

80 Ibid., 27 February 1915, p. 4.

81 Ibid., 14 July 1934, p. 6.

82 *Vapaus*, 30 September 1971, Part III, p. 5.

83 Interview with Ruth Svensk, Sudbury, 1995.

84 *The Sudbury Star*, 12 May 1928, p. 1.

85 Ibid., 9 May 1928, p. 1.

86 See Archives of Ontario (Toronto), Ministry of Natural Resources (1936-38), Land Files 85418, Vol. 1.

87 Township of Louise, *Daily Registers for School Section No. 3* (1934-44).

88 Ibid.

89 Eino Nissilä, *Pioneers of Long Lake* (Sudbury, 1987), p. 3.

90 Others who followed in the wake of the first pioneers included Isaac Niemi, John Kortesuo, William Peura, Kusti Järvi, Matti Vähämäki, Otto Kinnonen, Alexander Innanen, Kapriel Sävelä, Pekka Poutanen, Arvi Haverinen, August Pankkonen and Arvi Mäkinen. Among those who came around the World War I period were Alexander Majava, Jack Järvi, Jack Aho, Rev. Arvi Heinonen, Simon Hendrickson, Charles Kinnunen, David Haapala, Antti Kaksonen, Alexander Luoma, John Toivonen, Karl Nissilä, John Salomäki, Simo Purola, Antti Ahokas and Ella Marttinen.

91 *Vapaus*, 2 November 1937, p. 26.

92 Land registrations were made in the 1920s by Elis Lantto, Alfred Orrenmaa, Arthur Helin, Victor Hänninen, Ilmari Mäki, Nicholai Virtanen, John Kivi and Emile Ahola.

93 The new households included the Charles Lindström, Kusti Kangas, Jan Lammi, Mike Lambert, Edward Mäkinen, Venni Viita, Edward Hill, Ricki Pannanen and Erkki Hautamäki families.

94 *Vapaa Sana*, 14 April 1962, p. 5.

95 Long Lake Public School (Sudbury, ON), *Daily Registers for Long Lake Public School* (1914-85).

96 Interview with Arne and Kaarina Ritari, Sudbury, 1995.

97 These included subdivisions registered by Victor Hänninen, John Luoma, John Pulkkinen, Oliver Pennala, Arvid Mäkinen, Ida Finnila, Tyyne Kinnunen and David Häninen.

98 Nissilä, *Pioneers of Long Lake*, p. 1.

99 *The Sudbury Star*, 30 June 1933, p. 13, and 31 July 1935, p. 8.

100 *Vapaus*, 17 November 1921, p. 4.

101 *Vapaa Sana*, 14 April 1962, pp. 1 and 8.

102 Finnish Canadian Amateur Athletic Club *Voima* (Sudbury), Newspaper Archives (1940-84).

103 Nissilä, *Pioneers of Long Lake*, p. 23.

104 *Vapaus*, 27 September 1921, p. 4.

105 Among the new migrants were Alfred Hautamäki, Paul Korppi, Johan Koskela, Kustaa Laaksonen, Antti Lahtinen, Hjalmar Manninen, Adolph Pelto, Oscar Peltola and Otto Rautiainen.

106 Wanup Public School, *Daily Registers for Dill and Cleland (Wanup) Public School* (1923-51).

107 *The Sudbury Star*, 8 June 1932, pp. 1 and 20.

108 Ibid., 2 July 1932, p. 5.

109 Those who registered properties in the 1930s included Aksel Hakula, Miina Hill, Oiva Jouppi, Wiktori Rautianen, Kalle Simola, Kusti Varjonen, Einari Väliaho and Oscar Virtanen.

110 Wanup Public School, *Daily Registers for Dill and Cleland (Wanup) Public School* (1936).

111 Ibid. (1949-51).

112 Paul Tyni, *Wanupin Historia vv. 1925-1985* (Dill Township, 1985), p. 1.

113 *Vapaus*, 20 August 1921, p. 4; Estaire-Wanup Volunteer Fire Brigade, *Ladies Auxiliary Cookbook: Stories and the Kitchen Table* (Estaire-Wanup: Estaire-Wanup Volunteer Fire Brigade, 1997), p. 33.

114 Interview with William Kangassalo, Sudbury, 1995,

115 *Vapaus*, 28 February 1936, p. 4.

116 *The Sudbury Star*, 11 October 1922, p. 1.

117 Tyni, *Wanupin Historia vv. 1925-1985*, p. 119.

118 Interview with Wilf Salo, Sudbury, 1995.

119 Interview with Sulo and Bertha Heino, Sudbury, 1995.

120 Among the boarding-house operators were Mary Vähäniemi, Sirkka Heikkilä, Annie Peura, Väinö Kuja, Mrs. Matti Asunmaa, Elli Riutta, Mary Matson and H. Raudaskoski.

121 Inco Archives (Sudbury), Levack Real Estate Records.

122 *The Sudbury Star*, 7 January 1965, p. 3.

123 These included, for example, Arthur Mäki, Alli Kaukonen, Herman Perttula, M. Poutiainen, Armas Hook and Edna Lahti.

124 Interview with Wilf Salo, Sudbury, 1989.

125 Interview with G.O. (Gerry) Tapper, Sudbury, 1997.

126 Much of the information for this biography was derived from Lempi Johnson's autobiography. See Lempi Johnson and Raija Toivola, *Sisulla ja Sydämellä* (Sudbury, 1984).

127 William Copeland, "Early Finnish-American Settlements in Florida," in Michael G. Karni, ed., *Finnish Diaspora II* (Toronto: Multicultural History Society of Ontario, 1981), p. 135.

Chapter III

1 Peter V. Krats, "Limited Loyalties: The Sudbury, Canada Finns and Their Institutions 1887-1935," in Michael G. Karni et al., eds., *Finns in North America* (Turku: Institute of Migration, 1988), p. 190.

2 Jean Morrison, "Ethnicity and Class Consciousness: British, Finnish and South European Workers at the Canadian Lakehead before World War I," *The Lakehead University Review* 9, 1 (1976): 47.

3 J. Donald Wilson, "The Finnish Organization of Canada, the 'Language Barrier,' and the Assimilation Process." *Canadian Ethnic Studies* 9, 2 (1977): 105.

4 Jalava, "Radicalism or a 'New Deal'?"

5 Sillanpää, "A Political and Social History of Canadians of Finnish Descent in the District of Sudbury," p. 1.

6 Krats, "'*Sudburyn Suomalaiset,*'" pp. iii-iv; Edward W. Laine, "Community in Crisis: The Finnish-Canadian Quest for Cultural Identity, 1900-1979," in Michael G. Karni, ed., *Finnish Diaspora I* (Toronto: Multicultural History Society of Ontario, 1981), p. 6.

7 Varpu Lindström-Best, "Defiant Sisters: A Social History of the Finnish Immigrant Women in Canada, 1890-1930" (Ph.D. diss., York University, 1986), p. 418.

8 Ibid., pp. 32-33.

9 Interview with Sofia Pontio by Varpu Lindström, Sudbury, 1973.

10 Gary London, "The Finnish-American Anti-Socialist Movement, 1908-1918," in Michael G. Karni et al., eds., *Finns in North America* (Turku: Institute of Migration, 1988), p. 211.

11 A. William Hoglund, "Breaking with Religious Tradition: Finnish Immigrant Workers and the Church, 1890-1915," in Michael G. Karni and Douglas J. Ollila, Jr., eds., *For the Common Good: Finnish Immigrants and the Radical Response to Industrial America* (Superior, WI: Työmies Society, 1977), p. 27.

12 Sakari Sariola, "Socialism and Church: An Antinomian Impasse in Finnish-American Immigrant Communities," in Michael G. Karni et al., eds., *Finns in North America* (Turku: Institute of Migration, 1988), pp. 201-202.

13 Timo Orta, "Finnish Emigration Prior to 1893: Economic, Demographic and Social Backgrounds," in Michael G. Karni et al., eds., *The Finnish Experience in the Western Great Lakes Region: New Perspectives* (Turku: Institute of Migration, 1975), pp. 21-35; Kero, *Suureen Länteen,* pp. 120-21.

14 A. William Hoglund, "No Land for Finns: Critics and Reformers View the Rural Exodus from Finland to America between the 1880's and World War I," in Michael G. Karni et al., eds., *The Finnish Experience in the Western Great Lakes Region: New Perspectives* (Turku: Institute of Migration, 1975), p. 37.

15 Oiva W. Saarinen, "Spatial Behaviour of the State and of the Co-operative Movement in the Finnish Forest Economy" (Ph.D. diss., University of London, 1979), pp. 156-59.

16 Lindström-Best, *Defiant Sisters: A Social History of Finnish Immigrant Women in Canada,* p. 15.

17 *Vapaa Sana,* 26 June 1997, p. 15.

18 Ian Angus, *Canadian Bolsheviks: The Early Years of the Communist Party of Canada* (Montreal: Vanguard Publications, 1981), pp. 71, 253 and 295.

19 Kero, *Suureen Länteen,* p. 74.

20 Auvo Kostiainen, "Contacts between the Finnish Labour Movements in the United States and Canada," in Michael G. Karni, ed., *Finnish Diaspora I* (Toronto: Multicultural History Society of Ontario, 1981), p. 34.

21 Douglas Ollila, Jr., "The Work People's College: Immigrant Education for Adjustment and Solidarity," in Michael G. Karni and Douglas J. Ollila, Jr., eds., *For the Common Good: Finnish Immigrants and the Radical Response to Industrial America* (Superior, WI: Työmies Society, 1977), p. 90.

22 Sariola, "Socialism and Church: An Antinomian Impasse in Finnish-American Immigrant Communities," p. 207.

23 Carl Ross, *The Finn Factor in American Labor, Culture, and Society* (New York Mills, MN: Parta Publishing, 1977), p. 23.

24 Reino Kero, *Suomalaisina Pohjois-Amerikassa: Siirtolaiselämää Yhdysvalloissa ja Kanadassa* (Turku: Institute of Migration, 1997), p. 46.

25 Michael Karni, "Finnish Temperance and Its Clash with Emerging Socialism in Minnesota," in Michael G. Karni, ed., *Finnish Diaspora II* (Toronto: Multicultural History Society of Ontario, 1981), pp. 164-68.

26 Metsäranta, "The Workingmen's Associations, 1903-1914," p. 70.

27 Kostiainen, "Contacts between the Finnish Labor Movements in the United States and Canada," p. 34.

28 Hilja J. Karvonen, "Three Proponents of Women's Rights in the Finnish-American Labour Movement from 1910-1930: Selma Jokela McCone, Maiju Nurmi and Helmi Mattson," in Michael G. Karni and Douglas J. Ollila, Jr., eds., *For the Common Good: Finnish Immigrants and the Radical Response to Industrial America* (Superior, WI: Työmies Society, 1977), p. 200.

29 Varpu Lindström-Best and Allen Seager, "Toveritar and Finnish-Canadian Women, 1900-1930," in Michael G. Karni et al., eds., *Finns in North America* (Turku: Institute of Migration, 1988), pp. 133 and 140.

30 Michael Karni, "The Founding of the Finnish Socialist Federation and the Minnesota Strike of 1907," in Michael G. Karni and Douglas J. Ollila, Jr., eds., *For the Common Good: Finnish Immigrants and the Radical Response to Industrial America* (Superior, WI: Työmies Society, 1977), p. 78.

31 Kivisto, *Immigrant Socialists in the United States: The Case of Finns and the Left*, p. 157.

32 Auvo Kostiainen, "Finnish-American Workmen's Associations," in Vilho Niitemaa et al., eds., *Old Friends–Strong Ties* (Turku: Institute of Migration, 1976), p. 221.

33 Auvo Kostiainen, "The Tragic Crisis: Finnish-American Workers and the Civil War in Finland," in Michael G. Karni and Douglas J. Ollila, Jr., eds., *For the Common Good: Finnish Immigrants and the Radical Response to Industrial America* (Superior, WI: Työmies Society, 1977), pp. 230-31.

34 Arnold R. Alanen, "The Development and Distribution of Finnish Consumers' Cooperatives in Michigan, Minnesota and Wisconsin, 1903-1973," in Michael G. Karni et al., eds., *The Finnish Experience in the Western Great Lakes Region: New Perspectives* (Turku: Institute of Migration, 1975), p. 104.

35 London, "The Finnish-American Anti-Socialist Movement, 1908-1918," p. 214.

36 J. Donald Wilson, "The Canadian Sojourn of a Finnish-American Radical," *Canadian Ethnic Studies* 16, 2 (1984): 105.

37 London, "The Finnish-American Anti-Socialist Movement, 1908-1918," p. 223; Ollila, Jr., "The Work People's College: Immigrant Education for Adjustment and Solidarity," p. 112.

38 Kero, *Suomalaisina Pohjois-Amerikassa*, p. 61.

39 Sula et al., *Suomalaiset Nikkelialueella*, p. 18.

40 John Wargelin, *A Highway to America* (Hancock: The Book Concern, 1967), p. 43.

41 Koski and Mäkinen, *Wuoristo-St. Timothy's Lutheran Church, Copper Cliff, Ontario: 100 Years, 1897-1997*, p. 19.

42 Pikkusaari, *Copper Cliffin Suomalaiset*, p. 118.

43 Wargelin, *A Highway to America*, p. 40.

44 *Copper Cliff Courier*, Christmas Number 1903, p. 16.

45 Quoted in Jalava, "Radicalism or a 'New Deal'?," pp. 41-42.
46 *The Sudbury Star*, 8 March 1913, p. 8, and 28 June 1913, p. 1.
47 Ibid., 30 December 1914, p. 4, and 13 February 1915, p. 4.
48 Ibid., 24 March 1915, p. 4.
49 The provisional directors of the society were Anton Janti, Johan Kukkonen, Henry Mäki, Nestor Pethman and Alex Koskela.
50 *The Sudbury Star*, 21 December 1918, p. 4.
51 Wilson, "The Finnish Organization of Canada, the 'Language Barrier,' and the Assimilation Process," p. 114.
52 *Vapaus*, 20 March 1936, p. 3.
53 Krats, "'Sudburyn Suomalaiset,'" p. 136.
54 Wargelin, *A Highway to America*, p. 55.
55 Quoted in Krats, "'Sudburyn Suomalaiset,'" p. 131.
56 *Vapaus*, 28 October 1947, p. 13.
57 Ross, *The Finn Factor in American Labor, Culture, and Society* (New York Mills, MN: Parta Publishing, 1977), p. 210.
58 Graeme Mount, *Canada's Enemies: Spies and Spying in the Peaceable Kingdom* (Toronto: Dundurn Press, 1993), pp. 50-51.
59 United States National Archives (Washington, DC), Department of State, *Chapman to the Secretary of State*, Voluntary Report of 14 November 1931, RG59, Box 6167, Decimal File 1930-39, 842.00B/61.
60 Interview with Sofia Pontio by Varpu Lindström, Sudbury, 1973.
61 *The Sudbury Star*, 12 January 1929, pp. 1 and 3.
62 Ibid., 19 February 1930, pp. 12 and 19.
63 Allen Seager, "Finnish Canadians and the Ontario Miners' Movement," *Polyphony* 3, 2 (1981): 42.
64 *Vapaus*, 28 October 1947, p. 18.
65 *The Sudbury Star*, 23 October 1918, p. 1.
66 Barbara Roberts, *Whence They Came: Deportation from Canada 1900-1935* (Ottawa: University of Ottawa Press, 1988), p. 73.
67 Pilli, *The Finnish-Language Press in Canada, 1901-1939*, pp. 130-31.
68 William Rodney, *Soldiers of the International: A History of the Communist Party of Canada 1919-1929* (Toronto: University of Toronto Press, 1968), p. 51.
69 Gerry van Houten et al., eds., *Canada's Party of Socialism: History of the Communist Party of Canada 1921-1976* (Toronto: Progress Books, 1982), pp. 20-22.
70 Rodney, *Soldiers of the International: A History of the Communist Party of Canada 1919-1929*, p. 10.
71 *Vapaus*, 11 June 1921, p. 2.
72 Laine, "Community in Crisis: The Finnish-Canadian Quest for Cultural Identity, 1900-1979," p. 100.
73 John Kolehmainen, *The Finns in America: A Bibliographical Guide to Their History* (Hancock: Suomi College, 1947).
74 Raoul Palmgren, *Joukkosydän: Vanhan Työväenliikkeemme Kaunokirjallisuus* (Porvoo: Werner Söderström Oy, 1986), pp. 451-68.
75 *Liekki* (Sudbury), 2 April 1949.
76 *Northern Life* (Sudbury), 3 January 1997, p. 9A.
77 Van Houten et al., eds., *Canada's Party of Socialism: History of the Communist Party of Canada 1921-1976*, p. 29.
78 Jalava, "Radicalism or a 'New Deal'?," p. 193.

79 Donald Avery, *"Dangerous Foreigners": European Immigrant Workers and Labour Radicalism in Canada, 1896-1932* (Toronto: McClelland and Stewart, 1979), p. 143.
80 *Vapaus*, 2 November 1937, p. 9.
81 *The Sudbury Star*, 19 December 1928, p. 4, and 5 January 1929, pp. 9 and 11.
82 Ibid., 11 May 1929, p. 1.
83 Interview with Taimi Davies (Pitkänen) by Varpu Lindström, Toronto, 1997.
84 *The Sudbury Star*, 5 November 1930, p. 1, and 22 April 1931, p. 1.
85 Angus, *Canadian Bolsheviks: The Early Years of the Communist Party of Canada*, p. 296.
86 Van Houten et al., eds., *Canada's Party of Socialism: History of the Communist Party of Canada 1921-1976*, p. 59.
87 *Vapaus*, 16 November 1929, p. 1.
88 *Vapaa Sana*, 9 March 1972, p. 8.
89 Quoted in Angus, *Canadian Bolsheviks: The Early Years of the Communist Party of Canada*, p. 299.
90 *Vapaa Sana*, 31 October 1996, p. 3.
91 *Vapaus*, 9 June 1931, p. 2.
92 Mauri Amiko Jalava, "The Finnish-Canadian Cooperative Movement in Ontario," in Michael G. Karni, ed., *Finnish Diaspora I* (Toronto: Multicultural History Society of Ontario, 1981), pp. 95-96.
93 *Vapaa Sana*, 22 April 1936, p. 3, and 29 April 1936, p. 3.
94 *The Sudbury Star*, 21 June 1930, p. 1.
95 Yrjö Raivio, *Kanadan Suomalaisten Historia II* (Copper Cliff: Canadan Suomalainen Historiaseura, 1979), p. 361.
96 *The Sudbury Star*, 30 March 1932, p. 18; *Vapaa Sama*, 14 April 1962, p. 4.
97 Mauri Amiko Jalava, *Toronton Suomalainen Osuuspankki 1958-1978* (Toronto: Finnish [Toronto] Credit Union, 1978), p. 11.
98 *The Sudbury Star*, 7 November 1931, p. 1, and 11 November 1931, p. 1.
99 Ibid., 14 November 1931, p. 8.
100 Roberts, *Whence They Came: Deportation from Canada 1900-1935*, p. 140.
101 Ibid., p. 134.
102 Ibid., pp. 135 and 144.
103 Reino Kero, "Emigration of Finns from North America to Soviet Karelia in the Early 1930s," in Michael G. Karni et al., eds., *The Finnish Experience in the Western Great Lakes Region: New Perspectives* (Turku: Institute of Migration, 1975), p. 220.
104 *The Sudbury Star*, 19 September 1931, p. 1.
105 Alexis Pogorelskin, "New Perspectives on Karelian Fever: The Recruitment of North American Finns to Karelia in the Early 1930s," in Varpu Lindström, Oiva Saarinen and Börje Vähämäki, eds., *Melting into Great Waters: Papers from FINNFORUM V* (Toronto: University of Toronto Press, 1997), p. 169.
106 *Vapaus*, 27 June 1935, Part I, pp. 1 and 4, and Part II, pp. 1-2.
107 Pogorelskin, "New Perspectives on Karelian Fever: The Recruitment of North American Finns to Karelia in the Early 1930s," p. 178.
108 Jalava, "Radicalism or a 'New Deal'?," p. 245.
109 Interview with John Passi, Sudbury, 1995.
110 *The Sudbury Star*, 30 May 1931, p. 3.
111 Mayme Sevander, *Red Exodus: Finnish-American Emigration to Russia* (Duluth, MN: Oscat, 1993), p. 8; Kero, *Suureen Länteen*, p. 280.
112 Sevander, *Red Exodus: Finnish-American Emigration to Russia*, pp. 172-73 and 229.

113 Mayme Sevander, *Soviet Bondage: Sequel to "Red Exodus"* (Duluth, MN: Oscat, 1996), pp. 122-57.

114 *Vapaus*, 27 June 1935, p. 8.

115 Anita Middleton, "Karelian Fever: Interviews with Survivors," in Varpu Lindström, Oiva Saarinen and Börje Vähämäki, eds., *Melting into Great Waters: Papers from FINNFORUM V* (Toronto: University of Toronto Press, 1997), p. 181.

116 Sula et al., *Suomalaiset Nikkelialueella*, p. 50.

117 *Vapaus*, 17 December 1932, p. 2.

118 Ivan Avakumovic, *The Communist Party in Canada: A History* (Toronto: McClelland and Stewart, 1975), p. v.

119 Gregory Kealey and Reg Whitaker, *R.C.M.P. Security Bulletins: The Depression Years, Part I, 1933-1934* (St. John's, NF: Memorial University, 1993), p. 8.

120 Gregory Kealey and Reg Whitaker, *R.C.M.P. Security Bulletins: The Early Years, 1919-1929* (St. John's, NF: Memorial University, 1994), pp. 362-82.

121 Ibid., p. 176.

122 Kero, *Suomalaisina Pohjois-Amerikassa*, p. 98.

123 United States National Archives, Department of State, *Chapman to the Secretary of State*, Voluntary Report of 14 November 1931, RG59, Box 6167, Decimal File 1930-39, 842.00B/61.

124 *Vapaus*, 9 February 1921, p. 4; 16 March 1921, p. 4; and 20 August 1920, p. 4.

125 Yjrö Raivio, *Kanadan Suomalaisten Historia I* (Copper Cliff: Canadan Suomalainen Historiaseura, 1975), pp. 464-85.

126 Interviews with Laila Johnson, Sudbury, 1997, and Jules Päiviö, Sudbury 1995.

127 Kero, *Suomalaisina Pohjois-Amerikassa*, p. 83.

128 Varpu Lindström-Best, "Central Organization of the Loyal Finns in Canada," *Polyphony* 3, 2 (1981): 101.

129 United States National Archives, Department of State, *Chapman to the Secretary of State*, Voluntary Report of 12 March 1932, RG56, Box 6167, Decimal File 1930-39, 842.00B/71.

130 Edward W. Laine, "Finnish Canadian Radicalism and Canadian Politics: The First Forty Years, 1900-1940," in Jorgen Dahlie and Tissa Fernando, eds., *Ethnicity, Power and Politics in Canada* (Toronto: Methuen, 1981), p. 101.

131 Kealey and Whitaker, *R.C.M.P. Security Bulletins: The Depression Years, Part I, 1933-1934*, p. 60.

132 Avakumovic, *The Communist Party in Canada: A History*, pp. v-vi.

133 *Vapaus*, 2 July 1937, p. 5.

134 William Eklund, *Canadan Rakentajia: Canadan Suomalaisen Järjestön Historia vv. 1911-1971* (Toronto: Finnish Organization of Canada, 1983); Eklund, *Builders of Canada: History of the Finnish Organization of Canada 1911-1971*.

135 Lennard Sillanpää, "The Political Behaviour of Canadians of Finnish Descent in the District of Sudbury" (Licentiate thesis, University of Helsinki, 1976), pp. 113-15.

136 *Vapaus*, 28 October 1947, p. 13.

137 Laine, *Archival Sources for the Study of Finnish Canadians*, p. xix.

138 H. Kaskela, *Sudburyn Kansallis-Seuran 15 Vuotis Historiikki 1930-1945* (Sudbury: Finnish National Society of Sudbury, 1945), p. 2.

139 *The Sudbury Star*, 28 May 1930, p. 13. The first executive consisted of the following individuals: E. Vilska, V. Halonen, H. Sankelo, T. Toivonen, E. Wilson, A. Liukkonen and Rev. F. Mayblom.

140 Oiva W. Saarinen, *A History of the Finnish National Society of Sudbury 1930-1991* (Sudbury: Finnish National Society of Sudbury, 1991), p. 2.

141 Lindström-Best, "Central Organization of the Loyal Finns in Canada," p. 97.

142 Kaskela, *Sudburyn Kansallis-Seuran 15 Vuotis Historiikki 1930-1945*, p. 13.

143 Wargelin, *A Highway to America*, pp. 55-56.

144 Markku Suokonautio, "Reorganization of the Finnish Lutherans in Canada," *Polyphony* 3, 2 (1981): 19.

145 *Vapaus*, 27 February 1936, p. 6.

146 Viljo Nenonen, *Pyhän Matteuksen Suomalainen Evankelis-Luterilainen Seurakunta 40-Vuotias* (Sudbury: St. Matthew's Finnish Evangelical Lutheran Church, 1972), pp. 17-26.

147 Liisa A. Liedes and Uuno I. Vesanen, *Suomalainen Helluntaiherätys Pohjois-Americassa* (Vancouver: Mission Press Society, 1994), p. 65; *Todistaja* (Vancouver), Extra 1998, p. 6.

148 Liedes and Vesanen, *Suomalainen Helluntaiherätys Pohjois-Americassa*, pp. 51-52.

149 *Vapaa Sana*, 19 December 1936, pp. 1 and 3.

150 Ibid., 31 November 1931, p. 12.

151 Ibid., 9 March 1972, p. 2.

152 Ibid., 31 October 1934, p. 3.

153 Pilli, *The Finnish-Language Press in Canada, 1901-1939*, p. 223.

154 Ibid., p. 225.

155 *The Sudbury Star*, 4 May 1918, p. 5.

156 William Eklund, *Canadan Suomalaisten Sotilaiden Muistoalbumi* (Sudbury: Vapaus Publishing Company, 1946).

157 Pikkusaari, *Copper Cliffin Suomalaiset*, p. 91.

158 Sillanpää, *Under the Northern Lights: My Memories of Life in the Finnish Community of Northern Ontario*, pp. 62-72.

159 Interview with Jules Päiviö, Sudbury, 1995.

160 Interview with Sulo and Bertha Heino, Sudbury, 1995.

161 Oliver Korpela, *History of the Korpela Family* (Sudbury, 1986); *The Sudbury Star*, 28 May 1945, pp. 1 and 5.

162 *The Sudbury Star*, 13 December 1939, p. 11.

163 Ibid., 28 December 1939, pp. 1 and 8.

164 Kaskela, *Sudburyn Kansallis-Seuran 15 Vuotis Historiikki 1930-1945*, p. 18.

165 *Vapaus*, 6 June 1940, p. 1.

166 Eklund, *Builders of Canada: History of the Finnish Organization of Canada 1911-1971*, p. 238.

167 *The Sudbury Star*, 30 November 1939, p. 1.

168 Ibid., 15 February 1940, p. 6.

169 Ibid., 15 July 1940, p. 16, and 20 July 1940, p. 1.

170 Ibid., 7 February 1944, p. 3.

171 Eklund, *Builders of Canada: History of the Finnish Organization of Canada 1911-1971*, p. 244.

172 The first executive consisted of the following individuals: Bruno Tenhunen (president), Hannes Kaskela (secretary), Vaino Kuikka (treasurer) and Mrs. Fanny Heino, Rev. Lauri Pikkisaari, Antti Heiskanen and K. Asiala as directors.

173 Raymond W. Wargelin, "Finnish Lutherans in Canada," in Ralph J. Jalkanen, ed., *The Faith of the Finns* (East Lansing: Michigan State University Press, 1972), pp. 144-45.

174 Nenonen, *Phyän Matteuksen Suomalainen Evankelis-Luterilainen Seurakunta 40-Vuotias*, p. 55.
175 St. Matthew's Evangelical Lutheran Church, *Annual Report, 1995* (Sudbury: St. Matthew's Evangelical Lutheran Church, 1996).
176 *Vapaa Sana*, 6 June 1996, p. 2.
177 Koski and Mäkinen, *Wuoristo-St. Timothy's Lutheran Church, Copper Cliff, Ontario: 100 Years, 1897-1997*, p. 75.
178 St. Timothy's Lutheran Church, *Annual Report, 1996* (Sudbury: St. Timothy's Lutheran Church, 1997).
179 *Kaiku/Echo*, 15 August 1996, p. 11.
180 Ibid., 15 July 1996, p. 9.
181 Ibid., July/August 1997, p. 14.
182 *Vapaus*, 11 March 1991, p. 1; *Kaiku/Echo*, 15 August 1996, p. 14.
183 Lindström, "Finnish Canadian Culture in 1995: Toronto Perspectives," p. 87.
184 Raivio, *Kanadan Suomalainen Historia II*, p. 151.
185 *Vapaa Sana*, 6 July 1995, p. 11; Kanadan Suomalainen Kulttuuriliitto, *Toimintakertomus 1995* (Toronto: Kanadan Suomalainen Kulttuuriliitto, 1996), p. 3.
186 *Vapaa Sana*, 11 July 1996, p. 3; *Canadan Uutiset* (Thunder Bay), 13 November 1996, p. 5.
187 Robert W. Selvala, *FinnFest USA: The First Decade 1982-1992* (Owatonna, MN: FinnFest USA, 1992), p. ii.
188 *Vapaa Sana*, 3 July 1997, p. 10.
189 Ibid.
190 Wilson, "The Finnish Organization of Canada, the 'Language Barrier,' and the Assimilation Process," pp. 105-106.
191 Eklund, *Builders of Canada: History of the Finnish Organization of Canada 1911-1971*, p. 1.
192 Central Organization of the Loyal Finns in Canada, *Constitution* (Sudbury: Central Organization of the Loyal Finns in Canada, 1931).
193 Quoted in Wilson, "The Finnish Organization of Canada, the 'Language Barrier,' and the Assimilation Process," pp. 107-109.
194 Glad, "Planning Strategies for an Ethnic-Finnish Lutheran Congregation," p. 9.
195 Michael J. Maunula, "The Retention of Ethnic Culture among Thunder Bay Finns" (M.A. thesis, Lakehead University, 1984), pp. 190-95.
196 Laine, "Community in Crisis: The Finnish-Canadian Quest for Cultural Identity, 1900-1979," pp. 3-4.

Chapter IV

1 Keijo Virtanen, "Work as a Factor of Adaptation for Finnish Immigrants in the Great Lakes Region," in Varpu Lindström, Oiva Saarinen and Börje Vähämäki, eds., *Melting into Great Waters: Papers from FINNFORUM V* (Toronto: University of Toronto Press, 1997), p. 117.
2 Quoted in Krats, " '*Sudburyn Suomalaiset*,' " p. 67.
3 Eklund, *Builders of Canada: History of the Finnish Organization of Canada 1911-1971*, p. 21.
4 *Vapaa Sana*, 14 April 1962, p. 6.
5 Nicholson, "A Sordid Boon: The Business of State and the State of Labour at the Canadian Copper Company, 1890 to 1918," p. 46.

6 Interview with John Passi, Sudbury, 1995.

7 *Inco Triangle* (October 1952), p. 9.

8 Ibid. (February 1937), p. 1; (November 1938), p. 5; (November 1951), p. 5; (June 1957), pp. 8-9.

9 Ibid. (February 1947), p. 3; (April 1947), p. 3; (October 1950), p. 11; (December 1950), p. 12; (June 1951), p. 15; (October 1952), p. 9; (January 1954), p. 11.

10 Krats, " '*Sudburyn Suomalaiset,*' " pp. 231-32.

11 Guy Gaudreau, "Les Ouvriers-Mineurs de la Région de Sudbury 1886-1930," *Revue du Nouvel Ontario* 17 (1995): 22-28.

12 Paulette Gosselin, "Les accidents de travail à la Canadian Copper Company, 1900-1920," *Revue du Nouvel Ontario* 17 (1995): 102.

13 Ontario Bureau of Mines, *Annual Report for 1902* (Toronto: Legislative Assembly of Ontario, 1903), p. 45.

14 Ontario Bureau of Mines, *Annual Report for 1907* (Toronto: Legislative Assembly of Ontario, 1908), p. 33.

15 Ontario Bureau of Mines, *Annual Report for 1912* (Toronto: Legislative Assembly of Ontario, 1913), p. 89.

16 Donald Dennie, "Sudbury 1883-1946: A Social Historical Study of Property and Class" (Ph.D. diss., Carleton University, 1989), p. 71.

17 Ian Radforth, *Bushworkers and Bosses: Logging in Northern Ontario 1900-1980* (Toronto: University of Toronto Press, 1987), p. 33.

18 Donald MacKay, *The Lumberjacks* (Halifax: McGraw-Hill Ryerson, 1978), pp. 221-22.

19 *Vapaus*, 6 November 1924, p. 5.

20 Radforth, *Bushworkers and Bosses: Logging in Northern Ontario 1900-1980*, p. 55.

21 As quoted in ibid., pp. 46-47. Translation by Varpu Lindström. The original Finnish title of this "immigrant" version of the poem is *Kalle Kosken Kuolema Testamentti*. It appears to be a variation of Heikki Jylhä's poem *Kalle Kosken Kuolema*, which was published in Finland in 1936.

22 Virtanen, "Work as a Factor of Adaptation for Finnish Immigrants in the Great Lakes Region," p. 7.

23 Interview with Lennard Sillanpää, Sudbury, 1997.

24 G.O. Tapper and Oiva W. Saarinen, "Finnish-Canadian Migration and Cultural Patterns: A Northern Ontario Case Study," *Nordia* 20, 1 (1986): 87.

25 Quoted in Krats, " '*Sudburyn Suomalaiset,*' " p. 33.

26 *The Sudbury Star*, 12 April 1924, p. 3.

27 Ibid., 21 November 1925, p. 1.

28 Ibid., 4 August 1982, p. 8.

29 Ibid., 2 July 1932, p. 5.

30 Ibid., 12 April 1924, p. 3.

31 Ibid., 8 June 1932, p. 20.

32 Ibid., 20 August 1932, p. 1.

33 Interview with Eino Nissilä, Sudbury, 1996.

34 *Vapaus*, 11 February 1937, p. 3.

35 Nicholson, "A Sordid Boon: The Business of State and the State of Labour at the Canadian Copper Company, 1890 to 1918," p. 19.

36 Interview with Jules Päiviö, Sudbury, 1995.

37 *The Sudbury Star*, 19 September 1931, p. 23.

38 *Vapaus*, 7 March 1936, p. 4.

39 Mike Solski and John Smaller, *Mine Mill: The History of the International Union of Mine, Mill and Smelter Workers in Canada since 1895* (Ottawa: Steel Rail Publishing, 1984), p. 99.

40 Seager, "Finnish Canadians and the Ontario Miners' Movement," p. 38.

41 Eklund, *Builders of Canada: History of the Finnish Organization of Canada 1911-1971*, p. 67.

42 Nicholson, "A Sordid Boon: The Business of State and the State of Labour at the Canadian Copper Company, 1890 to 1918," p. 63.

43 Royal Commission on Industrial Relations, *Report of Commission* (Ottawa: Committee of the Privy Council, 1919), p. 47.

44 Seager, "Finnish Canadians and the Ontario Miners' Movement, " p. 39.

45 *The Sudbury Star*, 14 June 1924, p. 2.

46 H.V. Nelles, *The Politics of Development: Forests, Mines & Hydro-Electric Power in Ontario, 1849-1941* (Toronto: Macmillan of Canada, 1974), p. 491.

47 Nicholson, "A Sordid Boon: The Business of State and the State of Labour at the Canadian Copper Company, 1890 to 1918," p. 58.

48 Goltz, "Genesis and Growth of a Company Town: Copper Cliff, 1886-1920," p. 7.

49 Nicholson, "A Sordid Boon: The Business of State and the State of Labour at the Canadian Copper Company, 1890 to 1918," p. 79.

50 Ibid., p. 66.

51 Ontario Bureau of Mines, *Annual Report for 1913* (Toronto: Legislative Assembly of Ontario, 1914), p. 67.

52 Interview with John Passi, Sudbury, 1995.

53 Solski and Smaller, *Mine Mill: The History of the International Union of Mine, Mill and Smelter Workers in Canada since 1895*, p. 102.

54 Ibid., p. 95.

55 Edmund Bradwin, *The Bunkhouse Man* (Toronto: University of Toronto Press, 1972), pp. 102-103.

56 Radforth, *Bushworkers and Bosses: Logging in Northern Ontario 1900-1980*, p. 118.

57 Ian Radforth, "Finnish Lumber Workers in Ontario," *Polyphony* 3, 2 (1981): 29.

58 Satu Repo, "Rosvall and Voutilainen: Two Union Men Who Never Died," *Labour/Le Travailleur* 8/9 (1981/82): 101.

59 Quoted in Eklund, *Builders of Canada: History of the Finnish Organization of Canada 1911-1971*, p. 50.

60 Bruce Magnuson, *The Untold Story of Ontario's Bushworkers* (Toronto: Progress Books, 1990), p. xvii.

61 Radforth, *Bushworkers and Bosses: Logging in Northern Ontario 1900-1980*, p. 12.

62 *Vapaus*, 30 September 1971, Part III, p. 1.

63 Repo, "Rosvall and Voutilainen: Two Union Men Who Never Died," pp. 79-102.

64 *Vapaus*, 2 November 1937, p. 28.

65 Ibid., 3 April 1936, p. 4.

66 Sillanpää, "The Political Behaviour of Canadians of Finnish Descent in the District of Sudbury," p. 76.

67 Lennard Sillanpää, "Voting Behaviour of Finns in the Sudbury Area, 1930-1972," in Michael G. Karni, ed., *Finnish Diaspora I* (Toronto: Multicultural History Society of Ontario, 1981), p. 112.

68 Lindström-Best, *Defiant Sisters: A Social History of Finnish Immigrant Women in Canada*, p. 5.

69　*Vapaus*, 28 September 1971, Part II, p. 1; Varpu Lindström-Best and Allen Seager, "Toveritar and Finnish-Canadian Women, 1900-1930," in Michael G. Karni et al., eds., *Finns in North America* (Turku: Institute of Migration, 1988), p. 133.

70　Sula et al., *Suomalaiset Nikkelialueella*, pp. 27-28.

71　Quoted in Eklund, *Builders of Canada: History of the Finnish Organization of Canada 1911-1971*, p. 316.

72　Interview with Taimi Davies (Pitkänen) by Varpu Lindström, Toronto, 1997; *The Sudbury Star*, 4 May 1932, p. 1.

73　Among the first executive members were Signe Hotti (First Organizer), H. Niittynen (membership secretary), Martha Koski (secretary), Katy Mäkinen and Tyyne Neil (corresponding secretaries).

74　Joan Sangster, "Finnish Women in Ontario, 1890-1930," *Polyphony* 3, 2 (1981): 53. The district secretariat consisted of Fanny Lehtelä, Elizabeth Este and Lempi Mäki.

75　For an interesting account of these activities see Lempi Mäki, "Activities of the Women of the Labouring Class in the Nickel District," translated by V. Rinne, in *Finnish Yearbook 1937* (Sudbury: *Vapaus* Publishing Company, 1937).

76　Quoted in Krats, " 'Sudburyn Suomalaiset,' " pp. 69-70.

77　Lindström-Best, *Defiant Sisters: A Social History of Finnish Immigrant Women in Canada*, p. 89.

78　Lindström-Best, "Defiant Sisters: A Social History of the Finnish Immigrant Women in Canada, 1890-1930," p. 236.

79　Sangster, "Finnish Women in Ontario, 1890-1930," p. 47.

80　Sillanpää, *Under the Northern Lights: My Memories of Life in the Finnish Community of Northern Ontario*, pp. 25-26.

81　Pikkusaari, *Copper Cliffin Suomalaiset*, p. 182. Others who followed in their wake included Matti Mäkelä, Heikki Mäkinen, Mikko Jussila, Heikki Pynttäri, Kustaa Pakkala, Antti Salo, Matti Marttila, John and Pauline Lahti, Elias Kallio, Olivia Mäkelä, William Pöntinen, Antti Pleuna, Jacob Walli, Hemmi Lammi, Jaakko Kannisto, Elias Laitila, Emil Kallio, Antti Pakkala, Antti Jaakkola, Väinö Kamppi and Edward Lampinen.

82　These included Fannie Puska, Mrs. Niemi, Mrs. G. Walli and Mrs. O. Kauhanen.

83　Others included those operated by S. Hill (Lorne Street), O. Leppänen (Elm Street), U. Pihlaja (Regent Street), R. Lind and J. Hankaanpää (Pine Street) and T. Rintaluhta (Beech Street).

84　See Antti Tuuri, *Uusi Jerusalem* (Helsinki: Otava, 1988).

85　Quoted in Lindström-Best, *Defiant Sisters: A Social History of Finnish Immigrant Women in Canada*, p. 106.

86　Ibid., pp. 106-107.

87　Interview with Anita and Walter Mäki, Sudbury, 1995.

88　*Vapaus*, 12 March 1937, p. 4.

89　Lindström-Best, *Defiant Sisters: A Social History of Finnish Immigrant Women in Canada*, p. 113.

90　Among Inco's engineering and geological employees were Karl Lindell, Arvi Ristimäki, Arvo Sirkka, Onni Timber and Emil Walli. Surveyors included Olavi and William Este.

91　Among the first to enter the nursing field were Helma Anderson, Miriam Halonen, Bertha and Ingrid Penman, Eva Ristimäki, Selma Salo, Lempi Stevenson and Aino Tapper. Pioneers in the teaching profession included Saima Hakkarainen, Rauha Halonen, Sylvia Koivula, Bertha Lauttamus and Aino Manninen.

92 This influence is discussed in Pikkusaari, *Copper Cliffin Suomalaiset*, pp. 62-63.
93 Interview with Veikko and Meeri Kivikangas, Sudbury, 1996.
94 Interview with Hannu Hintsa, Sudbury, 1995.
95 *Canadan Uutiset* (Thunder Bay), 17 April 1996, p. 7.
96 Korpela, *History of the Korpela Family*, p. 10.
97 Interview with Viljo Kähkönen, Sudbury, 1995.
98 Interview with Roy Äyräntö, Sudbury, 1996.
99 Interview with Ron Kanerva, Sudbury, 1996.
100 *Northern Life* (Sudbury), 28 September 1997, p. 1.
101 Among the long list of Finns to enter the teaching profession at the elementary-school level can be included Martha Huhtanen, Ray Kaattari, Richard Kangas, Sandra Korpela, Bill Lehto, S. Manninen, Saimi Seppälä, Eila Talpiainen, Lillian Wahamma and Marty Varpio. At the secondary-school level, Finnish names such as George Häkojarvi, Bill Mäkinen, Jack Pajala, Douglas Santala, Peter Varpio and Reijo Viitala have become commonplace.
102 *The Sudbury Star*, 14 November 1978, p. 7.
103 These include Stewart Kallio, Antti Saari, Oiva Saarinen, Carol Stos, Gerry Tapper, Roy Kari, Maire Laurikainen, Oliver Mäki, Arlene Mäkinen, Irene Wallenius and L. Rantala.

Chapter V

1 Bruce Kidd, *The Struggle for Canadian Sports* (Toronto: University of Toronto Press, 1996), p. 160.
2 Michael Ondaatje, *In the Skin of a Lion* (Toronto: McClelland and Stewart, 1987), pp. 20-22.
3 Kidd, *The Struggle for Canadian Sports*, p. 161.
4 Jalava, "Radicalism or a 'New Deal'?," p. 122.
5 An interesting account of the sporting clubs associated with the FOC movement is found in Tester, ed., *Sports Pioneers: A History of the Finnish-Canadian Amateur Sports Federation 1906-1986*.
6 Kidd, *The Struggle for Canadian Sports*, p. 174.
7 Hannes Sula, *Suomalais-Canadalaisen Amatööri-Urheiluliiton 25-v. Toiminnan Johdosta* (Sudbury: *Vapaus* Publishing Company, 1950), pp. 60-62. This book provides a brief history of the first twenty-five years of FCASF.
8 Much of this information has been obtained from Finnish Canadian Amateur Athletic Club *Voima*, Newspaper Archives (1940-84).
9 *Vapaus*, 14 April 1962, p. 1.
10 Kidd, *The Struggle for Canadian Sports*, p. 161.
11 Pagnucco, *Home-Grown Heroes: A Sports History of Sudbury*, p. 3.
12 Ibid., p. 133.
13 *The Sudbury Star*, 7 September 1948, p. 1.
14 Quoted in Tester, ed., *Sports Pioneers: A History of the Finnish-Canadian Amateur Sports Federation 1906-1986*, p. 181.
15 Ibid., p. 29.
16 *Vapaa Sana*, 11 July 1996, p. 3.
17 Ibid., 4 July 1996, p. 2.
18 *Vapaus*, 11 March 1991, p. 15.
19 Interview with Leo Niemi, Sudbury, 1996.
20 *The Sudbury Star*, 12 May 1996, p. B5.

21 Quoted in *Northern Life* (Sudbury), 19 May 1996, p. 3A.

22 Pikkusaari, *Copper Cliffin Suomalaiset*, p. 75.

23 Eklund, *Builders of Canada: History of the Finnish Organization of Canada 1911-1971*, p. 254.

24 *Vapaa Sana*, 1 June 1995, p. 8.

25 Sudbury Finnish Male Choir, *Sudbury Finnish Male Choir Anniversary Concert* (Sudbury: Sudbury Finnish Male Choir, 1995).

26 Jalava, "Radicalism or a 'New Deal'?," p. 99.

27 Other well-known actresses included Senni Ahonen, Helen Grenon (Kuusisto), Irja Kouvula, Katri Kuikka, Aino Lukkonen, Maj-Lis Miettinen, Rauha Mäki, Laina Ojala and Aino Piirskainen. These actresses were often aided by professional directors imported from Finland.

28 Jalava, "Radicalism or a 'New Deal'?," p. 103.

29 Pikkusaari, *Copper Cliffin Suomalaiset*, pp. 83-84.

30 Lyn Cook, *The Bells on Finland Street* (Toronto: Macmillan, 1950).

31 Charles Sutyla, *The Finnish Sauna in Manitoba*, Canadian Centre for Folk Culture Studies Paper No. 24 (Ottawa: National Museums of Canada, 1977), pp. 106-107; *Canadan Uutiset* (Thunder Bay), 6 September 1995, p. 14.

32 Interview with Viljo Virtanen, Sudbury, 1996.

33 W.F. Kirby, *Kalevala: Land of Heroes*, Vol. 1 (London: Dent, 1907), p. 273.

34 Lindström-Best, *Defiant Sisters: A Social History of Finnish Immigrant Women in Canada*, p. 55.

35 *Vapaa Sana*, 7 March 1996, p. 11.

36 Eugene van Cleef, "The Finn in America," *Geographical Review* 6 (1918): 210; Cotton Mather and Matti Kaups, "The Finnish Sauna: A Cultural Index to Settlement," *Annals of the Association of American Geographers* 4 (1963): 494.

37 Saarinen and Tapper, "The Beaver Lake Finnish-Canadian Community," p. 179.

38 Terry G. Jordan, "A Reappraisal of Fenno-Scandian Antecedents for Midland American Log Construction," *Geographical Review* 73, 1 (1983): 90.

39 Radforth, "Finnish Lumber Workers in Ontario," p. 29.

40 *The Sudbury Star*, 17 December 1946, p. 9.

41 Ibid., 13 July 1946, p. 5.

42 The Finnish term for these birch branches in western Finland is *vihta*; in eastern Finland it is called *vasta*.

43 Lindström-Best, *Defiant Sisters: A Social History of Finnish Immigrant Women in Canada*, p. 45.

44 Ibid., p. 69.

45 Ibid., p. 65.

46 *The Sudbury Star*, 5 September 1923, p. 12.

47 *Canadan Uutiset* (Thunder Bay), 20 August 1997), p. 5.

48 Alfons Ukkonen, *Kalevan Ritarikunnan ja Kalevan Ritarien Historiaa 100 Vuotta Ajalta* (Lake Worth: Knights of Kaleva, 1996), p. 8.

49 Oiva W. Saarinen, *A History of the Knights and Ladies of Kaleva Lodges in Sudbury, Ontario, Canada (1965/66-1991)* (Sudbury: Knights and Ladies of Kaleva, 1991), pp. 1-2.

50 John Kolehmainen, *Epic of the North: The Story of Finland's Kalevala* (New York Mills, MN: Northwestern Publishers, 1973).

51 Ray Rinta, *Suomalais Canadalainen Lepokotiyhdistys 1958-1968* (Vancouver: Suomalais Canadalainen Lepokotiyhdistys, 1970), pp. 13 and 38.

52 *Vapaa Sana*, 3 July 1997, p. 7.

53 Ibid., 4 July 1996, p. 11.
54 Saarinen, *A History of the Knights and Ladies of Kaleva Lodges in Sudbury, Ontario, Canada (1965/66-1991)*, p. 1.
55 Saarinen with Tapper, *Sudbury* Suomi *Lions Club, Sudbury, Ontario, Canada, 1989-1995* p. 1.
56 Ibid., p. 18.
57 Erkki Kuutti, *Suomen Aseveljet Kanadassa* (Montreal: Suomen Aseveljet Kanadassa, 1995), p. 13.
58 *Vapaa Sana*, 4 July 1996, p. 14, and 4 December 1997, p. 8.
59 Ibid., 3 July 1997, p. 8.
60 Ray Kaattari, *Rubberboots in the Sauna* (Sudbury, 1993).
61 Anneli Ylänkö, "The Role of Heritage Schools in Ethnic Maintenance and Development," in Varpu Lindström, Oiva Saarinen and Börje Vähämäki, eds., *Melting into Great Waters: Papers from FINNFORUM V* (Toronto: University of Toronto Press, 1997), p. 73.
62 Herbert Gans, "Symbolic Ethnicity: The Future of Ethnic Groups and Cultures in America," *Ethnic and Racial Studies* 2, 1 (1979): 9.
63 Lindström, "Finnish Canadian Culture in 1995: Toronto Perspectives," p. 92.

Chapter VI

1 Laine, "Community in Crisis: The Finnish-Canadian Quest for Cultural Identity, 1900-1979," p. 6.
2 Lindström, "Finnish Canadian Culture in 1995: Toronto Perspectives," pp. 77 and 92.
3 Canada, Canadian Heritage, Policy Coordination and Strategic Planning: Citizenship and Canadian Identity, *Ethnic Origins in Canada 1986/91* (Ottawa: Canadian Heritage, Policy Coordination and Planning: Citizenship and Canadian Identity, 1994), p. 3.
4 Peter Kivisto, "Does Ethnicity Matter for European Americans?," *Siirtolaisuus-Migration* 4 (1994): 4; Peter Kivisto, "The Attenuated Ethnicity of Contemporary Finnish-Americans," in Peter Kivisto, ed., *The Ethnic Enigma: The Salience of Ethnicity for European-Origin Groups* (Philadelphia: Balch Institute Press, 1989), pp. 67-88.
5 *Vapaa Sana*, 28 August 1997, pp. 1 and 5.
6 Kivisto, "Does Ethnicity Matter for European Americans?," p. 176.
7 Rasmussen, "The Geographic Impact of Finnish Settlement on the Thunder Bay Area of Northern Ontario," p. 142.
8 Dallen J. Timothy, "Finnish Settlements in Rural Thunder Bay: Changes in an Ethnic Community," *Siirtolaisuus-Migration* 1 (1995): 23; Dallen J. Timothy, "The Decline of Finnish Ethnic Islands in Rural Thunder Bay," *The Great Lakes Geographer* 2, 2 (1995): 57.
9 Timothy, "Finnish Settlements in Rural Thunder Bay," pp. 19-20.
10 Douglas Ollila, Jr., "From Socialism to Industrial Unionism (IWW): Social Factors in the Emergence of Left-Labor Radicalism among Finnish Workers on the Mesabi, 1911-1919," in Michael G. Karni et al., eds., *The Finnish Experience in the Western Great Lakes Region: New Perspectives* (Turku: Institute of Migration, 1975), p. 170.
11 Kivisto, *Immigrant Socialists in the United States: The Case of Finns and the Left*, p. 147; Lindström-Best, *Defiant Sisters: A Social History of Finnish Immigrant Women in Canada*, p. 418.
12 David Robertson, "Finnish and Canadian Literatures: A Comparison Using Salme Orvokki Pinola's *The Fatherless* as an Illustration," in Varpu Lindström, Oiva Saarinen

and Börje Vähämäki, eds., *Melting into Great Waters: Papers from FINNFORUM V* (Toronto: University of Toronto Press, 1997), p. 147.

13 Lindström-Best, *Defiant Sisters: A Social History of Finnish Immigrant Women in Canada,* p. 162.

14 *Vapaus,* 11 March 1991, p. 1.

15 Pilli, *The Finnish-Language Press in Canada, 1901-1939,* p. 142.

16 Krats, "'*Sudburyn Suomalaiset,*'" pp. 239-40; Finnish National Society of Sudbury, Archives, Membership List for 1933.

17 Krats, "'*Sudburyn Suomalaiset,*'" pp. 244-47.

18 *Vapaa Sana,* 31 October 1996, p. 15.

19 Jalava, "Radicalism or a 'New Deal'?," p. 258.

20 Saara Karttunen, "*Syvempi Kuin Meri*" (Keuruu, Finland, 1992).

21 *The Sudbury Star,* 17 May 1996, p. A5.

22 Radforth, "Finnish Lumber Workers in Ontario," pp. 32 and 34.

23 Seager, "Finnish Canadians and the Ontario Miners' Movement," p. 43.

24 The use of this word as a blanket term for all leftist Finns is common in Raivio, *Kanadan Suomalaisten Historia I* and *Kanadan Suomalaisten Historia II.*

25 Lindström, "Finnish Canadian Culture in 1995: Toronto Perspectives," p. 77.

26 *Vapaa Sana (Sudbury and Toronto),* 2 October 1997, p. 2.

Bibliography

Primary Sources

Archives

Archives of Ontario (Toronto, ON). Arvi Iisakki Heinonen Papers (MSR 11554).
_____. Ministry of Natural Resources (1936-38). Land Files 85418, Vol. 1.
Finnish Canadian Amateur Athletic Club *Voima* (Sudbury, ON). Newspaper Archives (1940-84).
Finnish National Society of Sudbury. Archives (1940-84).
Inco Archives (Sudbury, ON). Creighton Rent Rolls.
_____. Garson Real Estate Records.
_____. Levack Real Estate Records.
Public Archives of Canada (Ottawa, Canada). Manuscript Census (1871-91).
United States National Archives (Washington, DC). Department of State, *Chapman to the Secretary of State*, 20 August 1931, RG59, Box 6167, 842.00B/46; 7 November 1931, RG59, Box 6167, 842.00B/57; 14 November 1931, RG59, Box 6167, 842.00B/61; 12 March 1932, RG59, Box 6167, 842.00B/71.

Public Documents

Canada. Canadian Heritage, Policy Coordination and Strategic Planning: Citizenship and Canadian Identity. *Ethnic Origins in Canada 1986/91*. Ottawa: Canadian Heritage, Policy Coordination and Planning: Citizenship and Canadian Identity, 1994.
_____. Citizenship and Immigration Canada. *Immigration Statistics*. Ottawa: Citizenship and Immigration Canada, 1968-94.
_____. Department of Mines and Technical Surveys. *Aerial Photograph* 46-15/204-9.
_____. Royal Commission on Industrial Relations. *Report of Commission*. Ottawa: Committee of the Privy Council, 1919.
_____. *Sessional Papers*. No. 14. Ottawa, 1884.
_____. *Sessional Papers*. No. 8. Ottawa, 1885.
_____. Statistics Canada. *Censuses of Canada* (1901-96). Ottawa.

City of Sudbury. *Assessment Roll 1938.*

Long Lake Public School (Sudbury, ON). *Daily Registers for Long Lake Public School* (1914-85).

Ontario Bureau of Mines (Legislative Assembly of Ontario, Toronto). *Annual Reports* (1902-13).

_____ . Ministry of Natural Resources. *Crown Land Registry Domesday Books and Patent Plans.* Land Files 85418, Vol. 1, 1936-38.

Royal Ontario Nickel Commission. *Report.* Toronto: Legislative Assembly of Ontario, 1917.

Sudbury and Nickel Belt Electoral District Federal Election Voters Lists. *Voters List 1980.*

Sudbury Land Registry Office. *Abstract Indexes.*

_____ . *Directory of M-Plans.*

_____ . *First Registration Books.*

Town of Copper Cliff. *Assessment Roll* (1915).

Township of Louise. *Daily Registers for School Section No. 3* (1934-44).

Town of Nickel Centre. *Assessment Rolls* (1911-36).

Township of McKim. *Assessment Roll, 1946.*

Township of Waters. *Assessment Roll, 1916.*

_____ . *Collectors Roll 1935.*

_____ . *Voters' List, 1909.*

Wanup Public School. *Daily Registers for Dill and Cleland (Wanup) Public School* (1923-51).

Interviews

By the Author

Äyräntö, Roy (Sudbury, ON, 1996).

Ceming, Maija (Sudbury, ON, 1996).

Duncan, Elvi (Sudbury, ON, 1995).

Erola, Judy (Sudbury, ON, 1996).

Fortin, Jim (Sudbury, ON, 1995).

Heino, Sulo and Bertha (Sudbury, ON, 1995).

Hintsa, Hannu (Sudbury, ON, 1995).

Johnson, Bill (Sudbury, ON, 1994).

Johnson, Laila (Sudbury, ON, 1997).

Johnson, Lempi (Sudbury, ON, 1995).

Kaitila, Keijo and Tuula (Sudbury, ON, 1996).

Kanerva, Ron (Sudbury, ON, 1996).

Kangas, Siiri (Sudbury, ON, 1995).

Kangassalo, William (Sudbury, ON, 1995).

Kivikangas, Veikko and Meeri (Sudbury, ON, 1996).

Korpela, Oliver (Sudbury, ON, 1996).

Kurso, Mary (Sudbury, ON, 1995).

Kähkönen, Viljo (Sudbury, ON, 1995).

Laamanen, Risto (Sudbury, ON, 1996).

Lehto, Bill (Sudbury, ON, 1995).

Lindström, Varpu (Toronto, ON, 1997).

Michel, Arnel (Sudbury, ON, 1996).

Mäki, Anita and Walter (Sudbury, ON, 1995).
Nelson, Henry (Sudbury, ON, 1996).
Niemi, Leo (Sudbury, ON, 1996).
Nissilä, Eino (Sudbury, ON, 1996).
Passi, John (Sudbury, ON, 1995).
Päiviö, Jules (Sudbury, ON, 1995).
Rintamäki, Laila (Sudbury, ON, 1997).
Ritari, Arne and Kaarina (Sudbury, ON, 1995).
Salo, Wilf (Sudbury, ON, 1985, 1989 and 1995).
Sillanpää, Lennard (Sudbury, ON, 1997).
Svensk, Ruth (Sudbury, ON, 1995).
Tapper, G.O. (Gerry) (Sudbury, ON, 1997).
Villgren, Paul (Sudbury, ON, 1995).
Virtanen, Viljo (Sudbury, ON, 1996).

By Others

Davies (Pitkänen), Taimi. Interview with Varpu Lindström (Toronto, ON, 1997).
Pontio, Sofia. Interview with Varpu Lindström (Sudbury, ON, 1973).

Newspapers and Magazines

Finnish

Canadan Uutiset (Thunder Bay, ON).
Emigrantti (Helsinki, Finland).
Kaiku/Echo (Toronto, ON).
Liekki (Sudbury, ON).
Todistaja (Vancouver, British Columbia).
Vapaa Sana (Sudbury, ON, and Toronto, ON).
Vapaus (Sudbury, ON, and Toronto, ON).

English

Copper Cliff Courier (Copper Cliff, ON).
Inco Triangle (Copper Cliff, ON).
Northern Life (Sudbury, ON).
Sudbury Journal (Sudbury, ON).
Sudbury Star, The (Sudbury, ON).

Secondary Sources

Unpublished Theses

Allen, Martha. "A Survey of Finnish Cultural, Economic, and Political Development in the Sudbury District of Ontario." M.A. thesis, University of Western Ontario, 1954.

Dennie, Donald. "Sudbury 1883-1946: A Social Historical Study of Property and Class." Ph.D. diss., Carleton University, 1989.

Glad, Leo. 1995. "Planning Strategies for an Ethnic-Finnish Lutheran Congregation in Transition to a Canadian Lutheran Congregation." Doctor of Ministry diss., Luther Seminary, St. Paul, MN, 1995.

Goltz, Eileen. "Genesis and Growth of a Company Town: Copper Cliff, 1886-1920." M.A. thesis, Laurentian University, 1983.

_____. "The Exercise of Power in a Company Town: Copper Cliff, 1886-1990." Ph.D. diss., University of Guelph, 1990.

Jalava, Mauri Amiko. "Radicalism or a 'New Deal?' The Unfolding World View of the Finnish Immigrants in Sudbury, 1883-1932." M.A. thesis, Laurentian University, 1983.

Krats, Peter V.K. "'Sudburyn Suomalaiset': Finnish Immigrant Activities in the Sudbury Area, 1883-1939." M.A. thesis, University of Western Ontario, 1980.

_____. "The Sudbury Area to the Great Depression: Regional Development on the Northern Resource Frontier." Ph.D. diss., University of Western Ontario, 1988.

Lindström-Best, Varpu. "Defiant Sisters: A Social History of the Finnish Immigrant Women in Canada, 1890-1930." Ph.D. diss., York University, 1986.

Maunula, Michael J. "The Retention of Finnish Culture among Thunder Bay Finns." M.A. thesis, Lakehead University, 1984.

Nicholson, Thomas. "A Sordid Boon: The Business of State and the State of Labour at the Canadian Copper Company, 1890 to 1918." M.A. thesis, Queen's University, 1991.

Rasmussen, Mark. "The Geographic Impact of Finnish Settlement on the Thunder Bay Area of Northern Ontario." M.A. thesis, University of Alberta, 1978.

Saarinen, Oiva W. "Spatial Behaviour of the State and of the Co-operative Movement in the Finnish Forest Economy." Ph.D. diss., University College, London, 1979.

Sillanpää, Lennard. "A Political and Social History of Canadians of Finnish Descent in the District of Sudbury." M.A. thesis, University of Helsinki, 1973.

_____. "The Political Behaviour of Canadians of Finnish Descent in the District of Sudbury." Licentiate thesis, University of Helsinki, 1976.

Books

Finnish

Canadan Suomalainen. Sudbury: Canadan Suomalaisten Historia Seura, 1963.

Canadan Suomalainen Järjestö 25 Vuotta, 1911-1936. Sudbury: Vapaus Publishing Company, 1936.

Canadan Suomalaisten Sotilaiden Muistoalbumi. Sudbury: Vapaus Publishing Company, 1946.

Eklund, William. Canadan Suomalaisten Sotilaiden Muistoalbumi. Sudbury: Vapaus Publishing Company, 1946.

_____. Canadan Rakentajia: Canadan Suomalaisen Järjestön Historia vv. 1911-1971. Toronto: Finnish Organization of Canada, 1983.

Jalava, Mauri Amiko. Toronton Suomalainen Osuuspankki 1958-1978. Toronto: Finnish (Toronto) Credit Union, 1978.

Kero, Reino. Suureen Länteen: Siirtolaisuus Suomesta Pohjois-Amerikkaan. Turku: Institute of Migration, 1996.

_____. Suomalaisina Pohjois-Amerikassa: Siirtolaiselämää Yhdysvalloissa ja Kanadassa. Turku: Institute of Migration, 1997.

Liedes, Liisa A., and Uuno I. Vesanen. Suomalainen Helluntaiherätys Pohjois-Americassa. Vancouver: Mission Press Society, 1994.

Lindström-Best, Varpu, and Sutyla, Charles. *Terveisiä Ruusa-tädiltä: Kanadan Suomalaisten Ensimmäinen Sukupolvi.* Helsinki: Suomalaisen Kirjallisuuden Seura, 1984.

Palmgren, Raoul. *Joukkosydän: Vanhan Työväenliikkeemme Kaunokirjallisuus.* Porvoo: Werner Söderström Oy, 1986.

Pikkusaari, Lauri. 1947. *Copper Cliffin Suomalaiset ja Copper Cliffin Suomalainen Evankelis-Luterilainen Wuoristo-Seurakunta.* Hancock: Suomalais-Lutherilainen Kustannusliike, 1947.

Raivio, Yrjö. *Kanadan Suomalaisten Historia I.* Copper Cliff: Canadan Suomalainen Historiaseura, 1975.

_____. *Kanadan Suomalaisten Historia II.* Copper Cliff: Canadan Suomalainen Historiaseura, 1979.

Rauanheimo, Akseli. *Kanadan-kirja.* Porvoo: Werner Söderström Oy, 1930.

Rinta, Ray. *Suomalais Canadalainen Lepokotiyhdistys 1958-1968.* Vancouver: Suomalais-Canadalainen Lepokotiyhdistys, 1970.

Sula, Hannes. *Suomalais-Canadalaisen Amatööri-Urheiluliiton 25-v. Toiminnan Johdosta.* Sudbury: *Vapaus* Publishing Company, 1950.

_____, et al. *Suomalaiset Nikkelialueella.* Sudbury: CSJ:n Osasto No. 16, 1937.

Tuuri, Antti. *Uusi Jerusalem.* Helsinki: Otava, 1988.

Vapauden Soihtu. Sudbury: *Vapaus* Publishing Company, 1919.

Vapaus 1917-1934. Sudbury: *Vapaus* Publishing Company, 1934.

Vaurio, Paavo. *Suomalais-Canadalaisen Amatööri-Urheiluliiton 40-v. Toimminan Johdosta.* Sudbury: *Vapaus* Publishing Company, 1965.

Virtaranta, Pertti. *Amerikansuomen Sanakirja.* Turku: Institute of Migration, 1992.

English

Angus, Ian. *Canadian Bolsheviks: The Early Years of the Communist Party of Canada.* Montreal: Vanguard Publications, 1981.

Avakumovic, Ivan. *The Communist Party in Canada: A History.* Toronto: McClelland and Stewart, 1975.

Avery, Donald. *"Dangerous Foreigners": European Immigrant Workers and Labour Radicalism in Canada, 1896-1932.* Toronto: McClelland and Stewart, 1979.

Bertulli, Margaret, and Swan, Rae, eds. *A Bit of the Cliff.* Copper Cliff: Copper Cliff Museum, 1982.

Bradwin, Edmund. *The Bunkhouse Man.* Toronto: University of Toronto Press, 1972.

Cook, Lyn. *The Bells on Finland Street.* Toronto: Macmillan, 1950.

Darcovich, William. *A Statistical Compendium on the Ukrainians in Canada, 1891-1976.* Ottawa: University of Ottawa Press, 1980.

Eklund, William. *Builders of Canada: History of the Finnish Organization of Canada 1911-1971.* Toronto: Finnish Organization of Canada, 1987.

Heinonen, Arvi. *Finnish Friends in Canada.* Toronto: United Church of Canada, 1930.

Houten, Gerry van, et al., eds. *Canada's Party of Socialism: History of the Communist Party of Canada 1921-1976.* Toronto: Progress Books, 1982.

Järvinen, Juhani. *From Finland to Canada: Siirtolaiselämää Sault Ste. Mariessa Vuosina 1890-1940.* Sault Ste. Marie: Sault Ste. Marie and District Finnish-Canadian Historical Society, 1993.

Karni, Michael, ed. *Finnish Diaspora I: Canada, South America, Africa, Australia and Sweden.* Toronto: Multicultural History Society of Ontario, 1981.

_____, ed. *Finnish Diaspora II: United States*. Toronto: Multicultural History Society of Ontario, 1981.

Karni, Michael, Matti Kaups and Douglas Ollila, Jr., eds. *The Finnish Experience in the Western Great Lakes Region: New Perspectives*. Turku: Institute of Migration, 1975.

Karni, Michael, Olavi Koivukangas and Edward W. Laine, eds. *Finns in North America*. Turku: Institute of Migration, 1988.

Kealey, Gregory, and Reg Whitaker. *R.C.M.P. Security Bulletins: The War Series, 1939-1941*. St. John's, NF: Memorial University, 1989.

_____. *R.C.M.P. Security Bulletins: The Depression Years, Part I, 1933-1934*. St. John's, NF: Memorial University, 1993.

_____. *R.C.M.P. Security Bulletins: The Early Years, 1919-1929*. St. John's, NF: Memorial University, 1994.

Kero, Reino. *Migration from Finland to North America in the Years between the United States Civil War and the First World War*. Turku: Institute of Migration, 1974.

Kidd, Bruce. *The Struggle for Canadian Sports*. Toronto: University of Toronto Press, 1996.

Kirby, W.F. *Kalevala: Land of Heroes*. Vol. 1. London: Dent, 1907.

Kivisto, Peter. *Immigrant Socialists in the United States: The Case of Finns and the Left*. Toronto: Associated University Presses, 1984.

Kolehmainen, John. *The Finns in America: A Bibliographical Guide to Their History*. Hancock: Suomi College, 1947.

_____. *Epic of the North: The Story of Finland's Kalevala*. New York Mills, MN: Northwestern Publishers, 1973.

Koski, Pat, and Bill Mäkinen. *Wuoristo-St. Timothy's Lutheran Church, Copper Cliff, Ontario: 100 Years, 1897-1997*. Sudbury: St. Timothy's Lutheran Church, 1997.

Kovac, Elsie. *Grandfather and the Northern Wilderness*. New York: Carlton Press, 1986.

Laine, Edward W. *On the Archival Heritage of the Finnish Canadian Working-Class Movement*. Research Report No. 5. Turku: Institute of Migration, 1987.

_____. *Archival Sources for the Study of Finnish Canadians*. Ottawa: National Archives of Canada, 1989.

Lindström, Varpu, Oiva Saarinen and Börje Vähämäki, eds. *Melting into Great Waters: Papers from FINNFORUM V*. Toronto: University of Toronto Press, 1997.

Lindström-Best, Varpu. *Defiant Sisters: A Social History of Finnish Immigrant Women in Canada*. Toronto: Multicultural History Society of Ontario, 1988.

_____. *The Finns in Canada*. Ottawa: Canadian Historical Association, 1985.

MacKay, Donald. *The Lumberjacks*. Halifax: McGraw-Hill Ryerson, 1978.

Magnuson, Bruce. *The Untold Story of Ontario's Bushworkers*. Toronto: Progress Books, 1990.

Mattson Schelstraete, Nancy, ed. *Life in the New Finland Woods: A History of New Finland, Saskatchewan*. Rocanville: New Finland Historical and Heritage Society, 1982.

Metsäranta, Marc, ed. *Project Bay Street: Activities of Finnish-Canadians in Thunder Bay before 1915*. Thunder Bay: Thunder Bay Finnish-Canadian Historical Society, 1989.

Mount, Graeme. *Canada's Enemies: Spies and Spying in the Peaceable Kingdom*. Toronto: Dundurn Press, 1993.

Nelles, H.V. *The Politics of Development: Forests, Mines & Hydro-Electric Power in Ontario, 1849-1941*. Toronto: Macmillan of Canada, 1974.

Ondaatje, Michael. *In the Skin of a Lion*. Toronto: McClelland and Stewart, 1987.

Pagnucco, Frank. *Home-Grown Heroes: A Sports History of Sudbury.* Sudbury: Miller Publishing, 1982.

Pilli, Arja. *The Finnish-Language Press in Canada, 1901-1939.* Turku: Institute of Migration, 1982.

Radforth, Ian. *Bushworkers and Bosses: Logging in Northern Ontario 1900-1980.* Toronto: University of Toronto Press, 1987.

Roberts, Barbara. *Whence They Came: Deportation from Canada 1900-1935.* Ottawa: University of Ottawa Press, 1988.

Rodney, William. *Soldiers of the International: A History of the Communist Party of Canada 1919-1929.* Toronto: University of Toronto Press, 1968.

Ross, Carl. *The Finn Factor in American Labor, Culture, and Society.* New York Mills, MN: Parta Publishing, 1977.

Scardellato, Gabriele, ed. *A Guide to the Collections of the Multicultural History Society of Ontario.* Toronto: Multicultural History Society of Ontario, 1992.

Selvala, Robert. *FinnFest USA: The First Decade 1982-1992.* Owatonna, MN: FinnFest USA, 1992.

Sevander, Mayme. *Red Exodus: Finnish-American Emigration to Russia.* Duluth, MN: Oscat, 1993.

_____. *Soviet Bondage: Sequel to "Red Exodus."* Duluth, MN: Oscat, 1996.

Sillanpää, Nelma. *Under the Northern Lights: My Memories of Life in the Finnish Community of Northern Ontario.* Edited by Edward W. Laine. Ottawa: Canadian Museum of Civilization, 1994.

Solski, Mike, and Smaller, John. *Mine Mill: The History of the International Union of Mine, Mill and Smelter Workers in Canada since 1895.* Ottawa: Steel Rail Publishing, 1984.

Sutyla, Charles. *The Finnish Sauna in Manitoba.* Canadian Centre for Folk Culture Studies Paper No. 24. Ottawa: National Museums of Canada, 1977.

Tapper, G.O., and O.W. Saarinen, eds. *Better Known as Beaver Lake: An History of Lorne Township and Surrounding Area.* Walden, ON: Walden Public Library, 1998.

Vernon Directories Limited. *Vernon's City Directory: Sudbury.* Hamilton: Vernon Directories Limited, 1911+.

Wallace, C.M., and Ashley Thomson, eds. *Sudbury: Rail Town to Regional Capital.* Toronto: Dundurn Press, 1993.

Wargelin, John. *The Americanization of the Finns.* Hancock: Finnish Lutheran Book Concern, 1924.

_____. *A Highway to America.* Hancock: The Book Concern, 1967.

Wild, Paula. *Sointula: Island Utopia.* Madeira Park, BC: Harbour Publishing, 1995.

Articles in Journals or Books

English and French

Alanen, Arnold R. "The Development and Distribution of Finnish Consumers' Cooperatives in Michigan, Minnesota and Wisconsin, 1903-1973." In Michael G. Karni et al., eds., *The Finnish Experience in the Western Great Lakes Region: New Perspectives*, pp. 103-30. Turku: Institute of Migration, 1975.

_____. "Finns and the Corporate Mining Environment of the Lake Superior Mining Region." In Michael G. Karni, ed., *Finnish Diaspora II*, pp. 33-61. Toronto: Multicultural History Society of Ontario, 1981.

_____. "Finns and Other Immigrant Groups in the American Upper Midwest: Interactions and Comparisons." In Michael G. Karni et al., *Finns in North America*, pp. 58-83. Turku: Institute of Migration, 1988.

Anderson, Alan, with Brenda Niskala. "Finnish Settlements in Saskatchewan: Their Development and Perpetuation." In Michael G. Karni, ed., *Finnish Diaspora I*, pp. 155-82. Toronto: Multicultural History Society of Ontario, 1981.

Cleef, Eugene van. "The Finn in America." *Geographical Review*, 6 (1918): 185-214.

Copeland, William. "Early Finnish-American Settlements in Florida." In Michael G. Karni, ed., *Finnish Diaspora II*, pp. 127-41. Toronto: Multicultural History Society of Ontario, 1981.

Gans, Herbert. "Symbolic Ethnicity: The Future of Ethnic Groups and Cultures in America." *Ethnic and Racial Studies*, 2, 1 (1979): 1-20.

Gaudreau, Guy. "Les Ouvriers-Mineurs de la Région de Sudbury 1886-1930." *Revue du Nouvel Ontario* 17 (1995): 13-28.

Goltz, Eileen. "Copper Cliff: The Pioneer Period." In *Industrial Communities of the Sudbury Basin: Copper Cliff, Victoria Mines, Mond and Coniston*, pp. 1-21. Sudbury: Sudbury and District Historical Society, 1986.

Gordon, Terry, G. "A Reappraisal of Fenno-Scandian Antecedents For Midland American Log Construction." *Geographical Review*, 73, 1 (1983): 58-94.

Gosselin, Paulette. "Les accidents de travail à la Canadian Copper Company, 1900-1920." *Revue du Nouvel Ontario*, 17 (1995): 77-104.

Hoglund, A. William. "No Land for Finns: Critics and Reformers View the Rural Exodus from Finland to America between the 1880s and World War I." In Michael G. Karni et al., eds., *The Finnish Experience in the Western Great Lakes Region: New Perspectives*, pp. 36-54. Turku: Institute of Migration, 1975.

_____. "Breaking with Religious Tradition: Finnish Immigrant Workers and the Church, 1890-1915." In Michael G. Karni and Douglas Ollila, Jr., eds., *For the Common Good: Finnish Immigrants and Radical Response to Industrial America*, pp. 23-64. Superior, WI: Työmies Society, 1977.

Jalava, Mauri Amiko. "Finnish Cultural Associations in Ontario, 1945-80." *Polyphony*, 3, 2 (1981): 104-10.

_____. "The Finnish-Canadian Cooperative Movement in Ontario." In Michael G. Karni, ed., *Finnish Diaspora I*, pp. 93-100. Toronto: Multicultural History Society of Ontario, 1981.

_____. "Radicalism or a 'New Deal'?: The Unfolding World View of the Finnish Immigrants in Sudbury, 1883-1932." In Michael G. Karni et al., eds., *Finns in North America*, pp. 227-35. Turku: Institute of Migration, 1988.

Jordan, Terry G. "A Reappraisal of Fenno-Scandian Antecedents for Midland American Log Construction." *Geographical Review* 73, 1 (1983): 58-94.

Karni, Michael. "Struggle on the Cooperative Front: The Separation of Central Cooperative Wholesale from Communism, 1929-30." In Michael G. Karni et al., eds., *The Finnish Experience in the Western Great Lakes Region: New Perspectives*, pp. 186-201. Turku: Institute of Migration, 1975.

_____. "The Founding of the Finnish Socialist Federation and the Minnesota Strike of 1907." In Michael G. Karni and Douglas Ollila, Jr., eds., *For the Common Good: Finnish Immigrants and the Radical Response to Industrial America*, pp. 65-86. Superior, WI: Työmies Society, 1977.

_____. "Finnish Temperance and Its Clash with Emerging Socialism in Minnesota." In Michael G. Karni, ed., *Finnish Diaspora II*, pp. 163-74. Toronto: Multicultural History Society of Ontario, 1981.

Karvonen, Hilja J. "Three Proponents of Women's Rights in the Finnish-American Labour Movement from 1910-1930: Selma Jokela McCone, Maiju Nurmi and Helmi Mattson." In Michael G. Karni and Douglas Ollila, Jr., eds., *For the Common Good: Finnish Immigrants and the Radical Response to Industrial America*, pp. 195-216. Superior, WI: Työmies Society, 1977.

Kero, Reino. "Emigration from Finland to Canada before the First World War." *The Lakehead University Review*, 9, 1 (1976): 7-16.

_____. "Emigration of Finns from North America to Soviet Karelia in the Early 1930's." In Michael G. Karni et al., eds., *The Finnish Experience in the Western Great Lakes Region*, pp. 212-21. Turku: Institute of Migration, 1975.

_____. "The Canadian Finns in Soviet Karelia in the 1930s." In Michael Karni, ed., *Finnish Diaspora I*, pp. 203-13. Toronto: Multicultural History Society of Toronto, 1981.

Kivisto, Peter. "From Immigrants to Ethnics: The Problem of the Third-Generation Revisited." In Michael G. Karni et al., eds., *Finns in North America*, pp. 84-98. Turku: Institute of Migration, 1988.

_____. "Does Ethnicity Matter for European Americans?" *Siirtolaisuus-Migration*, 4 (1994): 3-11.

_____. "The Attenuated Ethnicity of Contemporary Finnish-Americans." In Peter Koivisto, ed., *The Ethnic Enigma: The Salience of Ethnicity for European-Origin Groups*, pp. 67-88. Philadelphia: Balch Institute Press, 1989.

Kostiainen, Auvo. "Finnish-American Workmen's Associations." In Vilho Niitemaa et al., eds., *Old Friends—Strong Ties*, pp. 205-34. Turku: Institute of Migration, 1976.

_____. "The Tragic Crisis: Finnish-American Workers and the Civil War in Finland." In Michael G. Karni and Douglas Ollila, Jr., eds., *For the Common Good: Finnish Immigrants and Radical Response to Industrial America*, pp. 217-35. Superior, WI: Työmies Society, 1977.

_____. "Contacts between the Finnish Labour Movements in the United States and Canada." In Michael G. Karni, ed., *Finnish Diaspora I*, pp. 33-48. Toronto: Multicultural History Society of Ontario, 1981.

Kouhi, Christine. "Labour and Finnish Immigration to Thunder Bay, 1876-1914." *The Lakehead University Review*, 9, 1 (1976): 17-40.

Krats, Peter V. " 'Suomalaiset Nikkelialueella': Finns in the Sudbury Area, 1883-1939." *Polyphony*, 5, 1 (1983): 37-47.

_____. "Limited Loyalties: The Sudbury, Canada Finns and Their Institutions 1887-1935." In Michael G. Karni et al., eds., *Finns in North America*, pp. 188-200. Turku: Institute of Migration, 1988.

Laine, Edward W. "Community in Crisis: The Finnish-Canadian Quest for Cultural Identity, 1900-1979." In Michael G. Karni, ed., *Finnish Diaspora I*, pp. 1-9. Toronto: Multicultural History Society of Ontario, 1981.

_____. "Finnish Canadian Radicalism and Canadian Politics: The First Forty Years, 1900-1940." In Jorgen Dahlie and Tissa Fernando, eds., *Ethnicity, Power and Politics in Canada*, pp. 94-112. Toronto: Methuen, 1981.

_____. "The Finnish Organization of Canada, 1923-40, and the Development of a Finnish Canadian Culture." *Polyphony* 3, 2 (1981): 81-90.

Lindström, Varpu. "Finnish Canadian Culture in 1995: Toronto Perspectives." In Leena Rossi and Hanne Koivisto, eds., *Monta Tietä Menneisyyteen*, pp. 77-94. Turku: Turun Yliopisto, 1995.

Lindström-Best, Varpu. "Central Organization of the Loyal Finns in Canada." *Polyphony* 3, 2 (1981): 97-103.

_____. "The Unbreachable Gulf: The Division in the Finnish Community of Toronto, 1902-1913." In Michael G. Karni, ed., *Finnish Diaspora I*, pp. 11-18. Toronto: Multicultural History Society of Ontario, 1981.

_____. "'Fist Press': A Study of the Finnish Canadian Handwritten Newspapers." *Polyphony* 3, 2 (1981): 65-73.

_____, and Allen Seager. "Toveritar and Finnish-Canadian Women, 1900-1930." In Michael G. Karni et al., eds., *Finns in North America*, pp. 133-53. Turku: Institute of Migration, 1988.

London, Gary. "The Finnish-American Anti-Socialist Movement, 1908-1918." In Michael G. Karni et al., eds., *Finns in North America*, pp. 211-26. Turku: Institute of Migration, 1988.

Mather, Cotton, and Matti Kaups. "The Finnish Sauna: A Cultural Index to Settlement." *Annals of the Association of American Geographers* 4 (1963): 494-504.

Middleton, Anita. "Karelian Fever: Interviews with Survivors." In Varpu Lindström, Oiva Saarinen and Börje Vähämäki, eds., *Melting into Great Waters: Papers from FINNFORUM V*, pp. 179-82. Toronto: University of Toronto Press, 1997.

Metsäranta, Marc. "The Workingmen's Associations, 1903-1914." In Marc Metsäranta, ed., *Project Bay Street: Activities of Finnish-Canadians in Thunder Bay before 1915*, pp. 66-99. Thunder Bay: Thunder Bay Finnish-Canadian Historical Society, 1989.

Morrison, Jean. "Ethnicity and Class Consciousness: British, Finnish and South European Workers at the Canadian Lakehead before World War I." *The Lakehead University Review* 9, 1 (1976): 41-54.

Mäki, Lempi. "Activities of the Women of the Labouring Class in the Nickel District." Translated by V. Rinne. In *Finnish Year Book 1937*. Sudbury: *Vapaus* Publishing Company, 1937.

Mäkinen, W.H. "The Mond Nickel Company and the Communities of Victoria Mines and Mond." In *Industrial Communities of the Sudbury Basin: Copper Cliff, Victoria Mines, Mond and Coniston*, pp. 22-43. Sudbury: Sudbury and District Historical Society, 1986.

Ollila, Douglas, Jr. "From Socialism to Industrial Unionism (IWW): Social Factors in the Emergence of Left-Labor Radicalism among Finnish Workers on the Mesabi, 1911-1919." In Michael G. Karni et al., eds., *The Finnish Experience in the Western Great Lakes Region: New Perspectives*, pp. 156-71. Turku: Institute of Migration, 1975.

_____. "The Work People's College: Immigrant Education for Adjustment and Solidarity." In Michael G. Karni and Douglas Ollila, Jr., eds., *For the Common Good: Finnish Immigrants and Radical Response to Industrial America*, pp. 87-118. Superior, WI: Työmies Society, 1977.

Orta, Timo. "Finnish Emigration Prior to 1893: Economic, Demographic and Social Backgrounds." In Michael G. Karni et al., eds., *The Finnish Experience in the Western Great Lakes Region: New Perspectives*, pp. 21-35. Turku: Institute of Migration, 1975.

Pogorelskin, Alexis. "New Perspectives on Karelian Fever: The Recruitment of North American Finns to Karelia in the Early 1930s." In Varpu Lindström, Oiva

Saarinen and Börje Vähämäki, eds., *Melting into Great Waters: Papers from FINNFORUM V*, pp. 165-78. Toronto: University of Toronto Press, 1997.

Radforth, Ian. "Finnish Lumber Workers in Ontario." *Polyphony* 3, 2 (1981): 23-34.

Repo, Satu. "Rosvall and Voutilainen: Two Union Men Who Never Died." *Labour/Le Travailleur* 8/9 (1981/82): 79-102.

Robertson, David. "Finnish and Canadian Literatures: A Comparison Using Salme Orvokki Pinola's *The Fatherless* as an Illustration." In Varpu Lindström, Oiva Saarinen and Börje Vähämäki, eds., *Melting into Great Waters: Papers from FINNFORUM V*, pp. 145-54. Toronto: University of Toronto Press, 1997.

Roinila, Mika. "The Finns of Atlantic Canada." *Terra* 104, 1 (1992): 35-44.

————. "Finland-Swedes of Canada." *Suomen Silta* 314, 3 (1997): 36-38.

Saarinen, Oiva W. "The Pattern and Impact of Finnish Settlement in Canada." *Terra* 79, 4 (1967): 113-20.

————. "Perspectives on Finnish Settlements in the Sudbury Area." *Historic Sudbury* 1 (1979): 33-41.

————. "Geographical Perspectives on Finnish Canadian Immigration and Settlement." *Polyphony* 3, 2 (1981): 16-22.

————."Finns in Northeastern Ontario with Special Reference to the Sudbury Area." *Laurentian Review* 15, 1 (1982): 41-54.

————. "Ethnicity and the Cultural Mosaic in the Sudbury Area." *Polyphony* 5, 1 (1983): 86-92.

————. "Perspectives on Finnish Settlement in Canada." *Siirtolaisuus-Migration* 3 (1995): 19-25.

————. "Geographical Perspectives on Finnish Settlements in the Sudbury Area." In Varpu Lindström, Oiva Saarinen and Böje Vähämäki, eds., *Melting into Great Waters: Papers from FINNFORUM V*, pp. 19-32. Toronto: University of Toronto Press, 1997.

————, and G.O. Tapper. "The Beaver Lake Finnish-Canadian Community: A Case Study of Ethnic Transition as Influenced by the Variables of Time and Spatial Networks, ca. 1907-1983." In Michael G. Karni et al., eds., *Finns in North America*, pp. 166-200. Turku: Institute of Migration, 1988.

Sangster, Joan. "Finnish Women in Ontario, 1890-1930." *Polyphony* 3, 2 (1981): 46-54.

Sariola, Sakari. "Socialism and Church: An Antinomian Impasse in Finnish-American Immigrant Communities." In Michael G. Karni et al., eds., *Finns in North America*, pp. 201-10. Turku: Institute of Migration, 1988.

Seager, Allen. "Finnish Canadians and the Ontario Miners' Movement." *Polyphony* 3, 2 (1981): 35-45.

Sillanpää, Lennard. "Voting Behaviour of Finns in the Sudbury Area, 1930-1972." In Michael G. Karni, ed., *Finnish Diaspora I*, pp. 101-16. Toronto: Multicultural History Society of Ontario, 1981.

Simpich, Frederick. "Ontario, Next Door." *National Geographic* 62, 2 (August 1932): 131-84.

Suokonautio, Markku. "Reorganization of the Finnish Lutherans in Canada." *Polyphony* 3, 2 (1981): 91-96.

Tapper, G.O., and Oiva W. Saarinen. "Finnish-Canadian Migration and Cultural Patterns: A Northern Ontario Case Study." *Nordia* 20, 1 (1986): 83-93.

Tarvainen, Eino, and Varpu Lindström-Best. "The Finnish Immigrant Theatre." *Polyphony* 3, 2 (1981): 74-76.

Timothy, Dallen J. "Finnish Settlements in Rural Thunder Bay: Changes in an Ethnic Community." *Siirtolaisuus-Migration* 1 (1995): 16-24.

————. "The Decline of Finnish Ethnic Islands in Rural Thunder Bay." *The Great Lakes Geographer* 2, 2 (1995): 45-59.

Virtanen, Keijo. "'Counter Current': Finns in the Overseas Return Migration Movement." In Michael G. Karni, ed., *Finnish Diaspora I*, pp. 183-202. Toronto: Multicultural History Society of Ontario, 1981.

————. "Work as a Factor of Adaptation for Finnish Immigrants in the Great Lakes Region." In Varpu Lindström, Oiva Saarinen and Börje Vähämäki, eds., *Melting into Great Waters: Papers from FINNFORUM V*, pp. 117-24. Toronto: University of Toronto Press, 1997.

Wargelin, Raymond W. "Finnish Lutherans in Canada."In Ralph J. Jalkanen, ed., *The Faith of the Finns*, pp. 130-57. East Lansing, MI: Michigan State University Press, 1972.

Wilson, J. Donald. "The Finnish Organization of Canada, the 'Language Barrier,' and the Assimilation Process." *Canadian Ethnic Studies* 9, 2 (1977): 105-16.

————. "Matti Kurikka and A.B. Mäkelä: Socialist Thought among Finns in Canada, 1900-1932." *Canadian Ethnic Studies* 10, 2 (1978): 9-21.

————. "The Canadian Sojourn of a Finnish-American Radical." *Canadian Ethnic Studies* 16, 2 (1984): 102-15.

Ylänkö, Anneli. "The Role of Heritage Schools in Ethnic Maintenance and Development." In Varpu Lindström, Oiva Saarinen and Börje Vähämäki, eds., *Melting into Great Waters: Papers from FINNFORUM V*, pp. 72-78. Toronto: University of Toronto Press, 1997.

Other Sources

Finnish

Johnson, Lempi, and Raija Toivola. *Sisulla ja Sydämellä*. Sudbury, 1984.

Junkkari, Lari. *Pyhän Matteuksen Suomalainen Evankelis-Luterilainen Seurakunta 50 Vuotta*. Sudbury: St. Matthew's Finnish Evangelical Lutheran Church, 1982.

Kanadan Suomalainen Kulttuuriliitto. *Toimintakertomus 1995*. Toronto: Kanadan Suomalainen Kulttuuriliitto, 1996.

Karttunen, Saara. "*Syvempi Kuin Meri*." Keuruu, Finland, 1992.

Kaskela, H. *Historiikki 1932-1942: Sudburyn P. Matt. Ev. Luth. Seurakunta*. Sudbury: St. Matthew's Finnish Evangelical Lutheran Church, 1942.

————. *Sudburyn Kansallis-Seuran 15 Vuotis Historiikki 1930-1945*. Sudbury: Finnish National Society of Sudbury, 1945.

Kuutti, Erkki. *Suomen Aseveljet Kanadassa*. Montreal: Suomen Aseveljet Kanadassa, 1995.

Nenonen, Viljo. *Pyhän Matteuksen Suomalainen Evankelis-Luterilainen Seurakunta 40-Vuotias*. Sudbury: St. Matthew's Finnish Evangelical Lutheran Church, 1972.

Pikkusaari, Lauri. *Wuoristo-Seurakunta 60-Vuotias*. Copper Cliff: St. Timothy's Wuoristo Evangelical Lutheran Church, 1957.

Tyni, Paul. *Wanupin Historia vv. 1925-1985*. Dill Township, 1985.

Ukkonen, Alfons. *Kalevan Ritarikunnan ja Kalevan Ritarien Historiaa 100 Vuotta Ajalta*. Lake Worth: Knights of Kaleva, 1996.

Wuoristo Ev. Lut. Seuraakunta. *Juhla-Julkaisu: Copper Cliffin Wuoristo Ev. Lut. Seurakunnan 40-Vuotis-Juhlille*. Copper Cliff: Copper Cliff Wuoristo Evangelical Lutheran Church, 1938.

English

Anderson Farm Museum Project. *There Were No Strangers: A History of the Village of Creighton Mine*. Walden: Anderson Farm Museum, 1989.

Central Organization of the Loyal Finns in Canada. *Constitution*. Sudbury: Central Organization of the Loyal Finns in Canada, 1931.

Cross Country Canada. *Cross Country Guide 1985 and 1986*. Ottawa: Cross Country Canada, 1985-86.

Estaire-Wanup Volunteer Fire Brigade. *Ladies Auxiliary Cookbook: Stories and the Kitchen Table*. Estaire-Wanup: Estaire-Wanup Volunteer Fire Brigade, 1997.

Festival Committee. *Reunion Festival*. Sudbury and Wanup: Festival Committee, 1994.

Freed, Verna. *Historical Bells: Northern Ontario*. Sudbury, 1978.

Jalava, Mauri Amiko. "Pehr Kalm: First Contact (1749-1750)." Paper presented at the FINNFORUM V Conference, Sudbury, 1996.

Kaattari, Ray. *Voices from the Past: Garson Remembers*. Garson: Garson Historical Group, 1992.

————. *Rubberboots in the Sauna*. Sudbury, 1993.

Korhonen, Kyllikki. *St. Matthew's Evangelical Lutheran Church 60th Anniversary 1932-1992*. Translated by Michael Korhonen. Sudbury: St. Matthew's Evangelical Lutheran Church, 1992.

Korpela, Oliver. *History of the Korpela Family*. Sudbury, 1986.

Kovac, Elsie. *Memories of Grandmother Manda*. Sudbury, 1990.

Nissilä, Eino. *Pioneers of Long Lake*. Sudbury, 1987.

Saarinen, Oiva W. *History of the Recreational Use of Lake Panache*. Sudbury: Laurentian University, 1990.

————. *A History of the Finnish National Society of Sudbury 1930-1991*. Sudbury: Finnish National Society of Sudbury, 1991.

————. *A History of the Knights and Ladies of Kaleva Lodges in Sudbury, Ontario, Canada (1965/66-1991)*. Sudbury: Knights and Ladies of Kaleva, 1991.

————. *A History of the Sudbury Finnish Rest Home Society, Inc.* Sudbury: Sudbury Finnish Rest Home Society, 1992.

————. *Suomalaisasutuksen Kaavio ja Vaikutus Canadassa Huomioiden erikoisesti Sudburyn Alueen Suomalaisasutuksen*. Sudbury: Finnish-Canadian Centennial Committee, 1967.

————, with Gerry Tapper. *Sudbury Suomi Lions Club, Sudbury, Ontario, Canada, 1989-1995*. Sudbury: Sudbury Suomi Lions Club, 1995.

St. Matthew's Evangelical Lutheran Church. *Annual Reports*. Sudbury: St. Matthew's Evangelical Lutheran Church, 1982-96.

St. Timothy's Lutheran Church. *Annual Reports*. Copper Cliff and Sudbury: St. Timothy's Lutheran Church, 1989-96.

Sudbury Finnish Male Choir. *Sudbury Finnish Male Choir Anniversary Concert*. Sudbury: Sudbury Finnish Male Choir, 1995.

Tester, Jim, ed. *Sports Pioneers: A History of the Finnish-Canadian Amateur Sports Federation 1906-1986*. Sudbury: Alerts AC Historical Committee, 1986.

Waters Women's Institute. *The Story of Waters Township*. Walden Township, Waters Women's Institute, n.d.

Index

DEMCO, INC. 38-2931